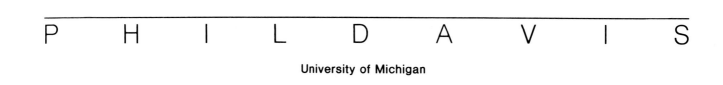

P H I L   D A V I S

University of Michigan

PHOTOGRAPHY

Fourth Edition

wcb
Wm. C. Brown Company Publishers
Dubuque, Iowa

Printed in the United States of America

Library of Congress Catalog Card Number:
81-66955

ISBN 0-697-03219-1

Book Team

Louise Waller
Editor

Patricia L. A. Hendricks
Production Editor

Anthony L. Saizon
Designer

James M. McNeil
Design Layout Assistant

Cover Image:
Hunting Island by Sam Wang

Contents

Preface

1

A Survey of the History of Photography 2
The Discovery and Evolution of
    Photography 3
The Art of Photography 31

2

**Introduction to the Photographic
    Process 52**
Light-Sensitive Materials 53
Image Formation 54

3

**Cameras, Accessories, and
    Operation 60**
Cameras: Types and Features 61
Accessories 70
Before You Buy 75
The Characteristics of Light 76
Lenses: Features and Functions 78
How Focal Length Affects Image Scale and
    Perspective 82
Depth of Focus and Depth of Field 86
Hyperfocal Distance 90
Focusing for Infrared 91
Relative Aperture—Lens Speed 92
How Exposure Is Controlled 93
Selecting and Using Black-and-White
    Films 95
Determining Exposure: Using Built-In
    Meters 98
How Aperture and Shutter Settings Are
    Related 103
EV Numbers 103
Light, Color, and Filters 104
Taking Care of Cameras and Lenses 110

6

Working with Light 180
Artificial Light Sources 181
Using Flash 182
Fluorescent Light 184
Ultraviolet and Infrared 185
Principles of Lighting 186
Available Light 190
Controlling Artificial Light 192

7

Color Photography 202
How Color Films and Papers Work 203
Film Color Balance and Filtration 205
Color Film Processing Outline 210
Color Printing 212
Cibachrome Printing 216
Printing from Negatives: Unicolor R-2 223
Filter Pack Adjustment 230

8

Special Camera Techniques 234
View and Field Cameras 235
Processing Sheet Film in a Tray 240
Using the View Camera 243
The Exposure-Development
    Relationship 251
Interpreting the Technical Literature 255
Using Average Gradient Information 259
Light Meters for View Cameras 259
An Incident Metering System 262
The Zone System 263
CI Charts 267
Close-up Photography 268
Copying Techniques 277

4

Developing Black-and-White Rollfilm 114

Rollfilm Processing Equipment 115
Processing Solutions: Ingredients and Their
  Functions 118
Developers: Types and
  Characteristics 120
Water for Chemical Mixing 121
Chemical Mixing and Preparation 121
Processing Rollfilm 123
Appraising Negative Quality 133

5

Printing 136

Facilities 137
Equipment 138
Printing Papers: Types and
  Characteristics 144
Preparing the Printing Chemicals 148
Proofing Negatives by Contact 150
Making Prints by Projection 156
Post-Development Controls 164
Mounting and Matting Prints 168

9

Special Darkroom Techniques 284

Process Manipulations 285
Dropouts, High-Contrast Techniques,
  Posterization 286
Masking, Tone-Line, Solarization 290
Screening 294
Color Manipulations 296
Introduction to Nonsilver Processes 299
Making Enlarged Negatives 300
The Cyanotype Process 302
The Gum-Bichromate Process 304

10

What Is a Good Photograph? 312

Subjectivity of Definition 313
Photographic Principles / Personal
  Expression 314
Composition 316
Visual Symbolism 318
Directing Your Image-Making Skills 319

Portfolio 320
Appendixes 342
Glossary 368
Bibliography 388
Index 392

Preface

My intent in writing *Photography,* in its original version, was (1) to provide students with some background in the history of the medium; (2) to present the necessary technical information in a logical sequence; (3) and to stimulate student interest in photography as a craft, an art, and a medium of personal expression. Those continue to be my aims in this fourth edition.

The text begins with a survey of the history of photography, which is followed by a brief introduction to the photographic process. The next three chapters are devoted to fundamental information and instruction in black-and-white photography: cameras and related equipment; small camera operation, including exposure calculation, selection of lens and shutter settings; film characteristics; and rollfilm processing and printing.

The chapter "Working with Light" has been given added emphasis in this edition with the inclusion of a new series of portrait lighting illustrations. "Color Photography," chapter 7, discusses the principles of color image formation and explains two popular printing procedures in detail. Chapter 8, "Special Camera Techniques," contains expanded coverage of the basics of view camera operation and discusses the exposure/ development relationship, the Zone System—a useful method

for incident metering—and close-up photography. The next chapter presents several procedures for technical manipulation of the image in the darkroom, plus step-by-step instructions for two nonsilver processes—cyanotype and gum-bichromate printing. The final chapter is an expanded attempt to cope with the knotty problem, "What Is a Good Photograph?", leading to a selection of what I consider to be good photographs in the Portfolio.

Although the content of this new edition is generally similar to that of the previous one, numerous detailed changes have been made in response to suggestions from users and reviewers. The new format and design are intended to improve both appearance and readability; some sections—notably chapter 3—have been extensively rewritten; and the popular marginal notes have been revised to provide a running summary of the text.

Illustrations have been given a more important role and many new ones have been added, but the emphasis of *Photography* continues to be on information and explanation, much of it drawn from my personal experience as a professional photographer, exhibitor, and teacher. Beginners and intermediate-level photographers will find answers to most of their questions here, and advanced workers should find useful information in the later chapters and the technical reference material.

The book contains several reference aids. Each chapter begins with a list of main topics that correspond with the major heads that appear throughout the chapter. The marginal notes permit rapid skimming of chapter contents, and chapter summaries facilitate review. Synopses—step-by-step reviews of technical procedures—appear at strategic places throughout the text. A bibliography is a categorical list of other books and periodicals that may be of interest. The appendix contains formulas, conversion factors, development charts, and much other useful information; and an extensive glossary defines and explains technical terms.

I am indebted to a number of individuals and organizations for supplying me with information or illustration material, among them Richard Rideout, Kenneth T. Lassiter, and Dr. Warren H. Jones of the Eastman Kodak Company; Dr. Edmund W. Lowe of Edwal Scientific Products Corporation; and Paul Graf and Sam Fox of Ethol Chemicals, Inc. I am especially grateful to Bob Chapman of Unicolor Corporation for his generous donation of materials and his patience in supplying technical advice, and to John Wilson, manager of the photo division of Home Appliance Mart in Ann Arbor, Michigan, for supplying product information and loaning equipment for illustration purposes.

I would also like to thank David Travis, director, Nancy Thrall, and Linda Cohen of the Museum Photography Department of the Art Institute of Chicago; Michael Kamins of International Museum of Photography, George Eastman House; and Brett Waller, former director of the Museum of Art at the University of Michigan, for their cooperation and assistance in supplying photographs.

Louise Waller, Pat Hendricks, Tony Saizon, and others at Wm. C. Brown Company, Publishers, deserve credit for their contributions to the design and organization of this edition. Finally, I must again acknowledge with affectionate gratitude the inspiration and support that my wife, Martha, continues to provide. Without her encouragement this book might never have been finished.

Phil Davis

PHOTOGRAPHY

A Survey of the History of Photography

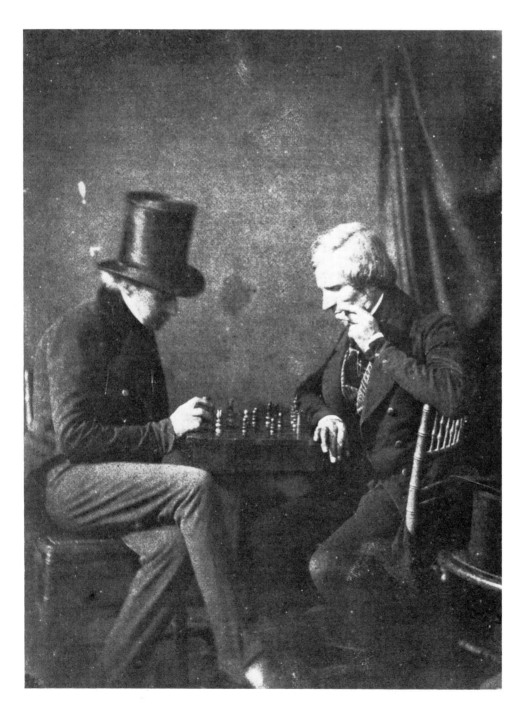

Outline

The Discovery and Evolution of Photography
    Discovery of Image Formation by Light
    The Chemical Investigations
    The Daguerreotype Period
    The Calotype Period
    The Collodion Period
    Applied Photography in a Commerical Enterprise
    The Gelatin Period
    Advancement of Color Techniques
    Post-War Advances in Photographic Equipment
    Editorial Photography
The Art of Photography
    Photography and Painting
    Photography Becomes an Art in Its Own Right
    The Post-War Era
    Photography Today
    The Future of Photography

It is almost impossible to imagine what the world would be like if photographs and photographic processes were suddenly taken from us. We take television for granted and accept motion pictures, photographic magazines, and newspaper illustrations as a matter of course, but these are only the more obvious signs of the influence of photography on our lives. It is involved, directly or indirectly, in almost everything we experience.

Photography is involved in almost everything we experience

It wasn't always like this. Newspaper and magazine reproduction of photographs was still a novelty at the beginning of this century. Color photography was in its infancy in 1910. Sound-on-film recording was introduced in the motion picture industry in the 1920s. And television, which seems to have made the whole world picture-conscious, was still new to most people in 1950.

Considering the fascination that image-making has always held for people, it sometimes seems surprising that it took so long for photography to be invented. In fact it wasn't just invented, it evolved; and that evolution was a long and painful process.

The Discovery and Evolution of Photography

Discovery of Image Formation by Light

The camera came into being long before there was any real use for it. It was probably inspired by the observation of some naturally formed image. Aristotle mentioned the images of a solar eclipse formed on the ground by sunlight passing through little gaps in tree foliage, and his comments indicate that he had some grasp of the principles involved.

No one knows when the first camera was constructed

No one knows when the first camera was constructed, but in view of Aristotle's obvious recognition of the principles, it could have been done by some unknown Greek. It's more likely, though, that it came more than a thousand years later. Roger Bacon discussed the camera obscura knowledgeably about 1267 and is presumed to have learned about it from the writings of tenth-century Arab scholars.

In its earliest form the camera obscura was what the name implies, a dark chamber or room. Leonardo da Vinci described one in some detail in about 1490, pointing out that the image was viewed through the back of a screen of paper which "must be very thin." He also specified that the hole "should be made in a piece of very thin sheet iron."

della Porta refined the camera obscura

In 1558 the camera obscura was described fully by Giovanni Battista della Porta who, in the first edition of his *Magiae Naturalis,* specified that a conical hole be installed in the shutter of a darkened room and that the image be shown on a white screen. He mentioned that the image will appear upside down and reversed from left to right and that the image size is proportional to the distance from the hole to the viewing screen—all of which are equally valid observations for the cameras we use today. Porta recommended that the camera obscura image be used as a guide for drawing and then went on to invent a method for producing an erect image using lenses and curved mirrors. With

Chess Players. William Henry Fox Talbot. (Courtesy of the Art Institute of Chicago)

Figure 1.1
Camera obscura. From an early print.
(Courtesy of the IMP, GEH)

and was accused of sorcery

this apparatus, he astounded viewers with the images of elaborate theatrical productions staged outside and is even supposed to have been accused of sorcery for his trouble.

The application of lenses to the camera obscura after 1550 was a significant step. The image could then be made both sharper and more brilliant because a lens can admit much more light than a simple hole and can also focus the light rays to finer points. Cameras began to be refined in design and construction as more and more people became interested in them, and by about 1575 the first movable cameras appeared. They were, at first, wooden huts or tents, still completely enclosing the viewer and viewing screen. Later more elaborate models, such as sedan chairs, were constructed.

Camera evolution was rapid

From that point on, the evolution was rapid. Smaller models were designed which permitted the operator to view or trace the image from outside the main enclosure, and finally completely portable cameras appeared. A *reflex* camera, one in which the image is reflected up onto a top-mounted viewing screen by an inclined mirror behind the lens, was built in 1676; a *ball-and-socket* mount (like some modern *tripod heads*) appeared in 1680; and a *telephoto* lens was installed in a camera obscura in 1685. The camera was ready, but for what?

The Chemical Investigations

but chemical investigations proceeded slowly

Photographic chemistry started late and proceeded slowly. In 1614 Angelo Sala noted that silver nitrate turned black when exposed to the sun, but apparently saw nothing significant in the change and did not ascribe it to the action of light.

Schulze made stencil prints

The first discovery of importance was made in 1725 by Johann Heinrich Schulze, a professor of anatomy at the University of Altdorf. He had mixed powdered chalk into a solution of nitric acid in an attempt to make a phosphorescent material (the "luminous stone" of the alchemist, Balduin) and was amazed to discover that the mixture turned dark violet in sunlight. He traced the discoloration to a contaminant in the acid, silver, and eventually proved that silver compounds were visibly changed by the action of light rather than heat or exposure to air, as had been previously suggested. Schulze made numerous stencil prints on the sensitive contents of his bottles but apparently never applied the solutions to paper or made any attempt to record natural images.

In 1777 Carl Wilhelm Scheele, the Swedish chemist, investigated the properties of silver chloride and made some interesting discoveries. Like Schulze, he established that the blackening effect on his silver salt was due to

Scheele overlooked the significance of his discoveries

Wedgwood almost invented photography

but couldn't fix the image: Davy was wistful

Niépce experimented with silver chloride

but had more success with asphalt coatings

In 1826 Niépce made the world's first camera image

light, not heat. He also proved that the black material was metallic silver and he noted that ammonia, which was known to dissolve silver chloride, did not affect the blackened silver. If Scheele had realized the importance of this last discovery, he could very well have become the inventor of photography, for by this time the essential processes were known. Silver chloride could be reduced to black metallic silver by exposure to light; ammonia could serve to preserve the image by dissolving the silver chloride without harming the image tones; and, of course, the camera was still waiting in the wings. But Scheele's investigations were only noted in passing. The world was not yet ready for photography. The fantastic possibility of producing images by the action of light had simply not occurred to anyone as a serious thought.

This essential idea finally came to Thomas Wedgwood, the youngest son of the famous potter Josiah, who, in addition to being an outstanding craftsman and artist, was a brilliant and respected member of the English scientific community. Thomas was familiar with the camera obscura because his father had used it as an aid in drawing scenes for use on his pottery. The Wedgwood family also owned the notebooks of William Lewis, who in 1763 had described Schulze's and his own experiments with the silver compounds. These circumstances and natural curiosity prompted young Thomas to begin experiments of his own, probably about 1795. Thomas Wedgwood narrowly missed becoming the inventor of photography for two reasons. He gave up attempts to make pictures with the camera obscura (his exposures were not sufficient), and he was not able to fix the silver images he did produce by direct printing.

It's strange that he failed to take note of Scheele's experiments with ammonia and silver chloride, particularly in light of his father's familiarity with things scientific and his own close friendship with Sir Humphry Davy, a famous young English chemist. Wedgwood's experiments with prints on paper and leather were published in 1802 with Davy's wistful summary, "Nothing but a method of preventing the unshaded parts of the delineation from being coloured by exposure to the day is wanting, to render the process as useful as it is elegant." This same problem continued to frustrate experimenters for the next thirty years. It was as if Scheele's work had never been done at all.

In France, meanwhile, Joseph Nicéphore Niépce and his son Isidore were busy experimenting with lithography at the family estate near Chalon. Then Isidore, who had been copying drawings onto the stones for his father, joined the army, and Nicéphore began to explore light-sensitive varnishes, hoping to find a coating for the stones which would record the drawings by exposure to light. He must have made some progress because, in 1816, he set out to take pictures from nature using a camera and paper sensitized with silver chloride.

He had limited success almost immediately, but he was displeased that the image tones were reversed from nature (they were negative), and that he could not make the image permanent. He realized that the tonal reversal was an inherent part of the silver process and tried to produce a positive print by reprinting one of his negatives, but his attempts were unsuccessful. He also found that nitric acid helped to preserve the image for a while, but it only postponed disaster and could not prevent it. He began to experiment with other materials.

Finally, in 1822, he produced a copy of an engraving by exposing through the original onto a glass plate coated with bitumen of Judea, a type of asphalt. Light hardens this material, so when Niépce washed his exposed plate with the usual solvents only the unexposed portions were floated away, leaving the image in permanent lines. He called his process heliography (sun-writing). He made a number of similar heliographs in the next few years and continued his efforts to record a camera image. At last, in 1826, he succeeded. The world's first permanent camera image shows the view from Niépce's second floor window and is little more than an impression. It is a bitumen image on pewter, showing only masses of light and dark tones. The exposure supposedly took about eight hours.

The Daguerreotype Period

Daguerre wrote to Niépce in 1826

In January 1826 Niépce received a letter from a Parisian painter, Louis Jacques Mandé Daguerre, who mentioned that he was also working with light images and inquired about Niépce's progress. Niépce was initially cautious, but after visiting Daguerre on a trip through Paris, his suspicions were somewhat allayed. After occasional correspondence, he finally suggested to Daguerre in 1829 that they form a partnership to do "mutual work in the improvement of my heliographic process." Daguerre accepted and visited Niépce to work out the details. They became friends and corresponded frequently but they never met again.

They formed a partnership and corresponded in code

Until the time of their partnership, Daguerre had not produced a useful light image, although he had implied that his work was rather well advanced. The agreement with Niépce seemed to spur him on. He became a tireless experimenter and mentioned in a letter of May 21, 1831, his growing interest in silver iodide. "I think after many new tests that we ought to concentrate our researches on 20," he wrote, "this substance is highly light-sensitive when it is in contact with 18." They were writing in code; "20" meant iodine, "18" meant silver plate.

Niépce died; Daguerre and Isidore Niépce continued

Niépce could not contribute much in this direction. His early experiments with silver compounds had left him prejudiced against them. Finally, impoverished and discouraged, he died. Daguerre was saddened but resumed his work with Isidore Niépce as his partner. He was now completely committed to working with the silver compounds.

In 1835 Daguerre discovered (quite by accident, if the story is true) that treatment with mercury vapor would produce a visible image on an iodized silver plate that had been briefly exposed to light. He also managed to stabilize the image with a strong solution of salt. In spite of the fact that Isidore had contributed nothing to the discovery, Daguerre included him in a new contract and set about trying to find a market for his process. He did not have much luck.

Arago announced Daguerre's discovery in 1839

Finally, late in 1838, he contacted a group of leading French scientists, among them François Arago, and solicited their help. Arago was immediately impressed with the invention and made a brief announcement of it at the Academie des Sciences in January 1839.

Daguerre had supported himself quite handsomely during most of the period of his research with the proceeds from his Diorama, a kind of light show which combined enormous paintings on translucent screens with some real objects, controlled light effects, and music to create illusions of famous scenes or ceremonies. It was a disaster for him, then, when the Paris Diorama was totally destroyed by fire in March 1839.

The daguerreotype was given to the world—except England

Arago immediately sprang to his aid and succeeded in convincing the government that French national honor was at stake. A bill was passed granting life pensions to Daguerre and Niépce, and the details of the process were announced to a frenzied public in August 1839. Although the French government had announced that the process was now public property, this was not entirely true. Daguerre had secretly patented it in England just a few days before the formal French announcement.

William Henry Fox Talbot was dismayed

News of the daguerreotype process spread like wildfire. Enthusiastic experimenters, French and foreign, were soon happily engrossed in the new technique. But there was dismay in England. A respected member of the Royal Society of London, William Henry Fox Talbot, saw the new process as a threat to his own investigations and, in an attempt to establish priority, had written Arago on January 29, 1839, to claim that he had been the first to find a method for taking pictures with the camera obscura and for fixing them. He overstated his case. He had not accomplished much more than Niépce had in his experiments with silver chloride, and his method of fixation was far from satisfactory.

Talbot was not an artist, but he was a brilliant, well-educated man. He apparently conceived the notion of capturing camera obscura images while trying to draw some landscapes in Italy and later wrote in his famous picture book, *The Pencil of Nature,*

> And this led me to reflect on the inimitable beauty of the pictures of nature's painting which the glass lens of the camera throws upon the paper in its focus—fairy pictures, creations of a moment, and destined as rapidly to fade away. It was during these thoughts that the idea occurred to me—how charming it would be if it were possible to cause these natural images to imprint themselves durably, and remain fixed upon the paper!

Talbot had begun experimenting in 1834

On returning to England in 1834, Talbot began experimentation. Having heard that silver nitrate was light-sensitive, he made his first attempts with silver nitrate-coated paper. He quickly found it unsatisfactory and turned to silver chloride, at first coating paper with the prepared salt, then producing it in the paper by successive washes of sodium chloride (common salt) and silver nitrate. He soon found that too much salt reduced the sensitivity of the paper and turned, as Daguerre had done, to the use of a strong salt solution for fixing the image. Before long, Talbot ran across the accounts of the experiments of Wedgwood and Davy and investigated them fairly thoroughly, apparently without discovering much of real value. He had not yet heard of the work of either Niépce or Daguerre.

He took pictures with "mouse traps"

Although his early experiments were confined to making prints of objects laid directly on the paper surface, Talbot had succeeded, by the summer of 1835, in taking pictures with a tiny camera obscura fitted with a microscope lens (his wife called his little cameras "mouse traps"). The pictures were only about an inch square, but he had found larger ones impossible to make due to the length of the exposure time required.

Talbot made little progress in the next three years. His attention was diverted to other things. His interest and concern were apparent, however, when he received word of Arago's announcement of Daguerre's fantastic discovery.

The Calotype Period

The news that stunned Talbot also greatly intrigued Sir John Frederick William Herschel, son of the famous German-born English astronomer and a prominent mathematician, astronomer, and chemist in his own right. Within a week, Herschel was at work in his laboratory near London investigating the various known processes and keeping careful notes of his procedures.

Herschel made the process practical— in two weeks

It is an indication of Herschel's intelligence and acuity as an investigator that in less than two weeks he successfully tested several silver salts for sensitivity, took several successful pictures, printed a negative to make a positive paper image, and fixed the images with a chemical he had described twenty years previously, which he called "hyposulphite of soda."

Talbot learned of hypo from Herschel

At the height of this investigation, less than two weeks after hearing about Arago's momentous announcement, Talbot visited Herschel at his laboratory, bringing with him samples of his work. Talbot begins to appear, at this moment in history, as a somewhat unlovely character. His treatment of the frank and generous Herschel was rather shabby. Herschel showed Talbot his results and described them in full detail, including his use of *hypo* for fixing. Talbot, on the other hand, revealed nothing. He referred airily to his own method of fixing the image, without explaining how it was done, and convinced Herschel that he should not mention the use of hypo until Talbot had announced his process. Herschel agreed, later writing admiringly that Talbot's method of fixing "must be a very chemical jewel," and gave Talbot permission to announce the use of hypo with his own process.

Figure 1.2
William Henry Fox Talbot (1800-1877).
Silhouette of Leaves.
(Courtesy of the Art Institute of Chicago)

Hippolyte Bayard also invented photography

His attempts to gain recognition were not very successful

In fairness to Talbot, it must be acknowledged that he credited Herschel with the application of hyposulphite of soda. In his letter of disclosure to a member of the French Academy, he outlined his own methods of fixing, then described Herschel's hypo as being "worth all the others combined." Daguerre immediately applied it to his own process.

Niépce, Daguerre, and Talbot can each be called the "inventor of photography" with certain justification, but so can a fourth man who is less well known, Hippolyte Bayard. Bayard lived in Paris and was a minor employee of the Ministry of Finance. His experiments with light-sensitive materials probably began about 1837 and, initially, seem to have paralleled Talbot's. His first images were negatives on silver chloride-treated paper. On learning of Daguerre's discovery, he set out to produce direct positive images. Within a few months he succeeded with a process that involved blackening a conventional silver chloride paper in light, then coating it with a solution of potassium iodide, and exposing it in the camera. The exposing light bleached this paper, producing a direct positive image, which was then fixed in hypo.

Bayard was apparently a very quiet, retiring man of modest means. Many of his pictures are still-life arrangements or details of his house and garden. In some of these views he appears seated in a doorway or in his garden, surrounded by flowerpots and garden tools. Although he did make a few tentative attempts to gain recognition and support, they were not very successful. Perhaps, too, he was unlucky in his choice of consultants. He showed some prints to Arago in May 1839 and asked for his help, but Arago was very interested in Daguerre's career at that point and arranged for a token grant of six hundred francs to

Figure 1.3
Moulins de Montmarte 1842. Hyppolyte
Bayard

**Bayard photographed himself as
a corpse**

Talbot patented his processes

help Bayard finance his experiments, counselling him to remain quietly in the
background until Daguerre's process had been publicly revealed. After that
revelation, of course, Bayard's work seemed anticlimactic and insignificant, and
he was virtually ignored by the public and the government alike.

Understandably bitter at this callous treatment, Bayard expressed his
hurt by photographing himself as a half-naked corpse and explained, in a long
and piteous caption, that this was the dead body of the unhappy Bayard who,
unrecognized and unrewarded, had thrown himself into the water and drowned.

Although he was never really given the credit he deserved during his
lifetime, he did eventually receive a little prize of three thousand francs. He is
now remembered as a significant figure, a victim of circumstances who might
have been as well known as Daguerre if things had worked in his favor.

Photography, a name generally credited to Herschel, languished in England. The daguerreotype process was patented, and Talbot immediately began
to secure his own processes by patents so restrictive that even amateur experiments were inhibited. Talbot improved his original paper negative process by
subjecting the exposed paper to development in gallic acid and silver nitrate
solution, thus shortening the necessary exposure time considerably. He called
the new process *calotype* (also later referred to as *talbotype*) and included in
its patent the use of hypo for fixing—blatantly appropriating Herschel's discovery.

Talbot must receive credit for inventing the photographic process as we
now know it, but he also must be remembered as a stumbling block in its
evolution. As new procedures were announced, Talbot promptly laid claims to

and controlled photography in England until 1855

them on the grounds that they were only modifications of the basic principles of his patented processes. Although these tactics created a great deal of antagonism and various suits were threatened, Talbot was generally successful in controlling photography in England until 1855.

The Collodion Period

Niépce's cousin invented the albumin process

The two decades following the invention of photography were years of rapid technical evolution and experimentation. The daguerreotype process was sufficiently refined to permit studio portraiture by about 1841. Talbot's calotype process was improved by Louis-Désiré Blanquart-Evrard; Gustave LeGray went a step further by sensitizing waxed paper to produce negatives of greater sharpness and translucency; and Claude Niépce de St.-Victor's glass plates, sensitized with an albumin emulsion, gave photographers still another alternative. All of these processes were in use in 1851 when Frederick Scott Archer announced the details of his collodion process and gave it freely for all to use.

Talbot claimed Archer's collodion process—and lost

The process was not free for long. Talbot, with typical lack of scruple, claimed that it was covered by his patents and announced that he would prosecute anyone who used it without his license. A number of challenges were made to this outrageous claim. Finally in December 1854 the courts found Talbot's claims illegal and his tyranny ended.

Applied Photography—A Commercial Enterprise

"We are daguerreotyping away like lions!"

By the 1850s photography was well established as a commerical enterprise. As early as November 1839 Noel Lerebours, a French optician and entrepreneur, had dispatched several crews of painters and photographers to various exotic places, such as Greece, England, America, and Egypt. The views that they collected, while "daguerreotyping away like lions,"—as one group reported—were copied by skilled engravers and Lerebours published them as *Excursions Daguerriennes.*

Talbot and Blanquart-Evrard: publishers

In England, Talbot had sold "sun pictures" of landscapes and other scenes and eventually set up a "glass house" at Reading where his several employees printed editions of photographs and sold calotype materials to Talbot's licenseholders. In 1844 the "Reading Establishment" began turning out the calotype illustrations for Talbot's famous" *Pencil of Nature,* the first book ever published with photographic illustrations. Several years later, Blanquart-Evrard opened a similar, but larger, printing establishment in France, where, using his improved process, his employees were able to produce several hundred prints per day. He also produced several booklets and albums illustrated with actual paper prints.

Morse and Draper became enthusiastic teachers

The paper processes were never popular in America, although various experimenters had worked with them unsuccessfully prior to the announcement of the daguerreotype. One of these men, Samuel F. B. Morse, had visited Daguerre in Paris (he was demonstrating his telegraph to Daguerre in the hour that the Diorama burned) and was enchanted by the images that Daguerre had shown him. After returning to America, Morse had a camera built and soon joined forces with John W. Draper in attempting to master the process. Morse and the other pioneers soon became enthusiastic teachers and many of their students, among them Mathew Brady and Albert Southworth, ultimately became famous as portrait photographers.

American daguerreotypists made spectacular pictures

The American daguerreotypist was not confined to the studio by any means. The Langenheim brothers of Philadelphia produced a panoramic view of Niagara Falls in 1845 by mounting five separate pictures edge to edge. An even more spectacular panorama of the city of Cincinnati, eight feet long, was assembled by Fontayne and Porter in 1848. A daguerreotypist named Platt Babbitt specialized in photographing tourist groups in front of Niagara Falls, and, in St. Louis, J. H. Fitzgibbon photographed riverboats, frontier scenes, and Indians, as well as maintaining a conventional portrait studio. A number

Figure 1.4
Platt D. Babbitt. *Group at Niagara Falls.*
(Courtesy of the IMP, GEH)

European photographers favored the paper processes

The collodion "wet plate" process was a demanding one

Roger Fenton used it to document the Crimean War

The Ambrotype and Carte-de-visite doomed the daguerreotype

Tintypes were also very popular

of adventurous men, such as Britt, Vance, McIntyre, and Carvalho, daguerreotyped the Far West, including the Rocky Mountains, the California gold fields, and San Francisco, a number of years before the better-known expeditions of Carleton Watkins, Timothy O'Sullivan, and William Jackson.

For somewhat similar work being done at about the same time, European photographers favored the various paper processes or albumin-coated glass plates. The calotype and the waxed-paper process were popular there until about 1855, and proof of their refinement is seen in the works of Charles Nègre, Henri Le Secq, John Shaw Smith, Roger Fenton, and others. Their landscapes, architectural views, and archeological records of Egypt, in particular, are frequently larger than one would expect and startlingly beautiful.

The collodion process offered photographers a negative material of greater sensitivity and better quality than paper, but the process was a demanding one. A glass plate had to be cleaned, then flooded with iodized collodion to form a uniform, blemish-free coating. It then had to be immersed in a bath of silver nitrate and rushed into the camera for exposure while still wet. Development in pyrogallic acid or a solution of ferrous sulfate had to follow immediately before the plate dried. For obvious reasons, it came to be known as the wet-plate process.

Roger Fenton was one of the first to use it for reportage, by covering the Crimean War in 1855. In spite of almost insurmountable difficulties, Fenton managed to produce a series of photographs which, although curiously unwarlike, do record the terrain and the camp life impressively.

J. A. Cutting's invention of the ambrotype (collodion on glass) and André Adolphe-Eugène Disdéri's popularization of the photographic carte-de-visite (albumin emulsion on paper), both in 1854, doomed the daguerreotype and disrupted the studio portrait business. Although the ambrotype was markedly inferior to the daguerreotype in clarity and brilliance, it was cheap and relatively easy to make. The carte-de-visite images, usually made eight-to-a-plate and then cut into individual pictures, were even cheaper. They became a worldwide sensation and were sold, traded, and collected by the hundreds of thousands.

The tintype (collodion on metal), also called *ferrotype* and *melainotype,* was patented by Hamilton Smith in 1855. It, too, became a quick, cheap and easy way to produce portraits and views and, although the image quality was

Figure 1.5
Roger Fenton. *Balaklava*.
(Courtesy of the Art Institute of Chicago)

Figure 1.6
Adolphe-Eugène Disdéri. Carte-de-visite,
uncut sheet.
(Courtesy of the IMP, GEH)

Figure 1.7
Mathew Brady (1823–1896). *Portrait of Lincoln*, carte-de-visite (obverse and reverse).
(Courtesy of William A. Lewis)

PUBLISHED BY
E. ANTHONY,
501 *Broadway*,
NEW YORK.
FROM
PHOTOGRAPHIC
NEGATIVE,
BY
M. B. BRADY.

**Stereo views were produced
in great numbers**

**Mathew Brady felt impelled to document
the Civil War**

poor, tintypes became popular. These cheap, mass-produced images were viewed with hostility and alarm by many "high-class" portrait photographers, but they had little choice; they could follow the trend or lose business. Most of them began producing the new, cheap images.

Stereoscopic views were also exceedingly popular. Although the principle of the stereoscope had been known for a long time, it was not adapted for photographic use until Charles Wheatstone suggested it in 1841. His early stereo viewer was effective but required careful adjustment and was rather clumsy to use. Sir David Brewster replaced the mirrors in Wheatstone's design with lenses in 1849, an improvement that allowed the paired images to be mounted on a single card, side by side. Before long, stereoscope views, both prints and transparencies, were being produced and sold in great numbers. By 1860 every wellfurnished American parlor featured an ornate album of carte-de-visite and tintype pictures and a stereo viewer, complete with dozens of slides.

Portrait photographers were doing a brisk business as the Civil War threatened. Mathew Brady, internationally famous as "Brady of Broadway," saw the impending conflict as a momentous historical event. Brady's sense of history was already well demonstrated. For years he had made it a practice to photograph famous people and had published *The Gallery of Illustrious Americans* in 1850. Now he felt impelled to document the war.

President Lincoln gave Brady his consent, but no financial backing. This was enough. Brady was a moderately wealthy man and he was willing to spend his own money for such a significant purpose. He assembled a staff of several men, outfitted them with the materials and equipment needed to make wet-plate photographs, and went to war. The pictures they made, under the most awkward and dangerous conditions imaginable, form a remarkable document of that desperate struggle.

Figure 1.8
Francis Frith (1822–1899). Stereo
transparency on glass.
(Courtesy of William A. Lewis)

Figure 1.9
Auguste Bisson. *Savoie 46—Mont Blanc,
vu de Mont Joli.*
(Courtesy of the Art Institute of Chicago)

Figure 1.10
Timothy O'Sullivan (1840-1882). *Cañon of
the Colorado River near the Mouth of the
San Juan River, Arizona,* 1873, Wheeler
Expedition.
(Courtesy of William A. Lewis)

**It left him heavily in debt; he died
penniless**

Francis Frith photographed in Egypt

**The Bisson brothers made Alpine
photographs**

Brady emerged from the enterprise practically destitute. There was little
market for his war pictures and their historical value was overlooked. His plates
were stored in warehouses and eventually auctioned off. Ironically, one lot of
them was bought by the government for storage charges. Brady, heavily in debt,
was forced to sell his portrait studio. Except for a belated government grant of
$25,000, he went unrewarded for his labors and died penniless in 1896.

The mid-nineteenth-century market for pictures of famous buildings, picturesque landscapes, and exotic foreign scenes kept many photographers employed. They were a hardy lot. The wet-plate process was difficult and awkward
and was complicated considerably by the demand for larger and larger images.
Francis Frith, one of the most enterprising travel photographers, journeyed
more than 800 miles up the Nile River in Egypt in 1856, carrying several
cameras, the largest of which accepted 16″ × 20″ plates. Flowing an even coat
of collodion over such a plate is difficult under the best conditions, but Frith,
and others like him, managed to do it in desert heat and mountain cold, in spite
of blowing dust, biting insects, and dripping rain. The fact that their pictures
turned out at all is amazing; in fact, many of them are of excellent quality even
by modern standards.

In 1860 the Bisson brothers, Louis and Auguste, photographed Mt. Blanc.
Climbing to more than 15,000 feet with cameras as large as 12″ × 17″, they
battled below-zero cold, which threatened to freeze the collodion on their plates,
and made a number of spectacular views of the windswept peaks and glaciers.

In America after the Civil War, exploration of the West began again in
earnest and photographers were in the vanguard. Timothy O'Sullivan, who had
been one of Brady's photographers during the war, joined an expedition exploring the 40th parallel in 1867 and was soon photographing the deserts and
mining areas of Nevada. Three years later he travelled to Panama with the

Figure 1.11
William H. Jackson (1843–1942). *The Rocky Mountains, Scenes Along the Line of the Denver and Rio Grande Railway* (Courtesy of William A. Lewis)

O'Sullivan and Jackson photographed the American West

Darien Expedition and, in 1871, joined the Wheeler Expedition. O'Sullivan's photographs are technically fine and frequently display considerable artistic sensitivity.

William H. Jackson's work is probably better known than O'Sullivan's, if only because Jackson's photographs of Yellowstone helped to persuade Congress to establish that region as the first National Park. As a child, Jackson was encouraged to draw and paint and was introduced to photography by his father. He served with the Vermont infantry during the Civil War, then—after being jilted by his fiancée—headed West with an ex-army buddy. They travelled with a wagon train to Montana where Jackson struck out on his own. After two years of wandering from job to job, he arrived in Omaha where he was hired by a local photographer.

Before long he owned his own studio but his wanderlust was still strong. Outfitting a horse-drawn wagon as a portable darkroom, he began to roam the country around Omaha photographing the prairies and the Indians who inhabited them. Soon he was attracted by the dramatic expansion of the railroads, and after redesigning his equipment to fit on packmules, he began to travel in earnest.

Jackson joined the Hayden expedition

In 1869 he met Dr. F. V. Hayden who was conducting a U.S. Geological Survey of the Territories. Jackson was persuaded to join him and during the nine years that he worked on the Survey, he produced thousands of magnificent negatives of both scientific and scenic value. An extract from his diary gives us some inkling of the difficulties of working in the mountains with the wet-plate process:

> Aug. 2, (1878) Upper Wind River Lake. Returned to upper lake. Wilson, Eccles, his man Payot and Richardson going with me. Fine morning and got good 11 by 14 exposure first trial. There were two or three small defects but impossible to take it over and get as good a lighting. Time 9 m. with Portable Symmetrical, single lens, at F. 32. Made 5 by 8 of same subject. Came up too thin, but intensifying made it as much too dense. Took camera up high for a general view. Exposed 2 m., F. 16, Portable Symmetrical, with some over-exposure. In packing up to return, I forgot to remove the two 11 by 14 plates that I had put in the bath holder to bring the solution up to its proper depth. Hoggie, the pack mule carrying the outfit, traveled so roughly that when I opened up the bath holder later I found the plates smashed to pieces and one side of the bath holder punched full of holes. It is going to bother me now to replace it. Was two or three hours making general repairs. I don't think I ever had so inconvenient an outfit.

Later Jackson specialized in photographing the railroads

In 1879 Jackson moved to Denver, set up a studio, and returned to his earlier interest, photographing the railroads. For twenty years he travelled through every state in the Union and from Montreal to Mexico City, often in "Jackson Special" cars supplied by the railroads, making photographs of all sizes from 20″ × 24″ to the popular stereo views. In 1898 he established the Detroit Publishing Company, specializing in views and postcards printed in color, derived from his vast store of negatives. When he "retired" in 1924, he took up painting again and did a series of pictures for the National Park Service. Still vigorous in his nineties, Jackson continued to tour, paint, and photograph the West each summer until his death in 1942.

Edward Muggeridge thought his name was really Eadweard Muybridge

Another Western photographer was English-born Eadweard Muybridge (who thought that this strange spelling was the correct Anglo-Saxon version of his real name, Edward Muggeridge). Muybridge was well known in the 1860s as a fine landscapist and industrial photographer but his fame now stems from his research in motion photography.

Almost from the beginning photographers were intrigued by the possibility of taking "instantaneous photographs." In 1851 Talbot used an electric spark to record the image of a page from the *Times* which he had fastened to a rapidly revolving wheel, and by 1860 several other photographers had managed to take outdoor views that showed walking figures caught in midstride.

He photographed Leland Stanford's horses

Muybridge was the first to attack the problem seriously though, when he was commissioned by Leland Stanford—one-time governor of California—to photograph a running horse. Stanford financed this experiment, so the story goes, to settle a bet he had made with a friend. Stanford claimed that all four of a trotter's feet leave the ground at some point in his stride; his friend insisted that at least one foot is always on the ground. Although his first attempts were failures, Muybridge finally managed to prove that Stanford was right.

and showed motion pictures with his zoopraxiscope

In 1874 Muybridge was tried and acquitted for murdering his wife's lover. He left the country for a time, returning to resume his work in motion photography with Stanford in 1877. By 1880 he had refined his procedures considerably and was able to project a crude motion picture sequence with a device he called the *zoopraxiscope*. In 1883 he was invited to continue his experiments at the University of Pennsylvania, an invitation that the painter Thomas Eakins may have influenced. In 1887 a set of his motion sequence photographs, analyzing both animal and human activities, was published under the title *Animal Locomotion*.

Although his work was denounced by a number of influential painters and photographers as "inartistic" and "untrue," Muybridge clearly influenced men like Etienne Jules Marey and Thomas Eakins, both of whom devised cameras for making multiple exposures of moving figures. Their work, in turn, clearly foreshadows the Futurist paintings of Duchamps, Balla, and others.

Figure 1.12
Eadweard Muybridge (1830–1904). *A Horse's Motion Scientifically Considered,* engravings after photographs.
(From a copy of the *Scientific American Supplement,* no. 158, January 11, 1879, in the collection of the University of Michigan Library)

The Gelatin Period

There was early interest in nonsilver processes

While most of the prints made for commerical purposes after 1850 were done on albuminized paper, the albumin process was not entirely satisfactory. The color was not altogether pleasing, and, as was true of other silver papers, the image was likely to fade or discolor, especially if the photographer was less than meticulous in his processing. For these and other reasons, considerable attention was devoted to the perfection of nonsilver photographic materials.

This was not a new thought. In 1839 Mungo Ponton had discovered that a solution of potassium dichromate spread on paper would be insolubly stained by exposure to light and he used this principle to produce simple images. Edmond Becquerel pointed out, shortly thereafter, that the reaction was largely due to the effect of the dichromate on the starch size in the paper. This soon attracted the attention of the ubiquitous Talbot, who, in 1852, patented *photoglyphic drawing,* based on the tanning effect of dichromates on a number of organic colloids, including glue, gelatin, starch, and various gums.

The honor of applying this technique to the production of photographic prints belongs to Alphonse Louis Poitevin, a French chemist and engineer. His research led to the eventual discovery of several methods of printing, including

Figure 1.13
Woodbury Process Portrait of Dr. W. H.
Russell. Lock and Whitfield

Poitevin's research led to the carbon and collotype processes

carbon and collotype processes. In the carbon process, a layer of gelatin containing powdered carbon and dichromate is spread on paper, dried, and exposed under a negative. The image, composed of hardened gelatin and carbon, remains on the paper after the unexposed (still soluble) portions of the gelatin area are washed away in hot water. This first form of the technique produced a black-and-white image without gradation, but later modifications resulted in a complete range of tones, making it one of the best of the nonsilver processes.

The collotype process also uses a dichromated gelatin layer, often on glass, but without the carbon pigment. Exposure tans the gelatin, making it less absorptive to water and therefore capable of holding a coating of greasy ink. When properly dampened and inked, the collotype plate can be used for printing, similar to a lithograph stone. The exposed portions, holding ink, print dark, while the unexposed portions, holding water and repelling the ink, print light in tone. When competently done, the process is capable of producing a complete range of tones, and is, in fact, still considered to be one of the finest methods of printing known, although it has practically disappeared as a commercial process.

The woodburytype was an ingenious and elegant process

Another interesting and ingenious process, which was used for production runs of a few thousand printed impressions, was the *woodburytype*. Making use of the fact that the image on an exposed dichromated gelatin film is in low relief, Walter B. Woodbury, an English photographer, devised a method that pressed the relief image onto a lead plate to form an intaglio image. The depressions thus formed were filled with liquid pigmented gelatin which was then impressed on paper. The image was formed by the varying thicknesses of the pigment. The woodburytype process is without a doubt the most faithful method of mechanical reproduction of images ever devised. In many cases, woodburytype prints are indistinguishable from actual carbon prints; there is no artifical grain or texture, and the original tonal scale and sharpness of detail are preserved.

Gelatin began to replace albumin by 1880

Although albumin paper continued to be used into the 1900s, the gelatin-coated papers, introduced before 1880, gave amateur and professional photographers a more versatile and stable print material. The "art" photographers, however, were not so easily pleased. The Naturalists, especially, sought a quality of surface and tone that the silver emulsions could not provide and began to look for alternatives. Two processes that suited them were photogravure and the platinotype.

Photogravure, which became popular in the 1890s, was derived from another early patent of Talbot's. In this process a positive transparency is printed on gelatin-coated paper, sensitized with dichromate. The paper is then soaked briefly and rolled onto a grained copper plate. Warm water rinses dissolve the unexposed gelatin, leaving the image in low relief on the copper surface. When dry, the copper is etched in ferric chloride to produce an intaglio image which can be inked and printed like an aquatint etching. While this procedure is a handcraft process, it was modified by Karel Klíč, a Czechoslovak, for use on rotary printing presses in 1895.

Platinotype: one of the most permanent print processes

Herschel's early investigations led to various photographic processes based on the light-sensitive properties of iron salts. These included numerous variations on the blueprint or cyanotype, the chrysotype, kallitype, and most importantly the platinotype, which was first made practical and patented by Willis in 1873. The platinotype image is composed of platinum metal and is considered to be one of the most permanent photographic prints. It is typically neutral gray to brownish in tone (although bluish grays are occasionally seen) with excellent, delicate highlight and midtone gradation. Platinum paper was manufactured and sold in Europe from about 1879 until World War I. It was still available in America as late as the early 1930s.

For almost thirty years after its introduction by Archer, the collodion process reigned supreme in spite of its obvious shortcomings. It was not sensitive enough, it had to be used wet, and the large glass plates were fragile and bulky to handle. In the mid-1870s gelatin began to be used, first as a coating for printing papers and then for camera materials.

The flexible film controversy

The first of these required elaborate handling. The emulsion was coated on a paper base for exposure in the camera, then developed and stripped off the paper to another support material, such as glass, for printing. Glass plates were also coated directly for camera use, but the growing public's desire for smaller, lighter cameras spurred experimenters in their search for glass substitutes.

The first commercial production of flexible film is credited to John Carbutt in 1888, but the Reverend Hannibal Goodwin had independently invented a similar film and applied for patent rights the previous year. Goodwin did not have enough money to produce his film and his patent application was so vague that it had to be revised several times.

By the time his patent was finally granted in 1898, the Eastman Company had also devised a flexible film, patented it, and gone into production. At Goodwin's death in 1900, his patent was taken over by Edward and Henry Anthony, who filed suit against Eastman for infringement. The litigation continued for twelve years, during which time the firms of Anthony and Scovill merged to form Ansco. In 1914 the courts found in favor of Ansco, and Eastman settled the claim for $5 million.

George Eastman selected the name "Kodak" arbitrarily

By this time the Eastman Kodak Company had captured the amateur market with a simple, portable camera that could be purchased, loaded with one hundred exposures of rollfilm, for $25. Eastman selected the name *Kodak* for it quite arbitrarily. He wanted a name that was easy to remember, one

"You press the button; we do the rest"

which was not liable to be mispronounced in any language and one which could be registered in the patent office without confusion. Additionally, he supposedly admired the "firmness" of the letter *K*.

In practically no time, the name Kodak and the slogan that accompanied it, "You press the button; we do the rest," were household words. The slogan was no idle boast. When the one hundred pictures were taken, the owner simply mailed the entire camera back to the company. For $10 the film was removed and processed, prints were made, and the camera was reloaded and returned with the finished pictures, ready for the next one hundred shots.

The "Photochemical Investigations" of Hurter and Driffield

With the formation of large manufacturing corporations like the Eastman Kodak Company, technical research in photography spurted ahead. The heyday of the amateur kitchen-chemist was definitely over. A significant step in this direction was the publication in 1890 of a paper by Dr. Ferdinand Hurter and Vero C. Driffield, entitled "Photochemical Investigations and a New Method of Determination of the Sensitiveness of Photographic Plates." This was the first serious attempt to analyze the effects of exposure and development and to organize the findings into useful form. This effort was not lost on the pictorialist leader, Henry P. Robinson, who in a magazine article in1892 said:

didn't impress H. P. Robinson

> Two very clever scientists, whom I much respect, Dr. Hurter and Mr. Driffield, have proved to everybody's unsatisfaction that photographers have no control over the gradations; but this does not alter the fact that— to put the simplest case—he (sic) knows when a negative is over- or underexposed or developed too dense or too thin to properly represent his idea of nature. . . .

Robinson, like most of his contemporaries, was under the impression that image density and contrast could be controlled equally well by modifying either exposure or development and that exposure errors could be corrected by suitable development. Hurter and Driffield's work was not accepted fully by many amateurs for almost fifty years.

The techniques of photography by 1910 were similar to those used today. Cameras of all shapes and sizes were available; films were sensitive enough to make action pictures possible; lenses of large relative aperture and good correction existed; and color photographs, long a theoretical possibility, became a practical reality with the commerical production of *Autochrome* film by the Lumière brothers, Auguste and Louis, in 1907.

Advancement of Color Techniques

Color! The Lumiere brothers' Autochrome film

From the earliest days of photography, fixing the colors was an intriguing problem. Color theory was still in a primitive state in 1839 and, of course, the simple silver compounds that formed the sensitive surfaces of the daguerreotype and calotype were almost totally blind to half of the visible spectrum.

It was generally believed that color was an intrinsic quality of a material's surface and that the different hues were due to differences in the molecular structure. Because of this, the early researchers spent a great deal of time compounding various mixtures of the silver salts known to be light-sensitive, coating them on paper and other materials, and observing their reaction to colored light. They were encouraged, occasionally, by the formation of colored compounds which seemed to relate to the light color which formed them. In a few cases, daguerreotypes were reported to have recorded traces of color, frequently reddish tints.

Early researchers in color photography

Robert Hunt, one of the more reliable and perceptive chemists of the time, reported one instance, in 1843, when he photographed (on calotype paper) a scene containing "a clear blue sky, stucco-fronted houses and a green field." After a fifteen-minute exposure in the camera he obtained

> a very beautiful picture . . . which held between the eye and the light, exhibited a curious order of colours. The sky was of a crimson hue, the houses of a slaty blue, and the green fields of a brick red tint.

The Rev. Levi Hill announced a special color process

In 1851 the Reverend Levi Hill, of Westkill, New York, announced that he had perfected a special daguerreotype process with which he claimed to have made

> a view containing a red house, green grass and foliage, the wood-color of the trees, several cows of different shades of red and brindle, colored garments on a clothes-line, blue sky, and the faint blue of the atmosphere, intervening between the camera and the distant mountains, very delicately spread over the picture, as if by the hand of a fairy artist.

but was plagued by "invisible goblins"

The excitement that this announcement generated was sufficient to bring ordinary daguerreotype to a virtual standstill, and according to a contemporary photographer, Marcus A. Root, "injured the heliographic artists to the amount of many thousands of dollars." Hill seems to have convinced many of his contemporaries that the process was genuine. However, as time went by and he failed to release details of the procedure, explaining that he was having difficulty with the color yellow and referring to the "invisible goblins" which were plaguing him, their suspicions grew.

Root, who had at first believed Hill's claim, ultimately discounted it as a trick and suspected that the few examples that Hill had actually shown were "probably common daguerreotypes, carefully colored by hand. " One that he examined revealed "dry colored powder . . . distinctly visible on the face and hair," and, he concluded, "As his endeavor succeeded but partially, if at all, and as there appears to have been deception in the matter, I shall meddle with it no further."

Maxwell and Sutton produced "a sort of photograph . . . in natural colors"

The idea that color is a characteristic of light rather than surface and the concept of *color separation* of white light were demonstrated in 1861 by Maxwell and Sutton. Sutton had photographed a colored ribbon through red, green, and violet filters (he also prepared a yellow separation which was not used) and made positive transparencies of the negatives. Using the same filters and three separate projectors, Maxwell projected the colored images in register on a screen to produce what Sutton described as "a sort of photograph of the striped ribbon . . . in natural colours."

which shouldn't have worked at all

Theoretically this shouldn't have worked, since the collodion plates used were not at all sensitive to red, but Ralph Evans, a hundred years later, proved, by recreating the experiment, that the red image had actually been produced by fluorescence of the particular dye used in the red stripes.

Louis Ducos du Hauron confused the color primaries

In 1869 Louis Ducos du Hauron described a method of producing color images by making a negative and viewing the subsequent positive through a screen covered with tiny dots or lines of red, yellow, and blue. This was an ingenious idea and the one that was eventually used in the very successful Lumière process. However, du Hauron mistakenly recommended the *subtractive* (pigment) primaries instead of the correct *additive* (light) primaries, red, green, and blue. He did, however, present a workable plan for making color prints or transparencies by using colored carbon tissues.

In 1873 Dr. Hermann Vogel made the initial discovery of dye-sensitizing, which extends the sensitivity of silver emulsions into the green, yellow, and red regions of the spectrum. This discovery was soon improved by Becquerel, Waterhouse, Eder, and others. The first panchromatic gelatin plates, sensitive to all the visible colors, were marketed in 1906 by Wratten and Wainwright.

Autochrome was the first of the screen processes

Panchromatic sensitivity finally made color photography possible. The Lumière brothers' Autochrome film, marketed in 1907, employed a screen of minute dyed starch grains coated with a panchromatic emulsion. The film, exposed through the screen, was developed to form a black-and-white negative which was, in turn, bleached out. Reexposure and development produced a positive transparency which, when viewed through the screen, appeared as a full color image of the original scene. Several other films subsequently appeared, based on a similar principle but using screens of ruled lines rather than the dyed starch grains. One such material, Dufaycolor, was available in both roll and sheet sizes until the 1940s.

The screen processes, good as they were, had their faults. They were relatively insensitive—Autochrome required fifty times more exposure than comparable black-and-white film—and the image could not be enlarged to any great degree without revealing the screen texture.

One solution to these problems was sought in the one-shot camera design. Three films were exposed simultaneously, each through its appropriate filter, by an ingenious arrangement of semitransparent mirrors. When developed, the negatives could be printed by any of several methods, such as *carbro* or *wash-off relief* (later called *dye-transfer*), to produce a full color print. Although these cameras could take color photographs of fine quality under ideal conditions, they were clumsy and slow.

Kodachrome: 1935

As early as 1912 Siegrist and Fischer had devised a process for producing color by chemically forming dyes in the emulsion during development. This method is employed by most modern color films but it was not reliable enough to be useful until about 1936. The early difficulties were largely due to the tendency of the dyes to migrate or bleed in the emulsion layers. Kodachrome film, introduced in 1935, avoided this difficulty by omitting the color couplers from the emulsions and introducing them during processing.

Ektachrome: 1942

With the appearance of Ektachrome film in 1942, positive reversal color film became both practical and convenient. Kodacolor, released for general use in 1941, and Ektacolor, in 1947, were designed to produce color negatives. With their introduction color became a relatively simple process and successive improvements, by various manufacturers, have brought color printing within reach of everyone.

Gasparcolor employed the principle of dye-destruction

A quite different approach to color was described by Christiansen in 1918 and by Gaspar in the early 1930s. Gasparcolor and the modern refinement of it, *Cibachrome* (see chapter 7), employed the principle of dye-destruction. In this process the image dyes are incorporated in the emulsion during manufacture and are bleached selectively as the silver image is removed during processing. This process results in images of relatively great stability and exceptional sharpness.

The "instant" color cameras

An almost incredibly complex and ingenious color film and camera system was announced in 1972 by the Polaroid Corporation. Called the SX-70, the camera features automatic exposure control and produces "instant" color prints that process themselves after ejection from the camera. The film, containing no less than sixteen layers of emulsion material, incorporates its own darkroom in the form of an opaque chemical layer that protects the developing image from light. At the end of the developing action and as the image becomes stable, the opacifier gradually disappears, leaving the image sealed under a plastic cover clearly visible against a white ground.

SX-70 cameras and film have proven to be extremely popular, as have the somewhat similar "Colorburst" products made by Kodak.

Post-War Advances in Photographic Equipment

Since World War II the technical evolution of photographic equipment has gradually accelerated. The single-lens reflex camera, exemplified before the war by the Graflex and the 35mm Exakta, was considerably improved by the addition of a pentaprism viewing system which corrected the lateral reversal of the image and increased its magnification and brightness. The first prism-reflex camera, the Contax S, was manufactured soon after the war by the East German half of the Zeiss Company and the new design quickly became a model for the industry.

Japanese cameras dominate the world market

In the early 1950s the Japanese camera industry began to complete in the world market with cameras that were rather obvious copies of the highly respected pre-war German cameras, Leica, Contax, and Rolleiflex. These designs evolved rapidly, however, and in a very few years the Japanese were producing quantities of excellent, relatively inexpensive cameras of original design. Their industry has continued to excel and dominates the world market today in numbers of camera models and lenses. Much of this success has been due to an aggressive research program. Japanese designers have consistently led the way in introducing such technical refinements as the instant-return mirror, automatic diaphragm, various forms of exposure automation, commercial production of multicoated lenses, and the metal blade focal plane shutter.

Figure 1.14
John Thomson (1837–1921). *The Crawlers,*
from *Street Life in London,* woodburytype.
(Courtesy of the University of Michigan
Museum of Art)

**Progress has been rapid;
there is no end in sight**

Improvements in lens design have been dramatic, too. Computers now do in seconds the optical calculations that used to take years of human figuring. New glasses, new construction techniques, and new testing procedures have resulted in a generation of lenses that are more versatile, more precise, and, in some cases, less expensive than comparable models of twenty years ago.

There seems to be no end in sight, either. Although recent improvements in design features, lens quality, miniaturization, and automation seem almost revolutionary, it seems likely that the cameras we admire today will seem primitive to the photographers of the next generation.

**Color materials are becoming
increasingly popular**

The changes in photographic materials over the years have not all resulted in obvious improvement, however. Certainly black-and-white films have become more sensitive, sharper and finer-grained, and are less easily damaged in processing than were pre-war films. Color materials, too, have improved in most respects, although there are some people who will argue that the quality of color reproduction is no better, and perhaps worse, than that of Lumière's Autochromes. The "instant" color films by Polaroid and Kodak are technical miracles, and Cibachrome has brought a new standard of image sharpness and brilliance within reach of the amateur printer.

But the improvements in color materials seem to have been made at the expense of the black-and-white, which, deliberately or not, the manufacturers

Figure 1.15
Jacob A. Riis (1849-1914). *Old House in Cherry Street, The Cradle of the Tenement.* (Jacob A. Riis Collection, Museum of the City of New York)

appear to be deemphasizing. Large sheet films are increasingly difficult to find and some have been discontinued entirely, but a good variety of rollfilms are available in most sizes, and resin-coated printing papers are plentiful. High quality fiber-based papers, which appeared to be headed for extinction in the mid-1970s, were apparently saved by the protests of art photographers. We now have a few very fine fiber-based papers to choose from—at premium prices. It seems likely that prices will continue to increase—perhaps dramatically—in the years ahead.

Editorial Photography

Lewis Hine saw photography's potential for effecting social change

By 1900, halftone reproductions of photographs were appearing frequently in magazines, books, and newspapers, and the photograph was beginning to be appreciated as an effective means of communication and persuasion. Lewis Hine, a trained sociologist, saw its potential for effecting social change and, teaching himself to use a camera, began to document the callous treatment of immigrants at Ellis Island and their painful entry into the melting pot of New York City's tenement district.

So had some earlier workers

Hine was not the first photographer to work in this vein. Mayhew and Beard had collaborated on a major social study *London Labour and the London Poor* in the early 1850s; Adolphe Smith and John Thomson had published a similar report, in words and pictures, called *Street Life in London* in 1877; and Jacob Riis had produced a series of books aimed at social reform, the first of which, *How the Other Half Lives,* was a scathing indictment of New York's slum lords and the festering conditions in their tenements in the 1880s.

***Street Life in London* was an important book**

Street Life in London was an important book for two reasons. It was a notable early attempt to use the camera editorially, and it was illustrated with woodburytypes, which gave Thomson's photographs authenticity and power. Beard's daguerreotypes for *London Labour and the London Poor* were copied and published as wood engravings, and Riis's photographs were similarly translated into print by a hand-engraver. In both cases the pictures suffer from a kind of esthetic distance. They lack credibility and take on a stylistic prettiness which contradicts their intended message.

Figure 1.16
Before about 1900, Riis's book, *How the Other Half Lives,* was illustrated with engravings like this one. The artists apparently felt free to "improve" the compositions, as has been done here.

Riis photographed with obvious passion—but had some problems

Hine's photographs undoubtedly benefitted from being published as convincing halftones, but they are also well-seen, well-crafted images which invite attention. Thomson's pictures, superb as they are, have a theatrical quality, occasionally flawed by clumsy retouching. Riis photographed with obvious passion and sincerity but the camera and the subject conditions were frequently too much for him to handle. His pictures are harsh in gradation, frequently out of focus or blurred, and rather haphazardly composed. It's probably remarkable that he managed to get any pictures at all, considering the awkwardness of the circumstances. On at least two occasions the flame from his flash powder set fire to the buildings he was photographing, and once he managed to ignite his own clothing. Regardless of his technical ineptitude, Riis's pictures accomplished their purpose. They awakened public sympathy and started a program of reforms which brought about real improvements. Hine's first work with the immigrants, then, continued the campaign that Riis had begun some twenty years before.

Hine's later work

In 1908 Hine began a series of pictures of Pittsburgh miners. He also worked for the Child labor Committee to expose the exploitation of children in various industries. These are some of his most powerful pictures and they helped to bring about new laws and reforms designed to protect children. During World War I, Hine served as a photographer with the Red Cross in Europe. Later he returned to devote himself to a series called "Men at Work," in which he documented the construction of the Empire State Building, climbing among the girders with the construction workers to capture both the spirit and the details of the project.

Arnold Genthe documented the San Francisco earthquake

In April 1906 San Francisco was virtually destroyed by a violent earthquake and the devastation was carefully recorded by Arnold Genthe, a resident portrait photographer. Genthe was well known for his idealized portrait studies and romantic landscapes, but his most significant early work was his extended

Figure 1.17
Lewis Hine (1874–1940). *Young Millworker.*
(Collection of the author)

Dr. Erich Salomon: the father of modern photojournalism

document of San Francisco's Chinatown. The first tremors of the earthquake destroyed Genthe's studio but he coolly borrowed a little box camera and proceeded to document the disaster as it occurred, displaying the courage and instincts of a true news photographer. This was probably the high point of his career. In later years he reverted to his pictorial style and his work, although competently done, was undistinguished.

After World War I, news photography was no longer a novelty. The unique power of the photograph to communicate ideas was just beginning to be appreciated.

Dr. Erich Salomon, sometimes called the father of modern photojournalism, was one of the first to concentrate in this field. Like many of the earlier workers, he began taking pictures rather late in life (at the age of about forty-two) more out of necessity than real interest. Employed by a German publishing house, he found that working with hired photographers was a time-consuming and expensive business, so he bought a camera and set out to learn to use it.

The camera that made him famous was the Zeiss Ikon (Dresden) Ermanox, which was introduced in 1927. It took 4.5 cm × 6 cm glass plates in individual holders and featured an amazingly fast f/1.8 Ernostar lens of 85mm focal length. (Salomon's own camera was equipped with an f/2.0 lens, according to his son.)

Salomon experimented briefly with artificial lighting, but soon gave it up in favor of the more natural and pleasing effect of available light. Using the little Ermanox on a tripod because of the long exposures required (usually from about 1/5 second to one full second), he specialized in photographing political notables, usually unposed, at their meetings and conferences. He had an uncanny knack for catching his subjects unaware in the midst of some characteristic or expressive gesture, somehow managing—in spite of the relatively long exposure times—to avoid excessive blurring of the image.

Figure 1.18
Erich Salomon (1886–1944). *Supreme Court, Chief Justice Hughes Presiding, 1932.*
(Courtesy of the IMP, GEH)

He was a master of persuasion and subterfuge

He was a master of persuasion and subterfuge when it was required to get the picture, often concealing his camera in a flower vase, in a briefcase, in a stack of books, or in his own clothing. He once smuggled a camera into the Supreme Court, where pictures were strictly forbidden, by putting his arm in an enormous sling and concealing the camera in the wrappings of the cast. He was so successful in these efforts that he eventually became accepted in international political circles; and a famous diplomat was once heard to remark, "Where is Salomon? If we begin without him people will think this conference is not important!"

Like Mathew Brady, Salomon had a great sense of the historical significance of his work. It is ironic that he died in a German prison camp, a victim of a political system that he had watched, documented, and opposed. Characteristically, he managed to conceal his precious negatives from his captors. Just before he was arrested, he arranged for some of them to be left with the librarian of the Dutch parliament and was able to bury the rest, safely wrapped and sealed, in a friend's garden.

The picture magazines appear

The 1930s were significant years in the history of photography. *Fortune* magazine was launched in late 1929 and did well in spite of the great stock market crash and the subsequent depression. *Life* magazine began in 1936, starting a whole new trend in journalism, based on the concept of the picture story. *Life's* Alfred Eisenstadt (who had worked beside Salomon in covering the Geneva League of Nations conferences) and Margaret Bourke-White were original staff photographers whose names soon became familiar to everyone. It was not long before other publishers got on the bandwagon. *Look* appeared in 1937, followed closely by a number of others, such as *Pic* and *Click*. Pictorial supplements were also added to Sunday newspapers and suddenly the nation was picture-conscious.

Advertising photography improved rapidly

Advertisers were relatively slow to employ photographic illustration. Although articles and stories in magazines like *Vanity Fair* were illustrated almost entirely with photographs before 1900, their ad illustrations were rarely photographic before about 1910, and advertising photography, as we think of it now, was not practiced until the 1920s. It quickly reached a high degree of quality and sophistication, however, in the work of Steichen, Beaton, Outerbridge, Hiller, and later Horst, Rawlings, Blumenfeld, Matter, Penn, and a great many others.

Figure 1.19
Russell Lee (1903–   ). *Sharecropper Mother Teaching Children, Transylvania, La.,* 1939.
(Library of Congress)

Roy Stryker and the FSA photographic unit

compiled a stunning document of the American poor

The earliest advertising photographs were often simply pictures, frequently of unrelated subject matter, that presumably attracted attention because of their novelty. It was not long, however, before photographs of the products themselves appeared, then the now-familiar pictures of models, frequently pretty girls and babies. Before World War I, though, exotic typography, art nouveau decoration, and outrageous verbal messages were the major elements of successful advertising.

The stock market crash of 1929, and the Depression following it, left millions of Americans impoverished. Various government agencies were established to provide employment and stimulate economic recovery. One of these, now known as the Farm Security Administration, included a photographic unit headed by Roy Stryker. Stryker was not a photographer himself, but he was appreciative of good pictures. He was also sensible enough to hire good people and let them work more or less in their own styles. The project began in 1935. Arthur Rothstein, Dorothea Lange, Walker Evans, Russell Lee, Ben Shahn, John Vachon, and Marion Post Wolcott were among the dozen or so photographers employed, and by the time America entered World War II, when the project was ended, they had amassed more than 250,000 negatives. These pictures, now filed in the Library of Congress Archives, are a stunning document of the suffering of the American poor during those dreadful times. The FSA project was successful in eliciting sympathy and support for the homeless and destitute victims of the Depression and proved again, as the work of Thomson, Riis, and Hine had done, the persuasive force of the photographic image.

Among the many photographers working in the photojournalistic style of the 1920s and 1930s, three names stand out: André Kertész, Brassaï (Gyula Halâsz), and Henri Cartier-Bresson.

Kertész was one of the first to use the Leica

Kertész, born in 1894 in Budapest, travelled to Paris in 1925 to make his way as a photographer. He had virtually no previous training and only an amateur's experience but his determination was strong. Before long he was selling some of his pictures to friends and managing to get a few assignments from local magazines. He was one of the first to buy and use the newly introduced Leica and immediately fell in love with it. By the mid-1930s he was successful and famous.

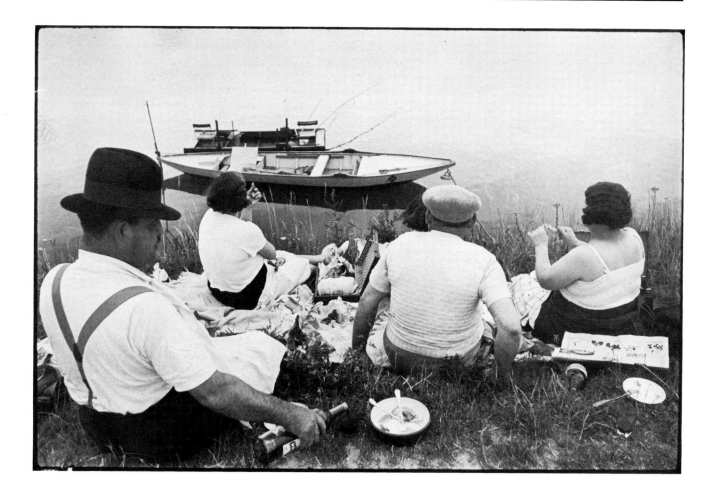

Figure 1.20
Henri Cartier-Bresson (1908–   ). *Sunday on the banks of the Marne, 1938,* from *The Decisive Moment.*
(Courtesy of Magnum Photos, Inc.)

He has been rediscovered as an innovative pioneer

Brassaï is an unusually versatile and talented artist

Cartier-Bresson called his Leica "the extension of my eye"

In 1936 he came to the United States to work for a commercial studio, a move that turned out to be a near-disaster. Unable to return to France because of the war in Europe, he found himself overwhelmed by the pressures of commercial photography and his natural sensitivity was stifled. He settled into semiobscurity for more than twenty years, supporting himself with competently done, but uninspired, work until illness forced him into temporary retirement in 1960. It gave him time to reflect and in 1962 he gave up commerical work to return to his own expression. Once again the wry humor and economy of design, which had characterized his work in Paris, appeared in his pictures and he has now been rediscovered as one of the most innovative of the pioneers of journalistic photography.

Brassaï (a name derived from his native Transylvanian town, Brasso) was a young painter, fresh out of art school, when he arrived in Paris in 1923 and immediately fitted himself into the community of artists. He soon met Kertész, who helped stimulate his interest in photography by lending him a camera. He immediately began a series of pictures that eventually became a book, *Paris by Night.* An unusually versatile and talented artist, Brassaï has alternately worked as a painter, sculptor, photographer, cinematographer, author, and stage designer and has done them all well. This same restless capability is evident in his photographs. They are impressively varied in style, from the Atget-like views of streets and parks and the candid vignettes of cabaret life, reminiscent of Lautrec's lithographs, to penetrating portraits and abstract compositions based on graffiti. Brassaï's work wears well and, although well known, he deserves more attention than he has been given.

Henri Cartier-Bresson dabbled in painting as a child before taking up photography. His first photographs were taken with a little wooden camera without a shutter, in a style inspired by Atget's pictures. He discovered the Leica in the early 1930s and said of it, "It became the extension of my eye. . . ." An adequate allowance made it possible for him to travel extensively and he began to work in the style that was to make him famous. He was, he said, "determined to 'trap' life . . . to seize the whole essence . . . of some situation that was in the process of unrolling itself before my eyes."

In 1947 Cartier-Bresson and four other free-lance photographers formed Magnum Photos, a cooperative organization which distributed their work. Since then Cartier-Bresson's photographs have appeared frequently in publications around the world, including more than twenty books—the most famous of which, *The Decisive Moment,* was published in 1952 and is now a rare and expensive collector's item. Although he is an avowed "photo-reporter," committed to the concept of the published picture story, Cartier-Bresson's work shows a greater sensitivity than is typical in photojournalism. His compositions are always based on the full frame dimensions of the 35mm format and are typically taut and graceful. He has a masterful sense of organization and pattern and his pictures frequently feature dramatic effects of light and shade. But the identifying characteristic of his work is suggested by *The Decisive Moment*—his ability to "preserve life in the act of living."

World War II brought advances in technology

World War II brought tremendous advances in technology. Photography played a vital part in every phase of the war effort and was extensively employed for aerial reconnaissance. But its greatest value may have derived from the work of the news photographers who, moving into combat with the front-line troops, brought the grim reality of war home to the people with unprecedented immediacy. The work of these photographers, Robert Capa, Eugene Smith, Carl Mydans, Margaret Bourke-White, Gordon Parks, and many others, raised photojournalism to a new level of effectiveness as a medium of communication.

Until about 1960 the photojournalists were major interpreters of the world's news. At the same time the photo-illustrators played a major part in moulding public taste and controlling buying habits. It was a serious blow to both groups when that lusty young medium, television, began to usurp their functions. *Look* magazine died rather quietly in 1971, a victim of increased costs and reduced advertising income—the same factors that had previously eliminated *Colliers, Saturday Evening Post,* and others. *Life* struggled gamely on but the handwriting was on the wall. In spite of a brave editorial policy of "more picture emphasis," waning public interest in the magazine picture story and loss of advertising revenue finally took their toll. The magazine published its last regular issue (in its original form) in December 1972.

Television is an effective influence

As the flow of advertising money began to shift from magazine space to television, a similar but less traumatic readjustment was forced on the illustrators. While some of the well-established photographers were relatively unaffected, a great many saw their profits dwindle. By 1970 it was clear that photographic journalism and illustration would never be the same again. Television has the public firmly in its grip and has become a frighteningly effective influence on our lives.

The Art of Photography

The nineteenth century saw rapid advances in science

In the early years of the nineteenth century, rapid changes were beginning to take place in science and industry. In the entire history of chemistry, for example, only about thirty elements had been identified before 1800 and by 1839 twenty-five new ones had been discovered. Fundamental electrical theory was being formulated by Ohm, Faraday, Ampere, Henry, and others. The steam engine, which had supplied power for the beginning of the industrial revolution, was being refined and installed in ships and railroad engines. Iron was being rolled into sheets and bars for structural uses. The inventors were busy, too. The telegraph, the Colt revolver, Portland cement, McCormick's reaper, the electric pile battery, the electromagnet, and vulcanized rubber, to name a few, were all invented between 1800 and 1839.

and the arts were in a similar state of flux

The arts in France, especially painting, were in a similar state of flux. The neoclassic influence still lingered, with Ingres at its head. Delacroix, as the leading Romanticist, was enthusiastically painting harem scenes and trading insults with Ingres at every opportunity, and the open air painters of Barbizon were setting their easels in the fields and forests to paint directly from nature.

Figure 1.21
D. O. Hill (1802-1870). *St. Andrews,*
calotype.
(Courtesy of the University of Michigan
Museum of Art)

Delaroche: "From this day painting is
dead!"

Painting and photography influenced
each other

Photography and Painting

The formal announcement of the daguerreotype process on August 19, 1839 and the sudden concentration of public attention on the photographic image was shocking to at least some of the artists of the day. When Delaroche saw his first daguerreotype he exclaimed, "from this day painting is dead!" but later he descibed photography as "an easy means of collecting studies" and decided that Daguerre had "rendered an immense service to the arts."

This ambivalence was typical. Ruskin, initially charmed by the daguerreotype, later became one of photography's sternest critics, and Ingres, who professed to despise photography (possibly because Delacroix was enthusiastic about it), is said to have worked rather frequently from photographs made for him by Nadar.

This uproar and confusion affected both painting and photography for many years. Many early photographers patterned their photographic compositions after the prevailing painting styles, while the painters, acutely conscious of the unique visual character of the photograph, were undoubtedly influenced by photography's incredible rendering of detail, its characteristic interpretation of light and shade, its informal compositions and its curious blurring of out-of-focus scenes and moving objects.

Although photography was probably a factor in the brief revival of interest in meticulously detailed painting such as that of the pre-Raphaelites, it was even more obviously an influence toward Impressionism and the freely composed snapshot vision of Daumier, Lautrec, and especially Degas. In this sense, painting profited tremendously from photography, while on the other hand the early photographers were hindered in their search for a genuinely photographic esthetic by the generally hostile art establishment.

Figure 1.22
Oscar G. Rejlander (1813-1875). *Two
Ways of Life.*
(Courtesy of the Royal Photographic
Society, London, and the IMP, GEH)

Hill and Adamson worked in calotype

**Rejlander's *Two Ways of Life* was
controversial**

H. P. Robinson's influence was enormous

It's hardly surprising, under the circumstances, that many of the early photographers were painters. Some of them, Delacroix, Corot, and Daubigny, for example, experimented a little with photography but remained essentially painters. Others, like Oscar Rejlander and Henry Reach Robinson, turned away from painting and concentrated on photography.

Some of the most notable work produced by an early painter-photographer was done by David Octavius Hill in partnership with Robert Adamson. The pair began their work in 1843 by making calotype portraits which Hill intended to use as reference material for a huge painting, depicting a conference of some four hundred Scottish churchmen. They soon began to photograph other people and scenes as well. Hill became so preoccupied that his painting was not completed for more than twenty years. Although they worked together for only about four years (Adamson became terminally ill in 1847), Hill and Adamson produced more than 2500 calotypes, many of which were portraits of enduring charm. Hill continued to work sporadically after Adamson's death but neither his later photographs nor his painting can be compared to the work done during his brief collaboration with Adamson.

Oscar Rejlander is best known for his large composite photographic composition, *Two Ways of Life,* done in 1857. Assembled from more than thirty separate photographs, this picture was an heroic allegory in the romantic style. Although it was a considerable success, it was highly controversial. The Photographic Society of Scotland refused to exhibit the photograph until it was agreed that the "offensive" half, depicting Dissipation, would be covered with drapery, leaving "respectable" Industry in view.

Rejlander made other composites but eventually turned toward "straight" photography and portraiture. Some of his work was remarkably inventive and advanced for his day and he deserves to be better known.

Robinson, like Rejlander, achieved immediate recognition for his montages. He was an extraordinarily prolific and extremely skillful photographer. He also was convinced that photography could be called an art, as long as it was governed by the same rules that had traditionally applied to painting. In promoting this view he wrote almost a dozen books and numerous articles, establishing himself as the spokesman for pictorial photography. His influence was enormous. So, apparently, was his ability to rationalize. Caught between the popular belief that "truth was beauty" and the obvious fact that the camera

Figure 1.23
Henry Peach Robinson (1830–1901). *Dawn and Sunset.*
(Courtesy of the Art Institute of Chicago)

Robinson and Emerson disliked each other's work

Emerson advocated a return to nature

recorded much truth that was not beautiful, Robinson solved the dilemma by declaring, in effect, that beauty was truth, and contended that combination printing (photomontage) permitted the photographer "greater facilities for representing the truth of nature."

Robinson's views continued to dominate photography well into the 1880s until he was challenged by Peter Henry Emerson, an avid amateur photographer, naturalist, and physician. Emerson and Robinson disliked each other's work intensely and Emerson, in particular, made no effort to be polite about it. Of combination printing he said: "this process is really what many of us practised in the nursery, that is, cutting . . . and pasting . . . though such 'work' may produce sensational effects in photographic galleries, it is but the art of the opera bouffe." Emerson advocated a return to nature and referred his readers to the work of the Barbizon painters. A naturalistic photograph, he declared must be

1. True in natural sentiment
2. True in appearance to the point of illusion
3. Decorative

To achieve these qualities he thought it necessary to use a slightly undercorrected lens, of relatively long focal length, at moderate aperture. Naturalistic focus was achieved when the background of the picture was thrown out of focus to an extent that did not produce "destruction of the structure," the principal object of the picture being either "sharp or just out of sharp."

Emerson's tremendous ego shows in his references to other photographers. Even in mentioning the three he most admired—Rejlander, Adam-Salomon, and Julia Margaret Cameron—he was careful to point out their limitations: Rejlander he thought of as a "trained painter (of) very second rate artistic ability"; Adam-Salomon, a sculptor "without first-rate ability"; and Cameron he described as "not an artist" and an "amateur."

and described Julia Margaret Cameron as "not an artist"

Julia Margaret Cameron was an amateur, certainly, but we now recognize her as an artist of significance. She was forty-eight years old when she began photographing in 1863, and within a year she had taught herself the rudiments of the craft. Using a rapid-rectilinear lens of 30″ focal length, she was a ruthless person to sit for, sometimes subjecting her subjects to extraordinarily long exposure times (in dim light) if she felt the visual effect was pleasing. Her portraits were her best work. They introduced a new directness and sensitivity to photography, which was ahead of her time. On the other hand, she was fond of illustrating biblical and literary themes and it's tempting to agree with Emerson's opinion of these, as "puerile and amateurish."

Figure 1.24
Peter Henry Emerson (1856–1936). *Setting the Bow Net,* platinum print.
(Courtesy of the University of Michigan Museum of Art)

Davison challenged Emerson's leadership

If the Impressionist painters were influenced by photography's treatment of atmosphere, soft-focus, movement blur, and halation (as it seems certain they must have been), some of the Naturalist photographers were, in turn, affected by Impressionism. One of them, George Davison, carried Emerson's naturalistic focus principles much farther than Emerson approved and, by promoting the virtues of soft-focus work, challenged Emerson's position as spokesman for art photographers. Emerson's reaction was immediate and spiteful. In a vitriolic renunciation of his previous views—as explained at great length in his book, *Naturalistic Photography for Students of the Art,* he declared that photography was not, and could never be, an art. The term *photographic impressionist,* which Davison was fond of, Emerson called "a term consecrate to charlatans, and especially to photographic imposters, pickpockets, parasites and vanity intoxicated amateurs." He then described Davison as "an amateur without training, and with superficial knowledge (who took) my old ideas . . . freely and impudently handed (them) about with no credit given me." Finally, he said, "when I have fully reconsidered the limited art possibilities of photography . . . I will write another book; in the meantime, let students avoid all spurious imitations."

and Emerson reacted spitefully

Emerson was clearly a difficult man to get along with but he was also a fine photographer of landscape and genre studies and an excellent craftsman. He worked almost exclusively in platinotype and photogravure.

Photography Becomes an Art in Its Own Right

A group of rebel pictorialists formed The Linked Ring

In 1892 a little group of rebel pictorialists broke away from the Royal Photographic Society and formed The Linked Ring Brotherhood. This group, which included most of the Naturalists, led now by Davison, was devoted to advancing the art of photography and included such notables as J. Craig Annan, Horsley Hinton, and Frederick Evans. Interestingly, H. P. Robinson was also a member, but Emerson, after his *Death of Naturalistic Photography* tirade, had returned to the venerable and conservative Royal. The Linked Ring lasted until 1910.

Figure 1.25
Julia Margaret Cameron (1815–1879). *Sir John Herschel.*
(Courtesy of the Art Institute of Chicago)

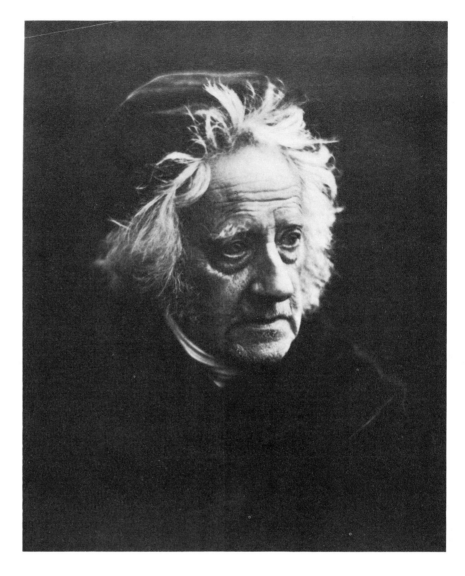

Emerson awarded prizes to Stieglitz and Fraprie

In 1887, while judging a photography contest, Emerson awarded the first prize to a young American, Alfred Stieglitz, and told Stieglitz that his picture, *A Good Joke,* was the only "truly spontaneous picture" in the exhibition. Similarly, in 1903 he gave first prize to a young American college student, Frank Fraprie. Fraprie eventually became a driving force in the Pictorialist movement in America, as editor of several photographic publications, including *The American Annual of Photography,* while Stieglitz was soon to assemble a little group of dedicated photographers who would call themselves the Photo-Secessionists.

Both remembered Emerson's appreciation with satisfaction

Although Fraprie and Stieglitz were poles apart philosophically (Fraprie later referred disparagingly to "Stieglitz and his crew" and the "Photo-Secession clique" in one of his articles), both remembered Emerson's appreciation of their work with satisfaction. It's interesting to note that Stieglitz carried on Emerson's philosophy of naturalism into straight photography, while Fraprie fixed superficially on Emerson's naturalistic focus and truth-in-sentiment recommendations and, with the other Pictorialists of the 1920s, 1930s, and 1940s, let those noble aims degenerate into out-of-focus images and contrived situation photographs of the most cloying sentimentality.

Alfred Stieglitz was born in New Jersey in 1864. He spent his student years in Europe and was introduced to photography in 1883 during his first year as an engineering student at the Berlin Polytechnic. He became obsessed with photography almost at once and experimented constantly while studying

Figure 1.26
Alfred Stieglitz (1864–1946). *The Terminal.*
(Courtesy of the Art Institute of Chicago)

**By 1890 Stieglitz was famous as
an exhibitor**

**"291" became a meeting place
for artists of all kinds**

chemistry under Vogel. He spent nine years in Europe, during which he studied and travelled on a modest income from his family, apparently leading a life that any young man would envy and taking pictures incessantly. By 1890 he was internationally famous as an exhibitor of photographs.

He returned to New York in 1890 and was fascinated by the city. An abortive attempt at business occupied him briefly, but he was soon out of it, devoting himself to photographing and promoting interest in photography by publishing *Camera Notes,* a quarterly for the Camera Club of New York. The group of sympathizers that soon surrounded him could have been called the "who's who" of American photography: Clarence White, Gertrude Käsebier, Alvin Langdon Coburn, Edward Steichen, Frank Eugene, Joseph Keiley, and others. In 1902 they formed their own informal group which Stieglitz, on impulse, named the Photo-Secession.

In 1903 Stieglitz published the first quarterly issue of *Camera Work,* a lavishly printed magazine devoted to the promotion of photography as an art form. The magazine and the Photo-Secessionists flourished for some time and their gallery, three rooms at 291 Fifth Avenue next to Steichen's room, became a meeting place for artists of all kinds.

The arts were united by Stieglitz as by no other individual. Although he was a photographer himself—and an extremely sensitive one—his passion transcended photography. He encouraged all artists who met his high standards of perception and dedication without caring what medium they chose to work in. As a seasoned traveller (and a member of the Linked Ring Brotherhood), he

Figure 1.27
Gertrude Käsebier (1852-1934). "Turner Family, Woburn, Mass."
(Courtesy of the IMP-GEH)

Stieglitz and Steichen imported European work

Stieglitz's efforts culminated in the Albright show

Stieglitz's strength and vision brought the arts together

Atget was a self-taught photographer

was thoroughly familiar with European photography and, with Steichen's advice and assistance, became acquainted with the work of many new talents in painting and sculpture, as well.

Together, he and Steichen began to import European work that seemed to them to be vital and significant. As a result many of the artists who are recognized as outstanding today were discovered and shown in America for the first time at 291—among them, Cezanne, Picasso, Braque, Matisse, Picabia, Toulouse-Lautrec, and Brancusi. He was equally supportive of promising American talent. The work of John Marin, Marsden Hartley, Arthur Dove, Max Weber, and Georgia O'Keeffe (whom Stieglitz later married) was shown frequently.

For the first three years, photographs dominated the walls of 291, but Stieglitz was discovering that the Photo-Secessionists were less vital than the young painters. During the year 1909 only three of the eleven shows presented were photographic. In the following years through May 1917, only three photographers were shown at 291: Steichen in 1910, Stieglitz himself in 1913, and Paul Strand in 1916. The other forty-seven exhibitions included paintings, drawings, children's art, sculpture, ceramics, lithographs, and caricatures.

Stieglitz's efforts to promote photography as a fine art culminated in a monumental exhibition of photographs in the Albright Museum of Art in Buffalo, New York, in 1910. In spite of the opposition of Frank Fraprie, who denounced the Photo-Secessionists as a "reactionary force of the most dangerous type," the exhibition (designed and hung by Max Weber) was a great success and a very significant step toward the acceptance of photography by the art establishment.

For fifteen years Stieglitz's strength and vision had brought the arts together and photography and painting had co-existed in an atmosphere of mutual respect. But it was painting that profited most immediately. The majority of photographers after World War I, as if in reaction to Stieglitz's influence, reverted to the fuzzy Victorian silliness of the 1890s. Photography did not become a vital art again, with a few notable exceptions, for more than thirty years.

In every period there seem to be a few photographers whose work is difficult to classify, and Eugène Atget is one of them. Born in France in 1856, he was raised by an uncle and went to sea as a cabin boy. Later he became an actor and toured the country playing minor roles until he was about forty-two. He began to photograph in 1898 and was self-taught. Using an old view camera and a simple set of lenses, he spent most of the rest of his life recording the city of Paris and its environs. Although he made a meager living by selling his views (many of them to local artists), he apparently knew very little about the work

Figure 1.28
Eugène Atget (1856–1927). *Un Coin de la Rue Reynie.*
(Courtesy of the University of Michigan Museum of Art)

Atget was a lonely figure but an important one

Lartigue began photographing at the age of seven

of other photographers and was, himself, similarly unknown during his lifetime. Much of his work was saved from discard after his death by the efforts of Berenice Abbott—also a fine photographer—who obtained a large number of his plates and published a book of his images. Atget was a lonely figure but an important one in the history of photography. His work was a personal, direct, intense, and unusually honest product of the photographic process.

At about the same time, another unknown photographer was beginning to exercise his unique vision. The absolute opposite of Atget in almost every respect, Jacques Henri Lartigue was seven years old when he took his first picture, a snapshot of his family. Lartigue's family was wealthy and they appear in his photographs as a very lively, fun-loving group of people. He recorded them in all sorts of activities but specialized in sports and action shots—swimming, jumping, attempting to fly, touring, and racing wheeled bobsleds. His other major interest was photographing fashionable women, usually strolling along the avenue, resplendent in silk and lace and feathers. These pictures have an immediacy and intimacy suggesting that the ladies considered the boy with the camera harmless, if not actually invisible. They could hardly have suspected that their images would hang in the Museum of Modern Art fifty years later, nor that they would become well-known visual symbols of the secure and affluent society of "La Belle Epoque."

The new freedom of thought and vision, which inspired painters to break away from the representation of subject matter, also affected a few photographers. Again, it appears that the two media fed on each other: the Futurists' attempts to express speed and motion obviously derived from the photographs

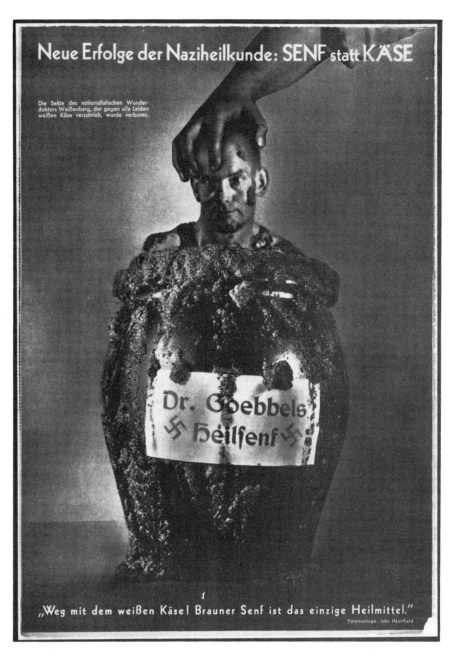

Coburn experimented with Vortographs

Dada: the anti-art of the irrational and absurd

of Muybridge, Marey, and Eakins, while the Futurists and Cubists, in turn, inspired Alvin Langdon Coburn to experiment with mirror-multiplied photographic images that he called *Vortographs.* Coburn, who had been a member of the Photo-Secession and the Linked Ring Brotherhood, was very interested in portraiture during most of his early career, but later turned to more diverse subject matter. He was a skilled printer in photogravure and personally made and proofed the plates used to illustrate four of his books.

Coburn was not the first man to experiment with distortions of the photographic image; Ducos du Hauron, at least, had preceded him by almost thirty years. Coburn was, however, the first photographer to work with distortion in a deliberate attempt to create a new visual direction for photography. Although his Vortographs were clearly limited, his exploration of new viewpoints and perspectives was ahead of his time.

The appearance of the Dada movement in art, just before World War I, was a direct attack on traditional values of all sorts. Dada proclaimed itself the anti-art of the irrational and absurd and produced such unsettling objects as a urinal displayed as *R. Mutt's Fountain,* a flat-iron studded with carpet tacks, and Marcel Duchamp's saucy distortion of a color reproduction of the Mona

Figure 1.30
László Moholy-Nagy (1895–1946).
Photogram.
(Courtesy of the Art Institute of Chicago)

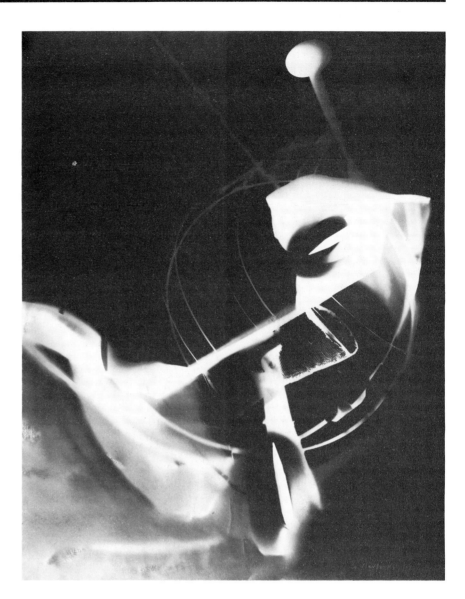

**Heartfield used photomontage to attack
the Nazi menace**

**Moholy-Nagy considered photography
to be an extension of vision**

Lisa, to which he added a pencilled beard and a moustache and the title, *L.H.O.O.Q.,* which spoken rapidly in French sounds like the phrase "Elle a chaud au cul" (she has hot pants).

The Dadaists and Surrealists were not interested in photography as such, but they frequently made use of photographic images in their collages. George Grosz, John Heartfield, and Hannah Höch were particularly adept at this art form and Heartfield, especially, used photomontage effectively to attack the rising Nazi menace in Germany. Dada eventually evolved into Surrealism and Constructivism, which, in turn, influenced some of the members of the Bauhaus in Germany in the early 1920s.

When the Nazis closed the Bauhaus in 1933, one of its members, László Moholy-Nagy, started the New Bauhaus (which later became the Institute of Design) in Chicago. Moholy-Nagy was convinced that photography was indispensible, not only as a scientific tool or means of expression, but fundamentally as an extension of vison. Like Christian Schad and Man Ray, Moholy-Nagy had reinvented the technique of shadow-printing which Talbot had called "photogenic drawing." Schad's prints were called *Schadographs,* Man Ray called his *Rayograms,* while Moholy-Nagy named his *photograms,* the term we usually use today.

Moholy-Nagy did not neglect straight photography but he was an experimenter and investigator by nature. Like Coburn he explored the visual effects of optical distortion and unusual viewpoint; but he went beyond Coburn by applying these techniques to graphic design and by pointing out the beauty to

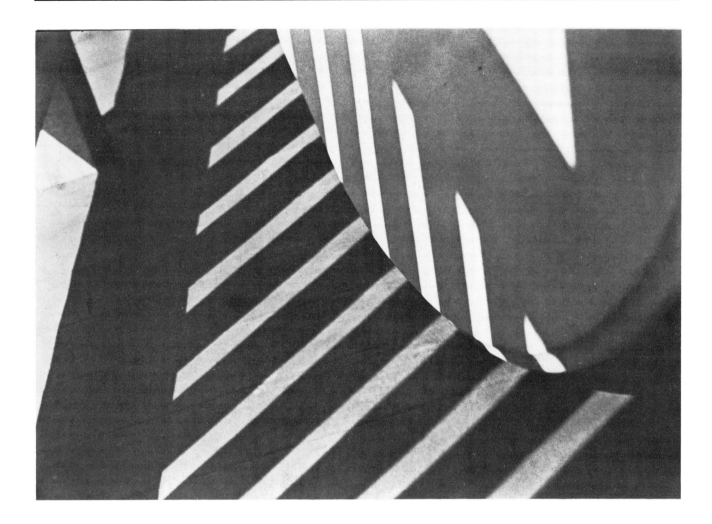

Figure 1.31
Paul Strand (1890-1976). *Shadows.*
(Courtesy of the Art Institute of Chicago)

be found in photomicrographs and other types of scientific photographs. Mo-holy-Nagy, like all the other Bauhaus artists, was committed to order, structure, and, to a degree, formula, but he was also a brilliant innovator whose teachings had a great deal to do with photography's acceptance as a visual language.

Meanwhile, photography was also evolving as an expressive medium. The final double issue of *Camera Work* in 1917 was devoted to the work of a young protégé of Stieglitz, Paul Strand. Strand had been introduced to Stieglitz while on a field trip to the 291 gallery with his teacher, Lewis Hine, and they formed an immediate friendship. Strand quickly worked his way through the soft-focus Pictorialist style and concentrated on straight photographs of New York and its street people, which Stieglitz described as being "brutally direct . . . devoid of trickery . . . devoid of any attempt to mystify. . . . These photographs are the direct expression of today."

Strand's photographs: "brutally direct. . ."

Strand worked as an X-ray technician and as a member of a medical movie crew during World War I. In the mid-1920s, after having supported himself for several years as a cinematographer, he returned to still photography and nature, first in Colorado, then in Maine and along the Atlantic coast. Later, in Mexico, Strand collected the images that ultimately comprised his gravure *Mexican Portfolio.* Alternating still and motion picture photography for several years, Strand did a number of documentary films and had a major exhibition in the Museum of Modern Art. Then, in 1948, he moved to France. He devoted the rest of his life to travelling and photographing, producing several books in collaboration with various authors. He died in 1976.

After the dissolution of the Photo-Secession group and the closing of 291 in 1917, Alfred Stieglitz withdrew to a more private existence for a while, but his crusade went on. He continued to encourage O'Keeffe and Marin especially, almost as symbols of an attitude in art that had to be protected and preserved.

Figure 1.32
Edward Weston (1886–1958). *Roses and Sunshine.*
From the *Platinum Print,* vol. 1, no. 5
August 1914.

Stieglitz called his "Songs of the Sky" *equivalents*

"An American Place" was a mecca for artists

In 1921 he prefaced a retrospective exhibition of his own work with a statement that ended, "I was born in Hoboken. I am an American. Photography is my passion. The search for Truth my obsession."

Later, in response to a comment that the power of his photographs resulted from his influence over the sitters, Stieglitz produced a series of cloud photographs "to show," he wrote, "that my photographs were not due to subject matter—not to special trees, or faces, or interiors . . . clouds were there for everyone—no tax as yet on them—free." These pictures, according to Stieglitz, inspired the composer, Ernest Bloch, to exclaim, "Music! music! Man, why that is music!" In an exhibition the next year, he showed another series of small cloud pictures entitled "Songs of the Sky." These two groups of photographs, which are very abstract and evocative, he called *equivalents,* meaning that they were intended to be seen not just as pictures of clouds but as incitements to perception, analogous to other experiences.

Although Stieglitz was not universally loved, by any means, no one can contest the fact that he was one of the most influential men in the history of art. Both painting and photography owe him a considerable debt. His final gallery, An American Place, opened in 1929 and continued to be a mecca for artists of all persuasions until his death in 1946.

On the West Coast, out of Stieglitz's immediate influence, the photography scene was less tempestuous. The Pictorialist influence was strong and, in 1906, when Edward Weston opened his first studio in California, he was completely committed to making soft-focus romantic portraits. He married and had four sons, but the marriage was not a happy one. He became increasingly dissatisfied with having to cater to the tastes of his clients, too, and in 1922 he travelled to New York where he met Stieglitz, O'Keeffe, Strand, and Sheeler. The meetings encouraged and stimulated him and, anxious to concentrate on

Figure 1.33
Edward Steichen (1879–1973). *Self Portrait.*
(Courtesy of the Art Institute of Chicago)

Weston sought personal expression in Mexico

a personal expression in photography, he travelled to Mexico with his oldest son Chandler and Tina Modotti, an artists' model. He lived there for almost two years, producing portraits, nudes, and cloud studies while working in quite close contact with Mexico's leading artists.

He returned to California in 1926 and in 1929 settled in Carmel, where he spent most of the remainder of his life. He worked with minimal equipment, an old 8″ × 10″ view camera and a primitive darkroom, but there is no hint of this in his photographs. They are still exceptional for their glorification of natural forms in light, their sharpness of detail, and their delicacy of texture.

His *Daybooks* are an inspiring record of his creative struggles

Weston kept a diary during most of his productive life and it has been published in two edited volumes, *The Daybooks of Edward Weston.* It is a revealing and inspiring record of the life and creative struggles of one of the major artists of this century. He was the first photographer to receive a Guggenheim Foundation Fellowship and was given a major retrospective exhibition in the Museum of Modern Art in New York in 1946. He died in Carmel in 1958.

In 1932 a little group of West Coast photographers banded together informally in reaction to Pictorialism. Calling themselves Group f-64, they worked to achieve sharpness and brilliance in their prints by careful selection of subject, camera position, light conditions, and focus. The title suggested their use of small lens apertures for greatest depth of field and good definition. Weston was a charter member of the group, as were Imogen Cunningham and Ansel Adams.

Adams was a trained musician before turning to photography

Adams had begun photographing only a few years earlier and was initially influenced by the prevailing Pictorialist style. He was a trained musician and photography was only an absorbing hobby until he happened to see some of Paul Strand's photographs in 1930. He was tremendously impressed and immediately decided to make photography his career. Within a very short time he was receiving international recognition, and in 1936 his work was shown in Stieglitz's gallery, An American Place.

Adams has spent much of his professional life photographing nature, concentrating on the Southwest and especially Yosemite. His photographs display a rare mixture of visual sensitivity and technical excellence and are notable for their dramatic effects of light, rich textures, and brilliant tonality.

Adams's Zone System has influenced a generation of students

He has been extremely productive and has published several books of photographs as well as a number of textbooks, the first of which, *Making a Photograph,* was published in 1935. He has also worked commercially and has been a consultant to the Polaroid Corporation for many years. As the acknowledged leader of the West Coast landscape photographers, Adams has influenced generations of students, many of them through his frequent workshops. But his fame as a teacher is due largely to his Zone System, a procedure for predicting and controlling the translation of subject tones into print values. Adams's place in the history of photography is secure; probably no other photographer has been more highly respected, more widely known, or more materially successful.

Steichen assembled "The Family of Man" exhibition

Edward Steichen, whose name had been intimately associated with photography since before 1900, became the director of photography for the Museum of Modern Art in New York in 1947. He brought to the post a variety of experience as painter, Pictorialist, Secessionist, aerial reconnaissance photographer during World War I, portrait, advertising, and fashion photographer, and director of photography for the Navy in World War II. During his directorship at the Museum of Modern Art, Steichen expanded and diversified the collection of photographs and put on more than forty photographic exhibitions, culminating in 1955 in a massive display of more than five hundred prints by photographers from all over the world. He called it "The Family of Man." Assembled from more than two million prints submitted, the exhibition was a notable success. In 1964 the museum established the "Edward Steichen Photography Center" in his honor and conferred on him the title of "Director Emeritus," which he held until his death at the age of 94 in 1973. Steichen's career in art and photography is almost without parallel. No other individual has combined so many talents, devoted so much energy, and achieved such success in so many branches of the medium.

It was a tour de force of photojournalism

In spite of its enthusiastic acceptance by viewers around the world, the "Family of Man," seen in retrospect, was impressive more for the statistics of its presentation than for its artistic significance. It told its story and was persuasive, but it used photography conservatively. Its real power lay in the sheer size and number of prints and the magnificence of its installation. It probably had to be done if only to complete the era of the picture story in a grand manner, but it was primarily a tour-de-force of photojournalism and had little to do with the "modern art" of photography in the 1950s. New, more personal and creative expressions were soon to appear.

The Post-War Era

The war's end brought sweeping social changes

The end of World War II brought sweeping social changes. With the post-war prosperity and the flood of consumer goods came the sobering realization that the world's last frontiers had been explored and that—for the first time in history—man had the physical capacity to exterminate himself with one grand gesture. To many young people of the 1950s and 1960s these factors combined into a ghastly paradox. They saw ahead of them lives full of comfort and plenty, but devoid of purpose, empty of human value, and threatened by atomic disaster, runaway population growth, and resource depletion. Their initial unease, heightened by the Korean War, became anguished rebellion with our involvement in Vietnam. Some of them looked at this new, crazy world with suddenly sharpened perception, and, while many were caught up in waves of semiorganized protest and demonstration, a few expressed themselves through their art, including photography.

Frank's book, *The Americans,* was new and startling

Robert Frank's book, *The Americans,* gave us a first shocked look at ourselves in 1959. The pictures seem quite ordinary now because Frank's work started a style that is still popular. In 1959, however, it was new and startling, direct, artless, and often irritating. It confronted us with things we had trained ourselves not to see, and we reacted with gut feelings of alienation, dislocation,

Figure 1.34
Robert Frank. *Elevator Girl.*
(Courtesy of Robert Frank, from *The Americans.*)

It seemed to deny the concept of the "fine print"

and a dismayed recognition of life's overwhelming trivia. Frank's work was a new, raw descendant of the social commentary approach to imagery, traceable through the Farm Security Administration documentary of the Depression to Hine, Riis, and Thomson. However, it had a new roughness of style which seemed to deny, or at least ignore, the older traditions of compositional elegance and the concept of the fine print. *The Americans* leads more or less directly to the work of Lee Friedlander, Gary Winogrand, Danny Lyon, and others, who have come to be known as the Social Landscape photographers.

Modern photography of the fifties still had some link with the past, however. The creative spark that Stieglitz passed on to Weston, Strand, and Adams persisted after World War II to inspire Harry Callahan, Minor White, and many others.

Callahan has been an important force in photography

Callahan, under whose later direction the Chicago Institute of Design's photography program became nationally known, first displayed an interest in pattern and design. Since the late 1940s he has worked in a variety of styles including experimental multiple exposure abstractions, nudes, street photographs, and formalistic patterns, all of which are characterized by an obvious interest in organization and structure, but which represent for him an intensification of the essential qualities of his subjects. Callahan has been an important force in photography as both artist and teacher for more than thirty years, but in a quiet way. He has seldom written or lectured on photography, but his numerous exhibitions attest to his continuing productivity and his appreciation by an ever-widening audience.

Minor White became interested in photography as a boy but put it aside during his college years in favor of writing. At the age of thirty, in 1938, he took up photography again and, resisting the prevailing Pictorialist influences, studied the work of Stieglitz, Adams, Weston, and Abbott. He quickly became a masterful technician and in 1938–39 completed documentary projects on the iron-front buildings and the waterfront areas of Portland, Oregon.

White developed an interest in philosophy and religion

He returned to writing during his army service and developed an interest in religion and philosophy which preoccuipied him increasingly for the rest of his life. After World War II, he became interested in the concept of "reading" photographs and, after meeting Stieglitz, Strand, Callahan, Adams, and Weston in 1946, he began working with Stieglitz's idea of the *equivalent* and images in series.

White's *sequences* are some of his best work

Photography began to find acceptance in the schools

Museums and galleries now exhibit photographs routinely

In the following years, he taught at the California School of Fine Arts, the Rochester Institute of Technology, and, finally, at the Massachusetts Institue of Technology. He was, meanwhile, a very active exhibitor, writer, critic, lecturer, and workshop instructor. Additionally, he found the time to join the staff of George Eastman House and to edit the magazine *Aperture*. His interest in religious experience, philosophy, and psychology eventually embraced various Far Eastern religions and astrology, and these principles became inseparable from his artistic expressions in photography and poetry.

White's *sequences*, photographs in series, frequently with accompanying poems, are some of his best work. He had a masterful command of technique, and his prints are rich and luminous. His images are always evocative, usually ambiguous, and frequently involve forms that are poetically suggestive of religious and erotic ideas. White was not without his critics, however. He inspired either admiration or scorn without much middle ground, but on the whole he was a genuinely constructive and powerful force.

The stylistic shift in the late 1950s, represented by Frank, Winogrand, and others, had some of the characteristics of the Dada movement in the teens and 1920s. Like Dada, it rejected the prevailing esthetic standards, involved subject matter that had been considered unfit, vulgar, trival, and banal, and displayed a fine lack of concern for technical polish. Unlike Dada, which was a violent outburst by a militant few, this photographic revolution was a relatively genteel reaction, which spread widely and resulted in gradual and progressive change. Although it inspired a great deal of interest in the street photograph and the snapshot, Frank's work was more effective in repudiating an old style than in establishing a new one. By finally disposing of the restrictive and ritualistic esthetic formula of the Pictorialists, the young rebels of the 1950s opened the door to experimentation and gave photographers a new freedom of expression.

By 1960 photography had begun to find widespread acceptance in high schools, colleges, and universities. This acceptance spread rapidly. In 1963 a group of teachers founded the Society for Photographic Education (SPE) to establish formal lines of communication between teachers of photography, to encourage the growth of photography in the schools, and to cooperate with other organizations, such as the Professional Photographers of America (PP of A), who were also interested in education. The SPE now has about 1,200 active members widely' distributed throughout the United States, as well as a few members in foreign countries.

Photography Today

Although a fairly recent phenomenon, this academic education of photographers is having unprecedented effects. One such effect has been the dramatic increase in interest in photography as a respectable art form and its consequent appearance in galleries, art museums, and extensive private collections. Until recently much of this professional interest was centered around vintage prints, work done personally by photographers who are no longer living.

Vintage prints are becoming rare and are, therefore, valuable, but the market has now become relatively stable as most of these prints have found their way through various dealers' hands to settle, finally, in the archives of museums or the files of wealthy private collectors. There is still substantial demand for the work of the better-known contemporary photographers but here, too, there are some signs that prices may be levelling off and that collectors are becoming more deliberate and selective.

There is no doubt, however, that photography has been accepted by the art community. Major museums and galleries exhibit photographs routinely, and critics treat photographers with the same respect they show artists in other media. Color photographs, which were considered a risky investment until about the mid-1970s, are now shown and collected without much reservation and it seems probable that this trend will continue as more and more photographers investigate and experiment with the color processes.

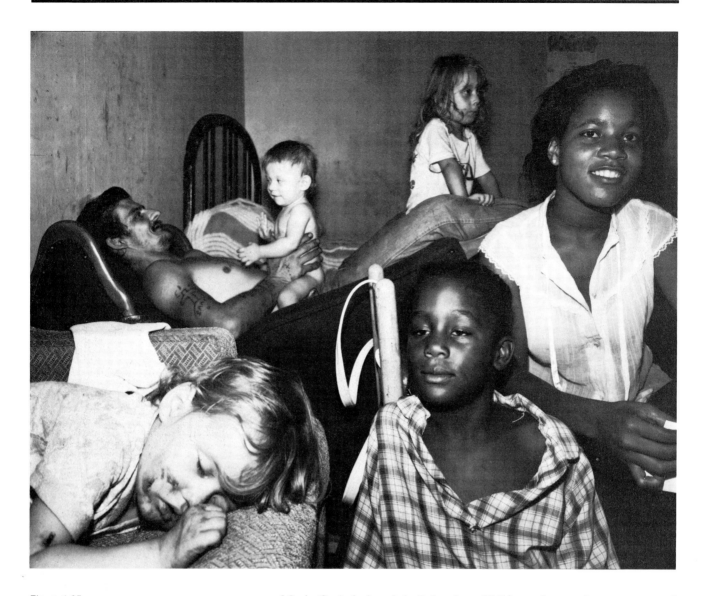

Figure 1.35
Cincinnati 1980. Nick Nixon

Despite growing interest in color, black-and-white is healthy

Marie Cosindas's subtle Polacolor still lifes and portraits were some of the first contemporary color photographs to be taken seriously as collectible art, although there had been some previous traffic in dye-transfer prints by masters of scenic landscape, such as Eliot Porter. More recently, the work of William Eggleston, Stephen Shore, Joel Meyerowitz, and others, have emphasized the potential of color photography and spurred its acceptance by collectors.

Despite the growing interest in color, black-and-white continues to be healthy and is used in a variety of ways. Technically, one extreme is represented by Nick Nixon, who combines a social documentary approach with the exquisite quality of the large format contact print; the other may be Nancy Rexroth's ethereal essay, "Iowa," done with the $1.50 "Diana" plastic camera. Between these two extremes, the majority of contemporary photographers seem to prefer 35mm cameras, and the prevailing style, in straight photography at least, seems to be casual, personal, informal, direct, and, not infrequently, pretentiously unpretentious.

There is still considerable interest in manipulated and mixed-media imagery. Jerry Uelsmann, Greg MacGregor, and others continue to produce amazing surrealistic blends of two or more images. Michael Teres melts and

Figure 1.36
Nancy Rexroth. *Boys Flying.*
(Courtesy of the photographer)

distorts the image gelatin itself to create complex fantasies, and Todd Walker's delicately multi-hued solarized nudes are still esoterically intriguing. Robert Heinecken's work is still unpredictably varied in material and style but is predictably shocking to conservative tastes. Betty Hahn, Bea Nettles, and others, work with variations of historic processes and embellish them with handwork, and there are many others who combine photographic imagery with other techniques, such as drawing or painting; for example, James Henkel, Patty Carroll, Christopher James, and Marcia Resnick. The Polaroid SX-70 images provide Lucas Samaras, Les Krims, and Ardine Nelson, among others, with raw material for bizarre transformations, and Jill Lynne, Ellen Land-Weber, and Sonia Sheridan are among those who work with "generated images" and "machine art."

The Future of Photography

We can only speculate about future trends

We can only speculate about future trends but a few possibilities are apparent. The present materials of photography are in short supply and will become more expensive. It seems likely that new processes, based on more readily available materials, will have to be devised if the steadily increasing interest in photography is to be satisfied. It also seems likely that our attitude toward making and consuming photographs must change, if only because our physical world, our culture, and we, as individuals, are changing. But of one thing we can probably be sure: man has a fundamental need to express himself in imagery and no matter what form photography may take in the future, it will continue to be used to satisfy that need.

Summary

The camera obscura was invented long before there was any real use for it. At first it was a curiosity, then an aid for drawing. Niépce is credited with producing the first camera image in 1826. He later formed a partnership with Daguerre to work toward an improved process. At the same time others, such as Talbot and Bayard, worked independently toward the same goal.

After the announcement of the daguerreotype process in 1839, the evolution of photography was rapid. Archer's invention of the collodion wet-plate process in 1851 established the basic procedures that are used today. Numerous methods were devised for producing photographic images in pigments and inks. Eventually this experimentation led to the introduction of such processes as carbon, collotype, woodburytype, and photogravure. Flexible film was introduced commercially in 1888 and in a few years George Eastman began to sell Kodak cameras with the slogan "You press the button; we do the rest." The introduction of Autochrome film in 1907 marked the successful end of a long search for a practical color material, a search that began almost as soon as photography was invented.

The popularity of photography has grown as rapidly as its technical advancements. Photojournalism had its roots in the documentation of the Civil War by Mathew Brady, the explorations of the West by Timothy O'Sullivan and William H. Jackson, and the studies of the immigrants and child laborers by Lewis Hine. By 1900 halftone illustrations were beginning to appear in books and magazines. This enabled the development of the picture story magazines and the fields of photo-illustration and advertising photography.

Almost from the beginning, art and photography had a tremendous influence on each other. At first photographers followed the current painting styles, which were undoubtedly influenced by photography's unique visual characteristics. Photographers, such as Alfred Stieglitz and Edward Steichen, encouraged many young photographers and promoted photography as an acceptable art form. Exhibitions of photographs in major museums, especially the Museum of Modern Art, have given the medium new status.

Technical advances in photography have been astounding. However, a crisis may result due to an increasing scarcity of raw materials as the medium's popularity increases daily. Photography will continue to fulfill the fundamental human need to communicate visually.

Introduction to the Photographic Process

Light-Sensitive Materials
Image Formation
    Using a Pinhole
    Using a Lens
    On Film and Paper

Light-Sensitive Materials

Light is a form of energy

Light is a form of energy. It affects many materials in various ways. Sunlight bleaches dyes, darkens freshly sawn pine, turns plants green, makes some plastic materials disintegrate, and reddens or tans human skin.

A negative image reverses the light effect

Photography takes advantage of this property of light. By shielding part of a sensitive surface and allowing light to act on the uncovered portion, a simple *photogram* can be produced. If the material is bleached by the action of light, as dyes are, the shaded portion of the surface will remain relatively dark and the illuminated area will be lighter in tone. This results in a *direct-positive* image, one in which the illuminated area produces a light image tone and the shaded area results in a dark image tone. A *negative* image results when the light effect is reversed; that is, when the illuminated area turns dark in tone and the shaded area remains light-toned. This is the photographic process that sunbathers unwittingly use to print photograms of bikinis on their bare skins.

In these examples the images are formed gradually, but directly, by the action of light alone. An image formed in this way is said to have been *printed-out*. Some modern photographic materials can be used to produce printed-out images; however, it's more satisfactory to *develop-out* the image by treating the exposed material with a chemical developer solution.

A latent image must be developed to become visible

It takes a relatively short exposure to form a developable image; in fact, the image is *latent* (invisible) until the developer makes it appear. A developed image is also stronger than a printed-out image; that is, its dark tones are darker and the contrast of the image is higher. Generally, a developed image is also more neutral in color. Printed-out images are usually brownish, pinkish, lavendar, or slaty-blue, depending on the material with which they have been sensitized.

Virtually all photographic films and papers currently used are coated with emulsions of silver compounds suspended in hardened gelatin. Gelatin has a number of unique properties that make it suitable for this purpose. It is easy to apply to the base material during manufacture. It absorbs the developing solutions quickly and evenly but is not dissolved. It protects the sensitive silver compounds, improves their image-forming efficiency, and, when dry, forms a tough, durable, uniform surface.

Most modern materials employ the halides of silver

A great many silver compounds are sensitive to light but most modern photographic emulsions employ the halogen salts or halides of silver. (The halogens are the chemical elements fluorine, chlorine, bromine, and iodine.) Silver chloride, bromide, and iodide are most commonly used and they are blended in various proportions to produce emulsions of widely diverse characteristics. In general, the *slower* (less sensitive) materials, such as *contact printing papers,* are sensitized with emulsion mixtures rich in silver chloride. *Faster* papers, such as those designed for *projection printing,* are likely to be coated with *chlorobromide* emulsions. Film emulsions contain higher proportions of silver bromide and iodide, as a general rule.

Untitled. Jerry Stratton. Stratton has had a long-continuing interest in pinhole photography and now manufactures and sells pinhole cameras in kit form. In this intriguing photograph-of-a-photograph he demonstrates some of the characteristics of the pinhole—very great depth of field, soft focus, and the possibility of subject movement due to the relatively long exposure time. (Courtesy of the Pinhole Camera Co., Box 19128, Cincinnati, Ohio.)

Figure 2.1
Half-image appearing in developer

It's a curious fact that the chloride emulsions, which are the least sensitive of the developing-out papers, are most satisfactory for printing-out experiments. They form a relatively rich and contrasty printed-out image quickly in strong light. Film emulsions, on the other hand, do not form satisfactory printed-out images under any conditions of exposure, although they are thousands of times more sensitive to light than papers are, when used in the conventional developing-out process.

Silver images are not stable until they have been fixed

Regardless of how they are formed, silver images are not stable until they have been *fixed* by a chemical treatment that dissolves the unused halides from the emulsion. If not removed these still-sensitive compounds will gradually discolor and darken, degrading the highlights of the image and eventually ruining it. There are a number of chemicals that can dissolve the unused halides without harming the silver image. They are all referred to commonly as *hypo,* in honor of Herschel's discovery of the chemical he mistakenly called "sodium *hypo*sulphite." Actually, it should have been named sodium thiosulfate; perhaps, if Herschel had named it correctly, we'd call the fixing bath "thio" now, instead of "hypo."

Image Formation

A simple pinhole can form a useful image

Photogram images are the shadow records of objects placed on or close to the paper surface. Camera images result from light patterns projected onto the sensitive film surface by the lens. Actually, it's possible to form a useful image in a camera without any lens at all; a simple pinhole will do the job.

Using a Pinhole

A pinhole forms images by allowing only a single, thin ray of light from each object point to reach the film surface. This is an easy concept to visualize if you consider, for example, photographing the stars in the Big Dipper constellation. Stars can be considered to be *point sources* of light because they are so far away that they have no measurable dimension. They are, however, radiating countless rays of light in all directions, so that each star illuminates the entire earth's hemisphere that faces it. If you point a pinhole camera at the Big Dipper, only those light rays that happen to be aimed straight toward the

Figure 2.2
a. If film is exposed directly to light from a single point source, such as a star, the uncontrolled rays affect the entire surface equally and the film is simply fogged without forming a useful image.

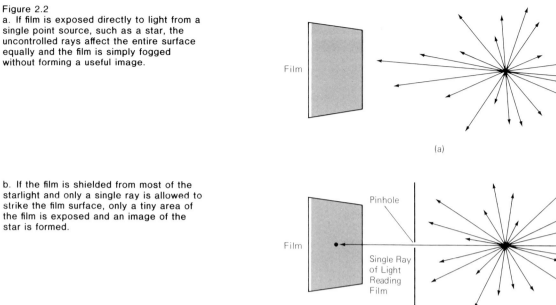

b. If the film is shielded from most of the starlight and only a single ray is allowed to strike the film surface, only a tiny area of the film is exposed and an image of the star is formed.

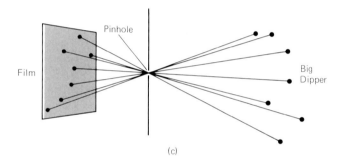

c. Each of the seven stars of the Big Dipper constellation projects a single light ray through the pinhole to the film surface to form an image of the constellation.

The image is formed upside-down and backwards

It is impossible to produce a truly sharp pinhole image

pinhole can pass through to the film. Therefore, each star in the constellation can contribute only a single ray of light to the image, and, since light travels in straight lines, the star images on the film surface form a miniature duplicate of the constellation.

Because the entering rays must cross each other at the pinhole, the image they form is upside-down and backwards. This is easily remedied, however. After the film has been developed, it can be turned right-side-up and, when viewed from the back, is seen unreversed.

As a device for forming images, a pinhole has two major drawbacks: its images are not really very sharp and it works very slowly. Unless the pinhole camera is very carefully designed, and used under optimum conditions, the image points can never be smaller than the pinhole itself; so, if the image is to be usefully clear and adequately defined, the pinhole must be very small. In practice, however, it cannot be made extremely small or image sharpness will actually be reduced by *diffraction*—a kind of turbulence in the light rays, induced by the edges of the aperture and somewhat similar to the water spray that results from a faulty hose nozzle. It is impossible, therefore, to produce a truly sharp pinhole image; image quality is degraded if the hole is either too large or too small.

Even the largest useful pinhole is tiny and the amount of light it transmits to the film is correspondingly small. A pinhole camera, therefore, would not be suitable for actually photographing the Big Dipper. The light from the constellation is extremely dim. After being attenuated by the tiny pinhole, there would be virtually nothing left to affect the film.

Figure 2.3
a. A very large pinhole will admit a bundle of rays and form a blurred image area (rather than an image point) on the film. A lens can concentrate these light rays to focus at a point. If the film is positioned accurately at the focus point, it can record a precise image of the star—much brighter than the image formed by a pinhole.

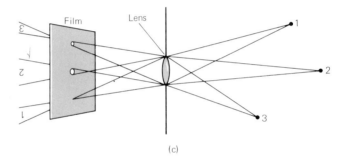

(a)

b. If the film is not placed precisely at the focal plane, the converging rays will form blurred circles of confusion rather than sharply defined points and we say the image is out-of-focus.

(b)

c. Light rays from very distant objects will focus on a single plane and will all be recorded sharply when the camera is focused at infinity. Objects closer than infinity, however, form images at different points behind the lens. No single adjustment of the camera focus will render them all equally sharp.

(c)

Lenses form sharper, brighter images than pinholes do

Using a Lens

Camera lenses were invented to solve these problems. A good lens can focus light rays to much finer points than can be formed by any pinhole and, because of its much larger aperture, a lens admits a great deal more light, possibly several thousand times more.

Consider the Big Dipper again and imagine that you have pointed a regular camera at it. If the effective diameter of the lens opening is one inch, for example, the lens will admit a cylindrical beam of light, one inch in diameter, from each star within its field of view. These cylinders of light do not reach the film directly. The lens converges each one into a cone, and if the camera is properly adjusted, just the tip of each light cone touches the film surface to form the star image. If the camera is not focused properly, the light cones fail to converge precisely on the film surface, and the resulting star images are visible as *circles of confusion*, rather than points.

Figure 2.4
In this photograph the camera lens was focused on the glass frame in the foreground. At maximum aperture the lens renders the foreground sharply but depth of field is shallow and the background greenhouses are badly blurred.

Figure 2.5
Although contrast in the shadows is reduced and fine details are blurred, this pinhole image is uniformly sharp from front to rear.

When photographing stars, or any other objects that are very far away, the lens is focused on *infinity,* and the image light cones all converge neatly on the surface of the film. When the objects are closer than infinity, but at different distances from the camera, the image points are formed at different distances from the lens. Under these conditions, if the camera is focused on a nearby object, its image will be sharp, but distant objects will be imaged as blurred shapes. In this situation a pinhole may be better than a lens. Although no portion of a pinhole image is critically sharp, it does not have to be focused and is, at least, uniformly sharp for objects at all distances. A lens can produce more precisely defined image details for objects at some specific distance but may not, at the same time be able to include closer or more distant objects within its *depth of field* (range of acceptable sharpness).

Figure 2.6
a. Positive transparency

b. Negative

On Film and Paper

Some cameras can be hand-loaded with sensitized paper, if you have any reason to do so; however, they all normally use film. In either case the image formed, after exposure and development, is negative. For camera use, film is preferable to paper for two reasons: we seldom have use for a negative print on paper, and most films are much faster than papers, and, therefore, require much less exposure to form a useful image.

Most films are "faster" than most papers

The term "negative," when used alone, almost invariably refers to a film negative image. Film negatives are generally not useful as finished images but are intended to be printed on sensitized paper, either by contact, which means that the negative is placed in contact with the paper emulsion and exposed to light, or by projection. A machine called an *enlarger* is used for projection printing and, as the name implies, the projected image is usually, but not necessarily always, larger than the negative itself. Most enlargers can also be adjusted to project images of the same size or smaller than the negative, but this is rarely necessary or desirable.

The term "print" usually refers to a positive image on paper

The term "print" usually means a positive image on paper. Strictly speaking, a print is a negative of the negative, which means, of course, that the subject tones, which were reversed in the film negative, are reversed again in the print. A positive image, therefore, resembles the original subject.

A positive image resembles the original subject

If, for some reason, we need a negative image on paper, we would normally refer to it as a *negative print*. Similarly, if we wanted to produce a positive image on film, we might describe it as a *positive,* a *film positive,* or a *positive transparency.* The term "direct positive," which was mentioned previously, also has a specific meaning. It refers to a positive image that has been produced without having gone through a separate or identifiable negative stage. Xerox prints are good examples of direct positive images. In conventional photography direct positive materials are rare and specialized.

Summary

In photography, light rays reflected from an object enter the camera through the lens and are focused onto the film surface. This surface is coated with a light-sensitive emulsion of silver halides, which absorb the light to produce a latent or invisible image. The film is then developed into a visible silver image and fixed to remove the unused halides. The developed film, called a negative, is then washed and dried.

The negative is printed either by placing it in direct contact with the paper or by projecting it onto the paper through an enlarger. This forms another latent image which is also developed and fixed. The result is a positive image which resembles the original object in tonality.

Cameras, Accessories, and Operation

3

Outline

Cameras: Types and Features
    Viewfinder-type Cameras
    Reflex Cameras
    View and Field Cameras
    Special Purpose Cameras
Accessories
    Tripod
    Cable Release
    Lens Accessories
    Flash Units
    Motor Drives
Before You Buy
The Characteristics of Light
Lenses: Features and Functions
How Focal Length Affects Image Scale and Perspective
Depth of Focus and Depth of Field
Hyperfocal Distance
Focusing for Infrared
Relative Aperture—Lens Speed
How Exposure Is Controlled
Selecting and Using Black-and-White Films
Determining Exposure: Using Built-in Meters
How Aperture and Shutter Settings Are Related
EV Numbers
Light, Color and Filters
Taking Care of Cameras and Lenses

Cameras: Types and Features

All cameras are basically alike

All cameras are basically alike. Regardless of its other features, every useful camera must be a lighttight box equipped with a lens on one side and a film-holding device on the other. It must provide a viewfinder function that allows pointing the camera and composing the image with some accuracy, and it must have a shutter mechanism that can be opened to admit light through the lens and closed to restrict light when it is not wanted. Additionally, most cameras provide some means of adjusting the lens-to-film distance so the image can be focused accurately. They also include an *iris diaphragm* or other device to constrict the lens aperture and thus reduce the light intensity on the film surface when that is desirable.

In addition to these essentials, modern cameras may incorporate a bewildering array of convenience features that make them easier to operate, enhance their various abilities, and, unfortunately, make them very expensive. Before you buy a camera, you should try to decide which features are important to you and which ones you can get along without. Then you can select, from the group of cameras that have the features you want, the one that feels best in your hands, is most convenient for you to operate, and gives you the best viewfinder image for focusing and composing.

Viewfinder-type Cameras

Simple cameras have simple viewfinders

Swimmers, 1967.
You'll find a long lens useful when you can't approach the subject closely. This photograph was made with a 200mm lens on Kodak type 2475 Recording film, from a distance of about 110 feet.
(Courtesy of the University of Michigan Press.)

The very simplest camera types may have either open-frame viewfinders or small optical finders like miniature reversed telescopes. In both cases you look *through* the finder at the subject. The finder image covers approximately the same area that the camera lens will record and provides a good indication of the picture shape. Finders of this type cannot be used to focus the camera, nor do they provide any indication of *depth of field*—the region of the subject from front to rear that will be acceptably sharp in the picture. They also suffer from *parallax error* because the lens and the viewfinder "see" the subject from slightly different points of view. Although *parallax* is usually insignificant for

Figure 3.1
Camera function diagram

subjects more than a few feet from the camera, it can, in some cases, lead to miscalculation of the exact boundaries of the image or, for example, let you photograph someone with a tree growing out of his ear, despite the fact that the viewfinder image may have shown tree and ear to be safely separated. An extreme example of parallax error is the possibility that you might forget to remove the lens cap and take a lot of pictures of nothing, assuming, because the viewfinder image was visible, that the lens was functioning normally.

They may not have any focusing adjustment

Very simple cameras of this type may not have any focusing adjustment. If not, they will have been set at the factory to focus most sharply somewhere in the middle distance and will usually take acceptably sharp pictures of any subject more than a few feet from the camera. They may not have adjustable lens openings or shutter speeds either. In this case they will be restricted to use in normal daylight conditions with general purpose films, although some of them will accept *flashcubes* or *electronic flash* units to permit their use in poor light conditions.

although some provide scale focusing

A few viewfinder-type cameras permit *scale focusing,* which means that you must measure or estimate the distance from camera to subject and adjust the focusing control manually. In some cases, especially on the small *pocket cameras* that use the 110-size film cartridges, the focusing scale is calibrated with visual symbols rather than specific distance numbers. For example, a stylized silhouette of a mountain may indicate the proper focus setting for distant objects; a full figure silhouette may indicate the setting for mid-range subjects; and a stylized head or head-and-shoulder silhouette may indicate the proper setting for close-up focusing. Although this may seem rather imprecise, these small cameras provide great depth of field and absolute accuracy of focus is not essential.

and others include rangefinders

The better cameras of this type include *rangefinders* for faster and more accurate focusing. A rangefinder consists of a pair of mirrors or prisms, placed an inch or two apart and arranged so the eye, in looking through one of them,

Figure 3.2
Frame or optical finder

Figure 3.3
Scale focus on 110 camera

Rangefinder focusing is fast and accurate

sees a double image of the subject. The other mirror can be pivoted to make the images converge and is connected to the focusing control of the camera so, as the lens is moved in focusing, the two images are always superimposed on the subject point of focus.

Rangefinder cameras, when well-designed and constructed, provide an excellent finder image, partially corrected for parallax error, and very brilliant. Focusing is fast and very accurate, and cameras of this type are particularly suitable for use in poor light conditions or in situations that require accurate framing of rapidly moving objects. The better rangefinder cameras will accept interchangeable lenses, automatically presenting the appropriate viewfinder field for (usually) one wide-angle and one telephoto lens, in addition to the normal field of view. In general, extreme *wide-angle* or *telephoto* lenses require accessory finders, and the inherent advantages of the rangefinder camera— operating speed, accuracy of focus and finder brilliance, may be compromised or lost.

Figure 3.4
Rangefinder camera

Figure 3.5
When a rangefinder camera is not focused
properly the image will appear something
like this. When the double image blends
into one—as you can make it do by turning
the focusing control—the image is in
focus.

Reflex Cameras

Reflex cameras make visualizing and composing easy

Reflex cameras reflect the viewfinder image onto a groundglass screen as a two-dimensional image to be looked *at* rather than *through*. This tends to simplify the problems of visualizing what the finished camera image will look like, makes composition easier and more precise (for most people), and makes it possible to appraise the sharpness of the image visually as the camera focusing controls are manipulated.

The TLR is really two cameras in one

In the *twin-lens reflex* (TLR) design, the lens that forms the viewfinder image is optically similar to the camera lens itself and the two lenses are mounted as close together as possible to reduce parallax. The TLR is really, therefore, two cameras operating as one; the upper unit serves merely to form the viewing image, while the lower unit contains the film and records the image. An inclined mirror, angled down behind the viewing lens, reflects its image up to the groundglass screen set into the top of the camera and, because the viewing and taking lenses focus together, the film image is in focus when the image on the groundglass appears sharp. The TLR is usually held at waist level and, looking down into the finder, the image is seen upright but laterally reversed, a characteristic that takes some getting used to. The groundglass image is partially shielded from outside light by a folding metal hood. A simple lens, built into the hood, can be flipped up to magnify the image, and when the eye is placed close to this magnifying lens, the image can be seen larger and more clearly for focusing and composing at eye level.

The SLR combines viewing and taking function in one lens

Single-lens reflex (SLR) cameras have become much more popular than TLRs. SLR design combines the viewing and taking functions in one lens, so there is no parallax error at all and the image seen in the viewfinder is, in most respects, identical with the image that the film will record. The mirror that reflects the image upward to the viewing screen is hinged in the SLR and flips up out of the way when the shutter release is pressed, allowing the image light to reach the film plane. During the actual interval of film exposure, the visual image in the finder is lost, but in almost all SLRs, the *instant return mirror* drops back into position as soon as the shutter closes and the viewfinder image is restored. In practice the brief loss of the visual image at the critical instant of exposure is usually only a minor annoyance. In some cases, however, the image blackout is troublesome, and in situations such as following erratically moving objects, a rangefinder camera is generally more convenient.

Figure 3.6
Twin-lens reflex

Figure 3.7
Single-lens reflex

Prism reflexes have many advantages

The lateral reversal of the viewfinder image, which is characteristic of simple reflex cameras, can be corrected by the addition of a *pentaprism* to the viewing system. *Prism reflexes* are necessarily bulkier and heavier than cameras without prisms but the prism system has many advantages. In addition to the fact that the image is oriented correctly, the prism assembly provides eye-level viewing of a magnified, brilliant image. Because the viewed image is formed by the same lens that takes the picture, it will show the effects of focus changes, depth of field, and any other factor that will influence the final picture. Wide-angle or telephoto lenses can be used without major difficulty. Very long telephoto lenses may crop off the top of the viewfinder image in some cameras, but the film image is not affected and will be complete.

Most incorporate a focusing aid such as

In spite of the fact that the SLR groundglass image is well shielded from outside light and is brightened (especially in the corners) by a built-in *fresnel lens,* it is not always easy to focus. The groundglass texture tends to obscure very fine image details and the concentric rings of the fresnel lens, although minute, contribute to this problem. In poor light the image becomes too dim to see clearly and things become even worse if the lens in use is slow (does not admit much light) or if filters or other lens attachments that absorb light are being used. To make focusing simpler under these conditions, most SLR groundglass screens incorporate some type of *focusing aid,* usually a *microprism grid* or a *rangefinder prism* assembly, or some combination of these.

a microprism grid

The microprism grid usually occupies a small circular area in the center of the groundglass and consists of dozens of minute pyramids of plastic. When the image is not in focus the pyramid faces disperse the image light, so the image seems to shimmer, especially when the camera is moved slightly. A well-focused image appears rather coarse-grained, but intact, and no shimmer is visible.

or a rangefinder prism

The rangefinder prism consists of two shallow wedges of glass or plastic laid side by side, pointing in opposite directions. Like the microprisms, the wedges refract light and react only to image light from the margins of the lens. These marginal rays are bent most sharply in focusing, so the image they form appears to go in and out of focus abruptly. The out-of-focus image appears divided, with each half displaced along the intersection of the prism wedges. Focusing the image brings the image halves into alignment, and the image form appears whole.

Figure 3.8
Cutaway view of the Olympus OM-1, a typical prism reflex 35mm camera. Courtesy of Olympus Camera Corp.

Neither device is as accurate as a real rangefinder but both are usually better than a plain groundglass. Unfortunately, when used with a lens of inappropriate focal length or when used with any lens at a small aperture, one or both halves of the rangefinder prism will appear black. Under the same conditions, the microprism grid simply darkens into a mealy-looking area of texture and refuses to fracture the image or shimmer. For this reason, most manufacturers offer separate prism-equipped screens for use with wide-angle and telephoto lenses. If you plan to specialize in working with one of these lenses, the special groundglass screen will be a good investment.

In some SLR finders the image appears to hang in space quite close to the eye. Other camera designs provide apparent image distances of up to several feet. If you are far-sighted, you will discover that even though you can't use some camera finders easily, you will have no trouble with others. Investigate several brands; they are not all alike.

Camera finders differ in "eye relief"

If you wear glasses but prefer to photograph without them, dioptric correction lenses can be added to most viewfinders to correct near- or far-sightedness, and special correction lenses, ground to your personal prescription, are offered by some manufacturers. You can, of course, wear your glasses while photographing but they may keep you from placing your eye close enough to the finder eyepiece to see the whole image area. Camera finders differ in this *eye relief* characteristic; so try several varieties. You may find one that allows comfortable full-field vision even with your glasses on.

Most cameras, 35mm and smaller, are now equipped with built-in exposure meters, employing one of three popular types of photocells, coupled to the lens and shutter controls. The cadmium sulfide cell (CdS), which made built-in meters and automated exposure systems practical, is commendably sensitive but suffers from slow response time, memory effects, poor color response, and temperature sensitivity. It is now being replaced by the *silicon*

Figure 3.9
a. This SLR viewing screen contains a central rangefinder prism focusing aid, diagonally divided; the next is a ring of fine-textured groundglass for visual focusing; the rest of the screen area is a fresnel lens, whose concentric line pattern shows in the corners of this detail. This picture shows the image focused on the crest of the snow-covered hill in the middle distance; the building corner is slightly out-of-focus.

b. When the camera is focused for close-up, both the building corner and the hill are out-of-focus.

c. Stopping the lens down renders both focusing aids useless and groundglass grain shows strongly.

Figure 3.10
Typical viewing screen illustrating the use of an LED readout instead of the older pointer. The indicated exposure is 1/250 second at f/5.6. The groundglass screen is equipped with a rangefinder prism (central divided circle) and a microprism grid (larger textured circle).

photo-diode (SPD) or the *gallium-arsenide-phosphide* (GaAsP or GAP) cell, commonly known as the *gallium photo-diode* (GPD). Both silicon and gallium photo-diodes have extremely fast response time, excellent sensitivity, good stability, and freedom from memory. Silicon photo-diodes when blue-filtered (*silicon-blue cells* or SBCs) have good color sensitivity. Gallium cells do not normally require filtering.

CdS cells function satisfactorily on simple battery power. SPDs and GPDs require complex electronic circuitry to amplify and stabilize their responses. Although this sounds risky and expensive, both systems have proven to be reliable.

There are four basic modes of exposure control

Modern SLRs may offer one or more of the four basic modes of exposure control: manual; semi-automatic, *aperture priority;* semiautomatic, *shutter priority;* and fully automatic, *programmed.* In manually operated cameras the meter scale or pointer (visible in the viewfinder near the margin of the image area) will indicate correct exposure when you have set the aperture and shutter controls appropriately for the film in use. In *match-pointer* or *match-needle* designs, the camera settings are correct when a pair of movable pointers—one sensitive to adjustments of the diaphragm, the other moved by changes in the shutter speed setting—are superimposed. Either one or both of these controls can be adjusted to align the pointers properly but these adjustments must be done manually. The camera meter merely tells you when you've made the right adjustments—it doesn't help you make them. Some cameras feature patterns of *light-emitting diodes* (*LEDs*), instead of moving pointers, to indicate correct adjustments. Others display the actual lens and shutter settings in illuminated windows in the dark margins of the image area. There is no significant difference in meter function or in the operation of the camera controls. Modern microcircuitry techniques are very sophisticated and the trend is toward more electric and electronic emphasis in camera design. In some of the more advanced cameras, built-in miniature computers calculate exposure, command the functioning of aperture and shutter, and time the exposure interval with a tiny quartz "clock." Even the mechanical shutter release has been replaced in some cameras; now the mere touch of a finger is sufficient to fire the shutter. These advances have provided us with smaller, lighter, more versatile cameras that are more reliable and less expensive than their mechanical counterparts. The major drawback is their dependence on battery power but that's a small price to pay for the advantages these new designs provide.

Some cameras feature LED displays instead of pointers

Semi-automatic operation

A semi-automatic camera allows you to select one scale setting; the camera will then choose and adjust the other. In the aperture-priority mode, you select and set the f-number, and the camera will immediately provide an appropriate shutter speed setting for the subject conditions and the film in use. Shutter-priority operation lets you select the shutter speed; the camera then sets the aperture at the appropriate f-number.

Programmed operation

In programmed operation the camera does it all; you merely focus, frame your subject in the viewfinder, and press the shutter release. The camera will select both lens and shutter settings.

There are two types of shutters in common use. Between-the-lens (BTL) shutters are part of the lens assembly and operate in a space between the lens elements. The thin metal leaves of the shutter are arranged coaxially with the lens axis and are pivoted so they can swing out to open and admit light, or swing in to overlap and restrict it.

There are two types of shutters in common use

Focal plane (FP) shutters are part of the camera body and usually operate just in front of the film surface. There are two types, *curtain* shutters and *leaf* or *blade* shutters. Curtain shutters are made of either thin metal foil or cloth. Two curtains are actually involved. In the closed position, their edges meet or overlap slightly to cover the film completely. During the exposure, the curtains separate and travel across the film surface in tandem, the space between their edges permitting light to reach the film.

Leaf or blade shutters typically consist of several thin metal leaves in each of two groups, one at the top of the film gate and the other at the bottom. In the closed position, one group of leaves is fanned out to cover the film, with the other group remaining folded. During the exposure cycle the first group of leaves retracts to its folded position, exposing the film. The second group then fans out to cover the film and terminate the exposure.

Figure 3.11
BTL shutter with blades partly open

Figure 3.12
Focal plane curtain shutter

Figure 3.13
Focal plane blade shutter

Because of its location near the optical center of the lens, the BTL shutter illuminates the entire film area uniformly throughout the complete exposure cycle, although the illumination is dimmed during the opening and closing phases. Focal plane shutters, on the other hand, expose the film progressively, wiping the image light across the film surface like a paint roller. BTL shutters, therefore, are more suitable for use with *synchronized flash.* FP shutters cannot be used successfully with electronic flash at high shutter speeds because only a narrow portion of the film surface is exposed at any instant during the exposure interval.

Focal plane shutters provide higher speeds, up to 1/2000th second in some models, but sometimes distort rapidly moving objects. BTL shutters are limited to a maximum speed of about 1/500th second, and while rapidly moving objects are undistorted they may be blurred. BTL shutters are relatively quiet and vibration-free and expose the film evenly. FP shutters, especially at higher speeds, may travel erratically leaving stripes or bands of uneven exposure on the film. Although this effect is usually insignificant, it may show up occasionally in otherwise uniform areas of image tone, such as clear skies. FP shutters, by separating lens and shutter functions, permit a wide variety of interchangeable lenses to be used with the camera body and simplify the design of aperture priority shutter automation.

View and Field Cameras

View cameras, in contrast with modern SLRs, are simple in design, unautomated, heavy to carry, clumsy and slow to operate, and expensive. Their lenses and shutters are relatively limited in speed. Their major virtue is their ability to make pictures of incomparable technical quality.

The terms *view camera* and *field camera* are rather arbitrary. Both types are basically *bellows* enclosures with *spring backs* (which accept the *film holders*) and removable *lensboards.* Both must be used on a *tripod,* or similar support, and are focused by inspection of the image, which is formed by the taking lens on a groundglass screen built into the back. The view camera design is usually sturdier and heavier, includes more adjustments, and permits greater interchangeability of parts. Field cameras usually feature light wooden construction, have somewhat limited adjustments, and can be folded into rather compact dimensions for carrying. Both cameras will accept a wide variety of lenses.

Special Purpose Cameras

There are quite a few special purpose cameras on the market. The Widelux, for example, uses a unique moving-lens mechanism to make very wide-angle pictures that feature (or suffer from, depending on your point of view) obvious perspective distortion. The Nikonos is a special waterproof camera to be used under water or in other wet or dusty environments that might damage a normal camera. The Gowlandflex is a limited production TLR that uses 4″ × 5″ sheet film. The Minox (about the size of a short, fat cigar) can be carried anywhere and takes fine snapshots on miniature rollfilm. There are many others.

In this category, the Polaroid cameras, and the somewhat similar Kodaks, deserve special mention. These cameras take color pictures that develop themselves outside the camera. They feature automatic exposure control and, in some models, motorized print ejection and film advance. Unlike the older Polaroid films, these newer materials are litter-free and, Polaroid prints, at least, are relatively stable and colorfast.

Accessories

Camera and lens accessories are expensive. Even though some of them are more trouble than they're worth, there are a few items that you should have.

Figure 3.14
View camera

Figure 3.15
Field camera (unfolded)

Figure 3.16
SX-70 camera

Tripod

You may not need a tripod for most of your photography, but when you do, you'll need it badly. Buy a sturdy one that will hold the camera steady at at least head height, even in a moderate breeze. It should have rubber feet to protect finished floors. Some also provide handy retractable metal spikes for use on rough or slippery surfaces. Some models provide extendable center columns to facilitate minor height adjustments, which is a desirable feature. Gear-operated columns are the best; they should operate smoothly and have a positive locking arrangement.

Most tripods intended for use with hand cameras have two or three leg sections that can be extended and secured in position by means of threaded locking collars. Check the collars for smooth operation and positive locking. Avoid any that bind, feel gritty as they're turned, or fail to hold the leg firmly in position. View camera tripods must be exceptionally strong and stable. Don't economize here; a flimsy tripod is worse than useless.

Cable Release

A *cable release* is another important accessory. Buy a good quality, flexible *cable* that is at least 10″ long. For view camera use, an even longer one is preferable. Some cable releases are provided with locking devices, which can be used with the camera shutter set on its B (*Bulb*) setting to make manually-timed exposures of any length. This is a useful feature if your camera shutter does not provide a T (*Time*) exposure setting, as most focal plane shutters do not. There are several types of locking devices. The best type has a knurled set screw, which can be turned in against the cable plunger to hold it firmly in any position.

Lens Accessories

There are many lens accessories, including caps, sunshades, filters, and close-up lenses, that are designed to clamp over or screw into the front of the lens mount. If you have several lenses in mounts of the same inside thread diameter, you can interchange screw-in accessories with a minimum of fuss. If some lenses are larger than others, buy threaded accessories to fit the largest one and use threaded *adapter rings* to match these accessories to the smaller lenses. Most of these accessories are double threaded, so they can be stacked. This will allow you to use two or more at a time, but there is some risk of vignetting the image and increasing diffusion and flare.

Years ago several standard sizes of filters were established and intended for use with slip-on adapter rings. These so-called "series" filters are not threaded and are normally less convenient than the screw-in variety, but they are valuable for use with lenses in unthreaded mounts or in mounts of non-standard size.

Some view camera lenses, especially the larger sizes, are difficult to fit with either screw-in filters or series-sized adapter rings. Usually these big lenses use gelatin filter holders and gelatin filter squares instead of the glass filters normally used on small cameras. Actually, many view camera users simply tape the flexible gelatin filters in place over the lens. They are relatively inexpensive and can be discarded when they become scratched or badly soiled.

A lens cap is one item you should have. If you have more than one lens, keep one on the camera with a front cap and provide caps for both front and rear elements of the other lenses so that they are never uncovered except when actually in use.

You should always use a good *lens shade* (*lens hood*) too. Buy shades deep enough to exclude side light but not so deep that they cause *vignetting* (shading) of the image corners. If you have an SLR or view camera, it's easy to check for vignetting. Focus the camera at infinity and check the extreme corners of the finder image as you stop the lens down to its smallest aperture. If the corners darken with the shade in place and lighten when it's removed, the shade is too deep for that lens. Try a shallower one.

Figure 3.17
a. Tripod

b. Cable releases

Figure 3.18
Lens shade

Figure 3.19
Vignetted corners result from the use of a too-deep sunshade, in this case a 24mm lens with a 35mm sunshade.

Flash Units

For work in poor light conditions consider using a flash

If you frequently work in poor light conditions or are interested in some control over light effects, you may want to investigate *flash* units. Some small 110-size pocket cameras have built-in sockets for *flash cubes* or *flipflash* bars and most can be purchased with matching plug-in *electronic flash* units. Many 35mm and larger cameras, which have *hot shoe* flash brackets, will also accept small, self-contained slip-on units but, for greater light output and versatility, larger and more powerful units are preferable.

Many modern electronic flash units have built-in *photocell sensors,* which can be set to monitor the light reflected from the subject and to adjust the exposure automatically, by limiting the duration of the flash. Thyristor circuits are useful in conserving battery power and in speeding up the recycling time under some conditions. Some units offer *bare bulb* attachments for more uniform distribution of light and some permit tilting the flash head for *bounce light* effects. Accessory filters, diffusion screens, and reflectors are also available.

Dedicated flash units control some camera functions

When used with the cameras for which they were designed, *dedicated flash* units automatically adjust the camera shutter speed. Some are designed to turn on an LED *ready light* in the camera viewfinder to signal when the flash unit is fully charged and ready to fire, and some provide an LED signal to verify proper flash exposure.

Electronic flash or flash bulbs? Consider both options

Unless you plan to do a lot of work with flash, *flashbulbs* may be better for your purposes than electronic flash. Although bulbs are relatively expensive per actual flash, the equipment cost is low. Bulbs also provide more total light output than any portable electronic flash unit can, and they won't deteriorate during prolonged storage. Electronic units have a fairly high initial cost but their operating cost is low if they are used frequently and regularly. Intermittent or infrequent use may reduce their efficiency, especially if they have rechargeable *ni-cad* (nickel cadmium) batteries. Electronic flash is certainly more convenient, provides a considerable degree of automation, produces little heat, and requires very short exposure times. Consider both options; then, if you decide to buy an electronic flash unit, be sure it is powerful and versatile enough to do what you want. The smallest ones are little more than toys.

Figure 3.20
Flash on hot shoe

Figure 3.21
Winder on Pentax

Don't buy a winder unless you really need one

Motor Drives

Motor drives, which replace the camera base-plate and permit automatic sequence photography at the rate of several pictures a second, have been around for a long time. Simplified versions, called *winders,* are also popular. Many of these winders, for 35mm cameras, permit automatic operation at about two frames-per-second but some simply advance the film and wind the shutter after each manual exposure. Lighter, smaller, and less expensive than regular motor drives, winders are useful in sequence photography and in special situations where manual winding would be difficult or impossible. Most of them can be electrically operated from a considerable distance, as for nature work, sports photography, or scientific purposes. Don't buy one unless you really need it. For ordinary work, a winder is an expensive luxury which substantially increases the size and weight of your camera.

Before You Buy

Before you buy a camera, try to decide what sort of pictures you want to make and what your standards of image quality are. Small cameras are easy to carry around and convenient to use. However, their negatives will have to be enlarged considerably, for most purposes, and their prints will consequently be somewhat less sharp than prints made from larger negatives. Very large cameras, on the other hand, can provide superb image quality but will be correspondingly difficult to carry and less convenient to use.

Small cameras, especially the better rangefinder types, are excellent for quick, spontaneous snapshooting. View cameras, the other extreme, must be used methodically and are best for pictures that require planning and thoughtful refinement. Medium-size cameras are intended to be universally useful, and some of them, at least, combine fairly convenient operation with fine image quality.

The 35mm SLR is probably best for the beginner

Although the medium-size cameras, most of which use 120 rollfilm, would seem to be the best choice for a beginner, the 35mm SLR is, in my opinion, a better one. First, many more models are available to choose from and most of them are less expensive to buy and operate than are rollfilm cameras of similar capability. Second, they are more convenient to use and offer a much greater variety of accessories. Third, there are more types of film available for 35mm cameras (135-size) than are available in rollfilm sizes. Finally, although the larger film size is inherently capable of producing prints of better quality, the differences in practice are frequently not great. If you are a careful craftsman, you can do fine work with a 35mm SLR.

Hardware doesn't produce photographs; people do!

Photographers are notorious gadget lovers and most of us own more equipment than we need or use. It's easy to convince ourselves that the road to better pictures is paved with money, but this simply isn't true. Hardware doesn't produce good photographs; people do! The moral is clear—buy only what you need; buy good quality equipment; and buy matched equipment, if possible, to permit interchangeability of parts and to avoid unnecessary duplication of accessories.

New camera equipment is becoming almost prohibitively expensive, but good used equipment is frequently reasonably priced. If you're in the market for a camera and have limited funds, you should consider "last year's models" of the better brands, particularly those whose newest models have been changed appreciably. Many photographers trade perfectly good cameras merely to get their hands on the "latest thing," and you can profit at their expense. SLRs with match-needle CdS cell meters are a good example. Although not as popular now as SBCs and GPDs, CdS meters are still functional. Similarly, the new, compact 35mm SLRs have made the older, larger models look like dinosaurs, although for picture-making purposes, they are just as good as the newer models. As their popularity declines, so will their prices.

If possible, buy from a reputable dealer and get some sort of warranty from him. Test the equipment thoroughly under your normal working conditions and inspect the results critically. If there is any hint of mechanical or optical defect in the equipment, return it with the pictures and ask the dealer to correct the problem. Don't make any repairs yourself or have them done by anyone else as long as the equipment is under warranty.

The Characteristics of Light

No simple theory explains all the effects of light

There is no single, simple way to explain all the effects of light. The photochemical effects (dye bleaching, latent image formation in films, etc.) are best explained by the theory that a luminous body sprays out streams of particles called photons which transmit energy and are capable of doing work on sensitive surfaces. Optical effects of light (color, lens action, etc.) are easier to visualize if light is considered to travel through space in somewhat the same way that ripples travel across a pond, in waves. However, unlike ripples, which vibrate only up and down as they move, light waves, and other electromagnetic waves, are thought of as normally vibrating in all directions perpendicular to their direction of travel.

Waves in water can vary in size from the mammoth ground swells in the Pacific, a hundred feet or more from crest to crest, to tiny ripples less than an inch long. The electromagnetic spectrum, by comparison, contains waves that must be measured in kilometers or miles (low-frequency radio waves) as well as waves so incomprehensibly tiny that they must be measured in millionths and billionths of a millimeter.

The visible spectrum is a minute band of wavelengths

The visible portion of the spectrum, which we call light, is a relatively minute band of wavelengths ranging in extent from only 700 nanometers (millionths of a millimeter), or the limit of visible red light, to 400 nanometers, or the last visible shade of deep violet. Above the 400nm boundary of the visible spectrum lies the region of ultraviolet (UV) radiations, which are invisible to the human eye but which tan skin, bleach dyes, and affect photographic emulsions strongly. Below 700nm lies the extensive region of infrared (IR) radiations, which are invisible to both the eye and most films but are capable of affecting some exposure meters to a troublesome degree. We perceive the longest wavelengths of infrared as heat.

Figure 3.22
a. Candle emitting photons

b. Candle emitting light waves

Figure 3.23
Electromagnetic spectrum

Candle Emitting
Photons
(a)

Candle Emitting
Light Waves
(b)

Gamma Rays

X Rays

Ultraviolet

Blue ——

Green —— Visible Light

Red ——

Infrared

Microwaves

Radio

Figure 3.24
a. Light transmitted through transparent material.

b. Light diffused by translucent (cloudy or milky) material.

c. Light absorbed by opaque surface.

d. Light partially absorbed, partially transmitted.

e. Light refracted in passing through a glass sheet.

(a)   (b)   (c)

(d)   (e)

A light ray may be absorbed, reflected, transmitted. . .

A light ray travelling through the air will continue to zip along in a straight line until it hits something or until its energy is gradually dissipated (in a perfect vacuum, presumably, it would go on forever). If it encounters an object of any sort, any of several things may happen to it. Almost certainly some of the light will be absorbed by any surface it touches. Part of it may be reflected, part may be transmitted if the material is transparent or translucent, and if the material is cloudy or milky, the light may be diffused or scattered. Light can also be diffused by reflection from a rough or matte surface, and if a ray is forced through a tiny aperture or made to graze a sharp edge, some of it will be diverted or disturbed, resulting in a special kind of diffusion, called *diffraction.*

When a light ray travelling in air strikes a plain glass surface at somewhat less than 90°, the transmitted ray will be *refracted,* or bent, more steeply into the glass (or toward the perpendicular). When leaving the glass at another surface, the ray will be bent away from the perpendicular.

diffused, diffracted, refracted, or dispersed

When white light is refracted in this way it is also *dispersed* into its component colors, because the various wavelengths of light are bent to different degrees. The shorter visible wavelengths (violet and blue) are refracted to the greatest degree; red and orange are least affected. In nature, dispersed rays display their colors when sunlight is refracted by falling raindrops to form a rainbow. (See plate 1.)

Light can also be split into its component colors by *interference.* Lens coatings, thin oil films on water, and soap bubbles operate on this principle. By trapping light between their closely spaced reflecting surfaces they fold certain wavelengths (colors) back on themselves and cancel them. Varying the spacing between the surfaces will change their color absorption; so, by controlling the thickness of the lens or filter coating, for example, any color of the spectrum can be eliminated from the reflected light.

A dichroic filter transmits one color, reflects its complement

In a somewhat similar manner, *dichroic* filters manage to separate the colors without actually destroying them; a portion of the light color is reflected back toward the source while the remaining color is transmitted.

Positive and negative lenses

When light passes through a transparent object with non-parallel faces, such as a common glass prism, the emerging rays are deviated from their original course. If you think of a simple lens as being derived from prisms placed base to base and then rounded into spherical surfaces, you can see how a lens manages to focus light rays. A lens of this sort—thicker in the center than at the perimeter—is called a *positive* lens and is said to form a *real* image because the image can be projected onto a viewing screen or captured on film. A *negative* lens—thinner in the center than at the perimeter—can form only *virtual* images, which can be seen in the lens itself but can not be displayed on a screen. Most camera lenses are composed of several simple lenses, some positive and some negative, but the lens assembly, as a whole, is positive. Light rays passing through the various lens surfaces are refracted many times but they eventually converge—or focus—to form the camera image on the film surface.

Lenses: Features and Functions

A good general-purpose lens should form a sharply defined image

A good general purpose camera lens must, first of all, form a sharply defined image, free from *color fringes* and other optical blurring effects. It must form this fine image on a reasonably flat plane in order for the film to record it, and the image should be free from obvious linear distortion. The image should be fairly uniformly illuminated, even in the corners (absolutely uniform illumination is theoretically impossible), and should not be marred by *flare* spots or streaks. Finally, the lens should be capable of covering a fairly wide field of view and should have a large usable aperture to admit a lot of light. No lens does all of these things perfectly but many modern lenses come satisfactorily close.

but may not because of aberrations

Lenses form less-than-perfect images because inherent defects in material, design, and construction show up as *aberrations*. Some aberrations are natural characteristics of simple lenses. For example, a simple lens tends to form its best image on a saucer-shaped plane. This *curvature of field* is identified as a problem because the image doesn't fit neatly onto the flat film surface. Simple lenses also disperse light into its component colors, forming the different colored images on different planes and in different sizes. We dislike color-fringed images and refer to the several varieties of this defect as *chromatic aberration. Spherical aberration* and *coma* result in image blurring because light rays striking the lens surface near its center don't focus precisely with the marginal rays or with rays entering the lens obliquely. *Astigmatism,* another troublesome aberration, causes image lines that are radial to the image circle to focus differently from the tangential lines. *Distortion,* still another problem, may turn large square shapes in the subject into *barrel* or *pincushion* shapes in the image.

Correcting aberrations requires careful design and assembly

Correcting these aberrations to a useful degree requires the use of at least two different kinds of glass and, frequently, several different lens *elements* of different shapes, very carefully assembled into a single functioning compound unit, the camera lens. The possible combinations of material, shapes, number of elements, and arrangement are almost infinite. Before the age of electronic computers, a new lens design might occupy mathematicians for months or years as they struggled through endless calculations. Now, with many new types of exotic glass and sophisticated computers to do the calculating, very complex lens designs can be completed in hours or days.

Many of the aberrations are related to the fact that lens elements are usually ground and polished with surfaces of spherical form. A few lenses, however, make use of one or more *aspheric* elements. Although they can simplify design and improve lens corrections, aspherical surfaces are difficult to manufacture and are consequently very expensive. Except where maximum performance is required and cost is no object, aspheric lenses are seldom worthwhile.

a

b

Figure 3.25

a. Spherical aberration is responsible for the soft-sharp quality of this photograph. This picture was made at the lens maximum aperture (f/2.9). When stopped down to f/4, or further, it is quite sharp.

b. This enlarged detail from the corners of a transparency shows how the lens focused blue light. Some of the blue streaking is probably due to ultraviolet light and could have been reduced somewhat by using a skylight (Wratten 1A) filter over the camera lens. In the color transparency, and prints made from it, the streaks show as red-yellow blobs with sharp blue tails.

c. You have to try hard to produce this kind of flare with modern coated lenses, but it's possible. The smaller spots, spaced randomly around the flare pattern, are caused by dust spots on the front surface of the lens, glowing in the sunlight. To avoid problems like this, keep the lens free from dust particles and always keep the lens shaded so direct light cannot strike it.

d. Here coma is used purposely to form these decorative candle flames.

c

d

Floating elements help to optimize lens correction

Coating lens surfaces reduces flare

A lens can be well corrected for the various aberrations when focused on distant objects but not perform well at close range. At one time this was unavoidable, but some modern lenses have been designed to work very well at all distances from close-ups to infinity. *Floating elements* within the lens structure accomplish this by adjusting themselves automatically to optimize lens correction as the lens focusing control is turned. The improvement is most noticeable at close range.

Some of the light entering the lens is lost by multiple reflections between the various glass surfaces. Frequently some of this wayward *flare light* reaches the film, not as part of the useful image but in streaks, geometric patterns, *or fog,* unrelated to the image. To reduce flare and increase the contrast of the image, modern lenses are *coated* with very thin layers of a hard, transparent material. A single layer of coating will absorb a large proportion of flare light, but not all colors are absorbed equally. *Multicoating,* adding several specially

Figure 3.26
Macro-lens

Figure 3.27
Super macro-lens on bellows

Figure 3.28
PC lens

Figure 3.29
Zoom lens

controlled layers of coating, can reduce flare of all colors satisfactorily and is a technique used in many lenses today. Multicoating is necessary only on certain types of lens elements. In some cases, a single coating is adequate or even preferable.

The focal length is an important dimension of a lens

The focal length of a lens is the approximate distance from the center of the lens to the film when the lens is focused on infinity. (See pages 82 and 273.) There is no obvious center measuring point in most modern camera lenses; in some instances the measuring point is not even contained within the lens structure. Fortunately, all lenses are clearly marked with their focal lengths, which makes actual measurement seldom necessary.

The focal length is important because it indicates something about the function and purpose of the lens. The *normal* lens for most cameras has a focal length approximately equal to the diagonal of the film image and will photograph objects in about the same way that the eye sees them, including about as much of the subject area as is perceived from the camera position.

Normal, long, and wide (or short) lenses

A *long lens* has a focal length appreciably greater than the film diagonal. It will form an image of larger scale than the normal lens but will cover a narrower field of view. *Wide* lenses (*wide-angle* lenses or *short* lenses) have focal lengths appreciably shorter than the film diagonal. Their images are small in scale but the subject area covered is substantially greater than normal.

Lenses of very *long* focal length are awkward to carry and use because of their physical length. Therefore, most long lenses are built as relatively compact *telephoto* designs, which implies that the effective focal length of the lens is greater than its physical length would appear to permit. Similarly, very wide-angle lenses for SLRs are of *reversed telephoto* or *retro-focus* design, a   b

Figure 3.30
a. Camera with a mirror lens

b. These light doughnuts are typical out-of-focus image points formed by a mirror lens. Because the light rays from the edges of the subject area pass through the lens system slightly obliquely, the circles near the image margins are deformed into pointed ellipses.

Special lens types: Macro lenses

PC lenses

Zoom lenses

which means that their effective focal lengths are substantially shorter than their *back focus*—the actual space between the rear element of the lens and the film surface. This construction is essential in SLRs to allow the reflex mirror space in which to move. A short lens of normal construction would block it.

There are several types of lenses designed for special applications. *Macro-lenses* (one manufacturer calls his product a *micro-lens*) are specially corrected for close-up photography, but will also work satisfactorily with subjects at any distance. These lenses come in several focal lengths, most commonly about 50mm, for 35mm cameras, and can be focused in a range from infinity to about 6″ or 8″ by simply turning the focusing ring. Most of them are supplied with an accessory life-size adapter or a special *extension tube* which can be fitted between the camera body and the lens to permit even closer focusing, so life-size images can be made directly on the film.

Some manufacturers offer specially corrected macro-lenses for different subject distances, each designed to work within a very limited range. Usually these special macros come in plain, nonfocusing barrel mounts and must be used with accessory bellows units for focusing.

A few manufacturers offer *perspective control* (PC) lenses, which are also sometimes called *shift* lenses because they can be shifted off-center in their mounts about one-half inch or more. PC lenses for 35mm SLRs are usually of fairly short focal length, making them moderately wide-angle lenses when used in the normal, unshifted position. They are corrected for a much wider field, though; so even when the lens is displaced as far off-axis as possible, the image quality is maintained at a satisfactory level.

PC lenses are especially suitable for architectural photography because the shift feature makes it possible to rectify, or at least reduce, the apparent convergence of parallel lines in perspective, and buildings can usually be photographed without objectionable distortion.

From a given camera position the focal length of the lens in use will determine the size of the image and the area of the subject recorded. If the camera cannot be moved and if the image must be very precisely composed, it is frequently convenient to use a *zoom* lens. The focal length of a zoom lens can be varied over a rather wide range by merely turning or sliding a collar on the lens barrel. *Zooming* can effectively magnify (or minify) the image, so it can be fitted neatly into the compositional space of the film frame, an especially valuable feature for color slide work. Although zoom lenses are typically not quite as well corrected as fixed-focal-length lenses, many of them are very good. Because the zoom feature necessitates *floating elements,* a number of manufacturers have doubled their function to include a measure of close-up correction in their *macro-zoom* or *close-focusing* (CF) designs. Zoom lenses are somewhat larger and more expensive than the longest fixed-focal-length lenses they replace, but they are extremely versatile and convenient to use.

Figure 3.31
Extreme barrel distortion is a
characteristic of fisheye images.

Catadioptric or mirror lenses

Some very long focal length lenses include spherical mirror elements, as well as lenses, in their design. These *catadioptric* lenses (referred to familiarly as *cats*) are more compact than regular telephotos of similar focal length and frequently have a greater range of focus adjustment. They do not have adjustable apertures. Light transmission through the lens must be reduced, when necessary, by the use of *filters*. A *mirror lens* appears to have a very large aperture, but its effective aperture is reduced considerably by an opaque disc, which is actually a small mirror cemented in the center of the front element. This construction causes the out-of-focus images of bright points of light in the subject to be formed as doughnut shapes rather than the usual *circles of confusion* formed by a regular lens. Cats typically produce images of slightly lower contrast than do regular telephotos, but the best ones can compare very favorably in image sharpness. They are very convenient to use, most are not excessively expensive, and they are available in extremely long focal lengths.

Fisheye lenses

Most lenses are carefully corrected to eliminate linear distortion but *fisheye* lenses emphasize it. They are usually of very short focal length and cover an extremely wide field. The image they form resembles the world as seen in the familiar mirror-surfaced garden balls; nearby objects are grossly distorted and straight lines appear as sweeping arcs. Some fisheye lenses form images that cover the entire film area, the corner-to-corner coverage approximating 180°. Others form a smaller, circular image with equal or even greater angular coverage. In either case the image is bizarre, and although the "fisheye effect" is no longer novel, the lenses are occasionally useful for very wide-angle shots or dramatic distortions.

How Focal Length Affects Image Scale and Perspective

Look for the focal length marking on your lens

When you turn the focusing ring on your camera lens until it stops at the *infinity* mark (∞), you've moved the lens back in its mount as far as it can go, and it is as close to the film surface as it can ever be while forming a usefully sharp image. At this infinity setting the distance from an optical measuring point in the lens structure to the film surface is called the lens *focal length*. You'll find this focal length marked on the lens barrel or on the front element retaining ring, in millimeters or inches. Look for it on your lens; if you have a 35mm camera, equipped with a "normal" lens, it will probably be marked "f=50mm," meaning that the focal length is 50mm, or about 2 inches.

a

b

c

Figure 3.32
a. Image size and angular coverage is determined by lens focal length; perspective is determined by subject-to-camera distance. Here the camera is close to the stop sign so the barn appears far away and small. The 24mm lens covers a large expanse of road and farmland.

b. A 50mm lens, twice as far from the sign as the previous picture, enlarges the barn and shows less of the road and fields, but leaves the sign the same size.

c. Doubling both the subject distance and the lens focal length keeps the sign the same size as before. The 100mm lens field angle is much narrower and the barn appears larger and closer.

d. Here a 200mm lens, at twice the previous distance, leaves the sign size unchanged. The coverage angle is again cut in half and the barn looms large in a shallow space.

e. Distance and focal length again doubled, this 400mm lens appears to compress the background space still further, and the lens coverage angle barely includes the barn width.

d

e

A normal lens is called "normal" because it pictures things "normally": when prints of average size are viewed at reading distance, perspective is believable and there is no obvious distortion of image scale or proportion. The subject area appears "normal," too, representing a subject field of about 45°, which includes about as much of the subject area as we consciously perceive from the camera position.

The normal lens is a good general-purpose lens but it isn't the best choice for every picture. In some instances you'll need to include more or less of the subject area; stand much closer, or farther away from, the subject; or alter the effects of perspective and image scale. In these cases you'll find lenses of longer or shorter focal length very useful.

The terms "long," "normal," and "short" are relative. By informal definition a "normal" lens is one whose focal length is approximately equal to the diagonal measurement of its image format. The popular 35mm cameras provide

The normal lens is a good general-purpose lens

Figure 3.33
a. The 25mm lens, used to take this picture, provides a wide view of the countryside and makes the parking lot attendant's structure (about 300 feet away) insignificantly small. This is a wide-angle lens for a 35mm camera.

b. The normal 50mm lens doubles the size of the structure and narrows the pictured field considerably.

c. A 100mm lens—moderately long for this format—again doubles the size of the building and further reduces the pictured area.

d. A 200mm lens again doubles the building size and restricts the field to the immediate area of the attendant's island.

e. A 400mm lens doubles the building size again, and frames it tightly. This is a very long focal length for 35mm cameras.

f. Focal length determines image size (on the negative) and angular coverage, but perspective is determined solely by the camera-to-subject distance. This enlarged section of a negative made with the 25mm lens is grainy and not very sharp because of the extreme magnification (16 diameters larger than A) but the perspective is exactly the same as that shown in E.

Focal length influences image scale and field coverage

an exception to this rule. They produce negatives that measure approximately 24mm x 36mm, with a corner-to-corner dimension of about 43mm. The normal focal length for this format is presumably about 40 to 45mm, so the 50mm lens, usually supplied with these cameras, is a little longer than normal.

Some popular rollfilm cameras produce square negatives with an image area diagonal measurement of about 76mm. These cameras usually come equipped with lenses having a 75 or 80mm focal length. Similarly, the normal lens for a 4″ × 5″ view camera is about 6 to 6½ inches; a close approximation of the film diagonal is 6.4 inches.

In general, a long lens (whose focal length is appreciably longer than the diagonal of the image format) will picture the subject in larger scale—but include less of it—than will a normal lens. A short lens will form an image in which details are small in scale, and if the lens is of *wide-field* or *wide-angle* design, it will also include more of the subject area than normal.

but the image format is also important

It's important to remember that a lens is classified as short, normal, or long depending on the size of the camera it's used with or, more specifically, on the dimensions of the usable image area it forms. Thus, while a 6″ lens is normal for a 4″ × 5″ camera, it will be considered a long lens if adapted to fit a 35mm camera or if only a small area of the 4″ × 5″ negative is selected to make the print. The same 6″ lens would be considered short for a 5″ × 7″ camera, but it's unlikely that it would be satisfactory for use with this larger format if its design and construction were normal. Normal and long (especially telephoto) lenses don't usually cover enough of the subject area to be useful for wide-angle work.

Wide-angle and telephoto "distortion"

If short, normal, and long lenses are used to photograph some subject from the same position, and if the resulting pictures are enlarged to the same dimensions and viewed from the same distance, at least two of the prints will appear to be distortions of reality. Which two depends largely on two factors: the size of the print and the distance from which you view it. Regardless of the lens it was taken with, an image will appear normal in scale and perspective if the ratio of print-width-to-viewing-distance is the same as the ratio of subject-width-to-camera-distance that existed when the picture was taken. In other words, if a subject 10 feet wide is photographed from 50 feet (width-distance ratio 1:5), the print will appear normal if it is viewed from a distance equal to five times its width; for example, a 2-inch wide print should be viewed from 10 inches and a 15-inch wide print should be viewed from 75 inches. To state the relationship in still another way, the print image will appear normal if it subtends, at the viewer's eye, at the same angle that the camera lens covered in photographing the subject.

is merely an illusion that you can use for effect

When you understand this relationship you'll realize that the so-called "wide-angle distortion" and "telephoto distortion" are not distortions at all. They're merely illusions resulting from unnatural viewing conditions. You can use this knowledge to add drama and emphasis to your photographs. By presenting a telephoto shot (or a considerably enlarged detail from a negative made with a normal lens) so that it is seen larger and closer than is natural, you can impress viewers with the illusion of flattened, shallow space. For deep space and dramatically emphasized effects of perspective, use a wide-angle lens (to keep image details small but include a large subject area) and make prints of only moderate size, not allowing viewers to approach them too closely.

Depth of Focus and Depth of Field

If you point your SLR or view camera at some very distant spot of light, such as a street light at night, the image is likely to appear, at first, as an indistinct, blurred circle. You can watch the circle get smaller and brighter as you focus the camera until, when the focus is precise, the image appears as a brilliant point without apparent shape or dimension. Moving the focusing control in either direction will now enlarge the image point again, re-forming the unfocused circle of light that we call a *circle of confusion.*

Figure 3.34
a. Here the distant street lights are rendered as tiny points of light, without apparent blur or softness of outline. When circles of confusion are large enough to become visible, they're responsible for the blurred outlines of the image forms. We rarely notice them in ordinary subject matter but when the street lights are thrown out of focus, in Fig. B, the circles of confusion are shown clearly.

a

b

Visible circles of confusion form out-of-focus images

Although we've used a single subject point—a distant street light—in this illustration, the principle also applies to the infinite number of points that can be identified on any subject surface. The beams of light reflected toward the lens from each of the subject points are focused to corresponding points behind the lens. If the focused points fall on the film surface, the resulting image is "in focus" and appears sharp; if the points fall an appreciable distance in front of or behind the film surface, the film records them as circles of confusion and we see a blurred, "out-of-focus" image.

Theoretically the film must be placed precisely at the point of focus to record a sharp image but, in fact, slight displacement forward or backward is usually tolerable. We call this little distance, through which the film can be moved without apparently affecting image sharpness, the *depth of focus*. It exists because a very slightly out-of-focus image can't be distinguished from a precisely focused one; in other words, we're not aware that the image is unsharp until the circles of confusion become large enough to be visible, which, of course, depends both on the size of the circles and on how closely we examine them. This is why a print may appear sharp at arm's length but look unsharp when held closer to the eye.

You can photograph a flat, two-dimensional subject without worrying about circle of confusion size, because if the camera is focused properly, the image points will all fall on the film plane and the image will be very sharp.

a

b

c

d

Figure 3.35

a. Focal length, 2 inches; aperture, f/2.8; distance, 12 feet; calculated depth of field, 2.409 feet. Compare this picture with C, F, and G.

b. Focal length, 2 inches; aperture, f/2.8; distance, 24 feet; calculated depth of field, 10.01 feet. Compare with A and D.

c. Focal length, 4 inches; aperture, f/2.8; distance, 24 feet; calculated depth of field, 2.39 feet. Compare with A and B.

d. Focal length, 4 inches; aperture, f/2.8; distance 48 feet; calculated depth of field, 9.71 feet. Compare with A, C, and G.

Depth of focus; depth of field

Don't take the scales too seriously

Three-dimensional subjects are another matter. The image of a three-dimensional subject is also three-dimensional; no matter where the film is placed in the image space, some of the image points will fall either in front of or behind the film plane and will be recorded as circles of confusion.

If all of the image points fall within the depth of focus, their circles of confusion will be acceptably small and the entire subject, from front to rear, will be recorded sharply. If, on the other hand, some image points fall outside the limits of the depth of focus, those portions of the subject that they represent will be pictured as unsharp.

The depth of focus, then, has a corresponding zone in the subject space, called the *depth of field*. Just as the film can be moved back and forth within the depth of focus without disrupting image sharpness, so can the subject be moved within the depth of field—either toward the camera or away from it—without apparently going out of focus. Normally, about one-third of the depth of field lies in front of the plane of sharpest focus, with about two-thirds extending beyond it, and all subject details that lie within the depth of field are considered to be acceptably in focus. They are not, however, *equally* in focus; sharpness gradually deteriorates as the near and far limits of the depth of field are approached.

As you can see, depth of field limits are determined by circle of confusion diameter and will obviously be affected by any conditions that alter our perception of sharpness, such as changes in viewing distance or enlargement of the image. You should therefore view with some skepticism the published tables of depths of field and the depth of field scales that are commonly found on lens mounts. They can be accurate only for certain specific conditions. Don't take them too seriously until you have discovered what circle of confusion diameter and image magnification they're based on.

e   f

e. Focal length, 4 inches; aperture, f/2.8; distance, 12 feet; calculated depth of field, 0.588 feet. Compare with A, C, F, and G.

f. Focal length, 4 inches; aperture, f/11; distance, 12 feet; calculated depth of field, 2.33 feet. Compare with A, C, E, and G.

g. Focal length, 4 inches; aperture, f/2.8; distance, 48 feet; calculated depth of field (based on a circle of confusion diameter of .00025″, then enlarged 4x, so sharpness is comparable to the other prints), 2.404 feet. Compare with A, C, D, and F. This is an enlargement of negative D.

g

There are a number of things that influence depth of field

"Acceptable sharpness" is a matter of perception

There are a number of things that influence depth of field. The most important one is lens aperture diameter: large apertures reduce depth of field; small apertures increase it. Lens focal length is important, too: long lenses produce relatively shallow depth of field; short lenses yield relatively great depth. Subject distance is also a factor: depth of field is shallow at close range; it increases rapidly as the subject distance increases.

We can lump all these influences together to arrive at two major conclusions: reducing aperture size will always increase depth of field; and any factor that reduces image size (short focal length, great subject distance) or makes the image difficult to see clearly (small print size, great viewing distance) will increase depth of field.

Depth of field, by definition, refers to the region of "acceptable sharpness" in the subject space and is, therefore, a matter of perception and judgment. Despite this fact, it's sometimes useful to refer to published tables of depth of field, or the formulas from which the tables are derived, to determine the *relative* effects of changes in focal length, aperture, subject distance, etc.

These photographs of a line of rural mailboxes were taken with focal lengths of 2 and 4 inches, apertures of f/2.8 and f/11, and subject distances of 12, 24, and 48 feet. In each case the camera was focused on the fifth mailbox and the depth of field is greater beyond the point of focus than before it. For example, in figure 3.35 the near plane of focus is calculated to lie 10.92 feet from the camera and the far plane is 13.32 feet away; thus the depth extends about 1.085 feet toward the camera from the plane of sharpest focus (12 feet) and about 1.325 feet beyond it for a total depth of about 2.409 feet. These depths are calculated for a circle of confusion diameter of .001″ and will not agree with tables based on some other sharpness limit.

Figure 3.36
Lens set for hyperfocal distance

Figure 3.37
Lens set for Zone focus

Hyperfocal focus and zone focus

These photographs should answer most of your questions about depth of field: What's the most effective control for increasing depth? Does a short lens at close range give greater depth than a long one at greater distance? At any given subject distance, is it better to use a long lens or enlarge a small image? Is a long lens at small aperture better than a short lens at larger aperture? Examine the photographs carefully, compare the numbers, and draw your own conclusions.

Hyperfocal Distance

When a camera is focused on infinity, the far plane of the depth of field is infinitely distant. The distance from the camera to the near plane, however, is measurable; it's called the *hyperfocal distance*. Hyperfocal distance varies with changes in the values of lens aperture, focal length, and circle of confusion size, but you can find its approximate values for the various apertures of your lens by consulting the depth of field scale. First, align the infinity mark on the focusing ring with the selected aperture number on the depth of field scale; then find the hyperfocal distance opposite the focusing index mark. In other words, the lens is focused on the hyperfocal distance. When the lens is set this way (called *hyperfocal focus*), the near plane of the depth of field falls at *half* the hyperfocal distance and everything will be sharp from there to infinity. Set your lens this way when you want the greatest possible depth of field or when you want to be prepared for quick response to any action that may occur beyond the middle distance.

You can also *zone focus* to provide adequate depth of field for subjects closer to the camera. For example, assume you want to prepare for some action that will occur somewhere between 30′ and 100′ from the camera. Using a 150mm Sonnar telephoto lens for the Hasselblad camera (for purposes of illustration), turn the focusing ring until 30′ and 100′ straddle the focusing index mark and align them with the movable markers that define the near and far limits of depth of field. This has been done in the illustration, which shows the 150mm lens, zone focused for 30′ and 100′ and indicates that the required aperture is f/16. The shutter speed is shown as 1/250th second but, in practice, it would be dictated by the film speed and the light condition.

Figure 3.38
Small lens scale

Zone focusing some small camera lenses is more of a guessing game. In some cases the marked distances are widely spaced and their exact positions are ambiguous. This is probably deliberate on the part of the manufacturer, to avoid the implication that depth of field can be controlled with real precision.

Focusing for Infrared

Lenses can't focus all wavelengths equally

If you were to photograph a collection of brightly colored objects with a simple lens, you might discover that some of them were out of focus in the picture, even though all the objects were the same distance from the camera. This is because the lens's ability to focus varies with the wavelength (color) of the light; short wavelengths (blues) are focused closer to the lens than are long wavelengths (reds). In other words, the lens has a slightly different focal length for each light color. Ordinary camera lenses are corrected well enough for this defect (a form of chromatic aberration), so they focus the colors together satisfactorily; however, they don't do as well with the infrared radiations that lie beyond red light, just outside the visible spectrum. Therefore, if you want to take infrared photographs, you'll have to make a slight change in your focusing procedure.

Your lens probably has a separate index mark for IR focusing

You'll probably find a small red dot or line beside the index mark on the focusing scale of your lens. If you want to measure the subject distance, instead of focusing visually, merely set the measured distance value opposite the red index mark instead of the normal one. If you prefer to focus visually, note the distance value opposite the normal index mark, then turn the focusing ring to shift that value to the red index mark. This adjustment will move the lens away from the film plane slightly, and if you were to make the picture by visible light, the plane of sharpest focus would be a little in front of the subject. Usually, though, when using infrared film, we exclude most visible light from the camera, and the slightly extended lens position brings the IR image into focus. If you use a view camera, or if your lens doesn't have an IR index mark on its focusing scale, you'll probably have to guess at the correction. As a rule of thumb, the lens should be extended beyond the point of visual focus by a distance equal to about 0.2% of the lens focal length. If you can't figure that out, just focus slightly in front of the subject and use a small enough lens aperture to provide considerable depth of field.

1.4   2   2.8   4

Figure 3.39
Lens opening front and top with
calibrations

Relative Aperture—Lens Speed

The various standard settings of the diaphragm scale are marked by f-numbers, taken from this standard series:

$$f/ \ \ldots 1.4, \quad 2, \quad 2.8, \quad 4, \quad 5.6, \quad 8, \quad 11, \quad 16, \quad 22, \ etc. \ldots$$

The f-numbers are in a standard series

Notice that every second number in the ascending series is doubled, so it's easy to extend the series in both directions: the number following 22 must be twice 16, or 32; and the number before 1.4 must be half of 2, or 1. The f-numbers are found by dividing the lens focal length by the aperture diameter:

$$f\text{-number} = \frac{\text{focal length}}{\text{aperture diameter}}$$

They are called *relative apertures* and indicate lens speed

The f-numbers are sometimes called *relative apertures* because they express the relative values of lens aperture diameter and lens focal length. You can see that as you move the diaphragm control on your lens from, say, f/2 to f/11, the numbers themselves become larger but the aperture of the lens is reduced in size. This, of course, reduces the amount of light that can be transmitted to the film, so *lens speed* is reduced.

Lens speed varies inversely with the square of the f-number

The relative aperture, or f-number, is an indication of lens speed but the relationship is not a simple one. Speed increases as the f-numbers decrease (and vice versa); also, f-numbers are computed from aperture *diameter,* but light transmission through the lens depends on aperture *area.* Therefore, speed varies *inversely* with the *square* of the f-number. It's easy to find relative speeds of f-numbers: simply divide the larger by the smaller, square the result, and remember that the smaller f-number represents the higher speed. For example, to find the relative speeds of f/2 and f/16, divide 16 by 2 to get 8; then, square 8 to find the relative speed, 64. Since f/2 is the larger aperture, it's the faster speed—64 times faster than f/16.

You'll probably find both the maximum relative aperture and focal length of your lens engraved on the lens barrel or on the front element retaining ring. Uniquely, in this application, the relative aperture is expressed as a simple ratio of diameter-to-focal-length, and the small letter f is used to designate the focal length. An f/2 lens of 50mm focal length, for example, is likely to be marked 1:2 f=50mm.

5.6   8   11   16

Aperture settings are called *stops*

Although this may seem confusing, the use of the small letter f to stand for focal length, is traditional. Years ago, before adjustable diaphragms had been invented, photographers controlled image light intensity by inserting perforated metal plates into their lens barrels. Since the hole in each plate reduced the effective size of the lens aperture, some of the light was "stopped" from reaching the film, and the plates became known as stops. The stop plates were identified by hole size, defined as a fraction of the focal length; for example, if the lens focal length was 8 inches and the stop diameter was ½ inch, the stop was said to be 1/16th of the focal length, or equal to the focal length (f) divided by 16. This was originally written as $\frac{f}{16}$ but eventually became f/16, the form we use today.

Originally, replacing one stop with the next larger one in the series doubled the exposure. This is still true, even though we now control light transmission through the lens by varying the setting of the iris diaphragm control. The marked aperture settings (f-numbers) are called stops—or sometimes f-stops—and we call changing from a larger aperture to a smaller one *stopping down*. For some reason we don't "stop up" a lens; we *open up* when we change from a smaller aperture to a larger one.

Changing from one stop to the next doubles or halves the exposure

Because changing from one marked f-stop to the next in the standard series either doubles or halves the exposure (depending on which way you're going), we've come to describe *any* doubled or halved exposure as a change of one stop, even if the change is made by altering exposure time or subject light intensity. Thus, we speak of one film as being "a stop faster" than another (meaning it's twice as sensitive and therefore requires only half as much light to form a satisfactory image). We also say the light has decreased "a couple of stops" (meaning it's only one-fourth as bright) when the sun goes under a cloud; and we may even say we've increased an exposure by "three stops" when we change the camera shutter speed setting from ⅛ to 1 second (from ⅛ to ¼ = 1 stop; ¼ to ½ = 1 stop; ½ to 1 second = 1 stop).

The term is used loosely

This may seem a little confusing at first, but you'll get along very well if you can remember that (1) the f-numbers indicate lens speed; (2) speed increases as the f-numbers decrease; (3) the exposure difference, or interval, between adjacent f-numbers in the standard series is one stop; and (4) an exposure change of one stop implies a factor of 2—in other words, the exposure has been either doubled or halved.

How Exposure Is Controlled

Film requires a certain quantity of light to form a good image, meaning that both the *intensity* of the light on the film surface and the *duration* of the exposure must be controlled quite carefully. In practice we control the image light intensity by adjusting the aperture of the lens with the iris diaphragm. The exposure duration is controlled by the camera shutter, which opens to admit light to the film and then closes—after a selected interval—to terminate the exposure.

The Reciprocity Law of exposure

In general the film can be exposed satisfactorily at any of several settings of the aperture and shutter controls, as long as each pair of settings provides the same *total* exposure. That is, if a large aperture is used to illuminate the film brightly, it must be matched with a brief exposure time. On the other hand, a small aperture, which allows only a dim light to reach the film, must be paired with a shutter setting that will provide a long exposure. This relationship is expressed by the *Reciprocity Law* of exposure, which states that the exposure effect on the film will remain constant if the product of exposure time and light intensity is constant.

Although the shutter setting is the only control that actually involves time, we use words such as *speed* and *fast* to describe films and lens apertures as well as shutter settings. Thus, a fast film is one that is very sensitive to light, and a fast lens is one that transmits a lot of light to the film. A fast shutter setting is obviously one that provides a very short exposure time, and all shutter settings are commonly referred to as *speeds*.

The shutter speed scale on your camera is probably calibrated with numbers from this standard series:

1   2   4   8   15   30   60   125   250   500   1000   2000

Shutter speed scale calibration

Some cameras will not have all these speeds and some older cameras are calibrated in a slightly different series:

1   2   5   10   25   50   100   250   500   1000

or perhaps:

1   2   5   10   25   50   100   200   400

In all cases these numbers stand for fractions of a second, and would be written out like this if there were room on the scales:

1   ½   ¼   ⅛   1/15   1/30   1/60   1/125   1/250   etc.

As you can see, the series progresses by a factor of 2; that is, each numbered speed will provide half as much—or twice as much—exposure as the next one in the series, depending on which way you're going. Obviously, the sequence is not precise; 1/15 is not twice as fast as ⅛, for example, but the discrepancy is negligible.

The additional shutter speeds, *Time* and *B*ulb

In addition to the fractional speeds listed above, most shutter speed scales include a setting marked *B*. Some shutters, especially those with which view cameras are equipped, also provide a speed marked *T*. The B setting stands for *Bulb* and is a hangover from the days when shutters were operated pneumatically. By squeezing a rubber bulb, connected to the shutter by a long rubber tube, the photographer could compress air to force the shutter open, and hold it open indefinitely. Spring tension closed the shutter when the bulb was released.

Now, shutters are usually held open when set on the B position by finger pressure on a cable release—a flexible plunger that can be screwed into the shutter or camera body—but the result is the same: the shutter stays open as long as it's held open. When you relax pressure on the shutter release, the shutter closes.

The B setting is useful for short *time exposures,* that is, exposure intervals longer than the automatically timed speeds provided by the shutter mechanism but not so long that holding pressure on the release is tiresome. Generally we use the B speed for exposures of just a few seconds.

For longer exposures we usually use the *T,* or *Time* setting. The T speed can also be used to hold the shutter open indefinitely but T permits you to leave the camera while the exposure is in progress. The shutter opens, and locks open, when you press the shutter release; you have to press the release a second time to close it.

Both *T* and *B* are useful for time exposures

Selecting and Using Black-and-White Films

Black-and-white films are sensitized with an emulsion of silver halide crystals suspended in gelatin. After exposure and development, some of these crystals are reduced to particles of opaque metallic silver to form the image. Although the individual particles are too small to be seen with the unaided eye, they overlap randomly to form visible clumps which, distributed more or less uniformly, give the film image a granular visual texture. When a *grainy* negative is enlarged in printing, the print image reproduces the film grain clearly as a pepper-and-salt texture, most apparent in the areas of middle tone.

The film image appears grainy

Although grain is inherent and unavoidable, some films form a coarser grain structure than do others. In general, highly sensitive films (*high speed* or *fast* films) are relatively coarse-grained; *slow* films are typically fine-grained. These terms are relative. Whether grain is coarse or objectionable, or even noticeable, depends on your personal perception and taste. Some photographers like grain and use fast films purposely to achieve it. Others are displeased by grain. They are likely to select slow films and use large film sizes to avoid having to enlarge their images.

For many years American manufacturers have assigned speed numbers to their films following testing procedures originally recommended by the American Standards Association (ASA). Now, however, an international standard has been established and, today, film speeds may be identified either as ASA speeds or ISO (International Organization for Standardization) speeds. The difference is in name only; the numbers are the same. Here is part of the familiar ASA standard film speed number series:

10 12 16 20 25 32 40 50 63 80 100 125 160 200
250 320 400 500 etc.

Film speed numbers indicate film sensitivity

These speed numbers are directly related to film sensitivity, that is, a film rated at ASA (or ISO) 100 is twice as fast as one rated at ASA (or ISO) 50. Notice, too, that every *third* number in the ascending sequence is doubled, which means that the sequence progresses in third-stop intervals. Thus, Plus-X film (ASA 125) is 1⅓ stops faster than Ilford Pan F (ASA 50), but 1 ⅔ stops slower than Tri-X, which is rated at ASA 400.

The ISO standard includes our ASA number series

When the ISO standard was formulated in 1974, it adopted both the American (ASA) system and the German (DIN) system and approved each for international use. Although they are equally valid and useful, the numbers are in different series: the ASA system progression is arithmetic and the DIN system progression is logarithmic. Since Kodak films are sold internationally, the Eastman Kodak Company now includes both speed numbers on its film packages so that, for example, Plus-X film, which is rated at 125 in the arithmetic (ASA) system and 22 in the logarithmic (DIN) system, is now labelled ISO 125/22°—the degree symbol (°) being used to indicate the logarithmic number. This is merely a label change; American users may simply ignore the last portion of the speed number and continental photographers will presumably ignore the first portion.

ASA numbers are printed on the information sheets packaged with the films and are usually printed on the outside of the cartons as well. Kodak color films include the film speed in the film title. Kodachrome 25, Ektachrome 64, and Kodacolor 400, for example, have ASA speeds of 25, 64, and 400 respectively.

a

b

c

d

Figure 3.40
This series illustrates the way black-and-white films reproduce subject colors. Figure **a** shows the color response of ordinary blue-sensitive emulsions; reds and yellows are rendered darker than you'd expect them to be and blues are lightened in value. Figure **b** demonstrates orthochromatic color sensitivity; reds are very dark but greens and yellows are rendered more naturally. Figure **c** shows how common panchromatic films react to subject colors; reds and greens are quite similar in value and all colors are shown as grays of various shades. Extended red sensitivity produces the rendering shown in Figure **d**; reds are unnaturally light in value and all the colors have a rather bland look. Compare these photographs with the color photograph of the still-life on Colorplate 2.

Although black-and-white films don't produce color images, they do respond to color in the subject by recording the different hues in various shades of gray. The natural color sensitivity of the simple silver halide emulsion is restricted to the blue, violet, and ultraviolet region of the spectrum. The emulsion is effectively blind to red, orange, yellow, and some of the green. Ordinary or noncolor sensitized emulsions of this sort produce images that, in final print form, render blues and violet shades as almost white. Red, oranges, and yellows show up in the print as black or dark gray tones. This effect is apparent in daguerreotypes and in prints from collodion negatives. Pale eyes, in nineteenth-century portraits of blue-eyed individuals, and blank white skies demonstrate the relatively great blue-sensitivity of these early materials.

Orthochromatic films have had their sensitivity extended into the green region. Their reproduction of the *cool* colors appears more natural, but red objects are still photographed as if they were black. Further extension of sensitivity into the red region of the spectrum has given us *panchromatic* emulsions. Their reproduction of the spectrum colors in various shades of gray is quite balanced and believable, and generally preferable to *ortho* or *ordinary* rendition. Most *pan* films match the color sensitivity of the human eye quite satisfactorily, but a few types have *extended red* sensitivity, rendering red and orange objects

Figure 3.41
Cobblestone House, Avon, New York,
1958. Minor White. Infrared film, heavily
filtered to eliminate blue light, is
responsible for the dramatic tonality and
dreamlike quality of this photograph.
Courtesy of the Minor White Archive,
Princeton University.

**When selecting film, consider conditions
of use**

much lighter than the eye normally perceives them. These films are typically very fast, coarse-grained materials, intended mainly for scientific use, although one of them—Kodak's Type 2475—is available in standard 35mm cartridges for general use.

Kodak also supplies an infrared film in 35mm cartridges. The film is almost always used with a red filter over the camera lens, to exclude blue and ultra-violet light—both of which will affect it strongly. IR images are typically very grainy and often distort the subject tonality in strange and interesting ways. The film has no ASA film speed rating but it comes with an information sheet that will help you estimate exposures. It is moderately sensitive to daylight and rather unusually sensitive to ordinary tungsten light—less so to fluorescent light.

In selecting a film type for use, consider what you want to use it for and what sort of quality you expect in the prints. In both color and black-and-white films, low speeds are likely to indicate fine-grained, high-resolution materials which are appropriate for use in situations where the light is good and the pictures must be exceptionally clear and sharp. Very fast films will permit more freedom of operation in dim light conditions but will produce grainier images which are somewhat less crisply delineated. Medium-speed films, logically enough, represent a compromise between these extremes. See the film chart in appendix 1.

Figure 3.42
a. Open the camera back. On this camera the back latch is released by pulling up on the rewind knob.

b. Be sure the camera interior is clean, then insert the film cartridge and push the rewind knob down to engage the cartridge spool.

c. Insert the film tongue into the slotted take-up spool and be sure it is fully engaged and straight.

d. Wind the film by working the advance lever and releasing the shutter until both rows of perforations are mated with the teeth of the sprocket wheels; then take up the slack film in the cartridge, gently, by turning the rewind knob until the film is under slight tension. Close the camera back and wind off two exposures to get rid of the exposed film leader.

e. Set the film speed into the camera ASA dial before you forget it.

f. If your camera is equipped with a reminder frame of this sort, insert the end flap from the film box in it so you won't forget what kind of film you have in the camera.

a

b

When you have made your selection and bought the film, open the film package in subdued light and remove the information sheet. Read it. It contains valuable information about the exposure and development of the film, which is up-to-date and valid for that particular roll. Save the sheet for reference until the film has been developed; then throw it away. Manufacturers change their recommendations from time to time, so referring to data from reference books (like this one) or old information sheets may be inappropriate for new film.

Determining Exposure: Using Built-in Meters

All exposure meters are designed to read "average" subjects

Using the film speed numbers could hardly be easier; simply set the appropriate number into the ASA dial on your camera meter (or separate exposure meter) and the meter is ready to provide you with pertinent exposure advice. All that's left to do is to measure the subject luminance (the light being reflected toward the camera from the subject). That's what your meter is designed to do but you'll have to use it sensibly to be sure it gives you the information you're interested in. All exposure meters, including the built-in meter in your 35mm SLR, are designed to read "average" subjects, that is, subjects that are either uniformly middle-gray in tone or composed of areas of light and dark tones, which—averaged together—equal middle-gray. The meter, therefore, treats every subject (whether average or not) as if it were average, and will give you exposure advice that's intended to reproduce the subject as middle gray. In almost all cases this works quite well; many subjects *do* contain a mixture of lights and darks that average approximately middle-gray. But there are some that don't. Snow scenes, for example, are typically

c

d

e

f

Examine the subject area carefully; you may have to override the meter

much lighter than middle-gray, and you'll occasionally encounter a subject area that is much darker than middle-gray—the proverbial black cat on the coal pile, for example. You'll have to help the meter deal with subjects like these because, if you take the readings it gives you without modifying them, you'll get pictures of gray snow and gray coal. The meter wants everything you point it at to turn gray in the print.

To cope with this problem effectively, you must first learn to recognize when it exists. As soon as you've selected your subject and framed it satisfactorily within the viewfinder format, examine it carefully to see whether it's average or not. If the areas of tone you see in the viewfinder seem to be more or less balanced between light and dark, you can probably use the meter's recommended exposure settings without modification. If, on the other hand, the subject area seems generally lighter than average in value, or if actual sources of light appear within the subject area, you can assume the meter will underexpose the scene in an attempt to "restore" it to a middle-gray average.

You'll get the opposite result if the subject values average darker than middle-gray. The meter will interpret the subject as a normal one in dim light and will try to "correct" the situation by suggesting that you overexpose. In both instances you'll have to overrule the meter if you want the subject to be reproduced in its normal value scale.

There are at least two ways to do this: you can point the camera at a more nearly average distribution of light and dark tones, and then use the reading from *that* area when you reframe your subject to make the exposure; or, you can *manually override* the meter by deliberately increasing the exposure it recommends for subjects of lighter-than-normal appearance and deliberately decreasing its recommended exposure for darker-than-normal subjects.

Figure 3.43
Override dial

Both methods include some risk. In the first instance you must be sure that the area you select for your *substitute reading* has about the same *extremes* of luminance that the subject has, but in a more uniform balance. It's unrealistic, for example, to take a substitute reading in a totally shaded area when the subject you intend to photograph is in full sunlight. In the second instance, you'll have to learn by experience how much deliberate adjustment of exposure is required, whether you do it directly by altering the lens and shutter settings, or by merely setting the *override dial* on your camera (if it has one). In general an adjustment of one stop will be sufficient to compensate for abnormally light or dark subjects if you're shooting color film—and may also suffice for black-and-white—unless the subject average value is unusually far from normal. A two-stop shift will make a dramatic change in color film exposure and will have a very significant effect on black-and-white films.

Meter sensitivity is "weighted"

As you gain experience with your camera, you'll probably find that its built-in meter doesn't respond uniformly over the entire area of the viewfinder. Most don't, even those that are described as *full-field averaging* types. *Center-weighted* meters concentrate most of their sensitivity in the center of the viewfinder image field; a few are *bottom weighted;* and some others can be switched from one sensitivity pattern to another.

Your camera instruction manual may tell you what sensitivity characteristic your meter has but, if it doesn't, remember that nearly all meters are more affected by tones that appear in the center area of the viewfinder image than by similar values near the margins of the field. Keep this in mind while you're trying to decide whether or not the meter is reading a "normal" mixture of subject tones.

Programmed operation is not always appropriate

If your camera permits you to select modes of operation—manual, programmed, or semi-automatic—you should understand the advantages of each so that you can choose intelligently. Programmed operation is ideal for general picture-taking because all you have to do is point the camera, focus, and press the button. It's quick, simple, and worry free, but it isn't always appropriate.

Consider, for example, a subject in rapid motion, such as softball players in action. A very high shutter speed—probably 1/500th second, or even less—will be required to record the scrambling figures without blurring them, but a a   b

Figure 3.44
Proper film exposure requires
complementary settings of the lens
aperture and the camera shutter, both of
which affect image quality. In (a) the
exposure of 1/1000 second at f/2.8
stopped the motion of the runner and the
first baseman satisfactorily and restricted
the depth of field to the immediate area of
the action. The picture would have been
improved with a still higher shutter speed
and larger lens opening—for even less
motion blur and shallower depth—but
these were the limits of the equipment. In
(b) the exposure was 1/15 second at
f/22; depth of field extends from the
coach in the foreground to the buildings in
the distance but the moving figures are
blurred. This is the worst possible
rendering of the subject; the background is
very confusing and the runner is practically
invisible.

**Semi-automatic operation has distinct
advantages**

camera operating in programmed mode can't be adjusted; it will select the
shutter speed and aperture listed in its program for that particular lighting
condition. You may not know whether the selected speed was adequate until
you see the finished picture.

In manual mode you can set the shutter on any speed you like, then
activate the meter to find out what the appropriate aperture should be. When
you've set the aperture scale as recommended, you can take the picture, confident that it will be well-exposed and satisfactorily free from motion blur.
Better yet, *shutter-priority* semi-automatic operation requires only that you set
the shutter at the desired speed. The camera will then provide the appropriate
aperture setting every time you press the shutter release. For subjects of this
sort semi-automatic operation is both faster and more convenient than manual
because the camera will make instantaneous adjustments to maintain proper
exposure if the light changes while you're shooting.

When subject or camera motion threaten to blur your pictures shutter-
priority automation is ideal, but in some cases—photographing still-life objects,
for example—motion may be less of a problem than sharpness of focus and
depth of field. In these cases, *aperture-priority* automation (or, of course, manual operation) is preferable.

Depth of field (as explained previously on pages 88–90) is dependent on
several factors, the most important of which is the aperture of the lens; depth
of field is always greater when the lens is working at a small aperture. Thus,
when a deep subject space must be rendered sharply, you'll probably have to
stop the lens down—perhaps all the way. On the other hand, a large aperture
is indicated when you want to focus sharply on some shallow plane of the
subject and subdue foreground and background details by throwing them out
of focus. Occasionally—as, for example, when photographing some finely detailed or textured subject—you'll want the sharpest film image the lens is
capable of forming. Since lens sharpness deteriorates somewhat at both very
large and very small apertures, you should choose a medium one. In cases such
as these, when the success of the picture depends on the use of a specific lens
opening, aperture-priority operation is ideal.

Figure 3.45

a. This is good form for shooting with a small camera: the right hand holds the camera body, releases the shutter, and advances the film; the left hand supports the camera and operates the focusing and aperture controls. Keep your elbows braced firmly against your body for good camera support.

b. Bracing your arm on your knee will help provide firm support for the camera.

c. A small table-top tripod, braced against some solid support, will help steady the camera for fairly long exposures.

d. Bean-bags or shot-bags make a fine camera support and dampen vibration very effectively.

e. A shot-bag hung on the tripod will help stabilize it.

f. Brace a long telephone with sticks, as shown, to reduce vibration.

a

b

c

d

e

f

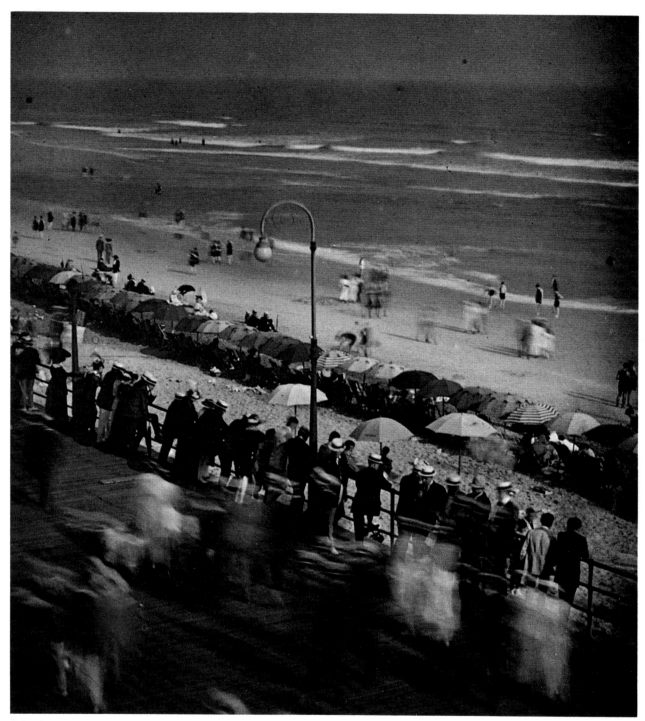

Colorplate 1

Karl Struss: **The Promenade,** Long Beach, Long Island, c. 1915. Lumiere
Autochrome. © 1981 by John and Susan Edwards Harvith. Reproduced by
permission.
For many years Struss's fame as a Hollywood cinematographer
overshadowed his earlier work as an innovative and respected member of the
Photo-Secession group. Now that he has been rediscovered, his photographs
are beginning to receive the attention they deserve.

Colorplate 2

Colorplate 3

Colorplate 4

a. Bruce Grukle, a student at Portfolio Center in Atlanta, works to arrange a still life. He has constructed a partial tent with dark sides to control the light direction and reduce reflected fill light in the shadows.
b. Bruce has arranged two light sources: a large-area source—the trans-illuminated screen at right—will provide soft, relatively shadowless illumination; the smaller, brighter light closer to the tent will establish the shadow patterns and model the contours of the subject. This combination will simulate strong window light while keeping the shadows open and detailed.
c. With the lights on and the window freshly sprayed to simulate raindrops, Bruce adjusts the lens and shutter controls. Notice the tilted position of the camera back and lensboard; this is necessary to keep the vertical lines of the subject parallel. The general studio illumination, which is necessary to make these pictures, will be turned off when the still life is photographed.
d. Here's the final picture; a handsome composition, skillfully controlled. Courtesy of the photographer and Portfolio Center.

b

c

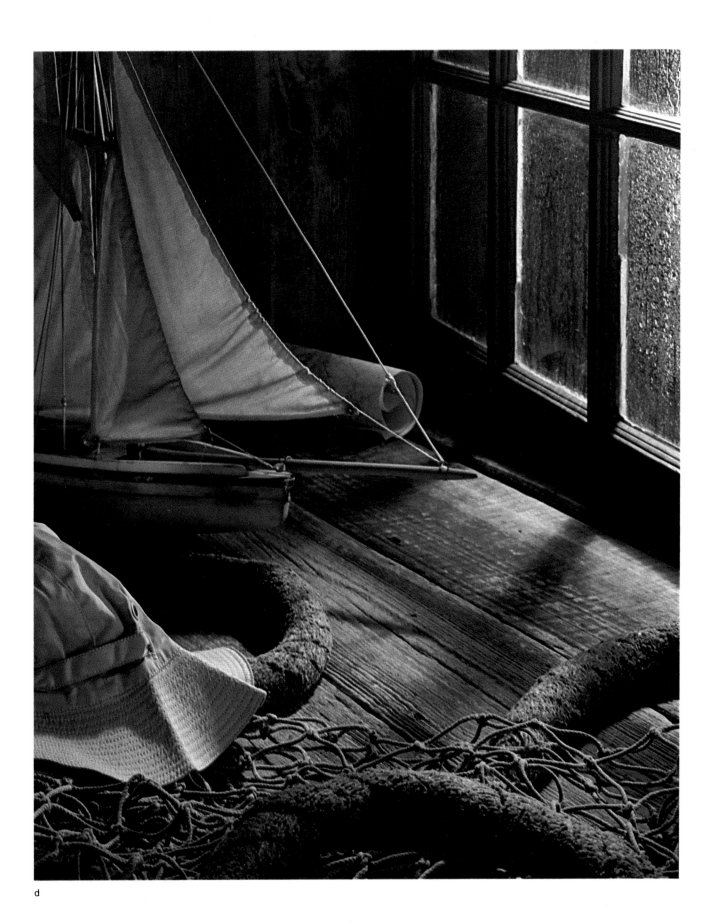

d

How Aperture and Shutter Setting Are Related

In both lens aperture (f-number) and shutter speed scales, a change from one number to the next doubles (or halves) the exposure. For example, if your camera is set on 1/60 at f/11, you can double the film exposure by either changing the shutter speed from 1/60 to 1/30 at f/11 or by changing the aperture from f/11 to f/8 at 1/60. You can keep the exposure unchanged if when you increase the aperture you decrease the exposure time by a similar amount. For example, if you decide to use a higher shutter speed than 1/60 without altering the exposure, you can select from any of the following combinations, all of which will expose the film equally:

1/125 at f/8.0
1/250 at f/5.6
1/500 at f/4.0
1/1000 at f/2.8 etc.

In every case, moving the aperture control one stop toward greater exposure can be compensated by moving the shutter control one stop toward less exposure. If, in the illustration above, you decide to use a smaller lens opening than f/11, any of these pairs of settings will keep the exposure unchanged:

f/16 at 1/30
f/22 at 1/15
f/32 at 1/8
f/45 at 1/4 etc.

EV Numbers

Because it's sometimes convenient to calculate exposures without worrying about specific aperture and shutter speed settings, some cameras—and most hand-held meters—are calibrated with a standard series of *exposure value* (*EV*) numbers, each of which stands for a specific quantity of exposure (and indicates all the possible pairs of aperture and shutter speed settings that can provide that exposure) with the film in use. The EV system, in other words, combines the exposure effects of aperture and shutter settings into single numbers. Table 3.1 shows a portion of the EV number series with some of the camera settings it represents.

You can select from several combinations of aperture and shutter speed

Table 3.1
f-Numbers Appropriate for the Various Shutter Speeds

EV Nos.	Shutter Speeds								
	1 sec	1/2	1/4	1/8	1/15	1/30	1/60	1/125	1/250
4	f/4.0	2.8	2.0	1.4	1.0				
5	5.6	4.0	2.8	2.0	1.4	1.0			
6	8.0	5.6	4.0	2.8	2.0	1.4	1.0		
7	11	8.0	5.6	4.0	2.8	2.0	1.4	1.0	
8	16	11	8.0	5.6	4.0	2.8	2.0	1.4	1.0
9	22	16	11	8.0	5.6	4.0	2.8	2.0	1.4
10	32	22	16	11	8.0	5.6	4.0	2.8	2.0 etc.

Figure 3.46
EV scale on camera

Figure 3.46
EV scale on camera

EV is frequently used in place of "stop"

As you can see, a change from one EV number to the next represents an exposure change of one stop; so the term "EV" is frequently used in place of "stop" to express exposure ranges or meter sensitivity. For example, a camera's built-in meter may be advertised as having an effective range of "EV O–18 at ASA 100". The EV range, alone, indicates that the meter can provide accurate camera settings ranging from, for example, 2 seconds at f/1.4 to 1/1000 at f/16—an exposure range of 18 stops, or about 256,000 to 1. When the film speed (ASA 100) is included in the specification, the actual range of subject illuminance that the meter can handle (with average subject matter) can be calculated (from about .25 footcandles to about 64,000 footcandles, in this example).

Light, Color, and Filters

In photography we are mostly concerned with the visible spectrum. Taken as a whole, we see it as white light. If portions of the spectrum are missing, we see the remaining mixture of wavelengths as color. We perceive narrow sections of the spectrum, seen alone, as relatively pure color, and if the spectrum is divided roughly into thirds, the colors are seen individually as red, green, and blue. We call these the *light primary* colors, and sometimes *additive primaries,* because they are basic colors (not mixtures of more fundamental hues) and because blending them together (adding them) makes *white*.

The light primary colors are called additive primaries

If the pairs of light primaries are mixed together, they form the *secondary* colors. Thus, red and green light (not pigment) blended together make yellow; green and blue make cyan (greenish-blue); and red and blue make magenta. In every case, mixing light colors together increases the brightness of the light. (See plate 2.)

Pigment primaries are called subtractive primaries

Pigments or dyes don't have any color of their own. They appear colored because they absorb portions of the light spectrum and reflect the rest. Thus a dye that absorbs blue light reflects red and green and will be seen as yellow. A dye or pigment that absorbs green will be seen as magenta, and a material that absorbs equal amounts of red, green, and blue will simply reduce the brightness of the light and appear gray. Because pigments absorb light color, they are called *subtractive colors,* and the pigment or dye primaries are *subtractive primaries.* Mixtures of the three subtractive primaries, if properly balanced, absorb virtually all the incident light and make black. (See plate 3.)

If a dye or pigment color completely absorbs some other light color, the colors are called *complementary,* or *complements* of each other. Thus, magenta dye, which totally absorbs green light, is the complement of green; blue is the complement of yellow; and red is the complement of cyan.

We use these principles, even in black-and-white photography, to control the pictorial quality of colored objects. A red filter placed over the camera lens, for example, will transmit only red light to the film, absorbing both blue and green light. Therefore, blue or green objects in the subject will be pictured in

a

b

c

Figure 3.47
a. These figures have black hair and are wearing yellow caps, red shirts, blue trousers, and dusty black boots. The grass is brownish green and the sky is hazy blue. In this picture no filter was used; this is the natural color response of Plus-X film.

b. A light yellow filter darkens the sky, the trousers, and the shadows slightly.

c. A red filter darkens the blue sky and trousers dramatically, darkens the grass somewhat, increases contrast, and lightens the red shirts to a light gray. See also colorplate 3.

d. A strong green filter darkens shirt and trousers, lightens the grass slightly, and leaves other areas practically unaffected.

e. A blue filter turns the sky almost white, lightens the blue trousers to gray, and darkens both the red shirts and the yellow caps.

d

e

Filters lighten their own color and darken their complement

the print as black, because none of their light reaches the film. Red objects, on the other hand, will appear as bright as white objects in the print because red light passes through the filter as easily as white light does.

Filters lighten their own color and darken their complement in the print. If the filter color is intense and saturated, the effect on the image will be dramatic. If the filter is a pale tint, or an impure color, the filter effect will be less pronounced.

Most film exposures are based on white light and therefore must be increased when a filter is used because the filter absorbs some of the image light. This necessary exposure compensation is called the *filter factor* and is usually expressed as a number by which the exposure must be multiplied. For example, the Kodak Wratten #8 is a yellow filter having a factor of 2x in daylight. When it is used, the normal (white light) exposure must be doubled, either by doubling the exposure time or by opening the lens up one stop. Similarly, the Wratten #25, a red filter, has a daylight factor of 8x and a

Synopsis

Filter Effect

For greatest filter effect, use a filter of pure, saturated hue on a subject whose colors are equally strong and pure, then underexpose slightly. For minimal filter effect, use a pale filter on a barely tinted subject with more-than-normal exposure.

Filters will lighten their own colors in the subject and darken their complements, as rendered in the final print image. Filtering the light source is just as effective as placing the filter over the camera lens. An exposure based on a white light meter reading will have to be increased when a filter is used, because the filter will absorb some of the image light. This increase is called the filter factor. The usual filter factor will not have to be applied if the meter reading is taken in filtered light or if an SLR through-the-lens meter is used to read through a filter on the lens. However, some compensation may be required; test your own meter by bracketing the settings it suggests.

Neutral density filters simply reduce light intensity without affecting color. Polarizing filters can reduce the intensity of glare from most reflecting surfaces without affecting the rest of the image substantially, in either value or color balance.

Filter factors may vary if light color changes

tungsten light factor of 4x. When used in daylight with panchromatic film, the exposure must be increased 8x, or 3 stops. In tungsten light (ordinary tungsten-filament light bulbs) the exposure must be increased only 4x or 2 stops. The difference in factors in the two light conditions is due to the color of the light. Daylight is relatively blue, while tungsten light is orange. The red filter restricts a large proportion of the bluish daylight but transmits the orange tungsten light with relatively little attenuation.

Obviously, there's no point in trying to use a red filter with either orthochromatic or non-color sensitized films, because neither film can respond usefully to red light—the only light the filter can transmit. It would be equally pointless to use a blue filter with blue-sensitive film, for example, because the film is sensitive only to blue and will form the same image, essentially, in either white or blue light. For most purposes, if you want to use filters to change the normal response of the film, you should work with panchromatic film. You don't have to worry about this too much; practically all the rollfilms you're likely to find at your local camera shop are panchromatic.

It isn't always necessary to put a filter over the camera lens to achieve a filtered effect on the image. Filtering the light source will do as well. Thus, covering your studio lights with blue *gels,* for example, will make blue objects photograph as very light in tone, just as using a blue filter over the camera lens would do. Caution—while in theory you should not have to apply any filter factor when the meter reading is taken in colored light, most meters are a little colorblind and it would be wise to bracket the indicated exposure by deliberately overexposing and underexposing a few extra frames. Bracketing is also a wise precaution when reading your SLR meter with a strongly colored filter in place over the lens.

Meters may not respond predictably to colored light

The filter effect on the film image is greatest on subject colors of high purity and is diminished for *tints* (colors diluted with white) and *shades* (colors diluted with black). Color filters have virtually no effect at all on black, white, and shades of gray. The filter factor must still be applied to the exposure, however, because the filter will absorb some of the image light whether its action alters the image tonality or not.

Finally, the filter effect depends to some extent on exposure. In general, underexposure tends to emphasize filter action and overexposure tends to reduce it.

Synopsis

Camera Operation Checklist

With this introduction you should be able to begin photographing knowledgeably and effectively. Here's a summary of the essential steps:

1. Select a film that's appropriate for your subject matter and light conditions (p. 95) and load the camera (p. 98-99). Be sure to set the proper film speed into the ASA dial on your camera or meter (p. 95).
2. Select the lens type (pp. 78-82) and focal length (pp. 82-86) appropriate for your pictorial purpose and interpretation.
3. Frame the subject area in the viewfinder and focus on the most important subject area (pp. 90-91).
4. Meter the subject area and determine the lens and shutter settings, making appropriate compensation if the subject is predominantly lighter or darker than average (pp. 94, 98-100).

5. If you use a filter, adjust the camera settings to include the filter factor (pp. 105-107).
6. Be sure the chosen settings—aperture and shutter speed—will provide adequate control of depth of field (pp. 88-91) and subject motion (pp. 100-101); if you change one of them, the other must be adjusted to compensate (p. 103).
7. Hold the camera steady (p. 102) and press the shutter release to make the exposure. Advance the film so you'll be ready for the next picture opportunity.

Neutral density filters simply reduce light intensity

Neutral density (ND) filters absorb all colors equally and appear gray. They are intended simply to reduce light intensity. Although they are not used as frequently as color filters are, they come in handy when it is desirable to change exposure without altering the camera settings, or when you wish to maintain normal exposure but use a large lens opening or a very slow shutter speed in bright light with fast film. Neutral density filters come in thirteen accurately calibrated densities, from .1 (requiring a ⅓ stop exposure increase) to 4.0 (which requires an increase of 13⅓ stops, or 10,000x).

When a light ray is reflected from a smooth surface (except polished metal), its normal multidirectional wave vibration is likely to be more or less restricted to one plane, and the light is said to have been *polarized*. This is practically an invisible effect; polarized light looks just like unpolarized light to the camera, the film, and to most people (some individuals can detect it under certain conditions). Polarization is a useful effect, however, because it provides us with a unique method of filtering one sort of light from another without distorting colors.

Polaroid filters help control surface glare

Polaroid filters (sometimes called Pola-screens) are capable of polarizing transmitted light; that is, they are transparent to light waves vibrating in one plane but are more or less opaque to waves vibrating in other planes. This characteristic permits the filter to reduce, or sometimes eliminate, the effect of reflected "glare" light. If you view a reflecting surface through a Pola-screen and slowly rotate it until its transmission axis is perpendicular to the vibration plane of the reflected light, the glare will magically disappear, without affecting the rest of the light at all.

They often improve color purity and increase contrast

By removing glare light from various areas of the subject, Pola-screens often seem to improve subject contrast and enhance the purity of colors. Since they are neutral gray in color, they do not affect color, as regular color filters do, and can be used with color films as well as with black-and-white materials.

Since the light from some areas of the clear blue sky is polarized, a Pola-screen can often be used to darken the sky dramatically. (See plate 8.) The greatest effect occurs in a broad arc of sky, 90° from the sun position; point your forefinger at the sun and your extended thumb will point to the sky belt of most complete polarization.

Figure 3.48
Polarized light, reflection, transmission

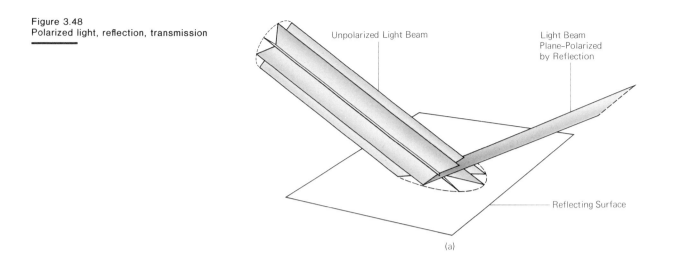

Unpolarized Light Beam

Light Beam
Plane-Polarized
by Reflection

Reflecting Surface

(a)

Figure 3.49
a. Surface reflections from surrounding displays almost obscure the fossil in this museum case.

b. Eliminating the reflections with a polarizing filter over the camera lens reveals this ferocious-looking fish skull and its descriptive caption.

a

Selective polarization can produce brilliant colors

Under some conditions white light can be dissected into its component colors by selective polarization. This effect can be demonstrated easily with a pair of polarizing filters and some scraps of cellophane (other plastic sheet materials may not work well). Place the cellophane scraps on one of the filters and cover them with the other one. When viewed against the light, the cellophane scraps will appear as brilliant colors which can be varied dramatically if one of the filters is slowly rotated. The effect is caused by the cellophane's ability to rotate the plane of polarized light and is related to wavelength. Some plastic materials have a similar ability; when they are strained or bent in polarized light, they form color patterns that indicate the distribution of the internal stresses. This technique is sometimes used by engineers to test models of machine parts or building structures to see where potential structural weaknesses may exist.

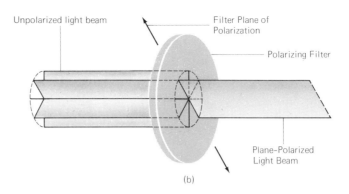

Unpolarized light beam

Filter Plane of
Polarization

Polarizing Filter

Plane-Polarized
Light Beam

(b)

b

Polarizing filters don't have a constant factor

Pola-screens do not have a single, constant filter factor because their absorption depends upon the amount of polarized light coming from the subject and the orientation of the filter axis relative to the polarity of the light. If no polarized light exists in the subject area, the filter factor for a typical Pola-screen amounts to about 3x, due entirely to its gray neutral density color. That same factor is approximately correct if the light is polarized in a plane parallel to the filter polarization axis. However, if much of the subject light is polarized and *not* parallel to the filter axis, the filter transmission will be greatly reduced and the necessary filter factor may amount to 6x, 8x or even more. It is a good idea, when using a polarizing filter, to make several exposures of any subject that is likely to be reflecting polarized light. Start with the 3x factor, or a little less, and then increase the exposures by a stop or two, just to make sure.

Figure 3.50
a. Clean loose dust particles from the inside of the camera with a rubber syringe.

b. Clean loose dust particles from the lens surface with a soft brush.

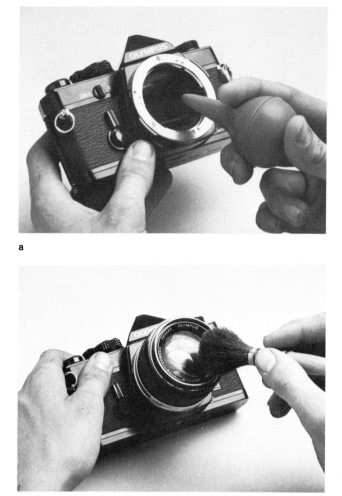

a

b

Taking Care of Cameras and Lenses

Cameras are precision instruments, but they can stand a fair amount of wear and tear. Protect them from dust, moisture, and excessive heat, however, and don't expect one to survive being dropped from any height onto a hard surface. Lenses are more delicate. Keep them capped at all times when not in use and carry them in padded cases to guard against hard knocks.

Keep lenses capped when not in use

Don't simply carry your camera around in your hands when you're out photographing; equip it with a neckstrap, and use it. Most neckstraps are much too long. The camera will be safer and more convenient to use if it hangs high on your chest. While you're not actually photographing, sling the strap over one shoulder with the camera lying snugly against your side, high up behind your arm. When transporting your equipment it should be packed in protective cases, but camera cases, even the (n)ever ready types, are usually more of a hindrance than a help when you're trying to work.

c

d

c. Or blow them off with a rubber syringe. Don't use canned air; it's an environmental hazard.

d. Moisten a clean, crumpled piece of lens tissue with a drop of liquid cleaner.

e. And rub the lens gently, with circular strokes, until the soil is loosened; then polish the surface dry with a fresh piece of lens tissue, crumpled into a soft wad. Be gentle!

e

Remove the batteries when you store your camera

If you are working in rainy weather, it makes sense to keep the camera covered as much as possible. Keep it under your shirt or jacket while it's hanging around your neck, and cover it with a coat or plastic sheet if it has to stand out on a tripod. Use a good deep lens shade and put a *skylight filter* or clear glass cap on the lens to protect it. When you get inside, wipe the outside surfaces of the camera as dry as possible, and leave it out of its case for at least several hours so it can dry out thoroughly.

If you aren't going to use your camera for several weeks or months, remove the batteries, if it has any, release tension on the shutter, and tuck the camera away in a reasonably cool, dry place. Don't wrap it tightly in plastic, because moisture may condense inside. Wrap it in cloth if you want to, or keep it in a *gadget bag* or equipment case. It's probably a good idea to exercise a stored camera occasionally. Take it out every few weeks and work all the controls a few times, or better yet, go out and take some pictures!

Summary

Every camera is basically a lighttight box, equipped with a lens, film chamber, viewfinder, shutter, and some provision for controlling light intensity, such as an iris diaphragm. Cameras vary greatly in size, design, and convenience features. The simplest types require manual adjustment of all controls; more complex designs may provide automatic operation of most essential functions.

Viewfinder and rangefinder cameras are easy to use, lightweight, and quiet in operation. SLR cameras provide accurate viewfinder images, but are less quiet and more complicated mechanically. Prism-reflex cameras provide excellent viewfinder image quality, are usually equipped with some sort of focusing aid, and frequently feature built-in exposure meters with either semiautomatic or automatic exposure control.

View and field cameras provide groundglass focusing. They are intended for use on a tripod, have almost no automatic features, and are slow and clumsy to operate. They are very versatile, however, and are capable of producing exceptionally fine image quality.

Among the many camera accessories are lens caps and lens shades, tripods, cable releases, filters, lens extenders or converters, flash units, and motor drives or winders. Consider your needs carefully before you buy.

Light sources may be thought of as transmitting energy in particles called photons or in waves of electromagnetic energy. Visible light occupies a very small band of wavelengths in the spectrum and is bordered by invisible ultraviolet and infrared. Light normally travels in straight lines but can be absorbed, reflected, transmitted, diffused, diffracted, refracted, or dispersed when entering media of different density or when encountering surfaces.

Simple lenses form less-than-perfect images because of various aberrations. Useful camera lenses are usually assembled from several elements. Floating elements in the lens structure can improve lens performance at close range. Coating the lens elements improves image contrast and reduces flare.

The focal length of a lens is the approximate distance from the center of the lens to the film plane when the lens is focused on infinity. Long lenses produce large-scale images but cover a narrow field of view; short lenses produce small-scale images, but include a wide field. Macro lenses are best for close-up work. PC lenses help control some perspective effects. Zoom lenses have variable focal lengths and are especially valuable for color slide work; some are useful for close-up photography. Mirror lenses are compact and available in extremely long focal lengths. Fisheye lenses feature extremely wide coverage and obvious linear distortion.

When a lens is focused at infinity it is as close to the film plane as it can ever be while forming a sharp image. The focal length of a "normal" lens is approximately equal to the diagonal of its image format. A lens is called "short" if its focal length is much less than the diagonal of its image format; "long" if its focal length is much greater than its format diagonal. Focal length and print viewing distance influence the apparent perspective of the image and can be altered for dramatic effect.

The out-of-focus image of a point light source can be seen as a circle of confusion. When the image circles-of-confusion are too small to be distinguished, the image is seen to be in focus. The depth of focus is the distance through which the lens-to-film distance can be adjusted in focusing without apparently reducing the sharpness of the image. Depth of field is the distance in the subject space, including the plane of sharpest focus, within which subject details are pictured as acceptably sharp. The hyperfocal distance is the distance to the closest plane of focus in the subject space when the lens is focused on infinity. When the lens is set on the hyperfocal distance (called hyperfocal focus), depth of field is maximum. Adjusting the focus and aperture settings to provide specific near and far limits of depth of field is called "zone focusing."

Infrared photography requires special adjustment of the camera focus. Use the special infrared index mark on the distance scale or simply focus slightly in front of the subject and stop down for plenty of depth of field.

The relative aperture of a lens describes the ratio of its aperture diameter to its focal length and is an indication of its light transmission ability, or speed. Relative apertures are calibrated in f-numbers. Small apertures have high f-numbers and low speed; large apertures have low f-numbers and high speed. Apertures are often called "stops," and a change from one stop to the next doubles (or halves) the previous exposure.

Film exposure results from the combined effect of light intensity (on the film surface) and time (duration of the exposure) and will remain constant if the product of intensity and time is constant. Shutter-speed scales are calibrated in fractions of a second and may also include settings marked B (for "Bulb") and T (for "Time"). Both are intended for manually timed exposure intervals.

Films are sensitized with emulsions of silver halides suspended in gelatin. Fast (very sensitive) films form relatively grainy images. Slow (less sensitive) films form less obviously textured images that are relatively sharp. Film speed is indicated by—and directly proportional to—ASA or ISO numbers. Black-and-white films record subject colors as shades of gray.

"Ordinary" emulsions are only blue-sensitive; they record red, yellow, and green as darker than normal. Orthochromatic films are sensitive to blue and green, but record red as a dark gray or black. Panchromatic films are sensitive to all colors and are the best choice for general use.

Exposure meters are calibrated for average subjects. If the subject is lighter or darker than average, the meter reading will be higher or lower than it should be and the film will not be properly exposed. In these instances, you can take substitute meter readings or manually override the meter. SLR meters are generally "weighted" to respond most strongly to tones in the central area of the viewing field.

Cameras may permit programmed or semiautomatic operation in addition to manual operation. Shutter-priority operation is best for rapidly moving subjects; aperture-priority is best when depth of field must be controlled. Programmed operation is totally automatic and is convenient for casual work in good light.

Exposure can be controlled by adjustment of either aperture or shutter speed, or both. EV numbers stand for specific exposure values. If your camera permits EV settings, you'll find them convenient for making adjustments of depth of field or subject motion without altering exposure.

Cameras should be protected from dust, moisture, heat, and shock. Protect your lenses with caps when not in use. If you store your camera for any length of time, remove the batteries (if it has any) and release the shutter. Exercise your camera shutter from time to time.

White light can be dispersed into the visible spectrum as primary colors or reformed by their combination. The light secondaries are pigment primaries; the light and pigment primaries are complements of each other.

Color filters transmit their own color and absorb its complement. The absorption light loss necessitates an increase in exposure called the filter factor. Filters cannot be used effectively with colorblind films. Filtering the light source is as effective as using a filter over the lens. The filter effect is diminished by overexposure. Neutral density filters simply absorb light without changing its spectral characteristic.

Light reflected at some angles from most surfaces is polarized and can be absorbed by a properly oriented polarizing filter. Polarizers can eliminate surface glare and darken blue skies in either black-and-white or color photography. Their factor is variable.

Developing Black-and-White Rollfilm

Outline

Rollfilm Processing Equipment
Processing Solutions: Ingredients and
Their Functions
Developers: Types and Characteristics
Water for Chemical Mixing
Chemical Mixing and Preparation
Processing Rollfilm
    Loading the Tank
    Development
    Stop Bath
    Fixer
    Clearing Bath
    Final Rinse
    Drying
    Clean-up
    Storage of Negatives
Appraising Negative Quality

Exposed film must be developed to make the image visible

Exposed film must be treated with a chemical developer solution to make the latent film image visible. It is then rinsed briefly in a stop bath (short-stop) solution and placed in the fixing bath (fixer or hypo). The fixing bath dissolves the undeveloped silver halides from the emulsion, leaving the developed silver image as a pattern of dark tones on the transparent film base to form the negative. After brief treatment in a *hypo-clearing bath,* the negatives are washed in running water and dried.

You must control time, temperature, and agitation

Because the film is extremely sensitive to light until it has been fixed in the hypo bath, the first few steps of the process must be carried out in complete darkness. Development must, therefore, be controlled by careful adjustment of *time,* developer *temperature,* and *agitation* (stirring of the developer or movement of the film through the developer during development) to avoid under- or over-development, either of which will produce negatives of poor quality.

Since development can't be watched anyway, it's customary to load exposed rollfilm in total darkness onto a spiral reel, and place the reel into a lighttight tank for processing. A light trap opening in the tank cover permits the various processing chemical solutions to be poured in and out without admitting light, so after the film is loaded and the tank cover is in place the lights can be turned on and the actual processing carried out in full light.

Rollfilm Processing Equipment

Buy a good quality tank

To develop rollfilm conveniently and efficiently you'll need a darkroom space, a sink with hot-and-cold running water, and a few items of equipment. The first piece of equipment you'll need is a rollfilm tank. There are several varieties on the market. The best ones, in my opinion, are made of stainless steel, but some photographers prefer plastic. Most tanks will work well enough, but don't get one that has lots of sculptured plastic shapes and many small parts—it will be hard to clean. The Nikor plastic tank with adjustable reels is especially suitable for 110 and other sub-miniature film sizes. Buy a good quality tank. There are some inexpensive stainless steel models that are rather flimsy and their film reels are not always accurately constructed; avoid them.

Calf, India. Jim Judkis.
In this dark environment the calf seems almost luminous.
(Collection of the author, courtesy of the photographer.)

Figure 4.1
Thermometers

Figure 4.2
Timer

Figure 4.3
Darkroom utensils

Figure 4.4
Film washer

You'll need a good thermometer, a timer. . .

You'll need a good thermometer for accurate control of solution temperatures. If you can afford a dial-type thermometer, buy it. If not, get a good quality glass one. Even though dial thermometers are more expensive, they will outlast several glass ones in ordinary use. They are also likely to be at least as accurate, much faster in reacting to temperature changes, easier to read, and easier to use in bottles and tanks.

You can use your watch or a clock to time the various processes, but an interval timer is much more satisfactory. The spring-wound models are cheaper and perfectly satisfactory if you keep hypo out of them. The electric models will probably last longer. They're larger and easier to read in the dark (be sure to get one with a luminous dial) and can also be used as time switches for controlling lights or other electrical devices.

and a variety of utensils

You'll need some utensils for mixing, measuring, pouring, and storing the various solutions. Plastic is a satisfactory material for graduates or measuring cups, stirring rods, and funnels; it is also fine for storage bottles for most of the solutions you'll use. Developers, particularly replenishment-types, should be stored in brown glass or plastic bottles and kept full and tightly capped. One-shot developers (stock solutions) should be stored in several small bottles, rather than one large one, to avoid the large airspace that will appear in the larger container as the solution is used. Regardless of how they're stored, try to protect developers from excessive exposure to air and bright light.

You can wash rollfilm in the developing tank, but if you can afford it, a special film washing tank will do the job faster. You can also make a good washing tank out of an old plastic jug; cut off the top and punch a few holes around the bottom edge. Stack the film reels in it and set it under the faucet. Water flowing in at the top will leak out at the bottom, taking the hypo with it—a cheap and effective solution to the problem.

Figure 4.5
Film clips

Figure 4.6
Sponge and chamois

Figure 4.7
Air bubbles in water

Try to keep your darkroom clean

You will need some film clips. You can buy either stainless steel or plastic clips, or you can use ordinary spring clothespins. Stainless steel clips are the best and most expensive; clothespins are cheap, but select them with some care. They should grip the film tightly. Don't use any that are warped or weakened, or they may let your film slip to the floor. Drill a hole through one of the flat wooden handles of each of the clothespins so they can be hung up conveniently.

You may want to have a clean, soft viscose sponge, chamois, or a soft rubber squeegee to wipe the film with if the wetting agent fails to leave it clean and free from streaks. The chamois is the better material, by far, but a good photo-grade chamois will be expensive and hard to find. Ordinary car-washing chamois skins are a cheaper, coarser grade but you may find a section of one that is soft enough to use. Don't use one that has been previously used for car washing, window washing, or household cleaning. Before you use a utility grade chamois for photographic purposes, wash it thoroughly in mild detergent and warm water, rinse it well several times, and squeeze (don't wring) it dry.

Finally, you should have a large, coarse sponge for general clean-up purposes and a couple of old towels. Use one of them for wiping up the various darkroom surfaces, and use the other as a hand towel. They'll get badly stained but that's no real problem. Just launder them periodically to get rid of accumulated chemicals.

It will take a little more than ordinary care to avoid problems of chemical contamination while you're working. You will soon discover if you're careless that spilled chemical solutions, dirty utensils, and unclean hands will cause lots of trouble. If you are serious about photography, you will have to become a careful craftsman. Try to keep your darkroom clean; be sure your chemicals are fresh and uncontaminated; wash all utensils immediately after use; keep all chemical solutions in the *wet area;* and never, *never* set trays or bottles or chemical containers on the *dry area* table surfaces where you'll be handling film or paper. Become a compulsive hand-washer. Never touch anything with developer (or especially hypo) on your fingers, and don't just wipe chemicals off your hands with a towel—rinse your hands first.

Wash everything; then wash your hands

Cleanliness is particularly important when you're working in a school situation or a community darkroom. If this is the case, you should also wash trays and other utensils routinely *before* use, whether they look clean or not. Wipe up spilled liquids, then wash the spots with several changes of water to prevent possible chemical scums. Be particularly wary of white powdery stains, which will probably indicate dried hypo; wash them up wherever they appear! It's impossible to get a darkroom too clean. Wash everything. Then wash your hands.

Processing Solutions: Ingredients and Their Functions

There are many useful developer formulas

A developer, to be satisfactory, must possess several special characteristics. It must actively *reduce* the exposed silver halide crystals of the latent image to visible particles of metallic silver but it should not affect the unexposed halides. In other words, it should produce a useful image without excessive *chemical fog.* It should work predictably, have a long useful life, be relatively economical to use, and be relatively nonstaining and nontoxic. No single known chemical in solution can fill these requirements, but there are literally hundreds of published formulas for mixtures and blends of chemicals that will serve as useful developers.

All contain one or more reducing agents

In a useful formula the work is done by the reducing agent or developing agent, the most common of which are Metol, hydroquinone, and Phenidone. Metol (also known as Elon, Pictol, Rhodol, Photol, etc.) or hydroquinone are occasionally used alone in developer formulas, but more frequently you will find both Metol and hydroquinone (MQ or MH developers) or Phenidone and hydroquinone (PQ or PH) specified. These pairs of reducing agents are sometimes called *super additive* because their mixtures are uniquely effective.

The accelerator is alkaline

Most reducing agents are inactive, or only weakly active, in neutral or acid solutions and must be activated or accelerated by some alkaline material. Almost any alkaline chemical will do, but the usual ones are borax (sodium tetraborate), Kodalk (Kodak's proprietary version of sodium metaborate), and sodium carbonate.

A simple mixture of a reducing agent and an accelerator would be an active developer, but it would oxidize and spoil very rapidly. Therefore, the solution must contain a preservative chemical, usually sodium sulfite.

A preservative and a restrainer are usually included

In some cases a solution containing a reducing agent, an accelerator, and a preservative would serve as a practical developer, but there is some danger that it might attack the unexposed silver halides to produce chemical fog. The addition of small amounts of a restrainer chemical, usually potassium bromide or benzotriazole, will minimize this difficulty and produce a *clean working* developer.

A few developers have fewer than four ingredients

Although most practical developers contain at least one chemical ingredient for each of the four basic functions just described, some successful formulas require only two or three. Kodak's D-23 developer, for example, contains only Elon and sulfite and functions satisfactorily because Elon (Kodak's brand of Metol) is inherently an active and easily accelerated reducing agent, and sulfite, being mildly alkaline, can serve as both preservative and accelerator. Elon needs no restrainer in this formula, partly because it is such a mild solution and partly because some of the natural by-products of the film developing action are bromide salts, which are effective as restrainers in the solution.

When the film has been developed sufficiently, the action of the developer can be arrested by placing the film into the short-stop solution or stop bath. Although some photographers feel that this solution is unnecessary (or even harmful) and can be replaced with a simple water rinse, most authorities now agree that a mildly acidic stop bath—typically about a 1% solution of acetic

The acid stop bath neutralizes the developer

The fixing bath dissolves the unused silver halides

Fixers also contain several ingredients

The hypo-clearing bath speeds washing

The wetting agent helps prevent water spots

acid—is preferable to plain water. This stop bath, by neutralizing the alkaline accelerator, halts development almost immediately. It also serves to rinse away the developer chemicals that might, under some extreme circumstances, cause staining of the film, and, by leaving the film in a slightly acid condition, helps to preserve the essential acid balance of the fixing bath.

The *fixing bath* is another mixture of chemicals dissolved in water. The major ingredient, in the ordinary fixing bath, is sodium thiosulfate, traditionally called *hypo*. In the so-called *rapid-fixing baths* ammonium thiosulfate is used, but all fixing baths are familiarly known as hypo and all are capable of dissolving the unused and still light-sensitive silver halides, without harming the silver image.

Sodium or ammonium thiosulfate and water will work as a fixer but the useful life of the solution is short and it is likely to decompose. Again, sodium sulfite acts as a preservative, extending both the storage life and the working capacity of the solution. When preserved with sulfite, the hypo solution can also be acidified slightly to help neutralize any developer alkali that might escape the action of the short-stop. This is usually accomplished by adding an acid sulfite, such as sodium bisulfite or potassium metabisulfite, to the solution. These three chemicals—hypo, sulfite, and bisulfite—make up a satisfactory *nonhardening fixer.*

It is, however, generally a good idea to harden film by toughening or tanning the gelatin emulsion. This helps to protect it from physical damage and improves image quality by reducing swelling during processing and hastening the drying of the finished negatives. The hardener usually employed is potassium alum, and since it must be in acid solution to work well (it may precipitate out of an alkaline solution), it is customary to include some acetic acid with it, instead of the bisulfite used in the nonhardening formula.

The hypo bath hardens more efficiently, is made more stable, is less likely to throw down a sludgy precipitate in use, and is less malodorous with the addition of some borax or metaborate. Without this ingredient the fixer develops a sharp, highly penetrating, sinus-torturing odor after standing a while, especially in the stuffy confines of the typical home darkroom.

Hypo contains a considerable amount of sulfur and produces some very complex sulfur compounds as it combines with and dissolves the undeveloped silver salts in the emulsion. The hypo itself (and these sulfur compounds) must be removed from the emulsion after its work is done to prevent eventual tarnishing, staining, or fading of the silver image. Because some of the sulfur products of fixation are relatively insoluble, they are not removed from the emulsion easily by simple washing in plain water. Under ideal conditions plain washing is adequate if done long enough and if the water circulates around the films freely; but films wash faster and more efficiently if they are treated before washing with a *hypo-clearing bath.*

There are a number of proprietary hypo-clearing baths on the market and any one of them is probably better than none at all. Presumably they all work when their instructions are followed, but some of them sound rather too magical to be believed. It would probably be wise to overdo the recommended treatment a little with most of them, since very little harm can result from *moderate* over-treatment, and the penalty for insufficient treatment is the probable, eventual deterioration of your negatives.

After the films have been washed, they should be treated briefly in a weak solution of *wetting agent,* which, by reducing surface tension, causes the water on the film to flow off evenly instead of forming droplets or beads (which might cause spots or scum deposits when they dry) on the film surfaces. There are a number of brands, all effective when used as directed, but some may produce a stronger solution than is necessary to do the job. Experiment with the brand you select and use the weakest solution that effectively prevents scum spots. Too strong a solution may leave greasy streaks on your negatives, especially if it is made with hard tap water. Distilled water is best, when available.

Developers: Types and Characteristics

Developers: Types and Characteristics

Some developers are intended to be replenished

There are several ways to use developers. One type is intended to be mixed in rather small volume, used, and then *replenished* by the addition of a small amount of developer concentrate. Replenishment is intended to restore the used developer to full strength, make up for the normal deterioration due to oxidation, and keep the solution at full volume. In practice, replenished developers can rarely be maintained at a uniform strength throughout their working lives, but the change in characteristics is so gradual that it can easily go unrecognized. An old solution usually works slowly and produces negatives of relatively low contrast; whereas, a new solution is full of "fire" and works rapidly and vigorously. To avoid problems when an old solution is replaced with a freshly-mixed one, most authorities recommend adding several ounces of the old used solution to the fresh new one to temper it.

but replenishment is an uncertain business

My recommendation is to avoid replenished developers entirely unless you are shooting enough film to wear the solutions out from use before they gradually deteriorate from sheer old age. Even then they're risky. Contamination from improperly cleaned tanks or reels (which, of course, should *always* be clean) can weaken the solution; oxidation rate is unpredictable; replenishment itself is based on average rather than actual requirements; and although proper replenishment might possibly be adequate to replace actual chemical loss, it can't compensate for the gradual build-up of restraining bromide in the used solution.

Some of the same criticisms can be levelled at any developer that is intended for repeated use, including the two-solution compensating types and the monobaths which combine the functions of developer and fixer in one solution. Although all of these developer types have their unique advantages and will certainly produce negatives of excellent quality under ideal conditions, they're likely to be more trouble than they're worth, especially for beginners.

One-shot developers are convenient and predictable

In my opinion, the simplest and most reliable way to develop film is to use a *one-shot* developer. Although almost any developer can be used this way, one-shots are usually supplied in highly concentrated stock solutions, a small volume of which is diluted for use with a much larger volume of water. The resulting working solution is used once and then discarded.

This procedure has many advantages: storage problems are minimized; the concentrated stock solutions are extremely stable and resistant to oxidation and will maintain their full strength for a very long time. The working solutions, therefore, are likely to be very consistent in strength, which makes it relatively easy to produce negatives of uniform quality. The procedure is quick and easy, too. Developer temperature is easy to adjust before use because the working solution will assume the temperature of the water used for dilution. After use, the exhausted developer is simply poured down the drain.

One-shots typically produce good image quality. Because of their high dilution they tend to be *compensating* in action; that is, they automatically restrain development in the areas of heaviest image density, so unprintable extremes of contrast are less likely to occur. They tend to enhance the apparent sharpness of the image, separating contrasting areas of image value with unusual crispness. They also emphasize sharpness and contrast (but not necessarily the size) of the image grain structure, giving the image a snappy pepper-and-salt texture, disliked by some photographers but admired by others. Unfortunately, some one-shots are rather expensive.

D-76 is a good developer to start with

If you are a beginning photographer, you will probably find that the old standard Kodak formula D-76 (identical with Ilford's ID-11) is an excellent general purpose film developer to start out with. It is available packaged in powdered form at any photo store, or if you prefer to mix your own developer from bulk chemicals, the formula is given in appendix 4. Another good general purpose developer is Kodak's HC-110. It is available only in highly concentrated, syrupy-liquid form; the formula is not available.

Although D-76 can be used *straight* (undiluted) as a replenished developer, many photographers like to use it diluted with an equal volume of water as a one-shot. Used this way, a gallon of D-76 stock solution will develop up to about 32 rolls of 35mm film. HC-110, diluted to make a one-shot solution of similar strength (dilution B), is slightly less expensive to use at current prices; however, both developers are at least as economical to use as any of the replenishment-type name brands.

Use any developer you like, but stick with it

There are many other developers to choose from. If you prefer not to use either D-76 or HC-110, start out with any developer you like, but stick with it long enough to learn how to use it before changing. The name of the developer you use is less important than the care with which you use it.

Some developers may cause skin irritation

Although most people can tolerate the chemicals involved in black-and-white photography, some individuals are susceptible to contact detmatitis or *Metol poisoning*. Metol affects sensitive skin the way poison ivy does, causing swelling, itching, scaling, blistering, and, in severe cases, cracking and open sores. Even if you are not sensitive to Metol now, you can become sensitized, so it's prudent to take some precautions. Avoid unnecessary contact with *all* reducing agents, especially in dry form, and don't let developer solutions dry on your hands. Rubber or plastic gloves provide good protection, and silicone protective hand creams will help to prevent drying and chapping, although they don't offer reliable protection against Metol, according to the Kodak medical authorities. If you discover any sign of skin irritation after a few sessions in the darkroom, stay away from developers for a few days. If the problem clears up but recurs when you go back to work, you should give up Metol developers entirely. A list of developers, which are relatively safe alternatives to conventional Metol formulas, is included in the appendix. Try one or more of these if Metol is causing you discomfort.

Whether you are affected by developers or not, you should treat all chemicals with respect. Some of them can stain or bleach your clothing; others can corrode metal or dissolve your plastic watch crystal. Some give off suffocating or unpleasant vapors and a few can irritate or burn your skin. Ordinary care in handling will avoid all these problems; photography does not need to be hazardous to your health.

Water for Chemical Mixing

General purpose developers can be mixed with ordinary tap water in most areas of the country without any harmful effect, but fine-grain developers and replenishment-type developers may require distilled water if your tap water is excessively hard or chemically treated. If there is any doubt in your mind, use distilled water. It's cheap and the quantities required are small.

Tap water is usually suitable for mixing chemicals

Tap water sometimes contains dissolved air, and air is detrimental to developers. Check your water supply by letting a freshly-drawn glassful of water stand quietly for a few hours. If a film of air bubbles forms on the inside of the glass, you should probably not use the water to mix developer stock solutions until it has either been boiled and cooled or allowed to stand loosely covered for a day or two. Tap water can be used right from the faucet for diluting stock solutions for immediate use or for making small volumes of developer that will be used within a few days. It will also probably be safe to use for mixing hypo or any of the other normal black-and-white film processing solutions.

Chemical Mixing and Preparation

Follow mixing instructions carefully

Mixing packaged developers is simply a matter of following the instructions on the package. Usually the instructions call for a partial volume of warm or hot water and these temperature recommendations should be heeded. Too cool water will make the chemicals dissolve with difficulty; too hot water may hasten oxidation or decomposition of the solution. Chemicals should usually be poured into the water with moderately vigorous stirring and the stirring should be continued until the solution is complete. Don't overdo it, though; whipping the liquid into a froth will mix air into it and encourage oxidation. Finally, the warm solution is brought to proper volume with cool water and poured into a clean brown glass or plastic bottle for storage.

Developers don't keep well if exposed to air

If the developer is a stock solution that will be used gradually, store it in several smaller bottles, each completely full, and keep them in a cool, dark place until needed. A small volume of developer in a large bottle will oxidize fairly rapidly. Most developers turn to a rich dark brown color when thoroughly spoiled and develop a kind of rotten garlic odor. Some developers have a rather pronounced tan color, even when fresh, but a distinctly yellowish or orangish tint almost always indicates the beginning of oxidation. Don't use any normal MQ developer that is approaching the color of weak tea.

If you decide to mix your developer from bulk chemicals, the routine is slightly different. Use the volume and temperature of water specified in the formula, but add each chemical ingredient separately and stir each until completely dissolved, unless otherwise instructed. The ingredients should normally be dissolved in the order given in the formula; if the proper order is not followed, the chemicals may not dissolve or, in some cases, they may decompose. See formulas in appendix 4.

The usual stop bath stock solution is 28% acetic acid

You can buy the stop bath stock solution already prepared, or you can buy glacial acetic acid and prepare your own stock solution. Stop bath stock is simply 28% acetic acid and is strong-smelling, but relatively harmless. Glacial acetic is 99% pure and should be handled with caution. It is fairly mild, as acids go, but still potent enough to burn the skin painfully, corrode some metals, and act as a powerful solvent for some plastics. It also has a breathtakingly sharp and penetrating odor. Mix it only in a well-ventilated area that is close to a source of running water, in case you spill it or splash some on your skin.

Contrary to popular belief, the rule "always pour acid into water" (which is vitally important with sulfuric acid) does not necessarily apply to acetic acid, but following this rule is probably good practice and will certainly do no harm. Treat acetic acid with respect, but don't panic; it is a friendly sort of acid, relatively speaking.

Make the stock solution from glacial acetic this way

To prepare the 28% short-stop stock solution, add three parts of the glacial acetic acid to eight parts of water. A *part*, of course, can be any volume you choose. If you want to make approximately one quart of stock, for example, you will need a total of eleven parts (three acid plus eight water) to make a total volume of about 32 ounces. Divide 32 by 11 to get about 3 ounces for the volume of each part. Then:

add:	3 parts acid (times 3 ounces)	=	9 ounces acid
to:	8 parts water (times 3 ounces)	=	24 ounces water
total:	11 parts (times 3 ounces)	=	33 ounces stock solution

Add the acid to cool tap water, stir until blended, and store in a plain glass or plastic container. This solution is stable and will keep indefinitely. Label the bottle "stop bath stock solution" and add the words, "28% acetic acid" if you want to.

Indicator stop baths contain a yellow dye

Commercial short-stop stock solutions frequently contain a yellow dye, called an "indicator." The stop bath itself, prepared from an indicator stock, is yellow as long as it remains in a useful acid condition, but when it becomes exhausted or neutralized, the yellow dye turns to purple as a visual signal that the bath should be replaced. Indicator stop baths are convenient for some purposes, but they are more expensive than plain acetic acid and are not suitable for use in some formulas (other than stop baths) that call for acetic acid. Plain acetic acid stop bath is perfectly satisfactory for film processing.

Dilute the stock solution to make a working solution

The working solution of short-stop is prepared from commercial stock solution or the 28% acetic acid stock solution by diluting one part of the stock with about 25 to 30 parts of water. Don't make the stop bath stronger than a 1 to 20 dilution nor weaker than about 1 to 50. One ounce per quart of water (1 to 32) is a good ratio for rollfilms, and it's easy to remember.

Although the fixing bath can be mixed from bulk chemicals, there is no particular advantage in doing so. Regular powdered fixer can be purchased readily and cheaply and is convenient to mix. Rapid fixers are even easier. They usually come as liquid concentrates. Fixers are quite sensitive to mixing conditions, however, and the instructions should be followed carefully. Two things are especially important: be sure the mixing water is not too hot, and when mixing the liquid concentrates, do not add the hardener solution (smaller bottle of clear liquid) until the thiosulfate solution has been adequately diluted with water and thoroughly blended. Failure to observe these precautions will probably cause the solution to form a milky precipitate.

Although this precipitate will not completely destroy the solution (in mild cases it may disappear after standing for a day or two), it will make the solution unsuitable for use with films or papers that you plan to keep for any appreciable length of time. You shouldn't use milky fixer for any purpose, actually. It's bad craftsmanship. Learn to mix it properly.

Regular fixing bath (not rapid) is generally used at the same strength for both films and papers. Rapid fixers are much more active, and if made too strong, they may bleach the silver image from the delicate paper emulsions. Rapid fixers are, therefore, mixed in two strengths. The stronger solution is used for film processing and—when carefully monitored—for archival processing of fine prints on certain papers. The weaker solution is preferred for processing ordinary prints. But regardless of the type you use, you should prepare separate volumes of fixer for films and for papers. A fixing bath that has been used for film fixing should not be used for paper. Mix the film fixer according to the package directions and store it in a plain glass or plastic bottle labelled "film fixer" or "film hypo." The solution is quite stable and will keep for a long time.

It is important not to use exhausted fixer for films (and even more important for printing papers) because the products of fixation formed by old, used fixing baths are relatively insoluble and cannot be removed from the emulsion easily by normal washing procedures. You can check the condition of your fixing bath with a commercial *hypo* test solution, following package instructions. Alternatively, you can make your own test solution by dissolving 2.0 grams of potassium iodide in 100 milliliters of water. A drop of this solution, introduced gently into a small volume of the fixing bath, will cause a dense yellowish-white precipitate to form if the fixer is exhausted. Throw it away and mix a fresh bath. No precipitation will occur in a fresh or still usable solution. Return this fixer to its storage bottle.

Hypo-clearing baths (also called hypo-neutralizing baths or washing aids) are sold as liquid concentrates in most cases, but the Kodak product comes in powdered form, which must be mixed to make a stock solution. Follow the instructions that come with the product you select; they are not all alike. In general the unused solutions keep fairly well, but some brands do not keep well after use. Although a slightly wasteful practice, it's convenient to mix the working solution in small volume just before use and discard it after one use, just as you would do with a one-shot developer. This will avoid uncertainty about the condition of the solution and simplify your storage problems.

The wetting agent does not ordinarily require any preparation except dilution to a working solution, just before use. In hard water areas, however, if may be necessary to use distilled water to prepare the wetting rinse and, in this case, the bath can be saved and reused. Be sure that the film is thoroughly washed before being treated in the wetting bath and discard the bath after just a few rolls of film have gone through it. Discard it after a week or so, whether it's been used or not; old wetting baths sometimes develop strange algae-like growths. Freshly prepared solutions are best. No storage is required.

Processing Rollfilm

Loading the Tank

Loading the film onto the tank reel is a skill that you'll have to acquire with practice. If possible, get a roll or two of spoiled or developed film and practice loading it in the light so you can see what the problems are. When you feel confident, take the practice film into the darkroom and load it a few times. Then, if things are going well, load your good exposed film in total darkness. Put the reel into the tank and put the cover on securely before turning on the lights. Figures 4.10 and 4.11 show the critical steps in loading various film sizes. Study them carefully while you're practicing.

Figure 4.8

a. Open the film cartridge with Kodak's special gadget or a hook-type can opener

b. Cut off the film tongue. Some films will tear, some won't. Scissors are recommended.

c. Palm the spool and squeeze the film edges together lightly to keep the extended end from rolling up.

d. Locate the end of the spiral film guides with your forefinger. They should be at the top of the reel, pointing toward the hand that holds the film.

e. The reel hub may be equipped with a clip to hold the film end or it may simply have a wide slot, as shown. Insert the film into the slot and center it between the reel flanges with thumb and finger of the left hand. This is important.

f. The start is critical; keeping the film slightly curled with the right hand and centered between the reel flanges with the left hand, pull on the film lightly and turn the reel counterclockwise so the film is bent sharply around the hub. It should slip smoothly into the spiral track. Let your left forefinger ride lightly on the back of the film to check for bulges and continue rotating the reel, feeding the film with the right hand.

g. If you detect any irregularity as you wind the film, go back at least a full turn and find the trouble; don't just try to force it. Correctly loaded film will feel loose in the reel grooves. When the reel is loaded cut off the film spool, tuck the film end into the tank. Be sure the cover is on snugly before turning the lights on.

a

b

c

d

e

f

g

a

b

c

d

Figure 4.9

a. Open the 110 cartridge (in the dark!) by breaking it in two, as shown.

b. Pull out the paper leader; the film will appear and can be pulled out. It is not fastened. Handle it carefully to avoid kinking or fingerprinting it. The emulsion side is inside the natural curl.

c. Align the flanges of the film reel, as shown, and insert the film end into the starting slot. Push it straight in for at least two or three inches. If the reel is dry and clean, you may be able to push the whole length of film into the tracks but usually you'll feel some resistance after the first few inches.

d. "Walk" the film the rest of the way by depressing the locking tabs with your thumbs, alternately, and twisting the reel flanges back . . .

e. . . . and forth, as shown. Practice this motion in the light, first, with a strip of spoiled film. It's not difficult, but it will take some coordination. Some types of reels don't have the locking tabs; you simply hold the edge of the film down with your thumb as you turn the flange.

f. Put the loaded reel into the tank and replace the lid before turning on the lights. This tank features an adjustable reel. The flanges can be spread apart to accommodate 35mm film as well as the 110 size shown here.

e

f

Figure 4.10
a. Check solution temperatures and set the bottles in a water bath if they need adjustment. If much change is necessary, pour the solution into a stainless steel film tank and set the tank in the water bath. Stir the solution with the thermometer stem, gently, until the temperature is satisfactory.

b. You can pour the developer into the loaded tank, like this, or you can fill the tank with developer before you load the film and place the loaded reel into the tank in the dark. Be sure to cover the tank before turning on the lights. In either case, start the timer as soon as the film is covered with developer.

c. Agitate continuously for the first fifteen seconds or so, then start a routine agitation procedure as described in the text.

d. When the developing time is almost up, pour the developer back into the storage jug if it's to be replenished. If it's a one-shot, dump it out. Time this operation so you can complete it before the timer rings.

e. Immediately pour in the stop bath. Ideally the tank should just be filled with stop as the timer goes off to signal the end of the developing step.

f. Agitate.

g. You can save the stop bath if you like. Some people do. I prefer to mix it fresh each time and throw it away after use.

h. Pour in the fixing bath and notice the time so you can determine the film clearing time.

i. Agitate for fifteen seconds or so.

j. Then remove the tank cover and inspect the film to see if it's clear. If not, replace it in the fixer and agitate it occasionally by lifting the reel out of the solution and replacing it. When it appears to be clear, note the time that clearing has taken and return the film to the fixer, with occasional agitation, for another similar time interval. (See text.)

a

b

c

d

e

f

g

h

i

j

k. Pour the fixer back into the storage jug. It can be reused until it fails the hypo test. (See text.)

l. Rinse the film briefly under running water to remove the surface fixer.

m. Pour in the hypo-clearing bath and agitate by picking the reel out of solution and replacing it periodically. Follow manufacturer's instructions for clearing bath use and storage.

n. You can save some clearing baths for immediate reuse, but they do not all keep well. I prefer to mix it fresh for each use and discard it afterward.

o. Wash the film in running water. If you use the film tank for this operation, as shown, empty it completely several times during the washing process to insure complete water changes. Follow washing instructions given for the clearing bath you use.

p. Treat the film with a wetting solution such as Photoflo diluted in distilled water. Let it soak for a few seconds, then . . .

q. . . . attach film clips to the film ends and see-saw the film through the wetting solution a few times and hang it up to dry.

r. Films larger than 110 will dry cleaner if they are held like this for a few seconds so the wetting solution can drain off to one edge. This will help to keep possible scums and spots out of the picture area. If the film strip is too long to handle this way conveniently, just hang it up.

s. Hang the film in a drying cabinet if you have one, otherwise find a dust-free place with adequate ventilation.

k

l

m

n

o

p

q

r

s

Development

The standard developing temperature is 20° C.

Although any temperature between about 18° and 24° Celsius (about 64° to 75° Fahrenheit) can be used satisfactorily with most developers, you should try to standardize. The generally recommended temperature for film development is 20°C (68°F). Although films and developers are not all alike in their sensitivity to changes in development temperature, the chart in appendix 11 will help you estimate a satisfactory developing time for temperatures other than the normal 20°C.

Whatever temperature you elect to use (remember, 20°C is recommended), be sure that the three main processing solutions (developer, short-stop, and fixing bath) are all about the same. Try to keep the developer within one degree of the desired temperature; the other solutions can vary by about two degrees without significant danger.

Avoid extreme temperature differences

An extreme *difference* in temperature between solutions should be avoided or you run the risk of *reticulation,* a fine net-like pattern of cracks or folds in the emulsion gelatin which coarsen the image texture and may even destroy it. Extreme cases of reticulation are very rare with today's tough emulsions, but a mild case can appear as an emphasized grain pattern and may pass unrecognized.

Agitate intermittently

Films should be agitated fairly vigorously when first immersed in developer to insure complete wetting of the emulsion and to dislodge any air-bells that might be clinging to the surface. Rollfilm tanks of the stainless steel variety can be agitated initially by picking them up, turning them over and back several times with a swirling motion, and then rapping them smartly a time or two against the heel of your hand or the sink surface. This initial agitation should not be prolonged more than ten or fifteen seconds, then the tank should be allowed to rest quietly for twenty or thirty seconds before beginning the *intermittent agitation* routine.

If the total developing time is to be more than about six or seven minutes, the film should be agitated briefly at one-minute intervals. If the total developing time is to be less than about six minutes, it is better to agitate briefly every thirty seconds. These brief agitation periods involve simply turning the tank over and back two or three times, with a final swirling motion. This can be accomplished in two or three seconds and should not be prolonged beyond about five. Do it gently, too.

Too much or too little agitation may cause streaks

Excessive or too vigorous agitation will increase negative density and contrast and may cause development streaks, usually along the margins of the filmstrip. Too little agitation can also cause problems: lowered contrast and density, and streaks that usually run across the width of the film. Try to be consistent with your agitation procedure. It is a critical part of the developing process.

Time development carefully

Development should be timed from the moment the tank is *filled* with developer (or the film is immersed in it) until the moment the tank is *filled* with the short-stop solution. Or, if you prefer, from the moment you *start to pour* developer onto the film until the moment you *start to pour* the short-stop. The actual time of development will depend upon film type, developer type and strength, developer temperature, agitation procedure, and degree of development desired. Follow the film manufacturer's recommendations or consult the development charts in appendix 14.

Stop Bath

Immediately after the developer is poured out of the tank, pour the short-stop in and agitate it continuously for at least ten seconds. The total treatment in the short-stop should last from about 30 seconds to a minute, but the film can remain in the short-stop bath for up to several minutes without harm if for some reason this is necessary. Agitate it periodically, then dump it out and pour in the fixing bath.

Figure 4.11
If you don't load the tank properly or if you handle the film roughly, your negatives and prints may suffer, as shown here. On the negative strip (seen from the emulsion side) the irregular black blob resulted from improper loading; adjacent layers of film touched, preventing the processing liquids from doing their work. The raw emulsion material, neither developed nor fixed in this case, appears on the negative as a milky-gray area which is virtually opaque to transmitted light. It prints as a totally white shape. The little black crescent shapes I call "fingernail marks" because they resemble nail trimmings. They result from kinking the film; they print white or light gray.

Fixer

The fixer temperature, like that of the other solutions, should be approximately 20°C (or whatever the developer temperature is). Agitate the tank for about ten or fifteen seconds immediately after filling it with fixer; then let it stand for a minute or so. This is a good time to wash the utensils you've used so far.

After the film has been in the fixer for a minute or so, it is safe to remove the tank cover. Lift the reel out of the solution part way and inspect the film. If the film has not been fixed yet, it will still contain undissolved silver salts which may appear as a solid or blotchy, creamy-white coating. The image may or may not be visible as a dark pattern, but it will gradually appear as the fixer dissolves the undeveloped halides. Let the film soak in the fixer for another half-minute with occasional gentle agitation, and check it again. If the film now looks totally dark with no visible trace of the whitish emulsions, it is *clear,* but not yet safe to remove! To be certain that all the silver halides are completely gone, leave the film in the fixer for two more minutes, or *(rule)* leave the film in the fixer for *twice* as long as it takes to clear.

Fix for "twice as long as it takes to clear"

Beginners seem to have trouble with this concept, so let's go over it again. If the film clears (looks black with no trace of white emulsion) after one minute in the fixer, give it another minute for a total of two. If it first appears clear after five minutes, give it another five. If you don't open the tank for four minutes after pouring in the fixer and the film is clear when you look at it, assume that it *just* cleared, and give it another four minutes. Overfixing the film by five or ten minutes is not likely to hurt it, but don't leave it in the fixer (especially rapid-fix) for more than ten or fifteen minutes, since there is some danger that some types of film might become slightly bleached.

Some films require considerably longer to clear than others. Panatomic-X, for example, will probably clear in fresh rapid-fix in less than a minute and should be taken out after a similar period. Type 2475 recording film, on the other hand, may not appear to be clear for five or more minutes, especially if the fixer is nearing exhaustion. If the clearing time for a given film is normally, say, two minutes in fresh fixer, you can reuse the fixer until the clearing time for that film is twice normal, or four minutes. Total fixing time will then be eight minutes (in this example) and the fixer should be discarded and replaced with fresh solution.

Figure 4.12
a. After 30 seconds in fixer, Plus-X film (left) and Infra-Red (right) are both still milky and opaque. Infra-Red appears lighter because it is on clear base material without antihalation dye.

b. After one minute the Plus-X is almost clear. The Infra-Red image areas are clearing but the leader is still milky and opaque.

c. After three minutes, Plus-X is clear and fully fixed. Infra-Red film is still showing traces of milkiness on the leader, particularly around the sprocket holes, but the image areas are clear. It cleared completely after another minute and was given four more minutes to insure complete fixing.

Clearing Bath

Treat the film in hypo-clear, then wash it

After pouring the fixer from the tank, fill the tank with fresh water, adjusted to match the temperature of the fixer within a degree or two. Agitate the film briefly. Pour the water out of the tank and pour in the hypo-clearing bath, mixed according to individual package instructions. It, too, should match the temperature of the previous processing solutions within a degree or two. Treat the film for at least the length of time and with the agitation specified for the product, and then wash the film in running water, at about the same temperature, for at least as much time as is recommended by the clearing bath manufacturer.

If you do not use a hypo-clearing bath, films should be washed for at least half-an-hour in slowly running water and agitated periodically to be sure the water is circulating to reach all areas of the film. Check for frothy coatings of tiny air bubbles on the film surface and rinse them off if they form. If running water is not available or if water is in short supply, you can wash film satisfactorily by soaking it for periods of two minutes, with occasional agitation in each of ten changes of water, draining the tank thoroughly each time before refilling it with fresh water.

Final Rinse

The final rinse bath consists of a wetting agent solution, mixed no stronger than is recommended in the package instructions. Distilled water is preferable to tap water for this bath; in fact, if your tap water is unusually hard or chemically treated, it is probably a good idea to agitate the film for a couple of minutes in a tankful of plain distilled water before treating it with the wetting solution. The preliminary rinse water should be discarded, but the wetting solution can be used for several rolls of film if they are done within a few days time. Don't reuse a wetting solution that has treated inadequately washed film; it will contaminate subsequent rolls. If there is any doubt in your mind about the condition of the solution, throw it away and mix a fresh bath.

Don't use a contaminated wetting bath

Soak the film, still on the reel, in the wetting solution for about a minute. Then remove the film from the reel, attach a film clip to each end of the film strip, and seesaw the film back and forth through the wetting solution, as shown in the illustration, to remove bubbles and surface particles. Then drain the wetting solution from the film, as shown, and carefully hang it in a dust-free environment to dry.

a

b

c

Figure 4.13
Soak the chamois thoroughly in clean
water, then squeeze it dry, stretch out the
wrinkles, fold it into a flat pad and wipe the
film gently.

d

e

**Wipe film only if necessary; then very
gently**

Clean up the darkroom

Drying

If you have not used a wetting solution, you will have to remove the water droplets from the film surfaces by wiping them. A dampened viscose sponge is better than nothing, but a folded piece of damp chamois skin is much more effective. Soak the chamois thoroughly to soften it, then *squeeze* it as dry as possible. Don't *wring* it or it is liable to shed its surface fibers and cover your film with tiny shreds of leather. Fold the chamois into a flat pad and, using moderate pressure, stroke the film from top to bottom, once on each side. It should be completely free from water droplets and visible moisture. If it is not, squeeze the chamois skin again, and repeat the wiping procedure *gently!* Alternatively, wipe the film surface dry with one stroke of a soft rubber squeegee such as a new (not used) windshield wiper blade. Although these are effective ways to treat film, there is some danger of scratching it. They are, therefore, not recommended unless the wetting agent treatment alone is ineffective.

Gentle circulation of warm, dry air will hasten the drying process, but avoid excessive heat and watch out for airborne dust. Commercial film dryers are available but you probably don't need one unless you have no suitable drying area or you're doing lots of processing on a daily basis.

Clean-up

If you have not already done so, now is the time to clean up the darkroom mess. Rinse developer-soiled articles with used or leftover short-stop, then rinse again with several changes of water. Rinse the tank cover under running water, paying particular attention to the light trap. Rinse the wetting solution out of the tank and off the reel until the water stops frothing, then set them in place to dry. Check the sink edge, light switches, and timer controls for chemical stains from unwashed fingers and wash these areas if necessary. Be very careful

Synopsis

**Rollfilm Developing
Process Steps**

Total Darkness

Load the film onto the appropriate tank reel and place it in the tank. Put cover on tank. Turn on lights.

Normal Room Light

In three clean containers prepare appropriate volumes of developer, stop bath, and fixing bath (of film strength). Adjust temperatures of all solutions to 20°C (68°F). Set an interval timer for the appropriate developing time for the film and developer in use (see developing charts in appendix 11).

Developer: Pour developer into tank until it starts to overflow. Start the timer, replace top cap on tank, and agitate vigorously for 10 to 15 seconds. Thereafter, agitate by turning the tank over and back two or three times, at intervals of thirty seconds (use one-minute intervals if total developing time will exceed about six minutes). About 30 seconds before end of developing time, pour developer out.

Stop Bath: Immediately pour stop bath into tank so tank is full just as the developing time is up. Agitate the stop bath continuously for 10 or 15 seconds, minimum. Pour out after about 30 seconds.

Fixer: Set timer running and note the time. Pour fixer into tank and agitate for 10 or 15 seconds, then let it rest for a minute or so while you wash the used utensils. Remove tank cover and wash it thoroughly. Inspect film. If film is not clear, replace it in fixer and check it at 30-second intervals until it clears, then replace it in fixer and leave it for another interval equal to the total clearing time. Then pour fixer back

into storage jug. Check fixer strength periodically.

Water Rinse: Fill open tank with clean water at about 20°C, agitate briefly, and pour out.

Hypo-Clearing Bath: Pour clearing bath at about 20°C into tank and agitate it two or three times. Repeat at frequent intervals during the clearing time recommended by manufacturer.

Wash: Allow slowly running water at about 20°C to flow into the center of the open tank for time recommended by manufacturer of clearing bath. At frequent intervals empty tank and allow it to refill to insure complete water changes. Alternatively, use film washer following manufacturer's instructions.

Wetting: Fill tank with wetting agent solution at about 20°C, preferably prepared with distilled water. In hard water areas, precede this bath with a thorough rinse in plain distilled water.

Dry: Drain wetting agent from film and hang the film strip to dry in a dust-free place. Avoid violent air movement or excessive heat. Wipe film surfaces only if necessary to avoid surface scums, but careful wiping with a clean, soft chamois, thoroughly soaked and squeezed very dry, is advisable if wetting agent is not used.

Store: Cut film into convenient lengths and store the negative strips in negative envelopes or sleeves to protect them from dust and fingerprints. Keep them away from heat and protected from moisture or high humidity.

not to let water get into the light switches or the timer mechanism. Rinse off the outside of the storage bottles and flush out the sink with water. Dry your hands, turn off the water, and turn out the lights before leaving the darkroom.

Storage of Negatives

When the film is dry, remove the film clips carefully so any water drops that they might be retaining will not fall on your new negatives. Cut 35mm negatives into strips of six to fit most standard negative envelopes or sleeves (some types take strips of five). Rollfilm negatives are usually cut into strips of two to four, depending on the image format. Buy negative envelopes to accommodate the strip lengths you find most convenient and cut the film to fit them.

Handle the dry negatives with care

Handle the dry negatives with great care. They will scratch easily and are susceptible to damage from fingerprints and water spots. Slip each strip of negatives into its own separate envelope or sleeve (don't double them up). Negative storage sheets punched to fit into a standard three-hole notebook are available; each sheet is capable of holding a full roll of negatives. Investigate them; they are convenient, offer good protection, and make the problem of locating a particular negative fairly simple.

Figure 4.14
Cutting and filing negatives

Appraising Negative Quality

Exposure primarily controls density

The quality of the negative image is influenced by both film exposure and development. In general, if development is normal and exposure is varied, the density of the negative will vary. Underexposure of the film will produce a thin, pale image, typically lacking in *shadow detail* because the shadow areas of the subject will have provided the least light for film exposure. Normal exposure will result in a negative of rather luminous quality, transparent enough to see some light through even the most dense areas, while retaining well-defined details in the thinnest shadow areas. Overexposure will result in heavy density overall; the highlight areas of the image may be virtually opaque in extreme cases and the image shadows will be well detailed but obviously dense.

Exposure, therefore, is said to control density. The other significant image characteristic is contrast. It is influenced strongly by development conditions.

Development primarily controls contrast

If film exposure is normal, underdevelopment (caused by insufficient temperature or time or excessive dilution) will result in a *weak* negative image which will appear thin (as an underexposed image would) but will contain visible traces of shadow detail. The image contrast (density difference between highlight and shadow areas) is low. Normal development will result in a negative of normal contrast and density, as described. Overdevelopment will produce dense highlights and relatively thin shadows; the negative will have a harsh appearance and contrast will be high.

But there is some interaction

Exposure and development are not entirely separate influences. Both control image density to some degree, and with some film types, both also influence contrast. Underexposure is easy to identify, however. If the negative highlights and midtones are thinner than normal and the shadow areas are transparent without useful image detail, the film exposure was insufficient. If, on the other hand, the shadows are unnecessarily dense and heavily detailed, the film exposure was overdone.

Development errors are not quite so easy to identify, but excessive contrast in the negative is an indication of more-than-necessary development for that particular subject condition. Low contrast, on the other hand, indicates that longer or more vigorous development would have been a good idea. Normal development will produce normal negative contrast when the subject contrast itself is normal. Abnormal subject contrast can be compensated for by modified development to produce normal negative contrast.

Good negative quality is essential for good prints

Good negative quality is essential if you want to make good prints. Expose and develop your film with care and treat the negatives tenderly. You'll soon learn to recognize "good quality" negatives if you understand the effects of exposure and development and make an effort to analyze and correct your technical blunders.

Summary

Exposed film must be developed in total darkness. Development is controlled by adjustment of time, temperature, and agitation, and is usually carried out in a tank.

For rollfilm processing you should have a darkroom equipped with a sink and hot-and-cold running water. Necessary or desirable equipment items include a tank, thermometer, timer, mixing and storage utensils and containers, a wash tank, film clips, and a soft sponge, chamois, or squeegee.

The developer typically contains chemicals that fulfill the functions of reducing agent, accelerator, preservative, and restrainer. Development is halted when the film is immersed in an acid stop bath, and the fixing bath removes the unused light-sensitive material and hardens the film emulsion. To avoid eventual image deterioration, the film must be washed thoroughly.

Developers can be used and replenished or they can be used as one-shots and discarded. One-shots provide good image quality and some are mildly compensating. Pick a developer and learn to use it well.

Photographic chemicals should be treated with reasonable caution. Some individuals are susceptible to Metol poisoning. Keep your darkroom and utensils clean and wash your hands immediately after contact with any dry chemical or chemical solution.

Most chemicals can be mixed with tap water. Follow mixing and storage instructions carefully. Some solutions are stock solutions, others are working solutions; don't confuse them.

Tank loading is a skill you'll have to acquire with practice. Use spoiled film while you're learning. When you are ready to develop, follow the process steps carefully. Time, temperature, and agitation are important and should be controlled quite precisely for best results. Film clearing time in the fixer is variable; learn to recognize cleared film. Don't use exhausted fixer; test it if in doubt. Use a hypo-clearing bath to speed washing and treat the washed film with a wetting agent. File the dry negative strips in separate sleeves.

Exposure is largely responsible for negative image density. Development is largely responsible for negative image contrast. Learn to recognize good negative quality.

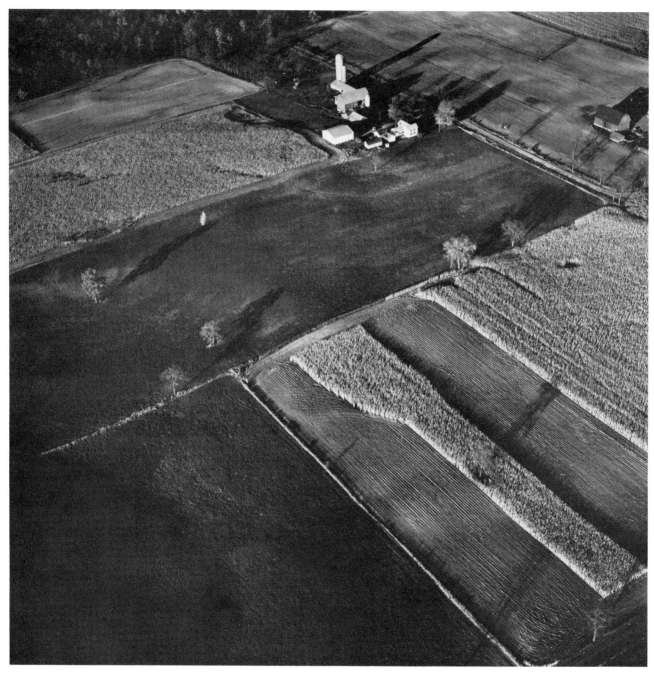

Untitled. Ken Baird.
By taking advantage of the brilliantly clear
atmosphere and slanting sunlight of a fine
October evening, Baird has rendered the
contours and textures of this Michigan
farmscape with dramatic clarity and
richness.
(Courtesy of the photographer.)

Printing

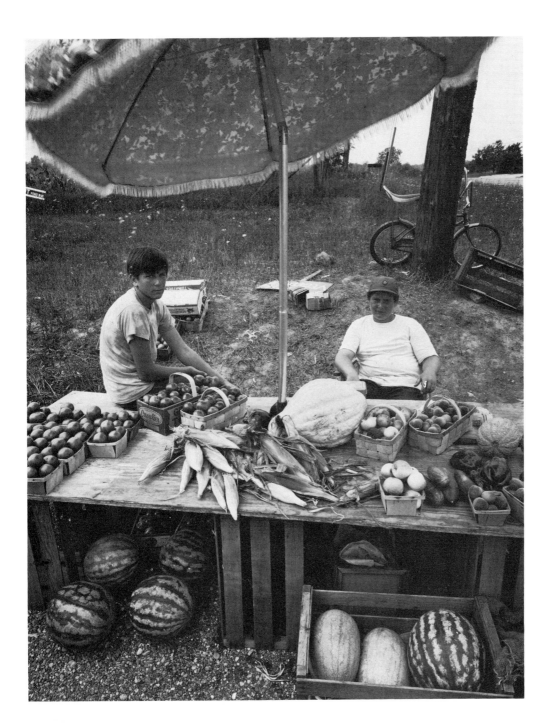

5

Outline

Facilities
Equipment
Lighting
Enlargers and Accessories
Dodging Tools
Trays
Tongs or Paddles
Mounting and Matting Materials
Printing Papers: Types and Characteristics
Resin-Coated vs. Fiber-Based Papers
Papers for Projection Printing or Contact Printing
Sizes
Color
Weight
Texture
Contrast
Preparing the Printing Chemicals
Developer
Stop Bath
Fixer
Clearing Bath
Proofing Negatives by Contact
Making Prints by Projection
Post-Development Controls
Reducing
Bleaching
Spotting
Mounting and Matting Prints

Facilities

Printing, like film processing, is easiest in a darkroom space with hot-and-cold running water. It's convenient to have a large sink to work in but a large table surface will do if it can be waterproofed so spilled solutions won't damage it or leak onto the floor. If you're building a darkroom, you can make an excellent sink out of plywood waterproofed with fiberglass cloth and acrylic or epoxy resin. These materials are available from boat dealers, who can also supply instructions for applying them. You can hardly make the sink too big; it should be at least six inches deep, two feet wide, and as long as possible. You'll find a six-foot sink cramped and, if you start making really big prints or getting involved in advanced color or nonsilver processes, you'll soon wish you had twelve feet of length.

Divide your darkroom into two areas: wet and dry

Divide your darkroom space into two well-defined areas, *wet* and *dry,* and keep them separate. The sink and an associated table space constitute the wet area. Do your chemical mixing, film and print developing, washing, and any other procedure that involves use or storage of liquids in this area. The dry area should include the printing area, film and paper storage, space for film tank loading, a paper cutter, negative filing folders or cases, and space for any other dry, clean operations you'll be involved in. Be sure to provide plenty of electrical outlets for timers, safelights, enlarger, and other needs. Don't neglect the ventilation—a closed darkroom can be very stuffy and unpleasant if you can't get fresh air into it.

You'll need lots of storage space, too. Cabinets with doors are preferable to open shelves because shelves collect dust. Try to provide a specific place for every item of equipment. It will simplify your housekeeping and make darkroom operations more efficient. A floor drain may come in handy but really isn't necessary unless you're a careless worker. If you enjoy comfortable working conditions, consider covering the floor with padded outdoor carpet, and pipe in some stereo music. An extension phone is a real convenience, too.

Roadside Vegetable Stand. Phil Davis.

Equipment

Most of your utensils will do double duty

Much of your film processing equipment will also serve for printing. The various measuring and mixing utensils (graduates, funnels, stirring rods, bottles, etc.) can do double duty. The thermometer and interval timer will occasionally be useful too, but a special timer for the enlarger is desirable. There are several varieties. The cheapest ones are spring wound, similar to inexpensive oven timers. They provide timed intervals of up to about one minute and turn the enlarger light off when the time interval has elapsed. Better models have electric clock-motor drive and frequently provide switched electrical outlets which can control both the enlarger light and a safelight. Some also provide automatic reset of the selected time interval so any given exposure time can be repeated by simply pressing a button. The best and most expensive timers are electronically controlled. They provide all the switching and convenience features of the mechanical and electric timers but offer a greater range of times and also permit accurate exposures of fractions of a second.

Lighting

Films, because they are extremely sensitive to light of all colors, must be handled and developed in total darkness. Papers are not nearly as sensitive, even to white light, and they are practically insensitive to red, orange, and yellow light. Consequently, light of any of these colors is considered *safe* for papers, and a light source suitably filtered to produce only safe light is called (reasonably enough) a *safelight*.

You will need at least two safelights

You will need at least two safelights in your darkroom; one near the enlarger and one suspended over the sink to illuminate the processing trays. Buy the largest ones you can afford and equip them with the orange-brown filters that are safe for variable-contrast papers. The Kodak designation is Wratten series OC, but equivalent filters of other brands will do as well. Other safelights can be placed strategically around the room to provide general room illumination, and if each is equipped with a bulb of the recommended wattage, the light will still be safe to work in. Don't economize on safelights. You'll enjoy your darkroom a great deal more if it is as light as possible.

Paint the darkroom walls yellow

If you have a large darkroom space, it may be worth considering a sodium vapor safelight. Although they are quite expensive, they are very bright and will replace several smaller conventional models. There are also special fluorescent tubes available, which are said to be both safe and bright. Regardless of the type of safelight you buy, you can increase the apparent illumination level in the room if you paint the walls and ceiling bright yellow. In yellow safelight illumination, the yellow walls will appear white or very light gray. Don't use white paint, though. White light which may leak from the enlarger will reflect dangerously from a white surface, but its reflection from the yellow paint will be safely yellow. Black paint is safe for the walls but it will make the darkroom a dingy place in which to work. You may, however, want to paint the wall area close to the enlarger black to subdue all reflections and protect panchromatic materials which you might occasionally want to use there.

Enlargers and Accessories

The major equipment item is the enlarger

The major equipment item in the darkroom is usually the enlarger. Shop carefully for your enlarger; a flimsy one that doesn't work well will be a continual source of frustration. Many models and styles are available to choose from but there are certain features you should look for. The entire machine should be solidly built and as free from vibration as possible, even when raised to full height. The illumination on the baseboard should be bright and uniform over the entire area, without obvious *hot-spots* or patterns. The light source should remain cool during prolonged exposure times. The negative stage, the lensboard, and the baseboard should be absolutely parallel.

Figure 5.1
Black-and-white enlarger

Figure 5.2
Color enlarger

Enlarger types: condenser and diffusion

The negative carrier should be designed to hold the negatives flat without scratching them and should be arranged so it can be turned to straighten a tilted image or to change from a horizontal to a vertical format. The enlarger head should be counterbalanced so it can be raised and lowered easily and it should lock firmly in the desired position. The focusing control should operate smoothly without blacklash and the range of adjustment should be great enough to permit projection prints of reduced size. Some enlargers can be tilted for horizontal projection and some provide a calibrated tilting lensboard for distortion control; both are convenient features, but they are not essential.

Until a few years ago enlargers could be classified easily into two groups, condenser or diffusion. Condenser enlargers provide even illumination for the negative by employing a system of large condensing lenses to collimate the light from the lamp into a parallel beam which then converges into a cone of light directed toward the enlarger lens. This system provides *specular* illumination for the negative and results in a projected image of relatively high intensity and contrast. Diffusion enlargers illuminate the negative evenly by scattering the light from the lamp through one or more layers of opal glass or groundglass, by multiple reflection within an integrating chamber or by using a light source of large area such as the cold-light heads which combine a grid of fluorescent or mercury-vapor tubing with some other diffusion. This diffuse illumination provides a projected image of somewhat lower intensity and lower contrast.

Figure 5.3
a. In a condenser system the light from the lamp is not diffused. The condensers focus the light through the negative and into the enlarger lens, with a minimum of scattering, producing a brilliant, contrasty image.

b. Diffusion enlargers provide a large source of light and diffuse it further by one or more layers of groundglass. The negative illumination is directionless, resulting in a relatively low intensity and low contrast.

c. Modern dichroic enlargers frequently combine the diffused light from an integrating chamber with a condenser system, to provide negative illumination of relatively high intensity and moderate contrast. The dichroic filters control light color and protect the negative from IR radiation. Dichroic heads are a great convenience in color printing and are also useful for controlling contrast of black-and-white variable-contrast papers.

A dichroic color head is a convenience

Photographers have rather strong prejudices and opinions about these two systems, but either one is capable of excellent results if it is used competently. In general, condenser enlargers have been thought to print faster and produce higher contrast, and some say they produce sharper images. Their critics say they emphasize image grain and surface blemishes and are likely to produce mottled images at very small lens apertures because of dust spots on the various condenser lens surfaces. Diffusion enlargers have been criticized for providing relatively dim illumination, giving images of low contrast, and tending to soften both grain structure and image details. These arguments are not as appropriate as they used to be because many modern enlargers combine some of the virtues of both designs.

If you intend to do any color printing at all, and if the added expense is not too serious a problem, buy your enlarger equipped with a *color head*. Color heads incorporate a system of filters which can be introduced into the light beam in any combination to tint the light color, a feature that is highly desirable for color printing and is also useful in black-and-white printing with variable-contrast papers. Modern enlargers used *dichroic* filters, which are much more heat- and fade-resistant than the older gelatin or acetate filter materials.

Color heads usually provide a printing light of high intensity and excellent uniformity, but don't feel that you can't manage with a regular black-and-white enlarger. A color head is a convenience, not a necessity, even for color work. Lots of photographers have worked very successfully in color by using acetate or gelatin filters with a black-and-white enlarger, and you can too, if you want to.

You obviously can't enlarge big negatives in a small enlarger but you can convert a big enlarger to accept small negatives. If you have more than one negative size to deal with, buy the enlarger to fit the largest one and convert it to work with the smaller negatives as required.

Figure 5.4
Easel

Figure 5.5
Focusing aids

The normal enlarging lens focal length for 35mm negatives is about 40 to 50mm; for 2¼″ × 2¼″ and 4.5 × 6cm negatives, about 75 to 80mm; for 2¼″ × 3¼″ negatives, about 100 mm; and for 4″ × 5″ negatives, about 135 to 160mm. Unless you need to make prints of maximum possible size, you can use somewhat longer-than-normal focal length lenses for your negatives (an 80mm lens for 35mm negatives, for example). You'll still be able to make enlargements of moderate size and the image quality is likely to be even better than that produced by the normal lens because you'll be using only the center portion of the lens field, where both lens correction and image illumination are at their best. Well-corrected enlarging lenses are essential for fine work; buy the best ones you can afford.

Buy the best enlarging lenses you can afford

A good enlarging easel is almost a necessity, too. Again, buy top quality. With reasonable care it will last a lifetime. In my experience the solid metal easels with adjustable margins on all four sides have proven most satisfactory. One model permits adjustments of margins on prints smaller than 11″ × 14″, but will also hold 14″ × 17″ paper for full-area prints when the adjustable mask assembly is removed. This size is big enough for most purposes. Don't buy the 16″ × 20″ size unless you make these big prints frequently. They're much more expensive and are awkward to use for the usual smaller print sizes.

A grain focuser is recommended

Focusing an enlarger sharply is even more difficult than focusing a camera. If you have trouble, buy a *grain focuser* magnifier. There are many models and the price range is surprisingly great. Price, however, is not necessarily an indication of efficiency; some of the least expensive types work very well (although you may have to adjust them yourself for best performance) and some of the most expensive models are not significantly better. Check out several types to find one that you can work with comfortably. If you wear glasses, you may find some grain focusers less convenient to use than others.

Figure 5.6
Proofing frame

Figure 5.7
Dodging and burning tools

**You can buy a proofing frame—
or make one**

You'll need a printing frame or something similar, for proofing your negatives and making contact prints. If you have enough room in your darkroom and can find a war-surplus contact printer at a real bargain price, buy it. Don't even consider a new one, though, unless you'll be specializing in contact printing large negatives. If you will make only occasional contact prints or proofs, you can get along with a homemade printer; cover a piece of smooth plywood or Masonite, about 8½″ × 10½″, with felt or thin foam plastic and privide it with a matching cover of double-strength glass. Hinge them together along one edge with plastic tape and you'll have a serviceable proofing frame. Look at the commercial proofing frames, too; they're neat, convenient, and not terribly expensive.

Dodging Tools

Make your own dodging tools

Dodging refers to the practice of shading part of the image area from the exposing light to prevent it from printing too dark. *Burning-in* the image is just the reverse; a portion of the image is given more light to make it darker in the print. You can make dodging tools easily by using music wire or any other thin, stiff wire for the handles and bits of black paper, cut to any desired shape and size, to produce the necessary shadow. For some purposes a little tuft of absorbent cotton, instead of the black paper shape, will produce good results. It

Figure 5.8
Print siphon

Figure 5.9
Tongs and paddles

will give a soft-edged shadow with some slight fogging and diffusion of the image. A sheet of black paper or cardboard with a small hole cut in it, near the center, will make a useful burning tool. You can improvise tools for special purposes as you need them.

Trays

Print processing is done in open trays

Print processing is done in open trays. You'll need three trays for the basic chemicals—developer, short-stop, and hypo. It's convenient to have at least two others, for a water rinse and for a hypo-clearing bath; and you'll need either a special print washer or a larger tray for the final wash.

Trays come in several sizes and styles. The best ones are made of heavy white or yellow slightly flexible plastic with large rolled edges and well-formed pouring lips. The cheaper hard plastic trays usually have more angular contours and sharper edges. They will serve for light-duty use but they are brittle and more likely to crack. They usually have ridged bottoms too, which, in my opinion, is an undesirable feature.

The washing tray should be larger

Trays come in nominal print sizes. Get at least four, but preferably six, $8'' \times 10''$ trays as a basic set, then buy at least four trays in each of the other print sizes you're likely to work with frequently. The washing tray should be at least one size, but preferably two sizes, larger than the prints you wash in it. Equip it with a *tray siphon* for automatic control of water level and good circulation. If you plan to do a lot of printing, it may be worth your while to buy a print washer, but consider this purchase carefully. Good print washers are expensive and bulky and will be neither economical nor convenient for only occasional use.

Tongs or Paddles

Tongs are useful for small prints

Many photographers like to handle prints with *tongs* or *paddles* during processing. These tools do have at least one advantage: they keep your hands out of the chemical solutions. They don't offer reliable protection from Metol poisoning, however, and they don't significantly reduce the risk of print stains or physical damage. In fact, they are more likely to bruise the print emulsion than your fingers are, especially when handling large paper sizes. In my opinion, tongs are occasionally useful for small print processing of up to about $5'' \times 7''$ size. For larger sizes they are a nuisance. If you prefer to use them, get the kind that have soft plastic or rubber tips and are clearly color coded so you won't confuse them. You'll need at least two, one for the developer tray and one that can serve for short-stop and hypo. Some photographers prefer to use three, one in each tray, to avoid any chance of contamination.

Figure 5.10
Plastic drying screens

There are several ways to dry prints

After the prints have been washed, they must be dried. Prints on *resin-coated* (RC) papers can simply be sponged surface-dry and hung up with clothespins to air-dry. Alternatively, they can be laid out on plastic screens (aluminum-framed window screens are fine). Conventional *fiber-based* papers can be dried in blotter books or rolls, laid out on plastic screens, or heat-dried in electric print dryers. Unless you are interested in *ferrotyping* fiber-based papers to produce a high-gloss print finish, or unless you do a lot of printing every day, a commercial heat dryer is probably an unnecessary expense. For most purposes, screen frames are entirely satisfactory. They are cheap, convenient, easy to store, and easy to keep clean.

Mounting and Matting Materials

And several methods for mounting them

Finished prints are usually mounted or matted for presentation. *Dry-mounting* has been a preferred method for general use because it is fast, neat, and permanent. A dry-mounting press is required. There are several models, all expensive, but this is another one-time purchase, which should last for years. Buy a big enough press to accommodate the largest print size you'll use frequently. You will also need a *tacking iron,* a small electrically-heated hand tool used for attaching the dry-mount tissue adhesive sheet to the print and mount board before heating them in the press. For some other methods of presentation, such as the use of pressure-sensitive tissues or art corners, a mounting press is not necessary.

Matting involves measuring and cutting the mount and mat boards and requires miscellaneous tools. A *print-trimmer* or *paper cutter* is a convenient accessory for cutting prints and tissue, but mat and mount board should be cut to shape with a *mat knife* and heavy metal *straightedge*. A special *mat-cutter* is essential if you want bevelled edges on your mats, and you'll find a T-square, a ruler, and a large draftsman's triangle (30°–60°) useful for measuring and marking the boards. You should also have a soft pencil (#2 or 2B), an eraser (art gum, kneaded, or Pink Pearl), and some linen or plastic tape. Don't use ordinary masking tape; it will dry out and discolor with age.

Printing Papers: Types and Characteristics

Resin-Coated vs. Fiber-Based Papers

Until a few years ago printing papers were really paper

Until a few years ago printing papers really were paper. Now the variety of fiber-based papers has diminished considerably and manufacturers are supplying more and more resin-coated (RC) papers. For commercial purposes and for prints that will be used and discarded, RC papers are usually satisfactory; in fact, they offer real advantages in ease of processing. Although this is a matter of individual preference, a great many photographers feel that RC papers look plastic and cheap. On the other hand, there are photographers who feel that the paper should be as neutral and unobtrusive as possible to avoid any competition with the image itself. You can make your own decision. Both groups recognize the advantage of fiber-based papers for long-term storage, however. RC papers are not yet considered stable enough to be archival.

RC papers are very convenient, but not yet archival

This is not as serious as it sounds. Despite the continuing interest in archival processing techniques, the most carefully pampered prints will survive only if they are stored properly, a factor that is out of the photographer's control. Further, it's probably true that a very sizable proportion of all prints, archivally processed or not, have little long-term value or significance and shouldn't be kept anyway. For almost all uses then, RC papers can be considered to be adequately permanent, and if you find a surface and image color you like in an RC paper, use it with no regrets.

Papers for Projection Printing or Contact Printing

You can't enlarge conveniently on contact paper

Most commonly available papers are designed for projection printing and are sensitive enough to respond to the relatively dim light produced by the enlarger. Contact papers are much less sensitive because they were originally intended to be used (in contact with the negative) in either subdued daylight or strong artificial light. Contact printing is not very popular anymore and many photographers, who still make contact prints, make them on projection paper, using the enlarger as a light source. Contact papers, therefore, are now fairly rare and difficult to obtain; the only variety generally available is Kodak's Azo.

Although Azo is a fine paper, it is useful *only* for bright light contact printing. Don't buy it for use under the enlarger, even in a printing frame; it is much to slow too be practical. You should, however, try contact printing at least once. There are many photographers who believe that a good contact print represents the ultimate in photographic quality and elegance.

Sizes

Printing papers come in sheet sizes from about $2'' \times 3''$ to $20'' \times 24''$, and in uncut rolls $20''$ or $40''$ wide. The most common sizes are probably $8'' \times 10''$, $11'' \times 14''$, and $16'' \times 20''$. Paper is commonly sold in packages of 10 sheets (for larger sheet sizes) to 500 sheets and is, of course, somewhat less expensive per sheet when purchased in the larger quantities. The two most common package sizes for $8'' \times 10''$ paper are 25-sheet double envelopes and 100-sheet boxes.

Color

Some papers contain a fluorescent brightener

Although we don't usually think of black-and-white papers as having any color, they are available in several subtle tints, such as white, warm white, natural, cream white, etc. Additionally, some papers contain a brightener which fluoresces in daylight or ultraviolet light, making the paper appear more brilliantly white than untreated paper. The silver image itself varies in color to some extent, too. Warm-tone papers produce a brownish image, while cold-tone papers give a bluish-black image. Most papers are neutral in tone. Their images appear uncolored or very slightly warm black. Image color is influenced by development conditions also and can be altered after development by special chemical *toning* treatment.

Weight

The thickness, or weight, of the paper stock is indicated on the package by terms such as single weight, double weight, medium weight, etc. Single-weight papers are less expensive than the heavier grades and are generally satisfactory for prints of normal size. Some photographers prefer double-weight papers because they are less easily creased or wrinkled during processing and drying and because they feel more substantial in the hand. This is largely a matter of choice. There is no significant difference in image quality.

Texture

The surface texture of printing paper is also specified on the package by some descriptive phrase, such as smooth, glossy; fine-grain, lustre; silk, lustre; rough; etc. In Kodak papers, the stock tint and surface characteristics are also symbolized by a letter designation, such as F for white, smooth, glossy or G for cream-white, fine-grain, lustre. Agfa paper packages display a combined letter and number code which expresses most of the essential information. BEH 1, for example, stands for Brovira, extra-hard, single-weight, white, glossy. BW 111 indicates Brovira, soft, double-weight, white, glossy.

Contrast

The descriptions extra-hard and soft refer to the inherent contrast characteristic of the paper emulsion (see appendix 2). *Hard* papers produce images of high contrast; *soft* papers produce low contrast. In addition to the letter symbols, Agfa papers indicate the paper contrast grade by another number series, from 0 through 5; the lower numbers stand for low contrast and the higher numbers indicate grades of increasing contrast. Number 3 (Brovira) is considered normal contrast, but number 2 papers are preferred for general use by some workers. Number 2 is the normal grade of Agfa Portriga paper. Ilford papers and some Kodak papers designate contrast grades similarly, but Kodak's Kodabrome projection paper carries word descriptions only—soft, medium, hard, etc.

Kodak's Polycontrast paper is a variable-contrast material. Coated with a mixture of high-contrast and low-contrast emulsions, the effective contrast of the print image can be controlled by varying the color of the exposing light. Green light (transmitted by a yellow filter) affects the low-contrast emulsion and will produce a low-contrast image. Blue light (transmitted by magenta filter) affects only the high-contrast emulsion and the paper produces a hard image. Mixtures of green and blue light produce intermediate grades of contrast.

In use, the desired contrast is produced by inserting a filter of the appropriate color into the enlarger light path. The filters are numbered to correspond with conventional paper grades, with the number 2 filter being considered normal. The paper also reacts with approximately normal contrast to the unfiltered incandescent enlarger light but cannot be used satisfactorily with some cold-light enlargers whose light is deficient in green. Polycontrast Rapid II SC is resin-coated and similar to Polycontrast, but it is faster and yields a more neutral image tone. Ektamatic SC is a fast, variable-contrast material, featuring white paper stock and a neutral image tone. It is intended for *stabilization processing* but also works very well in trays.

Stabilization papers, liks Ektamatic SC, include a reducing agent in their emulsion mixture. After exposure they can be processed in seconds by running them through a motorized stabilization processor, which first spreads a coating of strongly alkaline *activator* solution on the emulsion (developing the image almost instantly) and then coats the emulsion with a *stabilizer* solution which effectively renders the silver halides inert but does not fix the image in the usual sense. Stabilized prints emerge from the processor in about 10 seconds, thoroughly contaminated with chemicals, but damp dry and ready for immediate use. In this condition they are not suitable for long-term storage, nor should they be allowed to contact conventionally processed prints, for fear of contaminating them, but they can be made permanent, if desired, by 10-minute treatment in the fixing bath, followed by the usual clearing bath and wash. When processed in trays in the normal manner, Ektamatic SC reacts like any ordinary paper, producing fine image quality. Because of its versatility, it is an excellent paper for student use.

a. Kodabromide number 1

b. Kodabromide number 2

c. Kodabromide number 3

d. Kodabromide number 4

Figure 5.11
Printing paper contrast is indicated by
number. The low numbers indicate low
contrast; high numbers indicate high
contrast. These prints, all made from the
same negative, show the range of a typical
enlarging paper.

e. Kodabromide number 5

For the discriminating expert: luxury papers

There are at least four luxury-grade papers currently available, all aimed at the discriminating printer who is willing to pay a premium for quality products. In order of decreasing price: Ilford Galerie—a white base, neutral image tone paper, available in three contrast grades; Agfa Portriga Rapid—a warm ivory paper (although some batches are nearly white) featuring exceptionally rich brown-black image tones, available in three grades; Unicolor Exhibition—a white base paper with slightly warm black image tone, available in only two grades; and Oriental Seagull—a white paper of neutral image color, available in several grades and surfaces. Although these papers are capable of somewhat richer image quality than the less expensive varieties can manage, only skillful printers will be able to get the most from them. While you're learning to print, save your money and practice on any one of the fine, reasonably priced papers that are widely available. Until both you and your negatives become very good, no one will know the difference—most of the time.

Preparing the Printing Chemicals

Developer

Diluted print developers oxidize fairly quickly

Most print developers are either Metol-hydroquinone or Phenidone-hydroquinone formulas, accelerated with sodium carbonate. They are usually mixed into a stock solution for storage and are diluted with one or more parts of water to make the working solution. The solutions have considerable reserve strength and are normally used for a number of prints, one after the other, without replenishment; although in a few instances, replenishment is suggested as a means of extending their working life. Print developers, especially after dilution, oxidize fairly quickly; therefore, working solutions should not be saved for more than a few hours whether or not they have been exhausted by use. Stock solutions, on the other hand, are fairly stable and will keep for several months under ideal conditions.

Developing time recommendations vary from brand to brand of developer and will be different for different dilutions of the same developer. There's not much reason to experiment with different developers though, until you've learned the process fairly thoroughly. Get a good standard brand and use it according to the recommendations on the package.

Print development should be standardized

If you have no other guide, develop prints for about twice as long as it takes the image to become completely visible. This will be somewhat longer than is absolutely necessary, but slight overdevelopment is far better than slight underdevelopment. Most importantly, once you've established a workable development time, don't change it, regardless of what the print image is doing. *Development variations should not be relied on to correct improper print exposure.* If you're serious about fine print quality, expose the print so it can be developed normally—whatever you find that to be.

Stop Bath

Indicator stop baths are most useful for prints

A stop bath similar to the one used for film is also satisfactory for use with papers, but it may be made a little stronger, if desired. The working solution should not normally exceed about 1½% acid strength (slightly more than 1½ ounces of 28% acetic acid stock solution in 32 ounces of water). The yellow indicator stop bath is more appropriate for use with prints than for films because it is designed to be used in yellow safelight conditions. An indicator bath in good condition appears clear and colorless in the yellow light but will turn dark and appear almost opaque when exhausted. Although adding acetic acid to the exhausted bath will restore its clarity, it is better to throw the used bath away and mix a fresh one to avoid possible contamination.

The stop bath stops development and protects the fixer

The stop bath serves the same function in printing that it serves in film developing; it rinses the developer chemicals off the print surfaces, halts the action of the developer, and, most importantly, neutralizes the developer alkalinity so the essential acidity of the fixing bath will be preserved. The neutralizing action of the acetic acid on the sodium carbonate from the developer is sometimes accompanied by a high-pitched whining or whistling sound as tiny streams of carbon dioxide gas bubbles are forced out of the paper fibers. This sonnd (if it occurs at all) usually begins 10 or 15 seconds after the print is put into the short-stop and may continue for another 15 seconds or so. Leave the print in until it stops. You may not hear any sound at all. If you don't, don't worry about it. It only occurs with fiber-based papers anyhow. RC prints take their treatment in the short-stop without a murmur.

Fixer

Prints will fix satisfactorily in either regular or rapid-fixing baths. The regular bath, made with sodium thiosulfate, is used at the same strength for both film and papers. Rapid-fixer should be mixed at half-strength for most papers to avoid possible bleaching of the relatively delicate print image. Regardless of the kind of fixer used, films and papers should not be fixed in the same volume of solution. Film fixers rapidly accumulate complex silver-sulfur compounds which can be washed out of the film emulsions without too much difficulty but are extremely difficult to wash out of papers. Keep film and paper fixing baths separate and test them frequently; an exhausted fixing bath will eventually kill your prints.

Prints don't "clear" obviously, as films do

Prints don't "clear" obviously in the fixing bath the way films do, so there's no way to know for sure when fixing is complete. For this reason we usually leave prints in the fixer for longer than is probably necessary. Actually, most papers fix very rapidly and there is more danger of overfixing them than there is with films. Don't let them soak in the fixer for extended periods of time or they may begin to bleach out. This is especially important if you are using a rapid-fixing bath. Projection papers will fix adequately in a fresh fixing bath in 5 minutes or a little less.

Contact papers require even shorter times, try 3 to 4 minutes. RC papers need only about 2 minutes. In all cases these times apply only if there is an adequate volume of fixer and the prints are given frequent agitation. Discard the fixer after treating about one hundred 8″ × 10″ prints per gallon.

Two fixing baths are better than one

You can extend the fixing times to about twice the normal length to compensate for partial exhaustion of the bath, but don't exceed that amount of time and don't overwork the solution. For maximum economy and best results with ordinary fiber-based papers (not RC), you should really use two fixing baths in sequence. Agitate the prints in the first bath for 3 to 5 minutes, then transfer them to the second bath, and repeat the treatment. The first bath will do most of the work and wear out first, but it should be adequate for about two hundred 8″ × 10″ prints per gallon of solution. Then discard it and replace it with the second bath. Mix a fresh volume of fixer for the new second bath. This pair will be good for another two hundred prints and the cycle can be repeated once or twice more. Then both baths should be thrown out and new ones prepared.

Clearing Bath

Don't treat RC prints in hypo-clearing bath

Hypo-clearing or neutralizing baths are especially important for use with fiber-based papers, but are not recommended for RC papers. Follow mixing and use instructions for the product you select. Don't attempt to store and reuse a working solution of hypo-clearing agent unless the instructions suggest it. The stock solutions will keep indefinitely.

Proofing Negatives by Contact

Set up your processing trays in the sink

Set up your processing solutions in trays in the darkroom sink. From left to right the trays should contain working solutions of developer, short-stop, and fixer. If space permits and if you have enough trays, you can add a water rinse, hypo-clearing agent, and finally, of course, the washing tray or print washer. Prepare enough of each solution so you have a working depth of at least ½″ in the trays. An 8″ × 10″ tray will require about a quart. This much developer at standard working strength is sufficient for ten or more 8″ × 10″ prints. Smaller volumes can be used if you have only a print or two to make, but don't be stingy with chemicals. A quart of developer costs less than one 8″ × 10″ sheet of paper. Ruining paper to save chemicals is clearly false economy.

Within reasonable limits, temperature is not critical

The temperatures of the various processing solutions should, ideally, be about 20°C, plus or minus a degree or so. The actual temperature, within reasonable limits, is not terribly important in printing because the development goes to completion and the image characteristics are not changed much after the first minute or two in the developer. You should, however, try to establish a working routine and stick to it. If your darkroom maintains the solutions at a reasonably constant temperature of 21°C, then work at 21°C. If 18°C is easier to maintain, work at 18°C. Two or three degrees variation will not cause any serious problems, but excessively high temperatures increase the risk of fog and stains and may soften the print emulsion. Extremely low temperatures will certainly slow down the action of the developer and may also change its contrast characteristics.

The emulsion side of the negative is least glossy

When the chemicals have been prepared, wash your hands and dry them thoroughly before handling negatives or printing paper. Check the printing frame glass for dust and fingerprints and clean it if necessary. Lay the frame facedown on the table and arrange the negatives on the glass, emulsion side up. The emulsion side is the side that appears the least glossy, and the film usually (but not always) curls toward the emulsion. As a further check, you can look through the negatives and check the orientation of the images. When viewed from the emulsion side the images will be backwards. Dust the negative strips lightly on both sides but don't handle them any more than necessary. They'll have to be cleaned more thoroughly before they're enlarged.

Work in the yellow safelight illumination

Turn out the white lights and work, from this point on, in the yellow safelight illumination. Open the paper package and remove one sheet of paper, then close the paper package securely so the contents will be protected from accidental exposure to white light. Place the paper sheet in the printing frame so the emulsion side of the paper (usually the shinier side, inside the natural curl) is in contact with the emulsion side of the negatives. Clamp the hinged back of the printing frame securely in position and you are ready to make the exposure.

If you are using a contact printing paper, such as Azo, you can make the exposure by simply turning on the white room lights for an appropriate length of time (be sure your paper package is closed securely first, though). It's better to use a single light bulb without any reflector, about 3 or 4 feet away from the frame, however. The exposure time, using a 100-watt bulb at about 4 feet, should be about a minute. A medium-speed projection paper, such as Polycontrast, exposed under the same conditions would need only about ½ second, an impractically short exposure time for accurate measurement.

You can use the enlarger as a light source for proofing

If you want to use projection paper for proofing or contact printing, it's better to use the enlarger as a light source. As a rough guide to exposure, if the enlarger is set up to make an 8-diameter enlargement (8″ × 10″ print from 35mm negative) and the lens is stopped down to f/8, the exposure time for normal negatives will be somewhere around 15 to 30 seconds. Don't take this estimate too seriously; enlargers vary considerably in their effective light output and you'll have to determine your own best time by trial. The enlarger lens should be focused as if a negative were actually in the negative carrier, and for maximum working area the carrier may be removed from the enlarger when making proofs or contacts.

Keep prints submerged during development

After exposing the proof, remove the paper from the printing frame, and immediately after starting the interval timer or noting the time on a clock, slip the sheet into the developer solution with one smooth motion. Alternatively, you can flop the sheet into the developer facedown and immediately wiggle it back and forth in the solution as you pat it under the surface. As soon as it's submerged, lift it out by one corner and replace it in the solution, this time faceup. Push it under the surface again by patting it down lightly with your fingertips (or tongs) and continue to agitate it in the solution by rocking the tray. Keep the print submerged during development. It will tend to float to the surface and will have to be patted back down fairly frequently.

Again, DON'T vary development time

The time of development will depend on the kind of paper in use, the developer type and dilution, and your personal preference. In general, by using commonly available papers and a developer, such as Kodak Dektol or Ektaflo, appropriately diluted, contact papers should develop in 45 seconds to a minute and projection papers, such as Polycontrast, should receive from 1½ minutes to 2 minutes minimum. My recommendation is to use *1* minute for contact paper and *2* minutes for projection papers, unless the manufacturer's instructions specify a *longer* time. A slightly longer development than is absolutely necessary will insure against brownish, mottled tones and incompletely formed shadow details in the print. Again, don't vary the developing time in an attempt to save the print. If the image is not satisfactory at the end of the normal developing time, make another print and change the exposure or the paper grade to correct the problem. *Don't* change development.

RC papers can be processed very quickly

When development time is up, lift the print from the developer by one corner and let it drain briefly into the developer tray. Then place it in the short-stop and immerse it quickly with agitation. If you are using print tongs, it's considered good practice to avoid touching the short-stop with the developer tongs; handle the print in the short-stop with the stop bath-hypo tongs. There is no need to worry if you are using your fingers; in fact, the short-stop will rinse your fingers clean in the same way it cleanses the print. Agitate the print in the stop bath for 15 seconds or until it stops sizzling. Then place it in the hypo. Immerse it quickly and agitate it periodically, to be sure it stays submerged, for about 5 minutes (RC papers should stay in the short-stop bath for only about 5 seconds and in the fixer for 2 minutes with constant agitation). Rinse the hypo off your fingers before handling another print in the developer (or anything else, for that matter).

Keep prints separated in the wash; and wash in batches

RC papers should be washed for 5 minutes, immediately following treatment in the hypo, and then dried. Ordinary prints should be treated in the hypo-clearing bath according to the manufacturer's instructions. Those same instructions should be followed for washing the print after treatment. If no hypo-clearing bath is used, single-weight prints should be washed for an hour in running water, at a temperature between 15°C and 25°C. Double-weight prints should be washed for 2 hours. The water should be running fast enough to change the water in the wash tray every 5 minutes or so. The prints must be kept separated and moving so both surfaces are exposed to the water flow. Hypo-clearing treatment is highly recommended. It saves water and time and contributes to more efficient washing. Don't add unwashed prints to a trayful of partially washed prints. Wash them in batches. One unwashed print will contaminate a whole trayful of clean ones.

RC prints, after washing, should be sponged surface-dry and either hung by one corner or laid out faceup, on plastic screens or a clean cloth to air-dry. Gently circulating warmed air will hasten drying, but avoid strong drafts or excessive heat. In conditions of low to moderate humidity the prints should be dry in 30 minutes or less. Keep the prints from touching each other and protect them from airborne dust during drying. The emulsion is soft and tacky for the first few minutes and can be easily damaged.

Figure 5.12

a. Clean the printing frame glass.

b. Dust the negatives. Handle them carefully by the edges to avoid fingerprints.

c. There are several ways to identify the emulsion side of negatives—it is usually, but not always, on the inside of the natural curl; it is usually dull or matte compared to the more glossy back; the edge frame numbers are backwards when seen from the emulsion side; and the image itself is reversed, left to right, when viewed from the emulsion side. Here the left strip shows the emulsion side; the right strip is facedown and the back is showing.

d. Arrange the negatives on the glass, emulsion up, that is, with the backs touching the glass surface. Turn out the room lights and work from here on in safelight.

e. Remove a sheet of paper from its lighttight package and identify the emulsion side. It is usually, but not always, on the inside of the natural curl; it is usually, but not always, more lustrous than the paper back. Resin-coated papers may be especially confusing. When in doubt, expose a little strip and develop it.

f. Lay a sheet of paper over the negatives, emulsion down. Remember the printing rule, the materials should face each other, emulsion to emulsion.

g. Expose, using the enlarger as a light source, as explained in the text. The negative carrier has been removed here to provide a large area of illumination on the baseboard.

h. Develop the print, following the text instructions. The image will appear gradually after about 15 seconds in the developer. Be sure to agitate efficiently.

a

b

c

d

e

f

g

h

i. After the developing time is up, pick the print up with the developer tongs, transfer it to the stop bath, and handle it there with the stop tongs. Agitate.

j. After the stop bath, transfer the print to the fixing bath. Keep the tongs separate to avoid possible contamination.

k. The print can be placed directly into the clearing bath after it has been fixed, but the clearing bath will last longer and be more efficient if the prints are rinsed briefly before they are cleared. From here on you can handle the print with your fingers. Actually, I prefer fingers for all the operations. Don't clear RC prints.

l. Leave the print in the clearing bath for the recommended time, then wash it in running water. RC prints wash quickly without having been cleared. (See text.)

m. Squeegee RC prints lightly or wipe them with a dampened viscose sponge to remove surface droplets. Fiber-based prints can be wiped or blotted to remove surface moisture.

n. Hang RC prints or lay them out on some clean surface, faceup, to air-dry. Drying screens are excellent for both print types but fiber-based prints should be dried facedown to reduce their tendency to curl.

o. Alternatively, fiber-based prints can be dried between blotters or in blotter books or rolls. Don't dry RC prints this way.

i

j

k

l

m

n

o

a

b

c

d

Figure 5.13
a. Place well-washed prints face to face.

b. Squeegee both backs surface dry.

c. Roll them between blotters.

d. Separate the prints, lay them faceup on the dryer apron and mop the faces with a sponge soaked in glossing solution. The print emulsion must be thoroughly wet as it meets the drum surface to avoid possible freckles in the gloss.

Air drying is safe and effective

RC papers permit rapid processing because their plastic coating protects the paper base from becoming wet from the various solutions. Liquids do penetrate the paper along the cut edges of the print, however, and if RC prints are allowed to soak for very long, the paper margins may absorb enough water to cause them to shrink as they dry. If you find your RC prints drying into saucer shapes, try reducing their wet-time during processing.

Fiber-based prints should not be hung up or laid out faceup to dry because they will curl excessively. They should be dried facedown on the screens or a clean cloth-covered surface. If they tend to curl, they can be sandwiched between two screens or covered lightly with a layer or two of clean cloth. They can usually be dried satisfactorily between photographic blotters or in a special blotter book or blotter roll, but they may pick up lint from the blotters or become marked from the cover papers of the blotter book if the emulsion is soft. If this is a problem, it can sometimes be cured by treating the prints longer in the fixing bath to harden the gelatin emulsion more completely. In extreme cases, a separate hardening bath may be used but excessive hardening will make the print emulsion so brittle after it is dry that it may crack during ordinary handling. Air-drying on screens is safest.

Prints can also be dried in any of several varieties of electrically heated dryers. Glossy fiber-based (not RC) papers can be given a mirrorlike surface if they are *ferrotyped* on a drum dryer (although, since the introduction of the high-gloss RC papers, this is not often done any more). The wet prints are laid

Figure 5.14
Proof sheet with images marked

faceup on a moving canvas belt or apron which carries them into the machine where they are pressed between a rubber roller and the polished surface of a chromium-plated (or stainless steel) drum. As the heated drum slowly rotates, the prints dry and the soft gelatin emulsion is literally moulded smooth by the drum surface. After several minutes the prints emerge and drop off the drum surface into a basket.

Fiber-based prints can be ferrotyped to produce a glossy surface

Ferrotyping produces an immaculate surface, if all goes well, and gives prints the greatest possible brilliance and contrast. It is not always successful, however, and when it does not work well the prints may refuse to leave the drum or come off with a mottled or blotchy surface which is unacceptable. For best results the drum surface must be spotlessly clean and the prints must be properly hardened and well washed. The print emulsion must also be completely covered with a film of water as it meets the drum surface or tiny bubbles of air will become trapped between the surfaces, and the print gloss will be freckled.

Oyster-shelling can be troublesome

Ferrotyping can also be done by rolling wet glossy prints onto chrome-plated ferrotype tins or sheets of acrylic plastic, such as Lucite or Plexiglas, but unless drying conditions are ideal the prints may dry unevenly and become *oyster-shelled*. This can be avoided by covering the prints with two or three layers of clean, wrinkle-free cloth and drying the prints on the tins under moderate pressure. This will prolong the drying period considerably, but the results are usually good. RC glossy papers do not need this treatment. They will dry to a high gloss finish naturally in open air.

RC glossy papers don't need ferrotyping

Drum dryers can also be used to dry nonglossy fiber-based papers, or to dry glossy papers to a semi-gloss finish, if the prints are laid facedown rather than faceup on the dryer apron. The print emulsion then faces the canvas apron as it dries and its normal texture is undisturbed. In some cases, if the print emulsion is too soft or the apron presses on it too firmly, the dry print may show signs of the canvas texture or it may be marred by bits of lint from the canvas. Usually resoaking the print thoroughly, wiping its wet surface with a soft sponge, and air-drying it will restore its natural surface.

Heat-drying is not essential

For most purposes heat-drying is not essential. Unless you are making more prints than you can handle conveniently on screens, you don't need a heat dryer and shouldn't buy one. They're energy hogs, they require good ventilation, and they must be cleaned frequently to avoid contamination. Besides being cheaper, plain air-drying is more appropriate for archival prints and the image quality is at least as good. In fact, some photographers insist that air-dried prints are better.

After the negatives have been proofed, study the contact sheet to see which negatives are suitable for enlargement. This is a good time to consider composition, too. The basic forms and value patterns are often easier to recognize in small scale than they are in the full-size print. Try to decide how you want to crop the image; you may find it useful to mark the outlines right on the proof sheet with a grease pencil or a ball-point pen for future reference.

a

b

c

d

e

f

Figure 5.15
a. Inspect the enlarger, adjust it for the negative size in use, and clean the lens if necessary.
b. Insert the negative into the negative carrier and dust it carefully, using the enlarger light to show up the dust spots. If your enlarger permits it, raise the condensers and clean the negative after inserting it into the enlarger.
c. Open the lens to maximum aperture to provide maximum light for focusing and composing the image. Turn out the white lights; work in safelight from here on.
d. Adjust the image size and composition.
e. Focus carefully.
f. Stop the lens down to printing aperture.

Making Prints by Projection

Before you begin to print, give the enlarger a routine examination and select a lens focal length appropriate for the negative size. A 50mm lens is normal for 35mm negatives; a 75mm to 80mm lens for 2¼″ × 2¼″ negatives; a 100mm to 105mm lens for 2¼″ × 3¼″ negatives; and a 135mm to 160mm lens for 4″ × 5″ negatives. If you'll be making prints of only moderate size, you may want to use the next-longer-than-normal focal length for best results. Be sure the lens is clean and essentially free from dust.

If you have a condenser enlarger, be sure the condensers are adjusted to match the lens focal length. A mismatch may cause uneven illumination or a hot spot in the center of the image area. Be sure the condensers are reasonably clean. Any significant spots of dust or flakes of paint from the lamphousing,

g

h

i

j

k

l

g. Turn the enlarger light off. Cut a sheet of paper into test strips and return all but one to the paper package. Close the paper package to protect the paper from light.
h. Make a test strip as described in the text. Process it as previously described.
i. Inspect the test strip for density and contrast. If the contrast is not satisfactory, try another paper grade or change filters if you're using variable-contrast paper. It's best to make another test if you change contrast.
j. When you have determined the proper exposure and paper grade, make a full print, process it, and inspect it critically in good light.
k. If the print needs local control of density you can make another and dodge. . . .
l. . . . or burn, as indicated.

which may appear on the surfaces of any of the condensers, may show up in the image as light-toned blobs, especially if you stop the lens down to a very small aperture. If your enlarger has a glass negative carrier, clean it carefully.

If you have processed your film competently and protected the negatives in envelopes or sleeves, they should not need more than a light dusting. Dust them gently with a clean, soft brush before you insert the strip into a glass carrier. You can dust them in the glassless carrier itself; in fact, some designs allow you to get at them after the carrier has been inserted into the enlarger. That's the best way if it's possible. Turn the enlarger light on so the dust spots will show up clearly and pick them off, one by one, with the tip of a small brush. Wipe the brush across your forehead or the side of your nose to pick up a little "nose-oil." That will help dispel static electricity and make the brush slightly tacky so it will hold the dust particles better. If money is no object and dust is a real problem to you, you can buy a static-neutralizing gun, such as the Zerostat. It will be particularly valuable during winter when humidity is low. It will work well on your phonograph records, too.

Focus on white paper with the lens wide open

When everything is tidy and the negative is safely in place, turn on the yellow safelights and turn off the white room lights. Turn on the enlarger light and open the lens diaphragm to its maximum aperture. Set your easel margins to the desired size and proportions of the image and put a piece of plain white paper in the easel to focus on. Bring the image into approximate focus and check it for orientation and size. If it is not right side up and correct from left to right, remove the negative carrier and correct it. You may have to dust the negative again. Then raise or lower the enlarger to adjust the image size. You will have to focus it in order to do this with precision because focusing changes the size slightly. But with a little practice you should be able to control it easily. Adjust the focus with your grain focuser if you have one, stop the lens down to f/8 or f/11, and turn off the enlarger light.

Determine proper exposure by making a test strip

The next problem is to determine the proper exposure time and the correct paper grade for the negative you're using. Temporarily, assume the negative is normal in contrast and work with normal paper. The exposure must be determined by trial and there are several ways to go about it. The most direct and economical way is to make a *test strip,* a strip of paper bearing several different exposure areas. In yellow safelight illumination, open the package of projection paper, remove one sheet, and cut it into several strips, each about 1½″ to 2″ wide and 8″ long. Put all but one back into the paper package and close it to protect the paper from possible white light spills.

If your enlarger has a red safelight screen built into it, swing it into the light path and turn on the enlarger. Remove the white focusing paper from the easel (don't let the easel move) and position the paper test strip in the image area so it will record the most important areas of the subject. The red light image will be dim and hard to see, but you should be able to discern the image details well enough. Be sure the emulsion side of the paper is facing up. Turn out the enlarger light and swing the red screen out of the way.

The simplest way to make the sample exposures is to start with some time increment that you're reasonably sure will be too short to be useful. Repeat this exposure several times, covering a section of the strip after each exposure so the step exposures vary progressively. For example, suppose you decide to use an exposure of 2 seconds. Expose the whole strip for 2 seconds, then cover about one-sixth of it and expose it for an additional 2 seconds. Cover another sixth of the strip and repeat the 2-second exposure. Repeat this operation until the whole strip has been exposed. The first step, or the initial exposure of the entire sheet, had a 2-second exposure; the second step had two 2-second exposures for a total of 4 seconds; the third step received three 2-second exposures for 6 seconds, etc. The steps, in other words, increase in 2-second increments.

Making a "fixed increment" test strip

Develop the test strip, just as you developed the proof sheet, for 2 minutes (or your own standard time), regardless of what it appears to be doing. Rinse it in the short-stop for 15 seconds or so and place it in the hypo. After a minute or so (check your paper package to be sure it's closed) turn on the white lights and inspect your results. If your exposure estimate was correct, you should see image details on all the steps; the 2-second step will be obviously too light in tone and the 12-second step too dark. One of the intermediate steps should be almost exactly right. If so, the test was successful. Determine the exposure of the satisfactory step and proceed to make a print. If not, try again, correcting the exposures.

This *fixed increment* method of test exposure is generally a quick and effective way to determine exposure if you have some idea what the exposure is going to be. It is not a very good method if the probable exposure is in doubt, because it doesn't sample a very great range of possibilities. There is a danger, too, that the visual interval between adjacent steps may become too subtle to be perceived. The 2-second interval between the 2-second and the 4-second exposure represents an exposure change of a full stop (doubled exposure), but

Figure 5.16
a. Geometric test strip.

b. Fixed increment test strip. The steps are practically invisible.

a

b

Geometric test strips are simple, but there's a little trick involved

the same 2-second interval between exposures of, say, 16 and 18 seconds is almost negligible. To be usefully visible, the steps should all be separated by similar *geometric* intervals; in other words, the exposures should be increased by multiplying, rather than by simply adding, a constant factor.

Geometric test strips are simple enough to make, but there is a little trick involved, so pay attention. Each exposure (after the first) should be equivalent to the *accumulated total* exposure. In other words, if we give the whole sheet a 2-second exposure, the accumulated total is 2. Cover about a sixth of the strip and give it an additional 2 seconds. Now the accumulated total is 4 (2 + 2). Cover another sixth of the strip and give it 4 seconds. The total now is 8 (2 + 2 + 4), so give it 8 seconds; then 16, then 32. The six exposures given (2, 2, 4, 8, 16, 32) have accumulated to yield steps of 2, 4, 8, 16, 32, and 64 seconds. Regardless of the actual exposure time used, each step will always double the previous one and the last step will be equal to twice the last exposure given.

After you've done it a few times, you will find this method of testing just as easy as adding a fixed increment repeatedly, and it will be more useful for unknown or unusual exposure situations. The fixed increment method will be best for subtle adjustments of exposure, once you get the general range. Use either one, but learn how to use both of them.

Figure 5.17
First print: 16 seconds, #2 filter.

Adjust print density by varying exposure time; adjust contrast by changing paper grades or filters

Changes in print density or darkness are easy to make by varying the exposure time. Contrast adjustment is made by changing paper grades or, in the case of variable-contrast papers, filters. In either case it's a good idea to start with normal contrast and see what happens to the test image. If the test is harshly contrasty, displaying opaque blacks and bald whites without detail, the negative is much too contrasty for that paper grade and you should make a drastic change to a softer paper, which means a *lower* contrast number, like 1 or 0. If, on the other hand, the image turns out to be murky and gray without either black or white accent tones, it means that the negative is too *flat* (low contrast) for the paper and you should shift to a higher number, like 3, 4, or 5.

Changing paper grades or filters will probably change the exposure time at least slightly, so it will be wise for you to make another test strip, varying the exposures around the best test exposure on the normal paper. Check this test for both density and contrast, and if either one is unsatisfactory, make another adjustment and test again. Remember that prints on most papers will appear to darken a little as they dry.

Again, DON'T vary developing time

When the test strip image seems good, make a full-size print on the selected grade of paper, using the best test exposure but no other controls. This test is to confirm the exposure and paper contrast decision and also to see how the image tones relate to each other and to the basic composition. Again, develop this print using your normal developing time, regardless of what it appears to be doing in the developer. If the density and contrast are satisfactory, examine the print carefully in good light to look for areas of undesirable local tone. Try to visualize how this image would look if certain dark areas were lightened slightly or certain highlighted areas were darkened for richer texture. Possibly whole sections of the image should be modified. The sky in a landscape, for example, might not record clouds that are apparent in the negative. Extra sky exposure should bring them out. On the other hand, your concept might call for a totally white sky; less exposure will then be required to eliminate all tone and texture. These changes call for selective exposure, controlled by dodging or burning the image under the enlarger.

Figure 5.18
Dodging and burning diagram

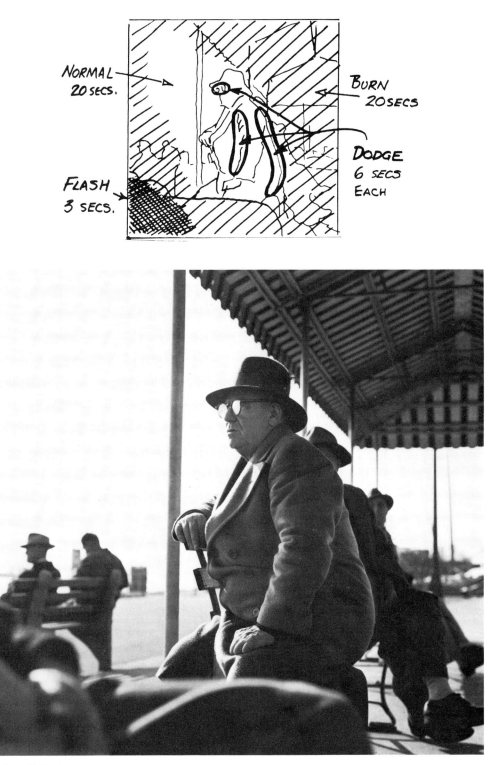

Figure 5.19
Final print 20 seconds, with dodging,
burning, and flashing as indicated in figure
5.18.

Figure 5.20

a. Polycontrast filter #1   b. Polycontrast filter #2

**Adjust tonal balance by dodging
or burning**

**Archival processing for increased print
longevity**

**Film-strength fixer for archival print
processing**

If the changes are extensive or elaborate, it will be wise to make separate test strips of the individual areas and make a little sketch of the image forms, labelling the areas you plan to modify, with the exposure times each should receive. The basic exposure will be the time appropriate for the largest area of the image. Areas that require less time will have to be *held back* or dodged for part of the time while the exposure is in progress. Then areas that require more time can be burned in by allowing beams of image light to fall on them through appropriately shaped holes cut in opaque cards. These techniques will require some practice but they are not particularly difficult if you work systematically. Beginners almost always fail to test and plan sufficiently before picking up their dodging tools and punching the timer button. Don't trust to luck this way or you'll waste a lot of time and paper and still not get good pictures.

Prints processed conventionally (as previously described) will probably last for many years without fading or discoloring, but they are not totally free from harmful chemicals and the silver image is not well protected from atmospheric contaminants, such as gaseous compounds of sulfur. *Archival processing* attempts to correct these problems as completely as possible by more efficient fixing procedures, by better washing, and by protecting the silver image with some sort of coating or by converting it, wholly or partially, to a more stable material—a process called *toning.*

The procedure is not basically different from the normal one but there is greater emphasis on the use of fresh chemicals, control of times and temperatures, general cleanliness, and avoidance of contamination. There are also a few extra steps in the process.

The developer and short-stop baths need not be altered but the chemicals themselves should be renewed more frequently than usual to avoid possible staining or contamination. It is important to develop the image fully; the usual 2 minutes is adequate (in Dektol, at least). Short-stop treatment should be sufficient to neutralize the developer alkali; 30 seconds is adequate with agitation. Make the prints a little lighter than normal. They will darken after they've been toned in either selenium or gold (most other toners will lighten the image, however). The two-bath fixer should be used but Kodak's 200-print cycles seem excessive; my recommendation would be to limit each bath to one hundred 8″ × 10″ prints per gallon for archival purposes.

An alternative fixing procedure is recommended by Ilford: fix prints for 30 seconds (some papers, such as Portriga Rapid, will require longer) with constant agitation in film-strength rapid-fix. Then treat with hypo-clearing solution and wash thoroughly—20 minutes or more—in running water, with frequent agitation. This treatment is said to reduce the necessary wash time and results in cleaner prints than can be produced by conventional methods. If you try it, be sure to use fresh fixer and fix one print at a time. Save the used fixer for later treatment of films. After fixing, Kodak recommends placing the prints directly into a normal-strength solution of Kodak hypo-clearing agent (prepared according to package instructions) to which Kodak Rapid Selenium Toner concentrate has been added at the rate of 2 ounces of toner per gallon of clearing bath. Agitate single-weight prints in this solution for at least 2

c. Polycontrast filter #3   d. Polycontrast filter #4

minutes (3 minutes for double-weight prints), then wash for 20 minutes in running water with frequent periods of agitation to insure good water circulation. Dry the prints on clean screens after sponging them to remove surface moisture.

For longest print life, hypo eliminator

Prints treated this way should last for a very long time under good storage conditions but they may still contain traces of dangerous sulfur compounds. Their life expectancy can be improved if they are given an additional hypo-elimination treatment and a final 10-minute wash. The formula for Kodak's hypo-eliminator, HE-1, is given in appendix 4.

Some photographers object to the use of a combined hypo-clearing and toning bath because the degree of toning is not very controllable and the selenium toner produces a rather sickly purple-brown color on some papers.

Toning protects the print image

If you want the protection that selenium toning can provide, without the excessive color change, use plain hypo-clearing bath and then treat the prints in a separate toning bath, made by adding one part of selenium toner concentrate to 20 or 30 parts of water. Some photographers prefer to dilute the toner concentrate with more clearing bath or with about a 2% solution of Kodalk (sodium metaborate). Suit yourself. Tone until you see some deepening of the dark tones; then re-treat the print in hypo-clearing solution, wash it thoroughly, and dry it on a screen. An excellent alternative procedure, using gold rather than selenium as the protective toner, follows.

Develop and fix the prints as described above, then rinse them briefly and treat them in any good hypo-clearing bath, following package instructions. Wash them also, as instructed. Then treat the prints, one at a time, in the hypo-eliminator bath (HE-1) with gentle agitation for six minutes at not more than 20°C. Handle the prints very gently in this and following operations, because the gelatin emulsion will become very soft in the HE-1 bath. Then wash the prints in running water for 10 minutes at not more than 20°C, and treat them, one at a time, in the gold protective solution given in appendix 4.

Some toners intensify the print blacks

Toning proceeds slowly at the recommended 20°C but the temperature should not be raised. Keep the print immersed in the solution with gentle agitation. Because of the subtlety of the color change, it is difficult to tell when toning has proceeded far enough. It will help a great deal to have an identical print, untoned, in a tray of plain water beside the toning bath so you can compare the images. The first visible effect of the toner (either gold or selenium) is a slight intensification of the deep blacks of the image. The print should be removed from the toner after this intensification occurs but before there is an obvious change in image color.

Toning may continue in the wash; don't overdo it

The toning action will continue for a little while in the wash tray, so don't overdo it. Gold-toned prints that have been treated too long will look distinctly bluish after they've dried. This is no problem if you like the effect, but it may come as a surprise to you if you are not familiar with the process. Wash the toned prints for at least 10 minutes in running water, sponge them surface-dry (gently!), and lay them out facedown on clean screens or cloth to air-dry. Don't use screens if the dry prints show any sign of the screen mesh texture; resoak the prints thoroughly and dry them on clean, lintfree cloth.

Post-Development Controls

Reducing

Occasionally the normal dodging and burning techniques are not adequate to adjust the image values to your complete satisfaction. Very small image areas, like highlights, or areas of unusual shape or sharp outline, are almost impossible to control during the print exposure. Occasionally, too, a print that looked great in the wash tray will *dry down* (look too dark when dry). Post-development chemical treatment may be helpful in these cases.

Farmer's reducer will lighten the image

Usually it isn't feasible to *intensify* (darken) a print image area, but *reducing* (lightening) an area of tone is relatively easy. There are several chemical solutions that can be used for this purpose but Farmer's reducer (formula in appendix 4) is one of the best and most reliable. Farmer's reducer is made from potassium ferricyanide and hypo, and it works in a kind of two-stage process. The ferricyanide converts the silver image back into a compound that is both light-sensitive and soluble in hypo, and the hypo dissolves it away in the normal fixing action. The solutions can be used separately, if desired, but the action of the ferricyanide alone is difficult to appraise. It's better, in my opinion, to use the combined solution.

The reducer must be fresh. Its useful life is fairly short once the ingredients have been combined but the separate solutions will keep indefinitely if protected from strong light and air.

Try it on a scrap print first

For use on prints the reducer should be diluted with water for slower, more controllable action. It's a good idea to try it on a scrap print first before attacking a choice one. Reduction is effective for prints that have turned out to be a little too dark overall. Soak the print in plain water for several minutes to soften it, then slip it into a tray of reducer that has been suitably diluted, and agitate it vigorously until it shows some signs of change. Get it out of the reducer and flood it with running water *before* it reaches the desired lightness. A print can always be given more treatment in the solution, but a too-light image can't be restored. Since the reducer contains hypo, follow it with a rinse, then the hypo-clearing agent, and the usual washing procedure.

Work slowly and rinse the print frequently

It's quite possible to reduce the image locally, too. Soak the print first, then flatten it out on the bottom of an inverted tray or a sheet of glass or plastic. Prop it up at a slight angle in the sink, close to a source of running water, and wipe the emulsion surface-dry with the edge of your hand or a dampened sponge. Saturate a ball of cotton or a small sponge in moderately strong reducer and squeeze it quite dry. It must not drip when handled. Rub the area of the image to be lightened with the cotton, using a random pattern of strokes and covering the entire area as quickly and uniformly as possible. Be very careful not to let drops of reducer stand on the emulsion surface for more than a second or two at most. Then, at the first sign of change, flood the print surface with water and inspect the result.

The change in image density should be barely perceptible and the treated area should be free from mottle, streaks, or spots. If there are signs of uneven reduction, it may be due to poor technique. Perhaps the cotton dripped reducer, perhaps it was too small to cover the area uniformly, or perhaps you missed part of the area. It could have also resulted from a too-strong mixture of reducer. If the problem is not too severe, further treatment may resolve it. Otherwise you may have to make another print. Be careful.

If the reducer is the right strength and your technique is good, it should take three or four cycles of wiping, reducing, and flooding to complete the job. But when completed, the area should be improved in value without obvious flaws. Be careful of light-toned areas or areas that contain light accents. The reducer will etch through light grays very quickly leaving yellowish white paper.

Don't use metal utensils with Farmer's reducer

There may be tiny areas of the image that need lightening. These can be treated in similar fashion but the reducer should be applied with a cotton swab (Q-tip) or a brush. Be very careful if you use a brush with a metal ferrule. The ferricyanide reacts with some metals to form a very intense and permanent blue dye (Prussian blue) which may stain the print and is very difficult to remove. For this same reason, Farmer's reducer should never be mixed, stored, or used in a metal container or in a chipped enamelled iron container.

Bleaching

For some purposes it is useful to remove the silver image from the emulsion entirely, which can be done with any of several *bleaches*. One of the best for this purpose is composed of potassium permanganate and acid (formula given in appendix 4). Although the solution itself is not dangerous to handle, the concentrated acid is. Be very careful and prepare the solution near a source of running water so you can flood the acid off your skin if it happens to splash or spill. The permanganate bleach must be mixed fresh and used within a few minutes. It spoils quickly, whether used or not. It is best for removing large areas of the image, either by careful local application with a swab or by immersing the print in the solution. Portions of the image that you wish to preserve can be protected with a brushed-on layer of Maskoid or thinned rubber cement.

The bleach works quickly and will stain the paper reddish brown. Remove the print from the solution when the image shows no further traces of black and then wash it in running water until the water runs clear, without any obvious pink stain. Then immerse the print in ordinary fixer or a nonhardening fixer (preferably), where the brownish-red stain and remains of the image will both disappear, leaving the paper pure white. Treat the print in hypo-clearing bath and wash it as usual.

Tincture of iodine is an effective bleach

Small areas of the image, and especially the occasional black blemishes that occur, can be bleached more conveniently with an iodine solution. Ordinary tincture of iodine, available at any drugstore, is effective. Using a toothpick or match stick, deposit a drop of iodine solution on the spot and allow it to stand for a minute or so. Then pick it up carefully with the tip of a moistened blotter or a wisp of tissue and inspect the spot. Occasionally the iodine will penetrate the paper, producing a bright blue stain in the paper itself. Don't worry about it. If any trace of black or gray remains, treat it again with iodine. The spot will be heavily stained with brown but, when the blackish appearance is gone, deposit a heaping drop of fixer on the spot and both the stains and the image should disappear. A second application of (or total immersion in) fixer may be required to complete the action. The bleached area should be pure white, without any tinge of stain. Treat the print with hypo-clearing bath and wash as usual.

If your first attempt is not completely successful and some silver remains in the bleached area after treatment with the hypo, you will have to rinse the area thoroughly to remove the hypo before it can be treated with iodine again. Iodine will not work if there is much hypo present in the emulsion.

Spotting

Spotting will take practice

Almost every print will have a few image flaws that will have to be corrected before it is fit to exhibit. Dust or abrasions on the negative will show in the print as white spots or lines, and scratches or cuts in the negative emulsion will probably show as black marks. Bleaching the black marks will make them white marks, and white marks will have to be *spotted*.

There are spotting colors and spotting dyes. The dyes are better for prints that are to be exhibited because they are invisible on the print surface. Spotting colors are really pigments that lie on the emulsion surface and are distractingly obvious. They are fine, though, for prints that are to be reproduced.

Tiny brushes make spotting more difficult than it has to be

Spotting will take practice and you'll need to experiment to find the method that works best for you. Provide yourself with a bottle of neutral spotting dye (Spotone is one brand), a small container for water, a white saucer or plastic palette for mixing dye, some facial tissues or paper towels, and a good red sable watercolor brush about size #4. Most authorities recommend much smaller brushes, like #00 or even #0000, but I can't believe they're serious. If you get a #4 sable that forms a good point (test it in the store before you buy it), it will make as delicate a mark as any smaller brush. Furthermore, because it holds a great deal more dye mixture, it will allow you to spot faster, longer, and more consistently, which will result in a superior job. Small brushes dry out very rapidly as you work and the dye changes tone and consistency. Spotting is tough enough when everything is working right; don't make it any more difficult than it has to be.

Figure 5.21
a. Saturate the brush in the appropriate
dye mixture and stroke it almost dry on
tissue. Rotate it as you stroke, to keep the
point well formed.

b. Greatly magnified view of a lint mark on
a medium gray area of a moderately grainy
image. Notice how fine the brush point is.
A smaller brush will form no better point
and will dry out much sooner, shifting the
dye color and laying dry dye on the print
surface.

c. Here the lint mark is partly spotted. Use
a stipple stroke to match the grain texture
and break the line into sections first, to
avoid the possibility of simply reinforcing
the linear appearance if your technique is
not perfect.

Practice for a while on spoiled prints

Practice for a while on spoiled prints. The easiest spots to deal with are
dust spots on a grainy image in an area of medium-light tone. The most difficult
spots to eliminate are fine, sharp white lines on black areas. After you've labored
over one of these, you'll learn to clean your negatives before you print them.

Place the dry print in good light, flat on either a table or a slightly tilted
surface, and arrange your equipment around it conveniently. Dip the brush into
the dye and deposit a brushful on the saucer, dividing it into three or four
separate puddles. Then dip the brush into the water and, without rinsing it,
deposit several blobs of "dirty" water on the saucer. Now stroke the brush on
the tissues, holding the handle low and pulling it across the tissue surface so

the brush hairs are straightened and brought to a point. Rotating the handle in your fingers as you stroke will help to form the fine point you need. Continue stroking the tissue until the brush leaves only a faint line of moisture and appears to be surface-dry. It now contains a light-toned dye mixture, suitable for use on a light gray image area.

Stroke the brush on tissue until surface-dry

Holding the brush almost vertically, bring the tip hairs into contact with the white margin of the practice print and draw a thin line. Notice that the dye color is pale when the brush moves rapidly and becomes darker when the brush moves slowly. Also, notice that going over the line twice darkens the color. Practice brush control by making thin lines in various directions, and try stippling an area of the practice print image with tiny dots. Be careful not to bear down on the brush; just use the tip hairs. You'll probably find that little stroking motions, which make little apostrophe-shaped marks, are easier to control than poking motions, which will tend to split the brush tip. Most spotting will require a gradual build-up of tone. Practice a blended-dot technique and avoid long linear strokes when working on a good print.

The dye will gradually get darker

After two or three minutes you will notice that the dye marks are getting darker and that they have a granular appearance (this will happen much sooner with a small brush). The brush is too dry. Stop and recharge it with dye. *Don't* simply touch the tip to a dye puddle, blend the dye and water on the palette to the desired tint, then saturate the brush with the mixture and stroke it dry on tissue. Failure to do this will result in uncertain dye color and improper wetting, and you'll regret it. Practice until you feel confident, then charge the brush with a very light tint and tackle a good print, beginning with the lightest areas.

RC papers will spot a little easier if the dye mixture contains a little acid and some wetting agent. Add one drop of Photoflo and one drop of plain 28% acetic acid (*not* indicator short-stop) to about 2 ounces of water. Work slowly on RC prints; because they're less absorbent than paper prints they take the dye much less readily at first. They can be spotted effectively, though, if you're patient with them.

Spotting is NOT like painting

Beginners have a lot of trouble with dye spotting because they think of it as painting and assume that the dye is being deposited on the surface like pigment. Wrong! The dye is *absorbed* by the gelatin and will only work well if it is applied in the right consistency, neither too wet nor too dry. If too wet, it will be hard to control and leave visible liquid traces on the print surface; if too dry, it will not take easily and will look coarse and ragged on the surface of the print, like pigment. It will also wipe off. When the dye is right it flows into the gelatin without a visible surface trace and simply becomes part of the image tone. It won't do this for you at first, but it will if you practice.

Work carefully; mistakes are hard to correct

The neutral dye color may not match the image color of your paper. Other colors of dye are available and you can blend them to match just about any image color that a black-and-white paper can be made to produce. Be careful not to work too dark too soon. The dye will naturally darken in the brush as you progress toward the darker print tones. If you make a mistake and overdo it, the dye can be lightened, but rarely removed completely, by rewashing the print. Try soaking it in a weak solution of sodium carbonate or water to which a few drops of ammonia have been added. Be careful; this treatment will soften the gelatin somewhat.

When you are through spotting, rinse the brush thoroughly in clear water and shake it dry. Form the hairs into a perfect point. It may be necessary to dampen them again slightly to get them to hold together. Then store the brush in some location where it will not be deformed and where it will be protected from dust and dirt. Use this brush only for print spotting and preferably only for dyes. Pigments will eventually grind off the fine tip hairs that form the delicate point you need. For long-term storage, wrap the brush in a paper cylinder and seal it; moths love red sable hair.

Mounting and Matting Prints

Mounting and Matting Prints

There are several ways to mount prints

Prints to be exhibited should be mounted in some way to hold them flat and to give them some body. There are several ways to do this. There are spray adhesives, liquid adhesives, adhesive sheets that can be stuck on the back of the print, and various thermoplastic adhesive sheets. Of these, the thermoplastic materials are best, in my opinion, at least for fiber-based papers. Adhesive sheets are fine for RC prints. The thermoplastic sheets are universally referred to as *dry-mount tissue.*

Thermo-plastic sheets are best for permanent mounting

Dry-mount tissue becomes adhesive when it's heated and sets as it cools. In normal use, a sheet of tissue is stuck to the back of the print with a light stroke of an electrically heated *tacking iron.* Then a loose corner of the tissue is similarly stuck to the mounting board to hold the print in position. Finally, print, tissue, and board, protected from surface damage by a heavy paper or card-stock cover sheet, are all inserted into a heated *dry-mounting press* and held under pressure for several seconds, during which time the tissue softens and cements the print firmly to the mount board. After cooling for a minute or two, the bond is complete and virtually permanent.

Too much press heat will damage RC papers

Fiber-based prints can tolerate more heat than RC papers or color prints can, so it's important that you use the right materials and set the press at the correct temperature for the kind of prints you're mounting. Press thermostats are not accurately calibrated, but for fiber-based papers the proper heat is about 250°F (121°C) and about 190°F (88°C) for RC papers and color prints. If you're using a press for the first time, with RC paper, try a spoiled print before you commit a good one. If the temperature is too low, the mounting tissue will not stick well; if the press is too hot, your print may be damaged. For best accuracy you can calibrate your press thermostat using Temperature Indicator Strips, manufactured by Seal, Inc., and available through photo stores.

Other than temperature control there are three features of the dry-mounting process that may give you trouble if you're not careful. Prints may not stick to the mount well if either the mount board or the foam-rubber press pad is damp. If the press platen (the flat metal plate that presses down on the print) is dirty, the print surface may be embossed or indented. If dirt particles are trapped between the print and the mount board, they will surely show on the print surface as little pimples.

DON'T use the press to dry prints!

The dampness problem is cured by heating the press in the closed position so the press pad is warmed thoroughly, and then opening it from time to time so any moisture can evaporate. Dry out the mounting board the same way; alternately heat it and air it until it feels reasonably dry when it is first removed from the press. Dampness will probably not be a problem in the wintertime when humidity is low, unless in a community darkroom situation, someone has thoughtlessly used the press to dry some wet prints (a *thoroughly* antisocial thing to do!).

A community-used press is also likely to acquire a dirty platen; therefore, you should check it every time you use the press. The most common problem results from fragments of dry-mount tissue that adhere to the metal. They should never touch the platen in the first place because you should *always* cover the print with a clean paper cover sheet before closing the press. RC papers and color prints should be covered with special silicone-treated paper (available from photo stores) which will not stick to the prints even if they soften excessively from a too-high press temperature. Don't *ever* mount a print without using a cover sheet.

Always use a cover sheet

A dirty platen surface is very difficult to clean, but if the material is not baked on too thoroughly, it may dissolve in alcohol or ethylene dichloride or some similar solvent. Use these solvents with great care to avoid breathing the fumes; they are very toxic. If you must resort to using one of them, take the press outside and work upwind of it. If the material is insolubly charred, it will probably have to be polished off, but this is a last resort. Use fine steel wool (#000 or #0000) and rub the whole platen surface lightly, concentrating on the

Figure 5.22
Drying press pad

dirty spots. When the surface seems clean, wash it thoroughly and dry it. A spray coat of silicone lubricant, rubbed dry, will help protect it from future abuse.

High-temperature dry-mount tissues (for fiber-based prints) and most low-temperature tissues (for RC and color prints) are paper-based. To repeat, a sheet of either of these materials is attached to the print by laying the tissue sheet on the back of the print and stroking it lightly (to avoid marring the print) near the center with the flat surface of the hot tacking iron. Then, any tissue that extends beyond the print edges must be trimmed off to protect the press and to prevent the print from sticking to the cover sheet. If the print is to be *flush-mounted* or *bleed-mounted* (trimmed without borders), the tissue can be tacked to the mount board; just raise a corner of the print out of the way so you can touch the tissue directly with the tacking iron. After heating in the press, the print and mount can be trimmed to size, preferably with a mat-knife and straightedge.

Mounting prints without borders

A print trimmed flush will probably look a little untidy until the cut edges have been smoothed. Using fine sandpaper (200 grit or so) and a small block, sand the edges on both faces of the print, stroking away from the image area to avoid flaking the emulsion. When the edges are nicely smoothed and rounded, rub them with paraffin or a china-marking pencil (black or white) and polish the edges with a folded facial tissue. After this treatment, people will enjoy handling your prints whether they like your images or not!

If the print is to be trimmed without borders but is to be mounted in some specific location on a large board, the tissue should be tacked to the back of the print before they are trimmed together to the final image dimensions. Then, hold the print in position, and while lifting a corner of the print only, tack the tissue to the mount. Protect the assembly with a cover sheet and clamp it in the press. The time required to complete the bond will have to be found by experimentation but somewhere around 15 to 30 seconds is a good place to start. Heavy mount board or a heavy-weight cover sheet will necessitate longer-than-normal times.

Insufficient time in the press or too-low temperature will produce a weak bond and the print may pop off the mount or loosen if the board is bent or twisted. Sometimes it's possible to lift a corner of the poorly mounted print and strip it partly or completely off the board. Reheating in the press at a higher temperature or for a longer time generally cures this problem. Overheating is rare with fiber-based papers. Overheated RC papers or color prints may be warped or their surfaces marred. There is no cure.

Figure 5.23
a. Lay the print facedown on a clean
surface and attach a sheet of dry-mount
tissue to it with a light touch of the hot
tacking iron. Tack it in only one spot,
preferably near center.

b. Trim off any tissue that extends beyond
the edges of the print. It's easiest to do
this if you take a narrow strip of the print
margin with the tissue but be careful not to
cut into the image area. The mat-knife and
straightedge technique shown here is
generally more satisfactory than using a
print trimming board or paper cutter. When
using a mat-knife, *always* keep a sheet of
heavy cardboard under the work to serve
as a cutting surface. *Never* cut on an
unprotected tabletop or desktop.

c. Lift a corner of the print and tack the
tissue to the mount board. Again, tack the
tissue in only one spot to avoid creating
folds or wrinkles in the tissue when it's
pressed. The tissue which overhangs the
mount board (right corner in the
illustration) will have to be trimmed off
before the board can be put into the
press; otherwise it will stick to the press
pad and make a mess.

d. Cover the face of the print with a clean cover sheet and slip it into the press. Time and temperature will depend on the type of paper in use and the mat board weight. See the text for details.

e. Trim the mounted print to finished size with mat-knife and straightedge. You can use a plastic triangle to keep the corners square and protect the print surface, as is shown here, but don't use it as a cutting guide; the plastic nicks easily.

f. Smooth the edges of the trimmed print on both faces with fine sandpaper and a block. Stroke away from the print face to avoid chipping the edge of the image gelatin. Then wax the smoothed edges and polish them with tissue. You can use wax crayons if you want toned borders; paraffin will finish the edges without leaving any visible trace.

Figure 5.24

a. If you want your print mounted with borders, but not matted, you'll have to trim it to finished size and place it carefully on the mount board. The actual procedure will depend on the mounting technique used, but in any case you'll have to determine the image dimensions and mark the print position carefully and lightly on the mount board face. Use soft pencil and light pressure so the marks can be erased.

b. If you plan to dry-mount the print, attach the tissue and trim both print and tissue to finished size. An alternative dry-mounting method, using Scotch brand adhesive sheets #567, is shown here. Lay the adhesive sheet dull-side down on a clean surface and carefully peel back the adhesive tissue from the release paper. Lay the print facedown on the release paper.

c. Lay the tissue back down to cover the print and squeegee firmly to attach the tissue to the back of the print.

d. Lift a corner of the adhesive backing paper and slowly peel it away from the print. The adhesive film adheres to the print back as it leaves the backing paper. It is self-trimming.

e. The print will stick to your fingers now but it can be moved around on the board without adhering. Position it carefully on the guide marks and press it down lightly with your fingers.

f. Now cover the print with a clean paper, preferably a silicone-release paper, and squeegee firmly. This pressure bonds the print securely to the board.

g. If traces of the adhesive show around the print edges, they can be removed easily with a rubber cement lifter or a kneaded eraser. This mounting adhesive is claimed to be safe for photographs, long lasting, and nonstaining. Prints can be removed from the mounts, if necessary, with rubber cement thinner.

a

b

c

d

e

f

g

Figure 5.25

a. Tack a piece of dry-mount tissue to the back of the print, then trim off any tissue which extends beyond the edges of the print. A print to be matted should not be trimmed to exact size before mounting but final image dimensions must be known. Determine the composition with L-shaped cardboard strips (cropping Ls) laid over the print. Then measure the image dimensions and jot them down.

b. Determine the mat and mount board size by adding the desired margin widths to the print dimensions. Cut the mount board very slightly smaller than the mat so the mat will cover it completely. Mark the image corner positions on the front of the mat board. Some mat boards will not tolerate erasure so make the marks as light and inconspicuous as possible.

c. Using a metal straightedge as a guide, cut the mat opening with a sharp mat-knife or utility knife. Always cut on the "waste" side of the straightedge so, if the knife wanders off line, it won't damage the mat itself. Cut just past the corner marks so the mat corners will be clean and free from tufts of uncut fibers.

d. Place the print on the mount board; place the mat board over it; and align the mat and mount boards carefully. Then slide the print into satisfactory position in the mat opening. Check to be sure the boards are still in exact alignment.

e. Holding the print in position on the mount, lift the mat carefully and, lifting a corner of the print, tack a corner of the dry-mount tissue to the mount board.

a

b

c

d

e

f. Protecting the print face with a cover sheet, insert the mount board into the press and heat the print to bond it to the board.

g. Align the top edges of the mount and mat boards; the mount board should be faceup, the mat board facedown. Tape the intersection together to form a hinge. Use fabric library tape for archival quality prints; plastic or paper tape for temporary use. Ordinary masking tape is not desirable; it will dry out and discolor with age and may damage the print itself if it comes into contact with it. You can, of course, dry-mount or glue the mount and mat together permanently, if you want to.

h. The finished print is neatly presented. Select mat boards in any color or texture that pleases you.

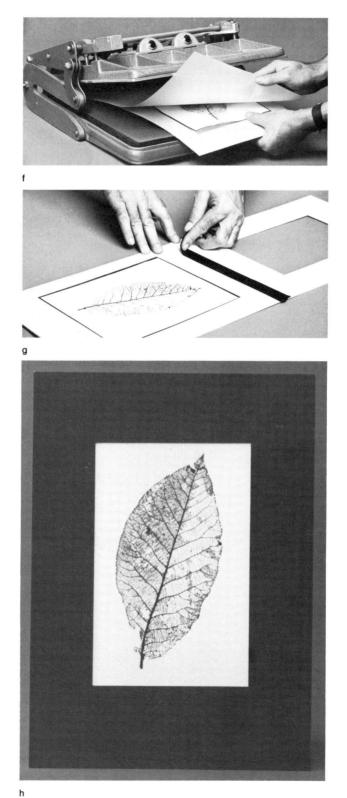

f

g

h

Figure 5.26

a. Cutting bevelled mats is not much different from cutting ordinary ones but a special mat-cutter makes the job easier. Here's one method, using the familiar and relatively inexpensive Dexter mat-cutter. Determine the mat opening dimensions and mark them on the *back of* the mat board. You can be bold with these lines and draw them well past the corners.

b. Place the mat board, facedown, on a sheet of expendable cardboard to serve as a cutting surface, and align both boards with the edge of your work table or drawing board. This allows you to use a metal T-square, both to keep the lines straight and to use as a cutting guide. The T-square is much easier to hold steady than an ordinary straightedge. Align the edge of the mat-cutter with the drawn border line and insert the knife point just behind the cross line, as shown. Press it down firmly.

c. Slide the T-square over to the cutter and allow it to square the cutter if it's slightly out of line. Check the board alignment again to be sure it is snug against the "T" of the T-square.

d. The Dexter mat-cutter is a strictly right-handed instrument. Place your hand on it naturally and, holding the T-square down firmly, push the cutter along the metal guide. If the knife blade is in good shape it should cut cleanly and easily without any tendency to wander away from the guide. Cut about ⅛-inch past the cross line to insure a clean corner. One authority suggests pinning the mat board down to help hold it in place—a good idea. Use a couple of pushpins in the waste center area of the board.

e. A finished mat corner.

f. Align mat and mount boards, as previously described, and center the print in the mat opening.

a

b

c

d

e

f

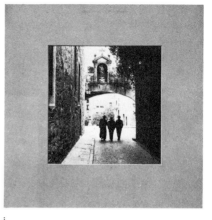

g   h   i

g. There are several ways to make paper corners for archival print mounting. This is the one I prefer. Simply fold narrow strips of acid-free paper as shown and fasten them in place with strips of linen tape. I recommend *museum barrier* paper if you can find it (some art supply stores carry it). It's safe and substantial enough to make corners that will support prints of any size.

h. Some people like to use gummed art corners for mounting. If you want to try this method, it's helpful to hinge the mat and mount boards before positioning the print. Then hold the print in position and open the mat. Moisten the gummed backs of the art corners, one at a time, slip them over the print corners and press them down firmly. They stick almost immediately. You can lick them if you like, but I suggest using a dampened sponge (the glue tastes terrible).

i. Art corners are fine for small prints and especially for RC paper, which lies quite flat. Large prints may need more support if you want them to stay in place without bulging or warping as the weather changes.

Place the straightedge so that it protects the margins

Although dry-mounting is considered to be archivally safe and is generally tolerated by collectors and museums, it's better practice to print your finest images on double-weight paper, displaying wide white borders. Mount the prints with "corners" made from tissue or *museum barrier paper,* held in place with linen tape. Then it's easy to remove the print for archival storage or for installation in a different mat or frame. You can buy gummed "art corners" for mounting small prints, but they are neither large enough nor archivally safe enough to be suitable for formal presentation of your best work. The choice is yours. If you plan to mat a print, whether it will be framed or not, first decide the exact dimensions of the image area by establishing the outlines of the image with cropping Ls and measuring the composition boundaries. Then decide on the width of the mat borders. It is conventional, but certainly not obligatory, to make the side margins equal, the top margin equal to or slightly wider than the side margins, and the bottom margin slightly wider than the top. The best guide is visual. Lay strips of paper or mat board around the print to simulate the finished mat and look at it critically. Then pick border proportions that seem most attractive.

Determine the size of the mat board by adding the print width dimension to the width of *both* side margins of the mat. Similarly, add the print image height dimension to the combined widths of the top and bottom mat margins. Cut a piece of mat board to these dimensions, being careful to keep the corners square and neat.

If you want the mat opening to have ordinary square edges, draw a very light outline shape of the image area, in exact position, on the *face* of the mat board, using pencil, T-square, and triangle. Lay the mat board faceup on a sheet of clean, smooth cardboard, and using a metal straightedge and mat knife, cut the mat opening by following the lightly pencilled image outline. If you prefer a bevelled mat opening, draw the image outline on the *back* of the mat board. Lay the mat board *facedown* on clean, smooth cardboard and use a mat-cutter with an angled blade to cut the mat opening.

Regardless of the tools you use, always place the straightedge guide on the mat so it covers and protects the margins. Then, if the knife should slip, it will simply wander off into the unwanted center of the board. Always use a sharp blade and cut slightly past the corners of the image area so the cut-out piece will fall out cleanly without leaving little fuzzy tufts of uncut fibers in the corners. It is important to have a firm, smooth surface, like cardboard, under the mat while cutting it. If the surface is rough or soft, the cut edges are likely

Synopsis

Print Processing Steps

1. In three clean trays prepare appropriate volumes of working solutions of print developer, short-stop, and print fixer, adjusted to about 20°C (68°F). If available, add a fourth tray of clean water and a fifth containing hypo-clearing bath, prepared according to manufacturer's instructions.
   No white lights: Safelight color, yellow (series OC or equivalent)
2. *Developer:* Immerse exposed paper in developer and note the time. Agitate continuously, keeping prints submerged, for standard developing time (my recommendation: 2 minutes in Dektol, diluted 1:2 with water, for projection papers; 1 minute for Azo). Drain briefly from one corner and transfer to short-stop.
3. *Short-Stop:* Immerse prints in short-stop with continuous agitation for 15 to 30 seconds, then drain and transfer to fixer.
4. *Fixer:* Immerse prints in fresh fixer with continuous agitation for about 15 to 30 seconds and periodic agitation for 4 or 5 minutes more. Increase time as the fixer ages, but do not exceed about 10 minutes. *Note:* RC prints get 2 minutes in fresh fixer (to maximum of 5) with frequent agitation. Drain regular fiber-based prints and transfer to water rinse. RC prints go directly to wash tray.
5. *Rinse:* Agitate fiber-based prints in plain water for about a minute, then transfer to hypo-clearing bath. Change rinse water frequently or use running water rinse.
6. *Hypo-Clearing Bath:* Treat fiber-based prints according to manufacturer's instructions. *Note:* RC prints don't need hypo-clearing bath.
7. *Wash:* Wash fiber-based prints as directed by manufacturer of clearing bath. *Note:* Wash RC prints for 5 minutes in running water. Wash prints in batches; don't add unwashed prints to partially washed batch.
8. *Dry:* Sponge or squeegee the prints' surfaces dry, and lay out on plastic screens or clean cloth; fiber-based prints facedown, RC prints faceup. RC prints can also be dried by hanging them by corners with clothespins. Fiber-based prints can be ferrotyped on a heated drum dryer or on plastic sheets, or dried to a natural finish in blotter books or rolls.
9. *Cleanup:* Discard developer, short-stop, and clearing bath (unless manufacturer suggests saving it). Save fixer until it has treated about twenty-five 8″ × 10″ prints per quart or until it tests negative. Wash all utensils thoroughly and wash up chemical spills and traces on timers, switches, door handles, etc. Rinse off chemical storage bottles and store away. Return trays to rack. Wash your hands and dry them. Turn off the water and the lights.

Watch your fingers; blood is very difficult to remove from mat board

to be ragged and uneven. If the surface is too hard, like glass or metal, the knife point may become dulled or broken. This is particularly serious with a mat-cutter; if the blade tip is damaged, the mat edges will probably be ragged. Finally, be careful. Stay in control and watch your fingers; blood is very difficult to remove from mat board.

When the mat is ready, brush the back of the print to remove dirt particles. Then, if you want to mount the print permanently, tack a sheet of tissue to it, and trim off the excess. Cut a piece of mount board to the exact size of the mat board (or very slightly smaller) and lay the print on it faceup in the chosen location. Align the top edges of mat and mount boards and, holding them slightly apart, reach through the mat opening and position the print precisely in the mat opening. When it is correctly placed, reach under the mat board and hold the print in position while the mat is removed. Then lift a corner of the print and tack the tissue to the mount. Heat the board and print in the dry-mount press, protecting the surface with a cover sheet.

When the mat is placed over the mount board and the top edges are aligned, the image should be precisely framed by the mat opening. Tape the mount and mat together along their inside top edges or fasten them together in some other way. Look over the mat face carefully and remove any smudges or marks with an eraser (kneaded eraser or art gum for minor marks, Pink Pearl eraser for stubborn marks). If the print is to be framed under glass, be sure the inside dimensions of the frame are large enough to permit the mat to expand a little.

This is your reward for all those hours in the darkroom. If you handled the camera well and followed the various process steps effectively, you should have a print you can show with pride.

Summary

Printing is easiest in a darkroom equipped with a large sink, running water, electricity, good ventilation, and lots of storage space. In addition to the usual darkroom equipment and utensils, you'll need timers, safelights, and an enlarger. Enlargers come in several sizes and designs; condenser or diffusion systems are available with or without color heads.

Buy a good lens for your enlarger. You will also need an easel and you may want to buy a focusing aid or grain focuser. Other necessary or desirable equipment items include a proofing or printing frame, dodging tools, trays, a tray siphon, print tongs or paddles, print dryer or drying frames, dry-mount press and tacking iron, a print trimmer, and mount- and mat-cutting tools.

Fiber-based papers are still available in some surfaces and grades and are preferred for archival storage. Resin-coated papers are becoming more popular. They offer processing convenience but are not considered archival. Both types are available in a variety of sizes, weights, image tones, base tints, surfaces, and contrast grades. Some papers provide a variable-contrast characteristic, controllable by varying the color of the exposing light. Some papers are designed for stabilization processing.

Print developers are usually strong solutions, mixed and stored as stock solutions and diluted for use. The stop bath for papers is similar to that used for film, but paper fixer is usually less concentrated. Papers don't clear in the fixing bath. They should be treated carefully and not overfixed. For best results, use two fixing baths in sequence.

The temperature of processing solutions is not critical in printing, within reasonable limits, but try to standardize for consistent results.

You can use either contact or projection paper for proofing or contact printing. Working under safelight conditions, place the negatives on the paper surface, emulsion to emulsion, and hold them in position in a printing frame. Expose through the negatives under an appropriate light source. Develop for the standard time and follow the other process steps carefully. Fiber-based and RC papers require different washing and drying treatment; follow the separate instructions.

Select images to be enlarged by examining the contact proof sheet. Be sure your enlarger is properly adjusted for the negative size and clean the negative, lens, and carrier, if necessary. Under safelight conditions, adjust the image size and focus; then make a test strip. Image density can be adjusted by changes in print exposure; contrast is adjusted by changing paper grades or by filtering the enlarger light.

Make a full test print and decide what adjustments are necessary. Dodging, burning, and flashing techniques are helpful for refining tonal balance.

For archival permanence, prints can be given special fixing, hypo-eliminating, and washing treatment, and the image can be further protected by toning. Since this treatment tends to soften the print emulsion, handle the prints carefully.

Print tones can also be adjusted by chemical reduction. Farmer's reducer can be used to lighten the entire print image or to treat small areas selectively. Bleaches remove the image completely. Permanganate bleach is recommended for large areas; iodine is effective for small areas. Bleached prints must be hypoed and washed thoroughly.

Spotting will remove small white blemishes in the print image. Use spotting dye and a fine-quality sable hair brush, and proceed carefully. Dyes can be blended to match almost any print image color and diluted to adjust the intensity of the tone.

Prints are usually mounted or matted for exhibition. Dry-mounting is one method; separate materials and press temperatures are required for fiber-based and RC papers. Dry out the mount board and the press pad. Always use a cover sheet over the print. Corner mounting is preferable for fine prints.

Mounted prints can be trimmed without borders, left with borders, or matted. Use cropping Ls to determine composition, then measure boards carefully and cut with mat knife and straightedge. Bevelled mats can be cut with a Dexter mat-cutter. Clean up the finished mat with art gum if necessary.

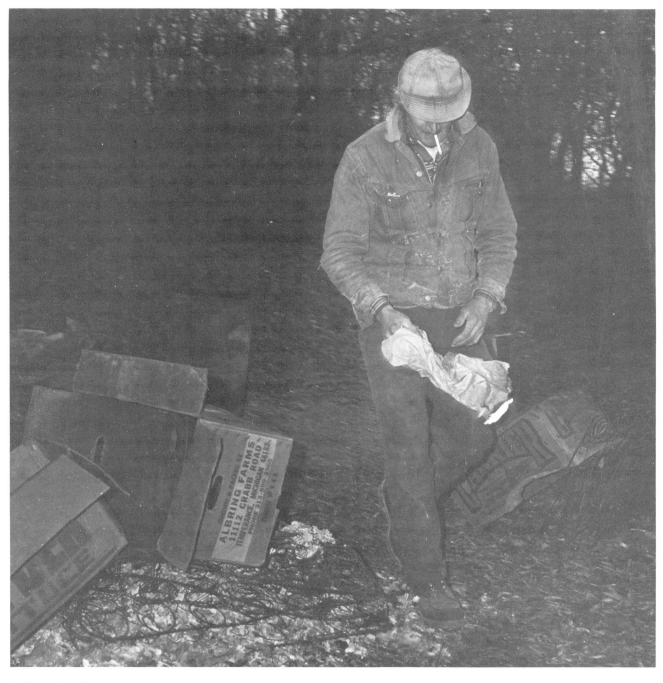

Untitled. Russ McKnight.
Using a small electronic flash, on camera,
McKnight has transformed this rather
ordinary situation—a man about to light a
trash fire—into a mysterious event. The
three light sources—fading cloudy
daylight, the weak flash, and the flaming
paper bag—are balanced to provide a
remarkable black-on-black composition in
which the brilliant flame and the man's
cigarette are dramatically emphasized.
(Courtesy of the photographer.)

Working with Light

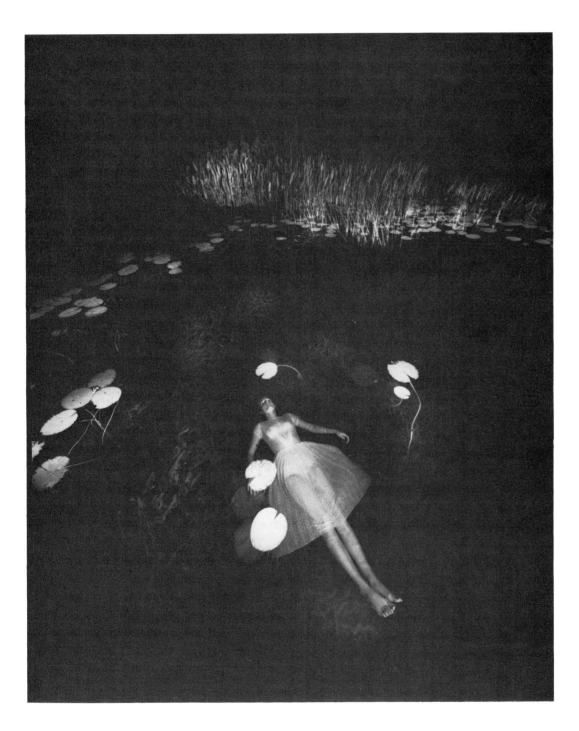

Outline

Artificial Light Sources
Using Flash
    Flashbulbs
    Electronic Flash Units
    Controlling Exposure
Fluorescent Light
Ultraviolet and Infrared
Principles of Lighting
    Characteristics of Light Quality
    Analysis and Control of Lighting Conditions
Available Light
Controlling Artificial Light

6

Artificial Light Sources

There are many different forms of artificial light

Sooner or later, at least some of your photographs will be taken in artificial light and, as you will discover, it exists in a great variety of forms. *Incandescent* light, the light produced by the hot tungsten filament of an ordinary light bulb, is common. So is *fluorescent* light. Occasionally you may have to cope with light from some *gas-discharge* source, like mercury-vapor or sodium vapor lamps which are often used for street lighting or industrial lighting. In the studio, tungsten-filament bulbs are universally used. Conventional flashbulbs are occasionally used, too, but electronic flash units are much more common.

One major difference is their color

One major difference between these various types of lights is in their color. Incandescent bulbs, including conventional flashbulbs, produce a *continuous* spectrum light, which implies that all the colors (wavelengths) of the spectrum are present in some amount. Gas-discharge bulbs, on the other hand, produce *discontinuous spectra,* from which certain light wavelengths are missing.

We use the term "color temperature" to describe light color

It is given in Kelvin degrees

The light produced by all incandescent bulbs is apparently orange in color (compared with daylight) but the actual color of the light is determined by the temperature of the glowing tungsten filament. If the bulb is designed for long life, as ordinary household lamps are, the filament burns at a relatively low temperature and its light is brownish and low in intensity. If the filament temperature is increased (as by raising the line voltage, for example), the light output is increased, the light contains more blue and appears "whiter." At this higher temperature the filament deteriorates faster, too, and the life of the lamp is considerably shortened. We frequently use the term *color temperature* to describe light color. The term refers to the color of the light radiated by a *black body* (a hypothetical, nonreflecting object) that has been heated to incandescence, and relates the light color to the actual temperature of the black body in degrees Kelvin (degrees Celsius above absolute zero). At the lowest temperature producing visible light, about 1000°K, the apparent color is a dull red. As the temperature is increased, the radiation increases in brightness and its color shifts gradually through orange and yellow toward an apparent white color. In theory, if the black body could be heated to about 6000° or 8000°K without vaporizing, its color would appear bluish white, becoming increasingly blue at still higher temperatures.

Professionals generally work with 3200° Kelvin bulbs

Incandescent bulbs intended for photographic use are designed to burn at either 3200° Kelvin or 3400°K. The 3200°K varieties are now the most common and are standard for professional work; 3400°K bulbs are brighter, but much shorter lived, and were originally intended for amateur use. Ordinary light bulbs, by comparison, burn at about 2700°K.

Incandescent bulbs give a slightly more blue light when they are new than they do after a few hours of burning time, and near the end of their lives, their light is comparatively brownish. Their light output decreases, too, as the burning filament metal is vaporized and deposited as a dirty film on the inside surface of the glass bulb. An improved bulb, which avoids these problems to a useful degree, is made of fused quartz, instead of glass, and is filled with a halogen vapor (bromine or iodine). During use the halogen gas prevents darkening of the quartz envelope and prolongs the filament life so the bulb burns at a more uniform color and intensity and has a longer useful life than a conventional

Untitled, 1976. Lorran Meares.
Lorran Meares assembles these haunting images by patiently painting selected areas of the subject with light and multiple-exposing with a stereo camera. Although they're intended to be seen in 3-dimensions for best effect, they're graphically strong and surreal in ordinary reproduction.
(Courtesy of the photographer.)

bulb does. Bulbs of this type were originally called *quartz-iodine* or *quartz-bromine* bulbs (quartz light) but they are now generally referred to as *tungsten halogen* or *halogen-cycle* bulbs. They are available in a wide variety of shapes and sizes and are generally much smaller, but more expensive, than conventional bulbs of the same wattage.

Clear flashbulbs burn at about 3800° Kelvin; blue ones at about 5500° Kelvin

Flashbulbs give a continuous spectrum light of relatively high color temperature (about 3800°K). Unlike more conventional incandescent lamps, however, they are designed to burn out almost instantaneously, producing a tremendous blast of light for a very brief period of time. Flashbulbs are valuable for work on location, where ordinary lights would be difficult or impossible to use, because they are easily carried, can be fired by small batteries, and produce a great amount of light for their size. Most of them now, including the popular flashcube, flipflash, and flashstrip units for amateur use, are covered during manufacture with a blue filter layer which raises their effective color temperature sufficiently to make them useful with daylight color film (approximately 5500°K).

Using Flash

Flashbulbs

Flashbulbs don't ignite instantaneously

Although the flash from a flashbulb seems to be instantaneous, it actually takes several milliseconds (thousandths of a second) for the light to reach useful intensity after the firing voltage is applied. This delay is typically from about 5 to about 15 ms (milliseconds) for M (medium peak) and FP (focal plane) bulbs, and about 20 to 25 ms for S (slow peak) bulbs. The useful flash duration for M bulbs is typically between 10 and 20 ms, and these bulbs produce a very high peak intensity. FP bulbs have an effective flash duration of 25 ms or more and, because they burn slower, produce a less intense light for the longer time. Type S bulbs are designed for maximum light output; they produce extremely high intensity at peak output and burn usefully for 20 ms or more. They are most effective when they are used in *open flash* technique; the camera shutter is opened on *Time* or *Bulb,* the flashbulb is fired manually, and the shutter is closed.

Open flash provides the greatest exposure

Open flash provides the maximum possible amount of light for the film exposure, but it is a clumsy way to work with a small camera. Usually, we use flash to permit instantaneous exposures in dim light so most flash pictures are taken with *synchronized flash,* which means that the shutter and the bulb are timed so the shutter is open only during the actual flash. Most cameras now are equipped with built-in synchronizers for this purpose; it is only necessary to plug the flash unit into the proper socket on the camera and set the synchronizer switch for the type of flashbulb in use. The camera will then fire the bulb at the right instant, so it will reach peak intensity while the shutter is open.

BTL shutters are easiest to synchronize at all speeds

Cameras equipped with between-the-lens leaf shutters are easiest to synchronize with flashbulbs because the flash will illuminate the full film area at any shutter speed if the timing is correct. M-type bulbs, with their short peak of high-intensity light, are best for use with BTL shutters. Focal plane shutters, especially the curtain types, open completely only at their slower speeds. At speeds above 1/60th second (1/125th for some metal blade shutters), the shutter exposes the film progressively through a relatively narrow opening. M-type bulbs may not burn long enough or evenly enough to expose the film fully and uniformly at these speeds, and it is safer to use FP bulbs (with the synchronizer set on FP) under these conditions.

Before using any sort of flashbulb with your SLR, you should check your instruction manual carefully for instructions. If you don't have a manual for your camera, or if the instructions are not clear, it will probably be safe for you to use M-type bulbs on the M setting (if the camera has one) at speeds up to 1/60th second or so.

Colorplate 5

Rainbow colors are caused by the refraction and dispersion of light by
raindrops.

Colorplate 6

Light primary colors blend additively, producing secondaries that are brighter and more pastel than the primaries themselves. Mixtures of the three primaries, in proper proportion, yield white.

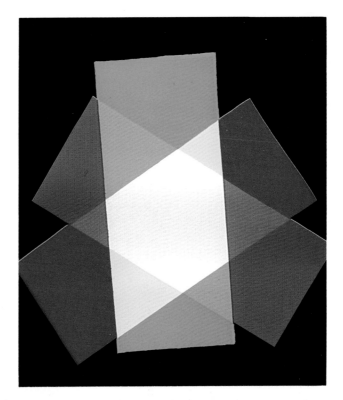

Colorplate 7

Pigment or dye primary colors are pure and bright. Their mixtures become less bright and more neutral, approaching black.

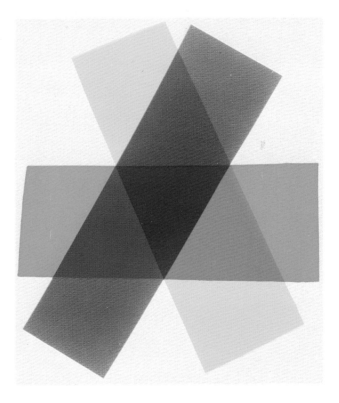

Colorplate 8

a. This photograph was taken without filtration.

b. A Polaroid filter was used to darken the sky in this photograph.

a

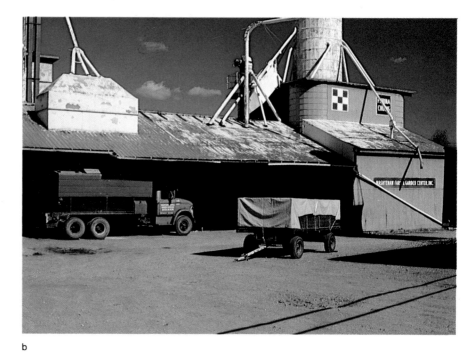

b

Colorplate 9

Mercury vapor streetlights appear greenish when compared to ordinary tungsten light. Filtration can't correct a situation like this.

Colorplate 10

a. Daylight color film, unfiltered in fluorescent light.
b. Filtered with special correction filter, FLD.

a

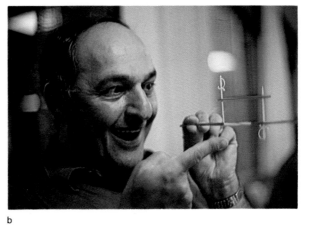

b

Figure 6.1
Camera synch controls

The X setting is intended for electronic flash

The X synchronizer setting is intended primarily for use with electronic flash. When set at X the synchronizer does not make firing contact until the shutter is fully open. If bulbs are used at the X setting, the shutter must remain open long enough to allow the bulb to kindle, flare up, and reach peak intensity—a minimum of perhaps 20 ms, or 1/50th second. Actually, because the useful flash persists for another 10 ms, or so, it is much better to use a shutter speed of 1/15th second or longer when M bulbs are fired at the X synch setting.

Electronic Flash Units

Electronic flash is very fast

Electronic flash units (frequently referred to as *strobes*) produce their light by passing a brief pulse of high voltage electric current through a glass or quartz tube filled with a mixture of gases, such as krypton, argon, and xenon. There is no firing delay of any consequence, so electronic flash units are always X synchronized. Typical small units for on-camera use usually provide an effective flash duration of about 1/500th second. Most of the more expensive and more powerful models contain *thyristor* circuits which can be set to quench the flash current automatically when sufficient light has been produced to make the exposure, or when reduced output is desirable. These flash units are capable of producing flashes of as little as 1/50,000th second duration, under some conditions.

Because of the very brief duration of the flash, electronic flash units synchronize easily at all speeds with BTL shutters, and with all speeds that provide a fully open shutter with focal plane types. In almost all cases the electronic flash duration determines the exposure time, and if there is no ambient illumination (light existing at the subject position), the effective exposure on the film is not affected at all by the camera shutter speed.

Flash and ambient light may combine to form "ghost" images

If there is any significant amount of ambient illumination, it will supplement the flash, and if the subject is moving, a double image or "ghost" image may be formed—one by the very brief pulse of the flash, the other by the longer exposure provided by the ambient light and slow shutter speed. This effect is particularly likely to occur with focal plane shutters because of their relatively low-speed X-synch, but it may occur at any speed if the ambient light is bright enough. It can be induced deliberately, if desired, by purposely setting the camera shutter at a low speed, or even opening it on Time or Bulb. Even when no subject motion is likely, this technique can be used to combine the existing light with the light from the electronic flash (or flashbulb) for special effects.

Controlling Exposure

Use a special flash meter or consult the guide numbers

Because of its very brief duration, the light produced by any sort of flash device cannot be measured with an ordinary exposure meter. Many electronic flash units now provide automatic exposure control and special flash meters are available for use with the larger, nonautomatic units. The exposure for flashbulbs is usually determined by consulting a chart of *guide numbers,* such as can be found on the information sheet that is packed with individual rolls of film.

A guide number represents the product of the lens f/ number multiplied by the distance in feet from flash to subject and can be found, for any given film speed, by matching a chosen shutter speed with the bulb type in use. Then, if the distance from flash to subject is known, the necessary aperture can be determined; if some specific aperture is desired, the necessary flash distance can be found. For example, if you are using Tri-X 35mm film, with a 25B bulb in shallow reflector, and you want to use a shutter speed of 1/60th second with M-synch, the published guide number is 220. If the flash-to-subject distance is 10 feet, divide 220 by 10 to find the necessary f/ number,

$$220 \div 10 = 22 \text{ or } f/22.$$

If you would prefer to use f/11, for example, divide 220 by 11 to find the proper flash distance,

$$220 \div 11 = 20, \text{ or } 20 \text{ feet.}$$

A similar chart is provided for use in estimating exposure for nonautomatic electronic flash, if you know the rated power of the unit in *beam-candle-power-seconds* (BCPS). For a flash unit rated at 1000 BCPS and Tri-X film, Kodak recommends a guide number of 140, for example. (See guide number charts in appendix 7.)

Guide numbers are intended for use under "average" conditions and may not be accurate for use in highly reflective rooms or totally nonreflective areas (outdoors at night, for example). Also, they apply only to direct flash from near the camera position and can't be relied on, without some educated guesswork, if the flash unit is pointed away from the subject or "bounced" from a wall or ceiling.

Strictly speaking, electronic flash tubes are discontinuous spectrum sources and, as such, do not have a real Kelvin temperature rating. Because of the mixture of gases used, however, the light they produce includes enough of the spectral colors in the proper proportions to appear, and photograph, as a slightly purplish "white," which normally requires only a little yellow or amber filtration to work well with "daylight" color films. Many small flash units are equipped with built-in filter screens which serve this purpose and obviate the need for any other color correction. For black-and-white work electronic flash light is perfectly satisfactory, whether filtered or not.

Fluorescent Light

Many artificial lights are not "white"

Most other light sources, which derive all or part of their light from luminous gas, concentrate all of their radiant energy into a relatively few bright lines of the spectrum, omitting large bands of color entirely. These lights can appear obviously colored, as do the familiar red-orange neon tubes, the strong yellow sodium-vapor streetlights, and greenish-lavender mercury-vapor industrial night-lights, or they can occasionally masquerade as "white." Without exception, however, they photograph as strongly colored, and because of their spikey spectral characteristics, they are almost impossible to filter back to anywhere near "normal." Rather than wasting your time trying to correct lights of this sort, make the best of the bizarre effect and try to use the color creatively. (See plate 9.)

Fluorescent lights are a little better, but generally not much. The gas with which fluorescent tubes are filled is designed to radiate strongly in the UV region of the spectrum, but produces very little visible light. The visible light results from the brilliant glow of *phosphors,* which coat the inside of the tube and are excited into fluorescence by the ultraviolet radiation. The color of the light can be controlled over a wide range by selection of the phosphors used, and some special combinations will produce a light that both looks and photographs like daylight. Unfortunately, these tubes are rarely encountered. The more common cool white, warm white, and daylight tubes tend to photograph in some shade of sickly pea-green and are poor sources of light for color photography, even when filtered as effectively as possible. (See plate 10.)

If you must include fluorescent light in your color photographs, and if reasonably normal color balance is important, you can try one of the special *fluorescent filters* marketed by several companies. Two types are available; one is intended for use with tungsten film, the other with daylight film. Another alternative is to use filters from the *color-compensating* (CC) series, marketed by Eastman Kodak in the form of dyed gelatin squares. Some authorities recommend combining magenta and blue filters in various strengths. My experience indicates that plain magenta, or even red, is preferable. In any case, filtering fluorescent lights is strictly a trial-and-error business and you must find your own solution. Color films of various types and speeds do not all require the same amount of filtration, even in the same light condition. I'd suggest starting out with daylight film and a CC 30M or 40M filter. Look over the resulting transparencies and go from there. Fluorescents are usually satisfactory for use with black-and-white films, without any filtration at all.

If you're wondering why gas-discharge and fluorescent lights are so widely used, despite their color problems, it's because they are much more efficient than incandescent lamps. Fluorescent lamps, for example, produce two or three times as much useful light as incandescents do, for the same amount of electricity consumed. They also last much longer and generate less heat, so they are an obvious choice for applications that don't require daylight color quality. As energy consumption becomes more and more of a national problem, you can expect to find these, and other "energy efficient" sources, becoming more and more popular. Learn to cope with them; they're here to stay.

Ultraviolet and Infrared

The invisible radiations (ultraviolet and infrared), which lie just outside the boundaries of the visible spectrum, can be troublesome at times. All silver-sensitized films and papers are strongly sensitive to ultraviolet and will record it as if it were blue light. This effect is most apparent in scenic views taken at high altitudes (where the percentage of ultraviolet is relatively high) and shows as an emphasized distance haze and an abnormally bright blue color in nearby shadow areas. It may also cause overexposure, because most meters don't react as strongly to UV as films do. These problems are easy to avoid, however; UV filters are available in several very light tints of pink (*skylight* filter) or yellow (*haze* filter) and can be used with either black-and-white or color films without any exposure increase.

Infrared light, on the other edge of the visible spectrum, does not affect most films to any appreciable degree. This is a blessing because IR is almost impossible to control with ordinary glass or gelatin filters. When it is necessary to exclude it, as for example, from enlarger light when color printing, a special dichroic or interference filter is the most effective type.

For some special photographic purposes; an ultraviolet light source can be used to illuminate the subject. If a very dark blue filter is used, either over the camera lens or over the light source, so as to exclude visible light from the camera completely. When used this way the results are occasionally similar to ordinary photographs, but contrast is usually low and the subject colors are likely to be translated into strange relationships of value. Frequently though,

Synopsis

Artificial Light Sources

Incandescent lamps give continuous spectrum light and are suitable for color photography when appropriately filtered; gas-discharge lamps produce discontinuous spectrum light and most are unsuitable for color work. They cannot be corrected by filtration.

Light color relates to the temperature of its source and is described as color temperature.

There are several types of flashbulbs; they are usually synchronized to reach peak intensity with the full opening of the camera shutter. Electronic flash units must also be synchronized. They provide light of very short duration, high intensity, and near-daylight color balance. Flash exposure can be estimated by consulting a table of guide numbers for the film and flashbulb type in use. Most fluorescent lamps photograph as a yellowish-green but their light can be partially corrected by filtration. Ultraviolet and infrared light can be used for special photographic purposes and effects.

UV and IR photographs show things that can't be seen

surface patterns and details that are normally invisible will appear, and this characteristic of UV photography is useful in such fields as medicine, science, and criminal investigation. Lenses made of special glass or quartz must be used for this work because ordinary optical glass absorbs UV very effectively.

Ultraviolet can also be used to stimulate certain materials into fluorescence—another method of displaying surface patterns or material differences that are invisible in ordinary illumination. In this application the material is illuminated by UV, but the UV itself is excluded from the camera by a filter over the lens. The filter should be selected to absorb UV while transmitting the color of the fluorescence freely. Ordinary visible light should not be used unless background details are needed to relate to the fluorescing material.

Infrared photography is also capable of displaying details and patterns that cannot be seen. However, ordinary film cannot be used. Special IR films (discussed previously on p. 97) are available in 35mm and sheet film sizes and they should be exposed through dark red or special IR filters to exclude visible light—especially blue and violet, to which the films are very sensitive.

Ordinary color film is sensitive to UV, but there is no advantage in using it because the filtration necessary for the UV effect will exclude all color from the camera. Color film *is* useful for recording fluorescence, but it must be filtered to exclude UV and transmit the fluorescent color, just as black-and-white film should be. Infrared does not affect ordinary color film usefully, but a special false-color IR film is available which, when properly filtered, produces unusual and gaudy distortions of the normal color relationships.

Principles of Lighting

Beginners are too concerned with light quantity

When appraising scenes they wish to photograph, beginning photographers—preoccupied as they are apt to be with the technicalities of film speeds, f/ numbers, shutter settings, and meter readings—are concerned primarily with light *quantity*. If there is enough light to produce a good meter reading and a clearly visible viewfinder image, they are likely to be satisfied. Sooner or later, though, the mere production of an image ceases to be a challenge, and light *quality* begins to assume real importance. At this point photography can begin to become at least a craft and perhaps an art.

Light quality is not easy to define, but we use the term to refer to the way light affects the appearance of the subject. In the simplest case, we consider the light quality to be satisfactory if the subject can be seen clearly against its background and if its form and texture are well-rendered. More specifically, light quality is good if it contributes to a personal interpretation of the subject, displaying it in a way that best suits our purposes, whatever they may be.

Figure 6.2
Focusing index for infrared light is the
small dot between f/16 and f/32 lines.

Characteristics of Light Quality

There are several characteristics that determine the quality of light. They are intensity, color, degree of diffusion, evenness, direction, and duration.

Intensity is not a particularly important consideration as far as the image itself is concerned. Moderate variations in light intensity are easily compensated for by adjustment of the camera controls or selection of the film speed, and barring extreme cases, the appearance of the finished image does not have to be dependent on the level of subject illumination.

Moderate variations in intensity are not usually serious

Light *color* is obviously important in color photography because the subject colors will be tinted by light that is not white and the image colors may appear stained or distorted. In black-and-white work, light color is significant only if it is fairly obviously not white. Even then the image may not be seriously affected unless the subject colors are strong and saturated and their value relationships must be preserved.

The AREA of a light source is important

The *degree of diffusion* of light is one of light's most important characteristics and is almost always ignored by beginners. As much as any other single factor, the degree of diffusion affects subject contrast, surface appearance, color saturation, and mood. In general, a diffuse light source is one that radiates more or less uniformly from a large area. Diffuse light produces low contrast, soft-edged shadows, muted colors, and a dull surface appearance. Small-area or point sources, on the other hand, produce high subject contrast, sharp shadows, bright and saturated colors, and a high surface sheen.

Except for rather special purposes the *duration* of a light is not particularly important. If the light persists for long enough to make an exposure possible, and if its intensity, color, and degree of diffusion are tolerable, it can be considered satisfactory.

Figure 6.3
We perceive depth and space in the real world by using our binocular vision; by observing the effects of light and shade; by noticing the overlapping of forms; and by analyzing the significance of relative size, position and motion of observed objects. Pictures—being two-dimensional—leave us with few spatial clues; if familiar perspective effects are not obvious, we must base our interpretation largely on effects of light and shade—and we are frequently deceived. When viewing unrecognizable subject matter we generally assume that the light is coming from the top of the image format. In this highly abstract picture, the forms are modelled strongly and the effect of depth is dramatic—but which forms are elevated and which sunken? Now turn the picture upside down and watch the valleys miraculously become jagged mountains. The picture is really a synthetic-aperture radar image of Greenland glaciers (the gray riverlike forms) flowing between mountains to the sea, then breaking up to form icebergs and floating ice chunks (the white particles in the dark ocean area). (Courtesy of the Environmental Research Institute of Michigan [ERIM].)

Light direction affects the illusion of depth and space

Intensity, color, diffusion, and duration are all characteristics of the light source itself. Two other factors that affect light quality, evenness and direction, are related to the manner in which light is used or manipulated and apply to any light source.

Evenness refers to uniformity of illumination level at the subject position. In the studio it is affected by "beam spread" (a spotlight illuminates a small area intensely, but a floodlight covers a wide area with relatively uniform illumination), and by the proximity of the light source to the subject (a distant light will provide more uniform illumination than a close one will). Indoors or out, uneven illumination can be caused by local areas of shade at the subject position.

Light *direction* is another very important characteristic that, like degree of diffusion, affects subject contrast and mood and also strongly influences the rendering of subject forms and textures. Light that grazes the subject surfaces from any direction will tend to emphasize surface texture and subject contours. Direct frontlight tends to subdue both form and texture, tends to reduce contrast, and may make the subject space appear shallow and flat. Toplight usually appears natural and so does sidelight; light from below eye level may appear theatrical or bizarre. Backlight will minimize subject details and tends to produce silhouette effects, rim light, and glare.

Light direction affects the illusion of depth and space, too. In real-life situations we rely mostly on perspective and our binocular vision for depth perception. In photographs we read deep space by looking for perspective clues, but subject form and surface contours must be interpreted from the pictured effects of light and shade. If the light direction cannot be determined from inspection of the image, or if several lights of approximately equal strength illuminated the subject from different directions when the picture was made, our perception of subject form and space is hampered and the forms may be ambiguous. This is particularly true if the subject matter is not readily identifiable, but it is a bothersome factor in the interpretation of any image forms.

Analysis and Control of Lighting Conditions

Any light condition can be analyzed and its probable effects predicted by determining its characteristics, as just described. Daylight is no exception; on a sunny day with no clouds you can expect the following photographic effects:

Intensity will be high. The sun is very bright and you can use slow film with fairly small apertures or high shutter speeds. Fast films may not be useful unless image light is reduced by filtration (either color or neutral density filter).

Color. Two colors are involved. The direct sunlight is distinctly *warm* (yellow) while the skylight is strongly *cool* (blue). In color photography this may show up as a noticeable contrast between the warm highlights (illuminated mostly by direct sunlight) and cool shadows (which receive most of their light from the blue sky). This is a natural and familiar effect and will probably not be unpleasant. In black-and-white photography it will pose no problem and may even be useful, since by filtering, the contrast can be either increased (yellow, orange, or red filter) or decreased to some extent (blue or green filter) if desired.

Degree of diffusion. Again, at least two sources are involved. The sun is apparently small and can be considered almost a point source. Its light is harsh and contrasty and will tend to form glaring highlights, sharply defined shadows, and crisply rendered textures. Color saturation will be high. The sky, on the other hand, is a very large source and provides extremely diffused light, but it is so much less intense than sunlight that its effect will only be visible in areas of shade or shadow. There it will produce very low contrast illumination, minimizing the effects of form and texture, and subduing color saturation.

Evenness. Daylight is inherently a very uniform light but there are frequently local variations of illumination to deal with. Areas of shade or cast shadows will be the chief problems.

Direction. Daylight is toplight, sidelight, or blacklight and is completely believable. It will produce a single set of highlights and shadows that will describe the subject form unambiguously.

Duration is not a factor to be concerned with; daylight is continuous.

You can "control" daylight by selection

You can "control" daylight, for photographic purposes, by selecting the time of day (or season of the year), by orienting your subject in the light, and by choosing your camera position to achieve the desired qualities of form and texture. Wait for passing clouds to obscure the sun if contrast is too high, or place your model close to a light-colored wall (snowbank, sandpile, or something) so reflected light can cause *fill light* in the shadows and therefore reduce the harshness of the illumination. Watch your subject carefully as the light changes and wait for the best effect. Don't forget to monitor the exposure, too; a cloud passing over the sun will probably reduce the light intensity by one or more stops.

If you pay attention to the way light works on things at various times of the day and in various weather conditions, you'll be amazed at the subtlety and variety of visual effects that are produced. (See plate 7.) Practice noticing light effects and analyzing them. Light is the raw material of your craft; as you become more conscious of it, your work will become easier and your pictures will certainly improve.

Figure 6.4
Available light shot
(Photograph courtesy of the University of
Michigan Press.)

**Available light is frequently difficult
to work with**

Make the best of reflections and glare

Available Light

The term *available light* usually refers to light conditions, other than
normal outdoor daylight, which are not arranged specifically for the purpose
of taking pictures. Usually this implies indoor daylight or artificially illuminated
conditions, indoors or out, that you can't adjust or control.

Available light is frequently difficult to work with. The intensity may be
very low, requiring fast film, slow shutter speeds, and large apertures. The color
will probably not be a problem in black-and-white, but may require filtration
for color photography. The illumination will probably contain a haphazard
mixture of direct and diffuse light and will typically be uneven. It may come
from any direction, or directions, and multiple shadows and confusing patterns
are typical. Finally, you may sometimes encounter intermittent or flickering
lights of very short duration (illuminated theater marquees, flashing signs, and
television images are a few examples).

There are no rules for dealing with these conditions but a few guidelines
are worth considering. Contrast will probably be high; if it is, be sure to expose
the film fully and develop for a little *less* than normal. (This advice is contrary
to the normal practice of *pushing* film to some unrealistic "speed.") Don't filter
in very dim light unless it is really necessary; the longer exposure required may
result in reciprocity failure and even increase color distortion. Pick your camera
position with particular care to achieve the best compromise between uniformity
of illumination, clarity, description of form and texture, and mood. If glaring
reflections or flare streaks are apparent, work with them for best visual effect;
they are not necessarily "bad." Brace the camera firmly (or use a tripod) to
avoid camera shake; or consider deliberate camera movement if the subject
matter is suitable and some blurring would enhance your interpretation. Focus
carefully; depth of field will be fairly shallow but out-of-focus forms can work
well in your composition if they are placed carefully. You can use the shallow
depth to subdue distracting background details or even to create interesting

Figure 6.5
Window light shot
(Photograph courtesy of the University of
Michigan Press.)

patterns in some situations. The relationship between subject and background is often awkward in this sort of photography; you may find that a change of lens focal length will improve the visual effect. Finally, bracket your exposures somewhat to be fairly sure you're covered and take a lot of pictures.

A good skylight is an almost ideal light source

Not all "available light" is bad or difficult to deal with. Room interiors illuminated by skylights or large windows can provide a beautiful quality of light, excellent for portraiture or figure studies, and often equally useful for still-life subjects. A good skylight is almost the ideal light source for many purposes. It combines good intensity, good direction, and a good compromise between direct and diffuse illumination (direct enough to model form strongly but diffuse enough to retain delicacy and softness of surface). Color can be a problem (skylight is frequently very blue), but it is usually possible to filter it successfully.

Place the subject and your camera with care

A very large window, not exposed to direct sunlight, can also be used to good advantage for portraiture or small still-life setups. The light will tend to be rather uneven and will fall off rapidly across the width of the subject, but if the subject is not too large the effect is controllable. If the room interior is light in tone, or if some other source of reflected light can be provided to fill in the shadow side of the subject, the contrast will not be excessive. Beware of small windows, though; they will tend to give higher contrast, especially if the subject is placed close to them and room reflectance is low.

You can control the appearance of the subject in both skylight and window light by your choice of camera position and subject placement relative to the light source. Additionally, you can use available materials for backgrounds and reflectors; a sheet pinned to the wall behind the model will serve as a neutral, light-toned ground (watch out for obvious wrinkles) and a large towel or a sheet of newspaper can be used to reflect some light into the shadow side of the subject, if it seems necessary. With a little ingenuity you can produce beautiful light effects with these simple materials. Best of all, this light consumes no energy, and it's free!

Controlling Artificial Light

Sooner or later you will probably have to work with some form of artificial light. This doesn't mean, necessarily, that your pictures will look different (artificial light can be made to resemble daylight if you want it to) but it does pose different problems of handling and arrangement. In natural light it is only necessary to recognize the quality of illumination you're after and take advantage of it; in artificial lighting you must first visualize the effect you want, then you must select and arrange light sources and reflectors to produce it. There is another difference, too. The sun is a single, very bright light source, which is very far away; so the light is powerful and uniform in intensity. Artificial light sources are relatively weak, are frequently used in multiples, and must be used fairly close to the subject in a confined space; their illumination varies perceptibly across the subject space and must be adjusted with great care to appear uniform and coherent.

Beginners make three immediate and serious mistakes

Beginners typically make three immediate and serious mistakes when they attempt artificial lighting. They tend to use lights raw (small sources, direct and without diffusion) and they place them too close to the subject (for maximum intensity). This will inevitably produce a harsh, glaring effect with burnt-out highlights and black shadow areas, which leads to the third mistake—adding more lights to "kill" the shadows. This rarely improves the picture and frequently makes it visually confusing.

A raw light will produce high intensity at close range but the intensity falls off rapidly at greater distances, according to the Inverse Square Law of illumination, which states that illumination decreases in intensity with the *square* of the distance from the source of the illuminated surface. Simply stated, this means that if you double the distance from the source to the surface the light intensity will be reduced by a factor of four; triple the distance and you'll have only one-ninth of the light left.

The Inverse Square Law is not as fearsome as it sounds

In practice the problem is not quite that serious. The Inverse Square Law is only completely effective for point light sources, like candle flames, electric arcs, and small clear glass light bulbs, used in an otherwise dark and unreflecting environment. Light from large sources, like fluorescent tubes, *umbrella* reflectors, or skylights, is much less seriously affected and can be used at relatively close distances with good results. Further, most photographs are taken in at least moderately reflective environments where some light, bouncing back at the subject from nearby surfaces, is returned to help illuminate the shadows. For these reasons the Inverse Square Law is not as fearsome as it sounds at first, but don't think you can ignore it entirely; light intensity *will* definitely diminish with distance.

Although lighting can be controlled almost completely in the studio, it is not unusual, even there, to simulate a natural light condition. Frequently this turns out to resemble a kind of diffused daylight with one main light serving to establish the predominant pattern of light and shade, and other subdued sources arranged to keep the overall contrast within bounds and to assist in defining edges and accenting forms and textures. At first, daylight is an excellent model to follow because it is both familiar and believable. Furthermore, it will tend to keep you from blundering into the confusion of too many light sources if you remember the basic characteristics of daylight—one relatively small, intense source (the sun) and one very large, less intense source (the sky).

A single source is the simplest lighting setup

The simplest possible lighting setup consists of a single bulb, usually placed above, in front of, and somewhat to one side of the subject. Try this arrangement and observe the results. If the bulb is bare, without a reflector, and if the surroundings are dark in tone, the light on the subject will probably look harsh and contrasty and the shadows will be fairly hard-edged and distinct. If the bulb is close to the subject, the illumination will be intense but will appear to fall off rapidly across the subject, increasing the effect of glare and harshness.

Probably the easiest and most dramatic improvement you can make in this arrangement is to enlarge the source by simply diffusing it. Hold a two-foot-square sheet of tissue paper between the bulb and the subject and observe the result. The glowing paper is now the light source. First, you will notice the loss of light intensity; then you should see a considerable improvement in the evenness of illumination, a softening of shadow edges, and a considerable reduction in contrast. If you can overlook the fact that the light is dim, you'll probably be pleasantly surprised by the quality of this softer light condition. It may even be good enough to use as is.

Now move the tissue paper close to the bulb. The shadow edges should become more distinct, the subject contrast will increase, and the light may appear to get brighter. By varying the position of the diffusing tissue between the bulb and the subject, you can exert considerable control over the subject contrast because, as you move the tissue, you are changing the effective *area* of the light source.

A "diffuser" works because it increases the AREA of the source

Most beginners (and quite a few experienced photographers) think that a diffuser works because it scatters the light. Wrong. It scatters light all right, but the scattered light is largely wasted, which accounts for the drop in intensity; the reduction in contrast and increased evenness are due entirely to the increase in the effective *area* of the source. Don't confuse "diffusion" with "area"; they are not the same. A small source is a contrasty source whether it is supposedly diffused or not.

If, in your experiments with the tissue paper diffuser, you find the light too soft for your taste, you can combine direct and diffused light by substituting the diffused tissue screen with a large white card placed *behind* the bulb as a reflector. This arrangement will retain the sharp shadow edges characteristic of a small light source, but will also provide the reduced contrast and greater evenness of a large light source. This is what the bowl-shaped metal reflector of a flood lamp accomplishes, but more effectively, because it captures more of the light from the bulb and directs it toward the subject with less waste. This makes for higher light intensity, but focuses the light somewhat and may cause a hot spot.

Use "bounce" light to "fill" the shadows

A single light source, small or large, may not illuminate the subject evenly enough to be satisfactory and it will frequently be desirable to fill in the shadow side of the subject with enough light to preserve shadow detail and avoid excessive subject contrast. At first you'll find it easiest and best to simply bounce some of the main light back into the shadows with one or more reflectors. Sheets of white cardboard or foamcore board are fine for this purpose; they can be propped up as close to the subject as necessary and braced or taped in position.

You can use reflectors freely, placing them almost anywhere (outside of the actual field of the camera) without having to worry too much about disrupting the lighting pattern. Reflected light from a matte-surfaced white card is less intense than the main light source and is highly diffused, so there is almost no danger of forming secondary shadow patterns. Stay away from shiny metal foil, or actual mirror reflectors, at least until you've gained some experience, because they reflect a hard *specular* light, which can look unreal and distracting if used without discretion.

Light the environment, not the subject

Although it would seem obvious that the way to illuminate a surface is to direct a light beam at it, that isn't always the best way to get results. In fact, you'll find your lighting problems are simplified if you assume that the subject surfaces are mirrors in which you see (and photograph) light reflected from the walls, ceiling, floor, and furniture in the room. The direct light from the source, falling on the subject, serves mainly to define form and provide bright, specular highlights. Put another way, it's sometimes more important to illuminate the environment than it is to shine light directly on the subject.

While this explanation is a little overdramatic for most sorts of subject matter, it is completely accurate for mirror surfaces, such as polished metal, glass, and liquids. You can demonstrate the principle quite easily—find a brightly polished silver (or plated) teaspoon and lay it faceup on a sheet of white paper in front of you. In normal room light you should be able to see much of the room reflected in the concave spoon bowl, and the details of windows, picture frames, other objects on the table, and so forth, should be clearly distinguishable. A photograph of the spoon would show the same details, but the contours and texture of the spoon would be poorly described, confusing, and irritating to the eye.

Figure 6.6
In this picture the photographer has used
the limited range of a small electronic flash
unit to illuminate the foreground strongly,
allowing background details to fade out
into black. The effect is stark and
surreal—an emphatic visual interpretation
of what is probably a rather unexciting
subject in daylight.
(Photograph courtesy of George
Schietinger.)

Tent lighting is best for shiny objects

Now stand a sheet of white paper beside the spoon and notice the result.
The confusing details of the room are replaced by a smooth gray tone where
the paper is reflected, and the metal surface appears matte and dull, but clean
and subtly modelled. By covering the spoon almost entirely with the paper sheet
and looking in under one edge of the paper, you will probably be able to see the
spoon completely "cleaned up" and totally free from distracting detail reflections. It will also be unnaturally dull and will look like paper or white plastic
rather than polished silver.

To complete the experiment, try to illuminate the spoon satisfactorily
without the paper cover, by bathing it with direct light from one or more
sources, either raw or diffused. You will find that the raw, small sources make
the silver look brilliant and polished, but produce glaring highlights and excessive contrast. There is no way to achieve the smooth gradation and subtle
modelling, produced by the paper *tent,* without shielding the spoon from its
room environment. In other words, any lighting setup you can contrive, which
provides *tent lighting,* will in fact be a tent.

In practice, neither the smooth, lifeless modelling of the plain tent lighting
nor the harsh confusion of direct light in an uncontrolled environment will be
satisfactory for most purposes. The best solution will probably be some compromise. Working with the spoon again, enclose it in its white paper tent and
shine a light on the tent from above. The spoon should appear brighter, but not
any less matte than before. Now lay a strip of black paper across the top of the
tent and observe the effect. By moving the strip you can "draw" a sharply
defined gray stripe almost anywhere on the spoon surface. Raising the paper
strip above the tent a little will soften the edges of the gray stripe on the spoon;
putting the black strip inside the tent will make the spoon stripe black and
crisp. By combining cast shadows on the top of the tent with bits of dark or
colored paper strategically placed inside the tent itself, you will find that you
can define the spoon contours and express its shiny quality without the confusion

Figure 6.7
This series illustrates the effects of the several lights employed in conventional portrait lighting. In (a) the main light—a flash tube in a twelve-inch reflector—is positioned high and 45° to the left of the camera to provide so-called "short" lighting, in which the near side of the model's face is in partial shadow. This relatively small light source, used alone, produces a harsh, glaring effect with sharply defined shadows and serious loss of shadow detail.

In (b) an "umbrella" *fill light* illuminates the shadows to one-fourth the highlight intensity—a lighting ratio of 4:1. For some purposes this arrangement might be considered sufficient.

In professional portraiture a *hair light* is generally thought to be desirable. In (c) it adds luster to the hair and increases separation from the dark background tone.

Some portraitists might stop here but, in this case, the model's dark hair is poorly separated from the background and her light blouse is too strongly emphasized. In (d) a background light shifts the visual emphasis back to the model's head and face. Adjustment of the relative intensities of these lights can provide a variety of expressive effects, but this is only the starting point. Don't feel that you must be bound by conventional techniques; you should know and respect the "rules" but learn to *see* the effects of light and use your own judgment.
(Courtesy of Nancy Stuart.)

a

b

c

d

**The subject must be adjusted
from the camera position**

Start with a "limbo" background

of its normal random reflections. This is the sort of game that professional illustrators play in order to produce the dazzling product photographs you see in magazine ads. You can learn to do it too, if you want to work at it.

In all situations, keep in mind that the subject must be groomed and adjusted to look right *from the camera position.* You can't judge any surface effect from off-camera, and if the camera must be moved, the whole process of "tickling" surfaces must begin again. You'll find it convenient to have a helper to hold reflectors and move things for you while you examine the image in the camera, especially for large setups.

Although matte surfaces will not show actual reflections of objects around them, they are affected by their environment to some degree. If you remember the principles involved, you can usually provide a satisfactory lighting condition for any sort of subject without too much wasted motion. As a rule, shiny objects will need a tent; matte objects will probably not need one. Lustrous objects, or arrangements containing a variety of surfaces, will probably be easiest to handle in a partially controlled space or open tent.

Tents can be constructed in many ways. You'll have to decide the best way to solve each problem. In many cases it's a good idea to begin by creating a *limbo* background—that is, a background that does not show any horizon line or any indication of a junction between floor and wall. This is easy to do— suspend a roll of paper on a crossbar between two light stands (or other supports) two or three feet above a suitable table surface, and pull the paper down to cover the table. Tape the paper down at its front edge and adjust it so that it hangs in a smooth curve from roll to table surface. Objects placed on the paper and viewed from the front in uniform illumination will appear to "float" in the space, and surface reflections will be partially controlled by the smooth background tone.

Figure 6.8
a. A small-area light source is a contrasty source, as is demonstrated by this series. A single, small electronic flash unit, pointed directly at the model from 45°, casts an unattractive nose shadow, deforms the face structure, and leaves the shadows black and empty. Notice the emphasized white of the model's right eye and the shiny skin texture.

b. When the shadows are filled by reflected light, contrast is reduced and some of the harshness is relieved; however, the nose shadow is still prominent, the eye is still strongly white, and the skin still seems glossy.

c. A single large source, used without added reflection, softens the shadow patterns, subdues the eye reflection, and gives the skin a satiny texture. Contrast is much less harsh, the shadows are satisfactorily detailed, and because the larger source illuminates the studio much more uniformly, the background tone is noticeably lighter.
(Courtesy of Nancy Stuart.)

a

b

Figure 6.9
a. Although dull-surfaced objects seem to be easier to light than shiny ones, all objects are affected by their environments. When you learn to light shiny surfaces well, you'll find matte surfaces easier to deal with, too, and the results will be better. Here a polished silver spoon, illuminated by diffused window light, reflects the room interior in confusing patterns.

b. Simply standing a white card beside the spoon "cleans it up" by blocking off part of the room reflections.

c. Here the spoon is completely "clean." Covering it with a translucent tent of tracing paper has eliminated the reflections but left the surface featureless and formless. The polished surface appears matte and gray.

c

d. To restore some of the form and surface quality, necessary to express the character of silver, controlled reflections are produced by applying black paper strips to appropriate areas of the tent, both inside and out. The cast shadow from the cardboard strip at upper right produces a soft gray reflection; the small black strip inside the tent adds a sharp black accent.

e. Here is one possible effect. The variations are endless.

f. Here is the spoon as it would appear with the tent removed. Simply directing a light at a shiny object (or any object) is rarely a good way to handle it.

a

b

Figure 6.10
a. A simple tent made by adding one side of tracing paper and a top of matte acetate to a limbo background.

b. Basic tent lighting. Accents can be added as desired.

You can make tents in various ways

Don't enclose them more than necessary

If a simple limbo background is not adequate, it may be necessary to enclose one or both sides. If the set is large, you can use large sheets of cardboard or painted canvas flats for this purpose, but for small, table-size still-lifes, it is usually preferable to use paper sheets hung from more crossbars constructed as before. If further enclosure is required, the paper background sheet can be extended forward across the top, over another crossbar and down the front to complete the cube. The camera lens can be poked through a small hole cut in the front wall of the tent, and adjustments of the subject can be made by lifting one of the sides temporarily. You can light the subject by illuminating areas of the tent walls from outside.

The basic cube tent will handle many kinds of subjects very adequately but occasionally you'll encounter some object, usually a very shiny, convex thing, which will show distressing reflections of the tent structure, its crossbars, and wall intersections. These problems will tax your ingenuity, but analyze the reflection problem and try to devise a structure that avoids it.

Sometimes the object can be placed in a paper cylinder and photographed through a hole cut in one side; perhaps you can build a paper cone and set it down over the object with the camera lens peering through a hole at the apex. If the camera lens shows in the surface of the subject as a black spot, try to position it so the reflection occurs on a corner or edge of the object where it will be relatively tiny and inconspicuous. Sometimes you can enlarge the lens reflection into a useful and decorative contour by surrounding the lens itself with black paper in some appropriate shape or pattern.

Frequently you will find that the object's own shadow causes unpleasant reflections in its surfaces or "ties it down" to the ground plane in an awkward manner. You can avoid this by supporting the object on some sort of concealed structure—a stiff wire or stick, for example, poked through the background paper. If the object is too heavy to be supported this way, you may be able to turn the whole setup (tent, lights, and all) over on its back and shoot down on the object as it rests on a solid floor stand protruding through the background wall. As a rule, don't enclose a tent any more completely than you have to in order to control the surfaces, because it's harder to light a closed tent than an open one.

Figure 6.11
An effective tent for small objects, made from translucent paper.

Regardless of the construction, remember that good modelling of forms requires one dominant light source; provide that first. Even a partial tent will provide a great deal of internal reflection, which will keep lighting contrast comfortably low and "open up" the shadows; but a single source may not be adequate to separate all the forms and edges, nor is it likely to provide those little accents of light that glorify surfaces and delight the eye.

Use reflectors rather than more lights, if possible

By all means try to provide these accents, but do it without turning on any more lights than you need to. It's safer and generally more satisfactory to provide the necessary lighting emphasis by reflecting the main light where you want it with little mirrors or reflectors made from aluminum foil. For relatively hard and bright reflection use cosmetic mirrors, propped up or taped into position inside the tent. Aluminum foil can be cut into any desired shape and held with tape in almost any position, even concealed between objects in the still-life if a little extra light is necessary to emphasize the space or accent some area of texture or color. In cases where extra drama is appropriate, you can make the subject glow or radiate light by concealing small light bulbs here and there, and running the wires through the paper walls of the tent, out of camera view.

And don't get carried away

Again, there are no rules for this sort of work; do whatever you have to do to make the picture sparkle and sing. Just don't get carried away. You can ruin a good basic setup with too much tickling, just as too many bay leaves or too much pepper can ruin a good stew. See pages 277–282 for a discussion of the special problems involved in lighting for close-up photography and copy work.

Figure 6.12
A single large-area light source at 45°
above the models was sufficient to
produce this informal portrait of two young
brothers. The bruised nose, sparkling eye,
broken finger, and the impish expressions
suggest that this is an impetuous and
irrepressible pair.
(Courtesy of Nancy Stuart.)

Summary

Artificial light sources vary greatly in spectral characteristic and in apparent color. Incandescent tungsten-filament bulbs emit continuous spectra containing all the visible colors; fluorescent and luminous-gas bulbs emit discontinuous spectra from which some visible colors may be missing entirely. Tungsten-filament bulbs are generally best for indoor color photography; they are available in two standard whites, 3200°K and 3400°K. Blue flashbulbs and electronic flash units are balanced for daylight color film, rated at about 5500°K.

Flashlight must be synchronized with the camera shutter. Synchronization is easiest with BTL shutters; FP shutters cannot be synchronized at all speeds with all flash units. Modern electronic flash units are capable of automatic or semiautomatic exposure. If the ambient light is bright enough when a flash is used or if the exposure time is prolonged, a ghost image may be formed.

Flash exposure calculation requires a special flash meter or the use of guide numbers. Electronic flash guide number charts are frequently based on the BCPS rating of the flash unit.

Luminous-gas sources cannot usually be filtered satisfactorily for use with color films. Some fluorescent lights can be filtered sufficiently to be useful but you will have to experiment.

Films are highly sensitive to ultraviolet light but special emulsions are required to photograph by infrared light. Both UV and IR have useful photographic applications but require special techniques for good results. Exposures must usually be established by trial.

Beginning photographers pay more attention to light quantity than quality. The important light characteristics are intensity, color, degree of diffusion, evenness, direction, and duration. Any light can be analyzed for potential effect by considering these characteristics. Daylight and available light can be controlled by selection of time, place, angle, lens focal length, and exposure. Available light is frequently contrasty; pushing film speed is not very effective and may be detrimental to image quality. Some available light, such as skylight and window light, may be very satisfactory and give excellent results.

Arranging artificial lights in the studio is easiest at first if you visualize normal daylight as a model. Consider the Inverse Square Law. Try some exercises with a single bulb, a diffusing screen, and some reflectors. Direct light from a small source is seldom the best way to get good results. Think of the subject surfaces as mirrors in which the room environment is reflected, then light the environment.

A polished silver spoon makes a good subject for experimentation. Build a tent around it for complete control, then add decorative reflections as desired. Tents can be constructed in many ways. Matte-surfaced objects may not require any sort of tent but shiny objects will almost always need one. Start with a limbo background, then add sides and a top if necessary. It's helpful to have an assistant adjust the lighting while you watch the groundglass image.

Color Photography

Outline

How Color Films and Papers Work
    The Light and Pigment Primaries
    Color Negative Films
    Color Reversal Films
    Film Latitude
Film Color Balance and Filtration
Color Film Processing Outline
Color Printing
Cibachrome Printing
Printing from Negatives: Unicolor R-2
Filter Pack Adjustment

How Color Films and Papers Work

The Light and Pigment Primaries

Any color can be produced by blending the primaries

It's a practical fact that light of any tint or shade of any color can be produced, quite satisfactorily, by blending together various proportions of the light (additive) primary colors—red, blue, and green. Similarly, if dyes or pigments of sufficient purity can be obtained, any paint color can be produced by mixing together various proportions of the pigment (or subtractive) primaries—cyan, magenta, and yellow. (See colorplates 6 and 7.)

We recognize the absence of all *light* color as being black. Adding light colors to black (no light) produces color of increasing brightness until, when all three primary light colors are present in the proper proportions, we perceive "white"—a color of greater brightness and less obvious hue than any of its components.

We perceive the absence of all *pigment* color as being white. Adding pigment colors to a white surface produces color of increasing darkness until, when all three pigment primaries are present in the proper proportions, we perceive "black"—a color of less brightness and less obvious hue than any of its components.

The light and pigment primaries are complements

The light and pigment primary colors are complements of each other, or opposites, just as black is the opposite of white and a photographic negative is the opposite of the positive (print) image made from it.

Color Negative Films

Although this photograph was made as a scientific document, it presents a surreal and strikingly beautiful version of Las Vegas, Nevada, and the surrounding area. This delightful visual bonus of the space program is one of the hundreds of thousands of images being made by the Landsat satellites that orbit the earth at an altitude of 575 miles and view most of the earth every 18 days, imaging a 115 × 115 mile square area in 25 seconds. The satellites observe the earth in four spectral bands (or "colors"): green, red, and two invisible infrared bands. The video signals of each of these bands are digitized and transmitted to earth where they can be computer-processed to recognize land-cover classes or to enhance features such as geologic patterns, water depth and turbidity, vegetation, and soils. They also can be combined to produce false-color images (like this one) for cartographic purposes. In these images, vegetation appears as various shades of red; bare soils range from light to dark gray; clear water is dark blue to black; water with sediment is light blue; asphalt roads and dense urban areas are blue to black; clouds, snow, and sand are white; and cloud shadows are black.

In color photography the appearance of full, natural color is achieved by separating the complex shades and tints of the original subject colors into their basic components, the light primary colors. Color film consists, essentially, of three separate black-and-white emulsion layers, coated one over the other on a common base. Each of the emulsions responds to a single primary color—the top layer to blue light, the middle layer to green light, and the bottom layer to red light. After exposure in the camera, color negative film is developed in a special color developer which, in one operation, produces a black-and-white negative image in each of the emulsion layers and forms, with each silver image, a negative dye image. The top film layer, in other words, contains a silver negative image plus a yellow dye image (the complement or "negative" of blue); the middle negative layer consists of silver plus magenta dye (the complement of green); and the bottom negative layer consists of silver plus cyan dye (the complement of red). Then a bleach bath removes all three silver images, leaving the three dye images superposed to form a color negative image of the original subject. In practice, controlled amounts of dye are allowed to form a color-correcting mask. This mask layer gives color negatives their typical orange or straw-colored overall tint. (See plate 13a).

Printing a color negative simply repeats the process (without forming a mask layer) on a paper base. The positive image is formed in silver and dye in each of the three layers; the silver is removed in a bleach step and the remaining dye layers, superposed, re-create the subject colors with commendable accuracy.

Color Reversal Films

The familiar color slides, or transparencies, are positive images formed on the original film base rather than being printed on paper. Their reversal processing procedure is a little different from negative color processing. Three similar superposed emulsion layers are exposed in the camera, but treatment in the *first developer* produces only a negative silver image in each layer, as in the ordinary black-and-white process. This leaves, in each layer, a residue of unexposed and undeveloped emulsion which constitutes a potential positive image. When this remaining emulsion material has been fogged (either by exposure to white light or by chemical action), the film is developed in a color-forming solution which produces positive silver and dye images in all three layers simultaneously. The film now contains three negative silver images, three positive silver images, and three positive dye images, and is totally opaque. After a bleach bath, which removes all the silver, only the positive dye images remain. Viewed against the light, the sandwiched dye layers blend together to present a reasonably faithful reproduction of the subject colors. (See plate 13b).

The Polaroid and Kodak instant-print films produce their images by much more devious and remarkable processes than those just described. Each sheet of Polaroid SX-70 film, for example, is a sealed packet containing all the ingredients required to produce a stable color print. Exposed through a clear plastic cover sheet, the image light is color-separated, as usual, on three emulsion layers. Development begins when the film packet is ejected from the camera, passing between a pair of steel rollers which rupture a capsule of activating chemicals and spread the mixture evenly between the plastic cover sheet and the film surface. An *opacifier* ingredient in the chemical mix protects the still-sensitive film from light while the developers are at work in the emulsion; then, as the image is formed and the alkalinity of the developer diminishes, the opacifier gradually lightens and recedes, allowing the image to be seen. The image is positive because the developed silver image in each emulsion layer suppresses its complementary dye color rather than producing it, as in the case of conventional negative color film. This entire chemical miracle is accomplished in minutes, without the use of a darkroom and without litter or waste. The dyes used are described as *metallized* and are said to be more stable and less subject to fading than those employed in ordinary color materials.

Film Latitude

Black-and-white films are comparatively tolerant of mistakes in exposure and development. Overexposure of two or three stops or underexposure of a stop or two is not always disastrous and may not even be serious in some cases. Development variations of 20% or 30% from normal can often be compensated for without much difficulty and the print results are usually tolerable, if not perfect.

You will find that there is much less latitude for error in handling color materials. Although modern films will produce an image of some sort, and occasionally an unusual or dramatic one, under less than ideal conditions, best results will usually follow correct exposure and accurately controlled processing. This is true because the three emulsion layers that are necessary for color reproduction do not react in quite the same way under abnormal conditions, and when one of the layers is out of balance with the other two, or when none of them match, the resulting image color will be unnatural and frequently unpleasant.

Color negative films will usually tolerate a little underexposure (perhaps as much as one stop) and somewhat more overexposure (perhaps one or two stops). Contrast can be varied to some extent by changing development times. Negative contrast increases with increased development just as in black-and-white, but negative contrast cannot be varied greatly from normal, nor should it be, because there is very little possibility for contrast compensation in color printing.

Reversal films have somewhat less latitude than negative films. Overexposure is likely to produce bleached-out highlights and pastel colors; underexposure increases color saturation and, if overdone, will block up the shadow details and make the colors murky. Most films will also exhibit some color shift in extreme highlights and shadow areas if the film exposure is not near normal. Unlike negative films, reversal materials are more tolerant of underexposure than overexposure and, if the first development is extended, they produce lower-than-normal maximum density and reduced contrast. Substantial changes in development will result in color shifts.

As is true with black-and-white films, high-speed color materials are grainier and less sharp than the slow films. This is less of a problem than it was a few years ago, because improvements are being made constantly and even the high-speed materials now provide good enough quality for most ordinary purposes. The sharpest, least grainy transparency film available for general photography, however, is still Kodachrome 25. Its special emulsion design and special processing procedure apparently permit a degree of image precision that some new films have approached closely but have not yet matched.

Film Color Balance and Filtration

When you first begin to work with color films, especially transparency materials, you'll probably be surprised by some of the results you get. Light conditions that seemed quite normal and ordinary while you were photographing may appear in your slides as distinctly off-color, as if the pictures had been tinted or toned. Actually, the pictures may be a fairly accurate record of the real light color, and you simply didn't notice the color cast.

This problem arises because the human eye and brain are remarkably accommodating and the film is not. We see color *comparatively,* to a large extent, and can identify rather subtle distinctions between hues, seen side-by-side, under widely varying conditions of illumination color and intensity. We do not have the ability to identify color accurately without some reference, however, and in these respects our color perception is similar to our ability to judge the pitch of musical tones. Most of us can distinguish a high note from a lower one or sing simple melodies without straying off-key, but very few individuals can tell that an automobile horn is playing an A-flat major chord, for example. The few who are blessed with this ability are said to have perfect pitch. It's doubtful that anyone has perfect color pitch (as film does), and that's probably a good thing; if familiar objects changed color every time the light color shifted, it would be unsettling, to say the least.

In almost any condition of illumination we can recognize and identify white objects, even though the entire scene may be strongly tinted with color. This perception of white provides us with a reference for judging both color and value of other areas in the scene. Interestingly enough, if a brighter white of more neutral color is introduced into the scene, we immediately perceive the first reference white area as tinted and degraded in value, but we may still be able to think of it as white. In other words, our perception of the color of familiar objects and surfaces is almost independent of illumination color, especially if the light contains representative amounts of all three of the primary colors in some reasonable proportion.

Color film doesn't have this ability. It is "balanced" during manufacture for a white light of very specific color, as indicated by its color temperature rating in degrees Kelvin (see discussion in chapter 6).

Normal sunny daylight is considered to have a color temperature of about 5500°K, and most daylight reversal color films are balanced during manufacture for that white standard. If daylight film is used in light other than 5500°K, some color shift or tint may be apparent in the pictures—a blue shift if the light color temperature is higher than 5500°K, a yellow shift if it is lower than 5500°K.

Table 7.1
Wratten Filters Chart

Color	Wratten Filter Number	To Obtain 3200°K from:	Filter Factor	Mired Shift Value
bluish	82	3100°K	⅓ stop	−10
	82A	3000	⅓	−21
	82B	2900	⅔	−32
	82C	2800	⅔	−45
yellowish	81	3300	⅓ stop	9
	81A	3400	⅓	18
	81B	3500	⅓	27
	81C	3600	⅓	35
brownish	81D	3700	⅔	42
	81EF	3850	⅔	52
blue	80D	4200 to 5500	1 stop	−56
	80C	3800 to 5500	1	−81
	80B	3400 to 5500	2 stops	−112
	80A	3200 to 5500	2⅓ stops	−131
orange	85C	5500 to 3800	⅓	81
	85	5500 to 3400	⅔	112
	85B	5500 to 3200	⅔	131

If this color shift is not too severe, it can be corrected by a filter of the appropriate color placed over the camera lens. The filter, if correctly chosen, converts the off-color light back to daylight, as far as the film is concerned. The filter will absorb some of the incident light, of course, and some increase in exposure will be required as indicated by the filter factor.

Color films are balanced for use in either daylight or tungsten light

While daylight film can be used in light of almost any reasonable color temperature, the filtration required to use it in tungsten illumination is rather excessive. It's preferable to use tungsten film under these conditions. There are presently two varieties—type A tungsten films were introduced originally to take advantage of the high-intensity 3400°K light output of photoflood bulbs, widely used by amateurs; type B films are balanced for 3200°K to match the standard professional tungsten spot and flood lamps. The 3200°K balance is now the most common.

With both daylight and tungsten films to work with, it is possible to get good color results in most light conditions by appropriate filtration. It isn't always easy, however; selecting the right filter even most of the time will require some understanding of the principles involved and considerable experience.

Filters are used to adjust their response

Eastman Kodak manufactures the Wratten filters in an extensive line which includes *conversion, light-balancing,* and *color-compensating* filters for color photography. In practice, the conversion and light-balancing filters are both used for making adjustments in color temperature, which means, of course, that they function in the yellow-blue range. Although there isn't any firm distinction between them, the term *conversion* is usually applied to filters in the 80 (blue) and 85 (orange) series and the term *light-balancing* is used to describe filters in the 81 (yellow-tan) and 82 (bluish) series. You will frequently hear the terms used interchangeably, but light-balancing is probably the most common.

Color shifts are described in degrees Kelvin or color temperature

As shown in table 7.1, each of these filters is capable of changing the color temperature of a light from one value to another. This color shift can be described in degrees Kelvin—the 80A conversion filter, for example, will adjust 3200°K tungsten light to 5500°K for use with daylight film. But this is a deceptive method of calibration, because the extent of the color shift in Kelvin degrees depends upon the color of the existing light. The 80A conversion filter produces a shift of 2300°K when used with a light source of 3200°K, but it will shift 5500°K daylight to almost 20000°K—a correction of 14500°K! On the other extreme, it will raise the color temperature of candlelight (about 1900°K) to only about 2530°K—a shift of only about 630°K.

**But using mireds simplifies filter
selection**

It is possible, however, to calibrate filters in such a way that their shift value is a constant for all light colors. If the color temperature in Kelvin degrees is divided by 1,000,000 and then inverted, the number obtained will express the light color in *"micro-reciprocal degrees"* or mireds (pronounced "my-reds"). A color shift expressed in mireds *is* constant for all light color temperatures and this simplifies the selection of conversion and light-balancing filters considerably. For example, suppose you are using daylight color film (5500°K balance) with an old model electronic flashgun which produces light with a color temperature of 6200°K. This will require *warming* the light source by some 700°K and indicates one of the yellowish light-balancing filters; but which one? If you consult table 7.1 to find a filter that will produce a yellow shift of 700°K, you might be tempted to select an 81EF, which will convert 3850°K to 3200°K; not quite 700°K, but the closest you can come with the information provided. This would not be proper correction for your flashgun, however. Working with mireds will give you the right information. First, convert the color temperatures 5500° and 6200° to mired values:

$$\text{Mireds} = \frac{1}{\dfrac{\text{Kelvin}°}{1,000,000}} \text{ or } \frac{1,000,000}{\text{Kelvin}°}$$

$$\frac{1,000,000}{5500°} = 181.8 \quad \text{and} \quad \frac{1,000,000}{6200°} = 161.3$$

Subtracting 161.3 from 181.8 gives 20.5, the desired color temperature shift in mireds. Consulting the mired values in the chart shows that the most appropriate filter is the 81A; its 18 mired rating is a little less than desired, but may be preferable to the 81B whose 27 mired rating would overcorrect the light and make it noticeably yellowish. The 81EF, which seemed to be the logical choice for a shift of 700°K, is obviously much too strong for this purpose. Its 52 mired rating would shift the 6200°K light of the flashgun down to about 4700°K, much too yellow to be satisfactory with daylight color film.

**The direction of color shift may be
confusing**

Working with mireds or decamireds (one decamired equals ten mireds) is a great convenience but it has one confusing aspect: the *direction* of shift (toward blue or yellow) is indicated by the *sign* of the mired number; that is, a *positive* number indicates a yellow or orange filter which will warm the light, and a *negative* number indicates a blue filter which will cool the light. Thus, the 85B, with a rating of 131 mireds, is orange in color; the 80A, rated at —131 mireds, is blue.

**Remember, subtract what you've got
from what you want**

If you keep your wits about you, you can usually figure out the filter color you need without worrying about the plus or minus signs of the mired numbers, but in some cases it can get confusing. For example, if you're using tungsten film, type B (3200°K), and photoflood lamps rated at 3400°K, what do you do? The color shift required is 18 mireds, but is it positive or negative, warm or cool? In the absence of any other clues, remember to *subtract what you've got from what you want*. In other words, subtract the mired value of the existing light (294) from the mired value of the light color you want in order to match the film balance (312).

$$312 - 294 = 18$$

The number 18 is positive, therefore the required filter is yellowish. The chart indicates the correct filter to be 81A.

If the conditions were reversed and you were trying to use a 3400°K film (type A) with 3200°K lamps, subtracting 312 mireds ("what you've got") from 294 mireds ("what you want"), will give you a minus number of —18. The chart indicates that this is most closely approximated by the 82A, a bluish filter, with a rating of —21 mireds. Kodak has not made the situation any simpler with their numbering system, either. The warming filters are in the 81 and 85 series; cooling filters are listed in the 80 and 82 series. Furthermore, the 80s, 81s, and 82s all get stronger as the letter designations increase (the 80C is a stronger blue color than the 80B or the 80A, for example). But the 85B and the 85 are both a stronger orange than the 85C.

In a laudable attempt to simplify this nomenclature, a number of manufacturers offer light-balancing filter sets calibrated in decamireds, with the colors indicated by letter. Hasselblad's CR 1.5 filter, for example, is a conversion red filter of 1.5 decamired (15 mired) strength, roughly equivalent to the Wratten 81A. In that same series, the CB 12 is a blue filter of 120 mired strength. It is intended to convert tungsten light to daylight quality and would fall between the Wratten 80A and 80B filters in strength. In filter sets of this type each color, warm and cool, is represented by decamired values of 1.5, 3, 6, and 12. By using the filters singly and in various combinations it is possible to obtain any strength up to 22.5 decamireds, in increments of 1.5. Although the 1.5 decamired will produce noticeable steps of adjustment in color, it is almost always possible to arrive at satisfactory color balance using these sets, and their convenience is certainly obvious. For the rare occasions when more accurate color balance is necessary, the Wratten gelatin filters offer more subtle control and greater precision.

Although it's sometimes possible to estimate the filter color required for light-balancing, it's obviously not the best way. The problem is considerably simplified if you have a way of measuring light color, and this can be done with a color temperature meter, such as the Gossen Sixticolor. Meters of this type work by measuring the relative amounts of warm and cool light present in the illumination and are quite accurate and useful for continuous spectrum light from about 1500°K or 2000°K to about 20,000°K. They are not reliable for measuring lights of discontinuous spectra; if this is necessary, better results, at much higher cost, can be obtained with a three-color meter, such as the Spectra.

For controlling colors in tints and shades other than those covered by the light-balancing series, a complete spectrum of color-compensating (CC) filters is available in an extensive range of strengths or color densities.

These filters are valuable for use over the camera lens to compensate for minor variations in film color balance which occur during manufacture. They can also be used to compensate for unusual color shifts in illumination or to produce interesting distortions of color for creative purposes. They are also effective in the darkroom for controlling the balance of color prints.

In contrast with the haphazard nomenclature of the light-balancing filter series, the color-compensating filters are described logically and effectively. Each filter is identified by the prefix CC followed by a number representing its density (actually its density multiplied by 100) for light of its complementary color and, finally, a letter indicating the dominant color of the filter itself. For example, CC 20R identifies a color-compensating filter of red having an average effective density of .2 for cyan light; CC 05M describes a magenta filter having an effective density of .05 for green light.

Color-compensating filters are available in the light primary colors, red, green, and blue, and their complements (the pigment primaries), cyan, magenta, and yellow. Densities of .05, .1, .2, .3, .4, and .5 are available in each color, and all colors except green and blue are also available in .025 density.

All six colors are useful and desirable for camera work, but for color printing applications it is only necessary to have magenta and yellow, and occasionally, cyan. The other colors can be produced easily by employing these three filters in various combinations, and although the mixed colors are not quite as pure as the individual primary colors are, the mixtures are very satisfactory. In using these (or any other) filters, it is wise to use the minimum number required to produce the desired color and density, especially when they are used in front of the lens. If more than two are required, as is sometimes the case in printing, it is best to use the larger acetate CP (color printing) filters some distance above the negative in your enlarger, rather than sandwiching a

A dichroic color head is best for color printing

number of CC gelatins below the lens in the actual image path. Better yet, if you can afford it, buy a color enlarger equipped with dichroic filters as an integral part of the head assembly. Color heads of this sort provide color densities of up to as much as 2.0 (200) in each of the three colors and permit stepless control of color and density mixtures in all combinations.

CC filters can be obtained in glass for camera use, but they must be specially ordered and are expensive. It is much more usual to use the gelatin squares mounted in metal frames or holders, or simply held in place over the lens with bits of tape. Although they are fragile and virtually impossible to clean, gelatins will last for a long time if they are given normal care and are protected from moisture and physical damage. With use they will gradually become abraded and soiled and when they begin to show obvious wear they should be replaced.

As is true with any filter, a CC filter will absorb some light which should be compensated for by an increase in the camera exposure. The filter factors are not the same for all the CC colors and many of them are awkward fractions of a stop (see table 7.1). Practically, for camera use, they can be rounded off to the nearest half-stop without serious effect on film exposure.

Color films suffer rather seriously from reciprocity failure

Color films suffer from the effects of reciprocity failure even more dramatically than black-and-white films do because each emulsion layer is affected separately. As a result, the normal color balance of the film is disrupted and a significant color shift occurs, accompanied by the usual loss of effective film speed. If the color shift is not too severe, it can be corrected by CC filtration and an exposure increase which must include the filter factors. Professional color films are tested during manufacture for color balance and reciprocity failure characteristics and come with an instruction sheet which gives the effective speed and filter recommendations for their particular emulsion batch. This is useful information, but not always accurate; age and storage conditions will change the film characteristics, and for critical applications, it is best to test the material yourself. This is especially true if the film is nearing expiration or has been subjected to heat or humidity during storage.

Correct color balance during camera exposure if possible

Reversal films can be filtered during camera exposure if any sort of color adjustment is required. The newest negative films for amateur use, however, combine fine quality and high emulsion speed with a universal color balance, which works well under most conditions of light color and simplifies correction in printing. Negative films for professional use are still supplied in two forms, but they are designated as types S and L rather than by a specific color temperature balance. In effect, type S (*short* exposure) is a daylight film and type L (*long* exposure) is intended for use in artificial light, but the exposure *time* is a more important consideration for these films than is the color of the illumination. Type S film should be used for exposures of less than about 1/10th second, even in tungsten light, and type L is the right film for exposures of longer than 1/10th second, even in daylight. In both situations the appropriate light-balancing filter should be used. If type S film is used for long exposures, or type L for short ones, reciprocity failure will cause a color shift which may not be correctable in printing.

Extreme color shifts may not be correctible in printing

As a general rule, if the negative film you are using does not specify a color balance, assume it is balanced for daylight, and for best results, filter it accordingly if you use it in tungsten light. If you plan to have the negatives printed by a commercial photo-finisher, however, it may be wise to use the film without any camera filtration, because commercial printers sometimes guess at the proper printing filter packs by inspecting the subject matter of the pictures. If the subject looks like an indoor one, they may filter it for tungsten light whether or not it needs it.

Color Film Processing Outline

Wear protective gloves when handling color chemicals

Developing color films is not much more difficult than processing black-and-white materials but in some processes there are more chemical steps involved and control of temperature is more critical. There is somewhat greater danger of chemical contamination, too, and you should be extra careful to wash the various containers and utensils thoroughly after each use. Color chemicals are somewhat more hazardous to handle than the normal black-and-white chemicals. The developers, especially the color-forming developers, are relatively strong sensitizers, are strongly alkaline, and should be handled with care. You should wear protective gloves when handling all the color chemicals, in either dry powder or liquid form. Get into the habit of washing your hands after every chemical contact. Dipping your hands into a regular short-stop bath (1% acetic acid) before rinsing them in water will help to neutralize the developer alkalis and make the rinse more effective.

Color chemicals have a relatively limited life

Color chemicals have relatively limited life, too. The developers, particularly, need protection from air and light and should be stored in a cool place. Avoid really cold storage conditions, however, to prevent the solutions from crystalizing. Although this will not usually affect the activity of the chemicals, they will have to be warmed and stirred to redissolve the crystals before they can be used effectively, and this is sometimes difficult.

Although the various manufacturers' chemical systems for color negative film developing are not all alike, most of them now combine the bleach and fixing baths into one solution and specify fairly high temperature processing to keep the total time short. The Eastman Kodak Company, however, takes a typically conservative approach. Their procedure, although it involves more chemical steps than some competing systems, is reliable and predictable and produces excellent results. The Kodak C-41 process for Kodacolor II and Vericolor II film is given in table 7.2.

A 30-second agitation is recommended at the beginning of each chemical step; after this initial agitation period, the film should be agitated for 2 seconds every 15 seconds during the developing period and 5 seconds every 30 seconds in the other chemical baths. As is true in all high-temperature processing, you should handle the film very carefully to avoid damage to the soft emulsion. Notice particularly that the film should *not* be washed after the stabilizer.

Color film processing is tedious

Reversal film processing involves more steps because the film must be developed twice—once to a negative, then again to form the positive image. The Kodak E-6 process for Ektachrome films is summarized in table 7.3.

Color film processing is a straightforward procedure which you will probably find rather tedious after the novelty wears off. There is very little advantage in doing it yourself usually, because the chemical cost is quite high, the capacity of the solutions is not very great, and their life is fairly short. Unless you have enough film to process so you can use up the chemicals completely within a week or so, you will not save much money by doing your own. You can, of course, control the effective speed of the film to some extent by varying the developing times, and this option is one of the best reasons for home processing. However, if you have only a roll or two to process, you'll save time and money and get good results (if you have a good commercial processor in your area) if you let the professionals do your film processing for you.

Table 7.2
Kodak Flexicolor Process C-41

Solution or Procedure	Time in Minutes	Temperature		Agitation			Remarks
		°F	°C	Initial	Rest	Agitate	
1. Developer	3¼	100 ± ¼	37.8 ± 0.15	30 sec	13	2	Total darkness
2. Bleach	6½	75 to 105	24 to 40.5	30 sec	25	5	Total darkness
Remaining steps can be done in normal room light.							
3. Wash	3¼	75 to 105	24 to 40.5				Running water
4. Fixer	6½	75 to 105	24 to 40.5	30 sec	25	5	
5. Wash	3¼	75 to 105	24 to 40.5				Running water
6. Stabilizer	1½	75 to 105	24 to 40.5	30 sec			
7. Dry	10 to 20	75 to 110	24 to 43.5				See instructions

Reproduced with permission of the Eastman Kodak Company.

Table 7.3
Kodak Process E-6

Timing: Includes time required to drain tank.

Solution or Procedure	Time in Minutes	Agitation	Temperature		Time Remaining at End of Step
			°F	°C	
1. First Developer	7	Initial & Subsequent	100 ± ½	37.8 ± 0.3	30
2. Wash	1	Initial & Subsequent	92–102	33–39	29
3. Wash	1	Initial & Subsequent	92–102	33–39	28
4. Reversal Bath	2	Initial	92–102	33–39	26
Remaining steps can be done in normal room light.					
5. Color Developer	6	Initial & Subsequent	100 ± 2	37.8 ± 1.1	20
6. Conditioner	2	Initial	92–102	33–39	18
7. Bleach	7	Initial & Subsequent	92–102	33–39	11
8. Fixer	4	Initial & Subsequent	92–102	33–39	7
9. Wash (Running Water)	6	Initial & Subsequent	92–102	33–39	1
10. Stabilizer	1	Initial	92–102	33–39	0
11. Dry	Film removed from reels; temperature not higher than 140° F (60°C)				

Reproduced with permission of the Eastman Kodak Company.

Figure 7.1
Processing drums

Figure 7.1
Processing drums

Color Printing

Color printing is worthwhile and simple

Color printing, on the other hand, *is* worth your while, and it is now remarkably simple. Whereas just a few years ago "doing color" was thought to require expensive equipment and professional skills, it is now within reach of any serious amateur, and in some respects, is less demanding than black-and-white. There are, of course, advantages in having a dichroic color head on your enlarger, a programmable electronic color analyzer, and an automatic color processor of some sort, but none of these lovely gadgets is really necessary; you can make perfectly satisfactory prints without any of them. All you really need is a good basic darkroom, adequately equipped for ordinary black-and-white printing; a reasonably good, color-corrected lens on your enlarger; and a set of filters. With this minimal equipment you'll not be very efficient but you *can* "do color."

You can work with minimal equipment, but extras help

A *little* extra hardware will make the process a lot easier and more efficient, however. Tray processing color prints is, in my opinion, rather tedious and uncertain, especially for beginners. Several manufacturers offer plastic drums for print processing and these have several advantages. They are light-tight, so after loading the exposed paper into the drum in the dark (or in the recommended dim brown safelight, which you don't need), all the process steps can be done in full room light. They permit economical one-shot use of the processing chemicals which helps to insure uniformity of results and also simplifies temperature control. They're also economical to use and not very expensive to buy in the first place—all in all, a recommended piece of equipment.

You'll need a good thermometer. If you don't already have a reliable and accurate one that reads to at least 40°C (105°F), buy one before you start to work in color. I recommend the metal stem, dial-indicating type, such as the Weston.

A water-temperature control is useful, but by no means necessary for amateur use. You will need a convenient supply of hot and cold water, though, and a large pitcher or graduate (2-quart capacity) for tempered water will come in handy.

You'll need an accurate timer

You'll appreciate a convenient and accurate interval timer. One inexpensive and ingenious model is supplied by Unicolor, Inc. Their Jingle-Bell timer is programmable, so all the intervals in any process can be preset. Simply push the "start" bar to begin a timing cycle; the bell will ring and the timer will stop when the preset interval is up. The next cycle will begin, at your convenience, when the "start" bar is pressed again. You can use your tape recorder as a timer, too, if you want to. Just record the processing instructions in detail, including such reminders as "turn off the lights" or "rinse your hands," and fill in the blank times with music.

Don't buy a color analyzer at first

Color analyzers are fascinating toys which can simplify color filter selection and save you time and materials, but unless you plan to go into the color printing business, don't buy one (at least not at first). Inexpensive ones aren't worth having and good ones are expensive. The prices are almost certain to come down, though, as new electronic miracles keep appearing, and it's probable that really functional analyzers will eventually be priced within reach of the average photographer. In the meantime, there are several ways of estimating filter requirements. One approach is to buy Kodak's *Color Dataguide* which contains a "standard" color negative and print (so you can see what it's supposed to look like) plus several dial calculators and a set of viewing filters, all designed to help you make a visual comparison of color balance alternatives.

Another good approach to the problem is to use a *color matrix* of some sort. One typical device is the Unicolor Mitchell Duocube, which is described and illustrated on page 229 and Colorplate 20. There are several similar devices available; all are useful and relatively inexpensive.

In the past, most authorities have insisted that you equip your enlarger with a heat-absorbing glass for color printing. This is now being questioned. The present attitude seems to indicate that dichroic infrared filters are desirable but that ordinary heat-absorbing glass screens may not be. My recommendation is to begin without one, unless your enlarger generates enough heat to damage your negatives.

Unless you have a color head, you'll need filters

You will need a set of printing filters. Kodak's CC or CP filters in values of 025, 05, 10, 20, and 40 in cyan, magenta, and yellow, plus an ultraviolet filter, Wratten 2B or CP2B, will make a reasonable starter set. Get the CP (acetate) filters if your enlarger has a *filter drawer* above the condensers. Get the CC (gelatin) filters if you must use the filters under the lens in the image light path. Both kinds are available in several sizes. Buy the smallest CPs that will work in your enlarger; the 2″ square gelatin filters are large enough for almost any under-the-lens application. Other manufacturers also supply printing filters in sets and they may even be less expensive than the Kodak product.

Color enlargers have several advantages

If you like equipment and have the money to spend, buy a color enlarger or a color head for your present enlarger. Modern color enlargers feature efficient, fade-resistant dichroic filters which can be introduced into the light path by means of external levers or dials to provide stepless filtration of 200 or more. They have several advantages—greater range of filtration; high intensity printing light; convenient, repeatable filter settings; built-in ultraviolet and infrared filters; and excellent heat protection for the negatives. In addition, some models offer voltage stabilization (for uniform light color) and have companion analyzers with matching filter characteristics. They are nice, but certainly not necessary.

If you live in an area where the electric power drain is irregular or poorly regulated, you may want to buy a voltage regulator for your enlarger light. An automatic regulator will keep the lamp voltage fairly constant, regardless of supply variations (within reason), which, in turn, will keep your enlarger light

Figure 7.2
Variable transformer

You probably don't need a voltage regulator at first

There are several ways to make color prints

white. Regulators are fairly expensive and come in several sizes, rated, usually, in volt-amperes, which means about the same thing as watts. If you buy one, be sure its V/A rating is the same as, or slightly higher than, the wattage of your enlarger lamp. Don't buy a much larger one than you need, even if it happens to be a bargain; regulators don't regulate very well unless they're loaded close to capacity.

If you need some voltage control but can't afford an automatic regulator, you can buy a variable autotransformer and a voltmeter. You can monitor the line voltage on the meter, then adjust it manually. Actually, except for color-matching or scientific purposes, line-voltage fluctuations may not be much of a problem. My recommendation is to start out under the assumption that the line voltage is going to be reasonably stable, and work without any sort of voltage control until it's apparent you need it. Plate 14 illustrates the magnitude of color shift you can expect if your line voltage varies from its typical maximum to a typical minimum without correction. Most variations will be less obvious than these.

There are presently four well-known and widely used methods of making color prints—prints from color negatives by exposure and color-forming (chromogenic) development of color-sensitive paper; prints from color slides or other positive transparencies by exposure and chromogenic reversal processing of color-sensitive paper; prints from slides on Cibachrome (a direct positive, dye-destruction or dye-bleach process); and, finally, the venerable old dye-transfer process which can produce beautiful prints from either positives or negatives, but in such a devious, painstaking, and expensive manner that it is out of the question for most amateurs. A fifth way to "get" color prints (rather than "making" them) is to use a Polaroid or Kodak instant-color camera, but this approach is so simple that it hardly needs description. Kodak's new Ektaflex process is a revolutionary departure from conventional color printing procedures. A color negative (or transparency) is exposed onto a sheet of special film in the regular way; but then the film sheet and a sheet of special paper are placed into the Ektaflex processor where the film is soaked briefly in an activator solution, then rolled into firm contact with the receiving paper. The film/paper sandwich "develops" outside the processor in room light in about 6 minutes, during which time the dye image transfers from film to paper. The entire process is completed in about 12 minutes and temperature is not critical. Although it is still necessary to test for proper exposure and color balance, the "wet" part of the printing processes has been eliminated, making the procedure, quick, clean, and semiautomatic.

Although Cibachrome is one of the most expensive color materials on the market, it offers unique advantages for the amateur—it is simple, relatively foolproof, relatively safe, and nonpolluting. It is capable of dazzlingly brilliant, saturated colors and it has no equal for detail rendering and sharpness. Additionally, it employs dyes of better-than-average stability and is considered one of the most durable and permanent of the color processes. Its main photographic disadvantage, aside from cost, is its rather high contrast characteristic.

Cibachrome is expensive, but it is a good first process

As a *positive-to-positive* process, Cibachrome shares with Kodak's Ektachrome paper type R-14 the distinct advantage of being suitable for use with color slides. For beginners in color work, particularly, this is good because slides are easy to appraise for image content, composition, and color balance. Negatives are much harder to judge. Working from slides is also simpler, at first, because the slide image serves as a convenient reference for color balance, and print filtration is relatively easy to determine when you can compare the print directly with the original color image. For these reasons, and its other advantages, Cibachrome is a good "first process."

You can buy the paper and chemical kit as separate items or you can purchase an introductory "discovery kit." You'll probably find this starter kit inadequate for any serious amount of experimentation and practice; I'd recommend getting the half-gallon P-12 chemical kit and a 20-sheet package of 8″ × 10″ type A paper.

Process it in a drum

Cibachrome is easy to process in its own special drum, but it can also be processed in other types of drums if you prefer. Liquids poured into the top of the Cibachrome drum while it is standing on end are retained in a cup built into the cap; at the same time, the used solution in the drum drains out of a vent at the bottom. The new solution is released into the drum when the drum is laid on its side and the fluid then spreads over the paper surface as the drum is rolled back and forth on a level surface. This drum design is fast and convenient for this process but is a little more likely to cause uneven development, particularly on large print sizes, than the horizontal-filling design, such as Unicolor's Unidrum II.

The Unidrum cylinder is larger in diameter than the Cibachrome tube and is equipped with plastic channel guides which permit its use with from one to four 4″ × 5″ prints, one or two 5″ × 7″ prints, or one 8″ × 10″ print. Solutions are poured into an end spout while the drum is resting on its stubby feet in a horizontal position. The solution flows into the drum immediately but lies in a trough at the bottom and doesn't touch the paper until the drum is rolled. Drums of this design can be completely filled with water for either prerinse or washing operations but they are not as easy to drain as the Cibachrome drum is. Investigate both types and see which one strikes your fancy. My recommendation is to buy the Cibachrome drum if you plan to do only Cibachromes, but buy the Unidrum (or equivalent) if you plan to do other sorts of prints as well as Cibachromes. You can do all sorts of prints in either drum type, but the Unidrum type is more versatile and probably the best compromise.

Cibachrome Printing

Cibachrome Printing

Follow mixing instructions carefully

Put on your rubber gloves, then follow the package instructions for mixing the chemicals and prepare one-quart volumes of the working solutions at first. Save the remaining chemical concentrates for later. Store the working solutions in clean glass or plastic bottles and label them clearly. Be careful of the bleach chemicals; pour the powder slowly to avoid raising too much dust and don't inhale any of it. If you spill any of the powder or the mixed solution, neutralize it with baking soda before you mop it up or before you flush it down the drain. The bleach is a strong and corrosive acid which is potentially harmful to you as well as to metal utensils and your darkroom plumbing.

The solutions are reasonably stable but they will work best when they are fresh. Try to use up the working solutions within a week or two at the most; the unused concentrates will keep for a month or two in partially full bottles. Very old chemicals will not produce good color results and are likely to cause mottled tones, degraded whites, streaks, and stains.

When you are ready to begin printing, stand the bottles of working solutions in a large tray of warm water (try about 30°C to 32°C, or 85°F to 90°F, at first) to bring them up to temperature. Cibachrome is remarkably tolerant of processing temperature variations, but it's wise to pick a convenient temperature within the acceptable 18°C to 30°C (65°F to 85°F) range, and stick to it. The recommended temperature is 24°C (75°F) and, since that's easy to maintain, you should probably try to work with it. By the time you're ready to process your first print, the chemicals in the water bath should have reached about the right temperature.

Cibachrome works best with low-contrast transparencies

Cibachrome works best with fully exposed, low-contrast transparencies. Heavily dense or contrasty images are not suitable and should not be attempted. Select a transparency; clean it carefully with a soft brush or compressed air (not canned air or freon) and put it into your enlarger. Cleaning is especially important with positive processes because dust spots show up in the print as black marks which are almost impossible to remove.

Adjust the image size, focus carefully, and stop the lens down to f/11. Then consult the back of the paper package for the *basic filter pack* recommendations. If you have a color head on your enlarger, you can simply dial in the recommended filtration; otherwise, select individual CC or CP filters to add up to the recommended totals and insert them into the enlarger—CP filters up in the condenser system somewhere, above the negative; CC filters below the lens, in the image light path. Although it is not specified in some recommendations, *always* use the Wratten 2B filter (or some equivalent UV filter) in any filter pack to exclude ultraviolet. You may be able to ignore this if you have a color head; the filter may already be in there.

Color filter selection can be confusing

Color filter selection can get confusing, and it will be discussed in more detail shortly. For now, remember that you can add filter numbers to arrive at the value you want (you can make a 30Y, for example, out of three 10Ys, or a 20Y and a 10Y, or any other similar combination). Also, remember that as a general rule you should not have more than *two* filter colors represented in any filter pack unless you are deliberately trying to reduce light intensity; all three primaries add up to *neutral density*. (More about this later.)

Don't use all three primary colors at once

Check your developing drum to be sure it's clean; dry it and lay it out with its cover so you can get at it in the dark. Turn out the lights and open the paper package. Cibachrome paper is protected by two envelopes, the outer one of heavy card stock and an inner one made of paper-covered plastic. There is also a sheet of heavy cardboard on each side of the paper stack. You will probably find it easiest to slip the entire stack partway out of the envelope so the paper sheets can be separated, rather than trying to extract a single sheet from the package with your fingernails.

After removing one sheet of paper, reclose the plastic envelope and replace it in the cardboard package, the folded end first. Then identify the emulsion side of the paper sheet by rubbing it lightly with a dry fingertip, first on one side, then the other. The emulsion side is glassy smooth and will make almost no sound when stroked; the back side has a fine matte texture and will make a light "whispering" noise as it is rubbed. Place the paper in the easel, emulsion side up, and make a conventional geometric test strip (see p. 000), beginning with an exposure of about 10 seconds @ f/11 and doubling the exposure total each time until it reaches 80 seconds. Then use the next larger aperture (f/8) at 40 seconds, and, finally f/5.6 @ 40 seconds to complete the series of six steps. In other words, expose: Step 1, f/11 @ 10 secs; Step 2, f/11 @ 10 secs; Step 3, f/11 @ 20 secs; Step 4, f/11 @ 40 secs; (total 80 seconds); Step 5, f/8 @ 40 secs; Step 6, f/5.6 @ 40 secs. This procedure will reduce errors due to reciprocity failure. (See plate 15.) Load the paper into the drum cylinder, emulsion side in; put on the drum cover; and turn on the lights.

Check the solution temperatures and adjust them, if necessary, by setting the bottles in hot or cold water and stirring the contents, one after the other, with the thermometer stem until they are correct. Be sure to rinse off the thermometer before going from one solution to the next; contamination is fairly serious in color processing.

Contamination is fairly serious in color printing

When the temperatures are suitable, pour three ounces of each chemical solution into the plastic cups provided in the kit. Each cup is clearly marked and should be used only for its own chemical. Set the filled cups in a shallow tray of 24°C (75°F) water to maintain temperature. If you are using the Cibachrome drum, stand it on end and pour the developer from the cup into the top opening. If you are using a Unidrum, stand the drum on its feet, horizontally, and pour the developer into the filler spout. Set your interval timer for two minutes, start it, and immediately lay the Cibachrome drum on its side on a flat smooth surface and begin rolling it back and forth, far enough to make at least a complete revolution on each pass. Agitate the Unidrum in the same way; knock it off its feet and roll it until it is stopped by the projecting feet, then roll it back until it stops. Continue this agitation routine, briskly but not violently, with either drum type, for 1 minute and 45 seconds. Then, with 15 seconds to go in the developing period, hold the Cibachrome drum drain over a large glass or plastic container and turn the drum to a vertical position. It will begin to drain immediately and you can, at the same time, pour the bleach solution into the filler opening at the top. Rock the drum back and forth a little to facilitate the draining (don't overdo this or you'll spill bleach into the tank prematurely). When the timer goes off, lay the drum on its side again and resume the agitation, rolling the drum back and forth for 3 minutes and 45 seconds. (Drain the Unidrum into the waste container through the filler spout, then set it on its feet to refill.)

Follow these instructions for P-12 chemistry

With 15 seconds (of the 4 minute bleach period) left, dump the drum as before, collecting the used bleach with the developer in the waste container. Pour in the fixer while the bleach is draining and, when the time is up, lay the drum down and begin the agitation of the fixer. Fix for 3 minutes, then drain the fixer into the waste container and pour a few ounces of water into the drum. Agitate it briefly, dump, then remove the cover and take out the print. Put the print into a tray of running water for 3 minutes, then wipe both sides lightly with a damp chamois, a soft squeegee, or a viscose sponge and hang it by one corner to dry. Wash out the drum thoroughly and wipe it dry. Rinse out the chemical cups and invert them over their respective bottle caps.

The used chemicals must be neutralized before they are discarded. Add two of the neutralizing tablets (supplied in the kit) to the waste container and let them fizz. You can continue to accumulate chemical waste in the container until you're through printing (or until it's full) if you remember to put in two tablets for each 3 ounces of used bleach that is added. After the last tablets have been in the waste liquid for half an hour or so (they will probably have disappeared), it is safe to pour the used chemicals down the drain. If you run out of tablets for some reason, use baking soda—adding it until the liquids stop fizzing. Chemical kits now being supplied omit this step.

P-30 chemistry, which will replace P-12, doesn't require the separate neutralizing step and times may be different. Follow manufacturers' instructions.

Figure 7.3

a. Cibachrome is relatively tolerant of temperature variations but, for best results, work at about 24°C (75°F). Wear protective gloves when mixing the chemicals, and set the bottles in a water bath to maintain temperature.

b. Be sure the drum is clean and dry. Set it out in a convenient location so you can find it in the dark.

c. Dust the transparency carefully, using the enlarger light to reveal the dust and lint.

d. Adjust the image to size and focus.

e. Stop the lens down to f/11.

f. Make up the recommended filter pack and insert it into the filter drawer. Now turn out the light and work in total darkness, no safelight.

g. Remove a sheet of Cibachrome paper from its protective package and place it in the easel. Be sure the emulsion side is up. (See text.)

h. Make a geometric test strip as described in the text.

i. Locate the drum and load it. The paper emulsion side must be inside the curl so the processing solutions can flow over it easily.

j. When the drum is loaded and the end caps are closed securely, turn on the room lights and pour out 3 ounces of each solution, using the plastic cups provided with the kit. They are clearly marked; don't mix them up. Set them back in the water bath to maintain temperature.

a

b

c

d

e

f

g

h

i

j

k. Stand the drum on end and pour the developer into the funnel opening. The solution flows into a cup in the end cap and will not contact the paper until the drum is laid down on its side.

l. Set the timer for 2 minutes, start it running and immediately lay the drum down on a flat, level surface and roll it back and forth continuously during the developing period. Be sure to roll the drum far enough each way to make a little more than one complete revolution, otherwise the print may not develop evenly. You can use an automatic agitator if you have one.

m. About 15 seconds before the end of the development time, stand the drum on the waste container so the developer solution can drain out while you are pouring the bleach bath in at the top. Let the drum drain until the timer rings, then set the timer for 4 minutes and immediately lay the drum on its side again and . . .

n. . . . agitate as before, continuously.

o. At 3:45, dump the bleach into the waste container while you pour the fixer into the funnel top of the drum. Let the bleach drain until the timer rings, then set the timer for 3 minutes and immediately lay the drum on its side and . . .

p. . . . agitate as before, continuously.

q. Fix for the full 3 minutes, then, when the timer rings, stand the drum on the waste container to drain and pour in a few ounces of water as a rinse. Roll the tank back and forth a few times, then remove the end cap, take out the print and slip it into a tray of clean water.

r. Wash the print for 3 minutes in running water.

s. While the print is washing, clean the drum, rinse the utensils, and add two of the neutralizing tablets to the waste liquid. This step is necessary to prevent possible damage to your drainage system and contamination of the environment.

t. Squeegee the finished print lightly and hang to dry. The color will be somewhat magenta while the print is damp. Wait until it dries to appraise color balance and exposure.

Note: As this book goes to press a new, improved Cibachrome process, P-30, is being announced. Handling of materials will be similar to the P-12 process, but processing times may be different. Follow the manufacturers' instructions.

k

l

m

n

o

p

q

r

s

t

This procedure should give you good results, but you may notice what the Cibachrome instructions describe as "an unpleasant odor" during or after the bleaching action. It is not likely to be a problem if the developer is well drained before the bleaching begins, but it can be avoided by using a brief water rinse after the developer. Three or 4 ounces of water, agitated for about 10 seconds just before adding the bleach bath, should solve the problem. You're more likely to need this with the Unidrum than with the Cibachrome drum; the Unidrum is harder to drain completely and will probably retain more of the used chemical solutions in each step.

Inspect the dry print for exposure and color balance

The prints will dry rapidly, especially in warmed, moving air. When your test print is dry, you can inspect it for exposure and color balance. (See plate 11.) The range of exposures sampled should certainly include a usable one and you should also be able to see the effects of extreme under- and overexposure. Remember, this is a direct positive process; overexposure will lighten the print and underexposure will darken it. Find the step or steps that seem closest to normal density and estimate an exposure for the next trial; then examine the color. Make exposure corrections by adjusting the aperture, if possible, to avoid reciprocity failure effects.

If the print appears strongly tinted with color, it may need a filter correction of 30 or more. If the tint is obvious, but not excessive, try about 20. If it is noticeable, but not obvious, try 10. A correction of less than 10 is harder to estimate without direct comparison with the original transparency colors.

This is a positive process: filters add their color to the print

Because this is a positive process, the print will react directly and positively to filter colors—for example, adding magenta to the filter pack will add magenta to the print and removing a yellow filter from the pack will reduce the yellow saturation in the print image. You can get some idea of the necessary correction, therefore, by viewing the print through various filters to see which one seems to balance the color most satisfactorily. This is a rather subjective and haphazard procedure, but with practice, you'll develop some skill at it. (See plate 12.)

There are two ways of using viewing filters

There are two ways of using the viewing filters—if you hold the filter to your eye and look at the print through it, you will see a relatively subtle color shift; if the filter is laid in direct contact with the print surface, the color shift is apparently greater. With Cibachrome, and also with Ektachrome R-14, holding the filter at the eye is the best way to appraise the probable effect of adding *that* filter to the filter pack. If you like the effect you see when the filter is lying on the print surface, you'll have to add a filter of *twice* its strength to the filter pack to get the desired correction. For example, if holding a 10M filter to your eye causes a pleasing effect, then add 10M to the filter pack. If it looks better when the 10M filter is lying on the print face, add 20M to the filter pack.

If you make substantial changes in the filter pack, you'll probably have to adjust the exposure to compensate, but exact calculation is practically impossible. As long as there are only one or two colors in the pack, the filter values can be combined and used as a rough guide for exposure estimation. Adding or subtracting yellow filters will not affect the total exposure substantially, regardless of their apparent density, so you need only concern yourself with changes in magenta or cyan filtration. As a very general guide, consider each

You can estimate filter factors this way

Some process variation is possible, but don't overdo it

10 value in either magenta or cyan to be worth about 1/5th stop, then increase the exposure an additional 10% for each filter *sheet* added, regardless of color. For example, if you add 10Y and 20M (to a pack that contains *no cyan*), ignore the added yellow filter factor; then, if the original exposure had been 30 seconds, the magenta factor (2/5 stop) would raise it to about 42 seconds and the two filter sheets would increase that an additional 20% for a final exposure of about 50 seconds.

Your next print, using the filter correction and exposure time estimated from the test, should be better, but will probably not be perfect. Process the print as before, and let it dry before appraising it (wet prints appear more magenta than they will when dry). Estimate the corrections again, if necessary, and make another print; this one should be nearly perfect. If it is not, review the previous instructions and try again. When you arrive at a satisfactory filter pack, record it for future reference. It will be valid for other prints made from similar transparencies on that particular batch of paper.

It is not usually wise to deviate very far from the manufacturer's instructions in the use of any material, and, of course, you do so at the risk of wasting your time and some expensive material. Still, if you have good control of the process and are a sensitive worker, you can manipulate Cibachrome to some extent. Its excessive contrast, for example, can be reduced a little, without serious loss of other qualities, if the development is also reduced somewhat. Don't attempt to do this by only reducing the time, however. It's better to weaken the developer by giving the paper a preliminary rinse with plain water for about a minute. Dump it out, add the developer, and continue normally. If you prefer, you can dilute the developer with up to about equal parts of water and develop normally, or for a little longer time. A third alternative is to use a milder developer, such as D-76 (any ordinary black-and-white developer will produce an image of some kind on Cibachrome) for 4 minutes or more. All these modifications will necessitate some increase in exposure, reduce contrast, and result in a color shift, which is generally correctable by filtration. If carried to extremes, however, reduced development will result in muddy colors, uncorrectable color shifts, and, worst of all, unacceptable putty-colored highlights. (See plate 16.)

One other deviation from the recommendations may be possible. If you are careful to level your working surface, you may be able to process the materials satisfactorily in less than the recommended 3 ounces of each chemical solution. A preliminary water bath will help prevent uneven development streaks. Obviously this is not the best procedure, but if economy is an overriding concern it may be worth a try. Weigh the possible savings in chemicals against the possible waste of paper, however. A single sheet of paper is worth more than the chemicals in which it's processed.

You can make small prints with the Unidrum by cutting the paper into 4″ × 5″ or 5″ × 8″ pieces before exposure, but the Cibachrome drum will not process these small pieces reliably. It's not difficult to make multiple prints on a single sheet, however, and you'll find this a convenient way to compare the filter requirements of two or more transparencies.

Synopsis

**Process Steps, Cibachrome P-12
Chemistry in Drum**

Developer (at 22°C to 26°C or 72°F to 78°F). Use 3 ounces and develop with rolling agitation for 2 minutes (including drain time). At 1:45, drain developer into a glass or plastic waste storage container. At 2:00, pour in 3 ounces of Bleach (same temperature range). Roll tank to agitate for 4 minutes. At 3:45, drain bleach into waste storage container. At 4:00, pour in 3 ounces of Fix (same temperature range). Roll to agitate for 3 minutes. At 3:00, drain fix into waste container and pour in about 4 to 6 ounces of water. Agitate briefly and drain. Remove print from drum and place it in running water to

Wash at about 24°C (75°F) for 3 minutes. Wash out the tank thoroughly and dry it with a clean towel. Add two neutralizing tablets to the used solutions in the waste container. When the wash time is up, wipe or squeegee the print surfaces carefully and hang the print to dry. Warm, moving air will hasten drying, but avoid excessive heat.

Note: This P-12 chemistry is being replaced by a new system, P-30. Follow manufacturers instructions for its use.

Figure 7.4
Cardboard mask on easel

You can print more than one image on a sheet

A simple cardboard mask (fig. 7.4) fastened to the easel margins will permit exposure of one-fourth or one-half sheet of paper at a time. Focus and compose the image in the mask opening, then before putting the printing paper into the easel, clip one (for instance, the upper right-hand) corner to identify its position. Make the first exposure in the mask opening, then (if you want more than one copy of the same image) turn the paper around so the clipped corner is in the lower left. Make the exposure, then remove the paper to a lightproof place and turn on the lights. Turn the cardboard mask over to shift the position of the mask opening, and recompose the image (or a new one) in the new position. Turn out the lights, insert the paper with the clipped corner in the upper right, and make the exposure. Turn the paper around and make the fourth exposure with the clipped corner in the lower left. Process the print and you should have four small prints, neatly spaced on the sheet.

After you have gained some experience, you should be able to make useful first tests of new transparencies by simply contact printing them, cardboard mounts and all. (See plate 17.) This is an excellent way to estimate exposure and filtration for the individual prints. It will be most useful if the enlarger is used as the printing light and is set at the right height and the right aperture for the prints you will make by projection, and if you can use a previously tested filter pack for the exposure.

Although this may sound complicated, you will find the process quite simple after you've tried it a few times. Keep notes on all details of exposure and filtration and on any other process details you feel may influence the results. Work logically; if something goes wrong, try to find out the cause and correct it before going on.

Printing from Negatives: Unicolor R-2

A color matrix calculator is a convenience

So is a motor agitator for the drum

If you plan to do very much color printing from negatives, you should probably buy one of the *color matrix* subtractive color calculators marketed by Omega, Beseler, or Unicolor. Unicolor's Duocube is typical, easy to use, and effective. You should also get a horizontal-filling drum like the Unidrum, mentioned previously. Similar products are available from a number of other manufacturers. A convenient (but not necessary) addition is a motor agitator unit which twirls the drum for you during processing. Again, several similar models are available; Unicolor's product is called a Uniroller. You probably don't really need a safelight, and it's safer not to use one; but if you think you must have one, get the Wratten #13, which is recommended for Ektacolor type 74 and 78 (a slightly higher contrast version of type 74) paper. It can also be used, with reasonable care, with Unicolor paper (but not with Cibachrome). Finally, of course, you'll need to buy a chemical processing kit.

There are several chemical systems available

There are several "two-step" processing kits on the market. By eliminating the usual stop bath, water rinses and stabilizer, these simplified systems reduce color processing to its barest essentials. The film is simply developed, treated in a combined bleach-fix bath, then washed and dried. Two-step processing obviously saves time but I don't recommend it for best results. If not carefully controlled, the abbreviated process is a bit more likely to produce stains or color variations than the regular processes are, and some authorities feel that eliminating the stabilizer may cause the image dyes to fade prematurely. I think you're likely to get better results with the regular processes, such as Kodak's Ektaprint 2 or Unicolor's R-2, at least while you're learning to work with color materials. You can process Kodak Type 74 and 78 papers and Unicolor RB paper in either of these chemical systems.

Before mixing the working solutions from your chemical concentrates, check them to be sure they have not crystallized (from being chilled or frozen in transit or storage). If crystals are present in any of the solutions, loosen the bottle caps, place the bottles in a warm water bath (about 32°C, or 90°F), and stir the contents occasionally until the crystals redissolve. Plan to use up the partially used concentrates within a month or two for best results. Don't deliberately freeze color chemicals to preserve them; they'll keep well in full bottles, protected from air and excessive heat.

All-liquid chemistry is easy to use and economical

With all-liquid chemistry, it is easy and advisable to make only as much working solution as you will use within a few days. Unicolor's R-2 kit makes this easy by including mixing instructions for as little as 8-ounce volumes of each solution. Smaller volumes than this are probably not advisable because of the difficulty of measuring accurately the very small amounts required of some of the concentrates. You should, of course, wear some sort of hand protection when mixing any color chemicals. Follow the instructions carefully and store the working solutions in very clean glass or plastic bottles of the appropriate size. Clean any chemical spills and wash all utensils and your hands after the chemical preparation.

When you are ready to begin printing, set the bottles of working solution in a water bath to bring them to the recommended temperature. Although tray development is possible, drum processing is easy and economical and allows most of the work to be done in full room light, a real convenience. My recommendation is to use trays only for very large or odd-size prints that won't fit into your drum.

Drum temperature is important

If you are using the Unicolor materials (other processes are generally similar but will differ in detail), bring the working solutions to about 24°C (75°F). The actual temperature of the individual solutions is not particularly critical in drum processing, because of the very small volumes used; the drum temperature itself is more important, and is established by a hot water presoak step immediately preceding development. While the chemicals are warming up, check your drum to be sure it's clean and dry and set it and its cover in a convenient spot for loading in the dark.

Figure 7.5

a. The temperature of the Unicolor solutions is not very critical because the drum will be hot when they're poured in and the small volumes involved will be warmed almost immediately; nevertheless, it's wise to standardize on a starting temperature of about 24°C to 26°C (75°F to 80°F). Be sure the drum is clean. You can leave it in the sink if you plan to load it "wet." (Unicolor representatives recommend this procedure.)

b. If you plan to load the drum "dry," be sure it is dry inside and out, and set it out in a convenient location so you can find it in the dark.

c. Clean the negative as previously described.

d. Adjust the image size and composition and focus.

e. Tape the cardboard mask onto the easel so it will provide four equal test areas. Move the easel so the mask opening is directly under the enlarger lens.

f. Make up the recommended filter pack or dial in the filtration if you have a color head.

a

b

c

d

e

f

g. Stop the lens down one full stop from maximum aperture. Now turn out all the lights and work the next four steps in total darkness.

h. Put a sheet of paper in the easel. Either Unicolor or Kodak papers are suitable. Notch one corner of the sheet so you can tell which exposures are which.

i. Place the Duocube on the paper. It will fit neatly into the cardboard mask opening. Expose through the plastic diffuser which is supplied with the Duocube kit. The enlarger shown here has a diffuser built-in. After the first exposure, turn the paper around and expose the second test. Then remove the paper to a lighttight place and turn on the lights.

j. Turn the cardboard mask over and retape it to the easel so you can expose the other two quadrants of the paper. Turn out the lights again. Replace the paper and the Duocube and make the final two exposures. The notched corner will help you identify the location of each exposure.

k. Still in complete darkness, load the drum. If you prefer the "wet" method, tuck the exposed paper away out of the light while you fill the drum with water at about 41°C (105°F), then turn out the lights again and load the drum. With either method, be sure the end cap is on and securely seated before turning the lights on.

g

h

i

j

k

l. If you loaded the drum "dry," now is the time to fill it with 41°C water for the presoak step.

m. While the paper is presoaking, measure out 2 ounces of developer. Presoak for 1 minute.

n. Dump out the presoak water . . .

o. Set the drum on the agitator (or on its feet if you don't have an agitator) and pour in the developer. In this tank design the solutions flow into a trough below the print and will not contact it until the drum is rolled.

p. Set the timer for 4 minutes, start it and the agitator. If you don't have an agitator, simply knock the drum off its feet and roll it back and forth until the feet stop it, continuously. Be sure the surface is flat and level to avoid uneven development.

q. While the development is proceeding, measure out 2 ounces of stop. At about 3:45, dump out the developer and drain until the timer rings.

r. Then pour in the stop, set the timer for 30 seconds and start it. Start the agitator at the same time.

s. Agitate the stop for the full 30 seconds.

l

m

n

o

p

q

r

s

t. Then dump the stop and drain thoroughly.

u. Pour in 2 ounces of Blix, set the timer for 2 minutes and start both timer and agitator.

v. Agitate the Blix for the full 2 minutes.

w. Dump out the Blix and agitate the drum a few seconds with several ounces of water. Then remove the print and slip it into a tray of running water.

x. Wash the print for 2 minutes.

y. Soak the print in a tray of stabilizer for about a minute.

z. Squeegee the print lightly and hang to dry. Wait until the print is dry before attempting to judge color balance or exposure.

t

u

v

w

x

y

z

Synopsis

**Process Steps, Unicolor R-2
Chemistry in Drum**

Presoak paper in Unidrum by filling drum with about 2 quarts of water at about 40°C to 43°C (105°F to 110°F), allowing drum to stand on end for at least 1 minute. Dump and then add 2 ounces of
Developer at about 21°C to 27°C (70°F to 80°F) and agitate by rolling drum for 4 minutes. Drain drum and pour in 2 ounces of
Stop bath at same temperature range as developer. Agitate stop bath for 30 seconds to a minute. Drain drum and pour in
Blix at same temperature range and agitate for 2 minutes. Drain drum and pour in about 8 ounces of

Water at same general temperature range. Agitate, then drain and refill every 15 or 20 seconds for at least 2 minutes—minimum of 6 times. Remove print and treat in a tray of
Stabilizer solution, at same temperature range, for 30 seconds to a minute, with agitation. Remove print; wipe or squeegee surfaces very gently and hang or lay out, emulsion up, to dry. Clean up drum, utensils, and sink area, and wash your hands. Wipe drum dry for next use.

Start out with the manufacturer's recommended filter pack

Consult the manufacturer's literature to find the recommended basic filter pack for the kind of negative film you are printing (different types of films require different filtration) and for the paper in use. For example, if you are planning to print a Vericolor II negative on Unicolor RB (resin-base) paper, the recommended filter pack is UV + 50Y + 40M. The UV filter is similar to the Wratten 2B used in the Cibachrome pack; they can be used interchangeably, but be sure to include *one* of them in the pack. You will probably notice some filter *color correction numbers* stamped on the back of the color paper package. Ignore them temporarily; we'll discuss them later.

For your first test, select a well-exposed negative that contains an average mix of color and density, such as an outdoor group or street scene. Clean your negative carefully and insert it into the enlarger, being sure that no white light can leak past it to dilute the color of the projected image. Focus and compose the image at the desired size, then either make a test strip or, preferably, use your Duocube (or equivalent) subtractive color calculator.

Make a test strip or

If you prefer to work with a test strip, follow the procedure suggested for Cibachrome testing on page 217 and process it. When it is dry, study the most nearly normal-looking area of the test image to determine whether there is an overall color cast or stain. If one is present, try to find a CC filter that, when laid on the white margin of the test print, appears to match the hue and intensity of the image color cast. For example, if you perceive an overall yellow tint on the test image and if a 10Y filter lying on the white print margin seems to match the image tint, *add that filter* to the filter pack. Estimate the correct exposure by inspecting the test strip segments and increasing the exposure by 1/5 stop for each CC 10 value of magenta or cyan (not yellow) and by about 10% for each filter you've added to the pack (there shouldn't have to be more than one or two). Make another print using the adjusted pack and exposure time, and process it. For further filter pack adjustment instructions, skip to page 230.

If you have the Duocube, proceed as follows (follow manufacturer's instructions for other brands).

Install the cardboard mask (fig. 7.4) on your easel and position the easel so the mask opening is directly under the enlarging lens. Don't worry about image position or composition at this point. Stop the lens down one stop from maximum aperture.

Use the color matrix calculator

Turn out the lights, place a sheet of RB or type 74 or 78 paper in the easel, and place the Duocube matrix on the unmasked quarter of the paper emulsion. Hold the diffuser (supplied) under the enlarger lens to integrate the image colors into one more-or-less neutral tone, and make a 10-second exposure. Reverse the paper sheet under the mask to reveal a new quarter of the sheet and make another contact print of the Duocube, this time using a 20-second exposure.

Expose the matrix through a diffuser

Tuck the paper sheet away in a lightproof container; turn on the lights and turn the mask over so it will expose the other two quarters of the paper. Recenter the mask opening under the lens and turn out the lights. Insert the paper in the easel and make a Duocube print through the diffuser, as before, with an exposure of 40 seconds. Repeat on the last quarter of the paper, for 80 seconds. Load the paper into the drum and install the lid; this will require a firm twist if the sealing gasket is new. Check it by feeling the position of the drum feet. If they are not aligned, the cover may not be seated properly. Correct it before turning on the lights.

In full room light again, check the temperature of the solutions. If they are not within the permissible 20°C to 27°C (70°F to 80°F) range, raise or lower the temperature of the water bath and stir the developer in its bottle until it is approximately 24°C (75°F). Then, fill the Unidrum with water at about 40°C (105°F) by holding the drum at about a 45° slant and pouring water into the spout until it runs over. This will take about two quarts of water. Stand the drum on end and let it soak for a minute. While you are waiting, pour out 2 ounces of developer in a small graduate or plastic cup.

Adjust the temperature of the solutions

And process the matrix test print

Dump the water out of the drum and shake it a few times to be sure it's empty, then set it down on its feet (or on the Uniroller motor agitator, if you have one) and pour the 2 ounces of developer into the drum spout. Set the timer for 4 minutes, start it, and immediately turn on the agitator or begin manual agitation by rolling the drum back and forth until its feet hit on a level surface. Continue the agitation for 3 minutes and 45 seconds. Dump the developer down the drain, and when the timer rings, pour 2 ounces of stop bath into the drum and agitate for at least 30 seconds. Dump the stop bath, add 2 ounces of Blix, and agitate for 2 minutes. Dump, and pour in about 8 ounces of water at about 21°C to 27°C (70°F to 80°F); agitate briefly and drain. Repeat this rinse-and-drain procedure at least five more times over a period of at least 2 minutes; then open the drum and remove the print. Rinse it briefly once more in a tray of clean water, then slip it into a clean tray containing at least 8 ounces of stabilizer solution and agitate the print for 30 seconds or so. Then wipe the print surfaces *gently* with a damp chamois or soft squeegee and lay it faceup to dry. Alternatively (and in my opinion preferably), wipe gently and hang by one corner in a film dryer. Return the stabilizer to its storage bottle and save it for future use. Discard the stabilizer when the other chemical solutions in that working set have been used up.

When the print is dry, you should have at least two or three usable test images of the Duocube color matrix to work with. Below the left-hand array of each set of color patches, you should be able to discern a row of blue-green squares. Select a sample image that shows from three to five squares (count the squares as visible if you can see all four corners), then lay the gray comparator card (supplied in the kit) over the left-hand color matrix and locate the color patch in the array that seems most nearly neutral gray, as compared to one of the gray comparator sections. Use a light gray section to match a light color patch and a darker gray section to match a darker color patch so tonal differences won't interfere with your color perception. (See plate 20.)

Locate a neutral patch with the comparator

None of the color patches will be a completely neutral gray, but you should be able to locate a "most nearly neutral" patch without too much difficulty. Identify this patch on the filter correction chart; let's assume it's patch D 10Y 15C, near lower left center of the left-hand array. This indicates that you should add 10Y and 15C filters to the existing filter pack in the enlarger before you make a print.

And count the visible blue squares

Now, suppose you have selected the test image that received the 20-second exposure and you can count 4 blue squares under the left-hand matrix. Consulting the exposure correction chart for patch D and square 4 leads you to the information −1f 1.0. This means that, after adding the recommended filters to the pack, you should reduce the lens aperture by one stop and multiply the exposure time by 1.0—in other words, don't change it; use the 20-second exposure that you used for the test.

Adding the new filters to the existing pack may produce some neutral density. In the illustration given, for example, the basic pack contains UV + 50Y + 40M and the new filters will make the pack

UV + 60Y + 40M + 15C. Because there are at least 15 of each primary color in this new pack, it contains 15 neutral density which will simply reduce the enlarger light intensity without doing anything to the color balance. Normally we would remove 15C + 15Y + 15M from the pack, leaving UV + 45Y + 25M; but when using the Duocube system, *leave all the filters in place.* The appropriate exposure increase, necessitated by the neutral density, is included in the exposure correction recommendations. Using the complete new filter pack, the reduced aperture, and the 20-second exposure time, make a print of your negative and process it.

Filter Pack Adjustment

When this print is dry, inspect it carefully for density and color balance. (See plate 17.) If the print is much too dark, it has probably received more than one stop *too much* exposure (remember this is a *negative* process); if much too light, it will need a stop or more increase in exposure. If the color balance is improved when the print is viewed through a 10 filter of some color, held at the eye, *remove half that value (05) of that color* from the filter pack, or add 05 of *the complementary color* to the pack. If the correction is best when the 10 filter is laid in contact with the print surface, adjust the filter pack by 10. (See plate 18.) If a 10 filter is not sufficient correction, even when in contact with the print surface, you will need to alter the filter pack by 15 or more (highly unlikely).

For example, the print seems best when a 10B filter is laid on its surface. This indicates that the print image needs 10 more units of blue which, in other words, means that we must *remove 10B from the negative* image or *add 10Y* (the complement of blue) *to the negative* image. Except when using the Duocube calculator, it's always advisable to remove filters from the pack rather than add them (if you can), so extract 10B from the pack. Again, the existing pack consists of UV + 60Y + 40M + 15C.

There's apparently no "blue" in this pack, but remember that blue is a mixture of magenta and cyan (just as green is a mix of cyan and yellow, and red is a mix of magenta and yellow). Furthermore, although the hue changes when you blend two different filter colors, the numbers don't add up (for example, 05Y + 05C = 05G, not 10G; and 10M + 20Y = 10R + 10Y, not 20R + 10Y, or 30R). To remove the 10B from the filter pack, therefore, we must first dissect it into its component pigment primary colors: 10M + 10C. Now it's easy:

$$\begin{array}{r} UV + 60Y + 40M + 15C \\ - 10M - 10C \\ \hline UV + 60Y + 30M + 05C \end{array}$$

Since we're beginning to make intuitive corrections in the pack, we really should remove the neutral density by taking out all of one of the colors and equal amounts of each of the other two. Cyan is present in the smallest amount, so out it goes, followed by equal amounts of magenta and yellow:

$$\begin{array}{r} UV + 60Y + 30M + 05C \\ - 05Y - 05M - 05C \\ \hline UV + 55Y + 25M \end{array}$$

Now we must include some exposure compensation for the filter changes. There are several ways to estimate this, and they don't all produce the same results. The charts and dial calculators in the *Kodak Color Dataguide* offer what are probably the most accurate methods of estimation. But, lacking those, you can use the rule of thumb given earlier—ignore the yellow filter factors entirely (but count them as "sheets") and assume that a value of 10 in either magenta or cyan is equivalent to 1/5th stop; then make an additional adjustment of 10% for each filter added to or subtracted from the old pack.

Figure 7.6
Duocube correction chart.

For example, if we ignore the yellow filtration, the new pack differs from the old by −15M −15C. Together this represents about 3/5ths of a stop *less* density and indicates, therefore, that the new pack will require less exposure. The original exposure was 20 seconds, so the new one should be about 14 seconds, or approximately 3/5ths of a stop less than 20. If we assume that the two filter packs contained the same number of filters, there is no "filter sheet" correction to apply. If the new pack contains, say, one less filter than the old, a further 10% exposure reduction to about 12.5 seconds is in order. This method is obviously rather approximate, but it will serve reasonably well in the absence of a better one.

This print should be reasonably good

Make another print and check it carefully. It should be reasonably good, but if it needs further correction, review the previous instructions and try again.

When you have arrived at a satisfactory filter pack for the negative type and paper lot that you're using, it should be satisfactory for other negatives of the same type, printed on paper from that emulsion batch; the emulsion number is printed on the paper package. Obtain the same emulsion number, if you can, when you buy your next supply.

Keep careful records of your procedure

Although you may have arrived at your present working filter pack by personal trial, it will include some filtration necessitated by the paper balance itself. A new paper lot will probably be somewhat different. You can compare the old paper with the new by checking the filter recommendations on both packages. Then, remove from your working pack the filters recommended for the old paper lot and add to the pack the filters recommended for the new paper. A single print on the new paper will probably be sufficient to appraise the color balance and make a satisfactory adjustment in the working filter pack.

There are many approaches to color printing control but most workers would agree that it is important to proceed methodically and consistently and to keep careful records of details like filter packs, exposure times, paper characteristics, and so forth. It will help a very great deal if you have a "standard" negative, preferably one containing some neutral grays and some relatively pure colors. You can make your own standard negative or you can buy one. A useful one, with matching reference print, is included in the *Kodak Color Dataguide*. (See plate 19.) Comparing your print with the reference print will give you a quick and accurate check of color balance.

Although only two methods of color printing have been covered in any detail, the basic principles discussed will apply to others, as well. You do not need lots of expensive equipment or extensive experience to "do color." Simply follow the instructions for the process you select; use reasonable care in handling the chemicals and other materials; use fresh materials; work from good original slides or negatives; study the effects of filtration until you understand the principles involved; and keep careful and complete records of your procedures. Good results are sure to follow!

Summary

The absence of all light color is black; the absence of all pigment color is white. Blending light primary colors can produce other colors or white light; blending pigment primaries can produce other colors or black. The light and pigment primaries are complements of each other. Colors in photography are reproduced by separating the subject colors into their light primaries by filtration to form a negative record; recombining them in pigment primaries produces a positive image. Color films accomplish this by employing three separate emulsion layers, each sensitive to one of the light primaries. Color-negative films must be printed on color-sensitive paper to produce the color-positive image; color-positive films produce the color-positive image in a two-stage process in the film itself.

Color films are less tolerant of exposure errors than are black-and-white films, and they permit very little contrast control. Fast films are more grainy and less sharp, in general, than slow films. Color films record colors objectively and most are balanced for some specific white standard. If exposed to light of some other color, they record it as a tint. Color balance is expressed in Kelvin degrees as color temperature. Daylight films are balanced for $5500°K$; tungsten films are either $3200°K$ or $3400°K$. Light of nonstandard color can often be adjusted by filtration.

Conversion and light-balancing filters are intended to adjust color temperature in the blue-orange range. Computing filter correction in Kelvin degrees is mathematically awkward; mired correction is easier to deal with. Positive mired numbers indicate warming filters; negative numbers indicate cooling filters. Color temperature can be measured with a special meter. For most accurate results, all three primary colors must be measured.

Color-compensating filters are logically calibrated and identified by the prefix "CC" and a number indicating the filter strength. They are available in six colors in several densities. They are useful for both camera work and printing. For color printing, however, many workers prefer dichroic color enlargers which provide a greater range of stepless control over color balance.

Color films suffer from reciprocity failure, just as black-and-white films do, and they react by exhibiting signs of underexposure and color shifts. Special negative color films are available for long (L) and short (S) exposure times to minimize reciprocity failure effects.

Developing color films is simply a matter of following instructions carefully. It is not economical to develop them yourself unless you use up the chemicals completely. Printing, however, is interesting and well worthwhile.

In addition to the normal black-and-white darkroom equipment, there are a few desirable equipment items—among them, controls for water temperature and line voltage, printing filters or a color head for your enlarger, and some device for estimating print exposure and filtration. There are four common color printing methods: color negative; color positive—dye-forming; color positive—dye-bleaching; and dye-transfer. Most recently, Kodak has applied the "instant print" principle to color printing. Their Ektaflex process, using a special processor, produces damp-dry color prints from either negatives or positives in minutes. Cibachrome is a dye-bleach procedure and a good first process.

It is convenient to use the Cibachrome drum for processing. Mix the chemicals carefully and use them fresh. Follow the process step instructions carefully and produce a test print. Collect the processing chemicals in a large plastic container and add the indicated number of neutralizing tablets to the mixture before pouring it down the drain.

View the dry print through the various CC filters to see which one seems to produce the best color balance; then add that filter to the filter pack for the next print. Some exposure compensation may be necessary.

Cibachrome contrast is normally high. It can be modified somewhat by reducing development, but there is danger of excessive color shifts and muddy highlights if this is overdone. Prints smaller than $8'' \times 10''$ can be made in the drum by printing several images on one paper sheet, using a cardboard mask in the easel.

Color negative printing requires special chemicals and paper but drum processing is convenient. The Unicolor (or similar) drum is easy to use, and a motorized agitator is helpful. A color matrix calculator, such as the Duocube, will simplify testing.

Mix the solutions carefully and use them fresh. Follow the manufacturer's filter pack recommendation and make a Duocube test, as described. A safelight is neither necessary nor desirable; work in total darkness. Process the test as instructed and view the dry print through the viewing filters. The filter color that seems to provide the best visual balance should be *subtracted* from the filter pack, or its complement *added*. Some exposure adjustment will probably be required; follow the instructions for refining the filter pack and for calculating exposures. Printing from different negative material or using a different emulsion lot of paper will require filter pack adjustment.

Special Camera Techniques

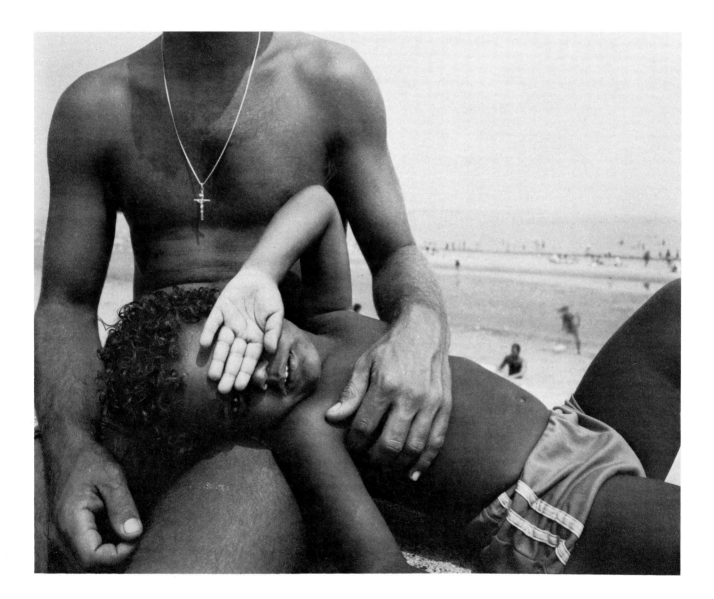

Outline

View and Field Cameras
    Operating
    Using Sheet Film
    Loading
Processing Sheet Film in a Tray
Using the View Camera
    Shifts and Swings
    Lens Types
The Exposure-Development Relationship
Interpreting the Technical Literature
Using Average Gradient Information
Light Meters for View Cameras
    Wide-field Averaging Reflectance Meters
    Spotmeters
    Incident Meters
An Incident Metering System
The Zone System
    What It Is and What It Can Do
    The Concept of Zones
    How the Zone System Works
    Zone System Calibration
CI Charts
Close-up Photography
Copying Techniques

8

View and Field Cameras

In recent years, there has been a considerable revival of interest in large-format photography and a substantial number of people have turned to the field camera as a reasonable compromise between the image quality of the view camera and the portability of the hand camera. Field cameras are basically view cameras, with somewhat restricted capability, very lightly constructed, usually of wood, and designed to fold up very compactly for carrying. The lightest models in the 4″ × 5″ size are not very much larger (in their folded state) and are no heavier than some full-size 35mm SLRs.

View and field cameras require firm support

Like view cameras, field cameras must be used on a tripod or other firm support. Most of them will accommodate wide-angle lenses or moderately long-focus lenses without difficulty and will provide enough bellows extension to permit life-size close-ups. Although they don't provide as great a range of adjustments as do view cameras, and cannot be adapted or added onto to anywhere near the same degree, they handle most view camera chores very adequately and are much more convenient to carry and use outside the studio.

Operating

If their various specialized adjustments are set at the neutral position, view cameras and field cameras are relatively simple to operate. For ordinary work, the lensboard and the camera back should be centered and parallel to each other. The camera should be mounted straight on the tripod head, so tilting the head forward and backward will not deflect the image horizon. Both front and back standards of most view cameras are equipped with focusing knobs (most field cameras have only front-focus controls) and they should be adjusted if necessary to balance the camera on the tripod. Be sure to lock all adjustments securely, but not so tightly that they bind.

Don't extend the tripod center column farther than necessary

Adjust the tripod height by lengthening or shortening the legs. A minor change in height may be made with the tripod central column, but it is risky to operate a view camera on a column extended more than just a few inches because of probable vibration.

Revere Beach, Massachusetts, 1980.
Nick Nixon.
Nixon has an extraordinary knack for photographing strangers at pointblank range without apparently disturbing them in any way. In this photograph he combines an expression of relaxed intimacy with the exquisite rendering of detail, texture, and gradation that are characteristic of the large-format contact print.
(Courtesy of the photographer.)

Point the camera in the general direction of the subject. Open the shutter by using the time setting or the press-focus lever and open the diaphragm fully. Cover your head and the camera back with a black focusing cloth and look at, not through, the groundglass. The image will appear on the groundglass upside down, backwards, and in full color.

a

b

c

d

e

Figure 8.1

a. Open the camera shutter. Here the press-focus button is being used. You can also use Time.

b. Open the diaphragm fully. This makes the visual image bright and reduces depth of field for most critical focusing.

c. Point the camera at your subject, focus and compose. You can use either the front or rear focusing controls in normal situations. The dark cloth or focusing cloth shields the groundglass image from extraneous light.

d. Stop the lens down to shooting aperture. Some lenses may exhibit some focus shift when they are stopped down. For extremely critical work it is wise to check the focus at the shooting aperture with a magnifying glass. This will not usually need to be considered.

e. Close the shutter and, if it is not already cocked, cock it now.

f

g

h

i

f. Pry (don't pull) the spring back open and insert the holder. Be sure it is seated properly to avoid light leaks.

g. Pull out the front darkslide. Don't pull the rear one or you'll miss your picture and fog your next film.

h. Use the darkside to shield the lens from light and make the exposure. Be sure to leave some slack in the cable release to avoid jarring the camera as you press the plunger.

i. Replace the darkside. Be sure that you have turned it around so the black side of the metal end clip is facing out.

j. Pry the back open and remove the holder. It will interlock with a shallow groove in the camera back; pull it back slightly before you try to lift it out. Store your holders in the shade or, preferably, in a closed case in the shade. Most holders will leak a little light in direct sunlight and heat is not good for the film.

j

Figure 8.2
Opened film box

Figure 8.3
Notches in the corner of each film sheet
identify the film type and indicate the
emulsion side.

Camera operation summarized

Loosen the tripod head controls slightly, and while watching the image on the groundglass, move the camera as necessary to adjust the composition. Image size can be adjusted by moving the camera toward or away from the subject or by changing lenses. When the composition is satisfactory, lock the tripod head controls firmly.

Adjust either the front or back focusing controls until the image is in focus, or sharp. You may find that it is not possible to get all of the image in focus at one setting. If this is the case, focus the most important area. Lock the focusing controls.

Close the shutter and set it on the desired speed. Cock the shutter if necessary. Set the diaphragm pointer on the selected aperture number. Insert the film holder in the camera back, being careful not to move the camera out of position. Pull out the front dark slide. Shade the lens. Press the cable release to make the exposure. Insert the dark slide, with the black side showing, to indicate exposed film. Remove the holder from the camera and mark it if you'll want to identify that film later for special development.

Using Sheet Film

**Notches in the upper right; the emulsion
is facing you**

Although some models can accept rollfilm holders, both view and field cameras primarily use sheet film. As the name implies, sheet film (occasionally called cut film) is usually supplied in boxes of twenty-five or more sheets. The stack of sheets is typically wrapped and sealed in a vinyl-foil envelope, then enclosed in a box composed of three interlocking "halves," which seal out the light entirely. After the envelope has been opened (in the dark, of course), it can be discarded and the unused films can be stored in the box without any other protection. Almost all sheet films are so sensitive that they must be handled entirely in the dark until they have been developed and fixed. They must also be handled with considerable care to avoid damage to the sensitive emulsion surface. You can identify the emulsion side of a film sheet by code notches (fig. 8.3) that are cut into one of the short sides of the sheet. When you hold the sheet with the long sides vertical and the notches are in either the upper right or the lower left corner, the emulsion side is facing you. For simplicity, remember to hold the film vertically; the emulsion faces you when the notches are in the upper right-hand corner.

The number and shape of the notches are a clue to the identity of the film. For example, Tri-X pan film sheets can be identified by three closely spaced V-shaped notches. Plus-X film sheets are marked with one V-shaped notch, a space, then two closely spaced nearly square notches (reading from left to right). These notching codes are printed on the bottom of the film boxes and on the information sheets included in the film boxes. Save the sheets for reference. You must know who made the film before it can be identified by the notches, but the position of the notches does identify the emulsion side of the sheet, regardless of the manufacturer.

a

b

Figure 8.4
a. Clean the holder and position its slides, silver side out, like this. Hold the film by the edges, lightly, to avoid fingerprints. The film notches in the upper right-hand corner of the sheet indicate that the emulsion is facing you.

b. Place your thumb and fingertips over the ends of the film guides. When you feel the film slip under your fingers you can be sure it is entering the guides properly.

c. Push the film sheet all the way into the holder. If it is not all the way in, the end flap will only close with difficulty, if at all, and the slide may not close completely. If the film is loaded properly the end flap and the slide will interlock easily to seal the holder against light.

c

Shiny side of slide means fresh film in the holder

Loading

For use in view or field cameras, sheet films are loaded into sheet film holders (fig. 8.4). Holders must be loaded in total darkness. But first, clean them thoroughly in the light. Remove and insert the slides a few times to clean any dust out of the light trap slot and dust the holder interiors thoroughly. Remove possible chemical traces with a dampened cloth. Don't let any moisture get into the light trap and let the holders dry completely before proceeding. Arrange the holders on a clean, dry table surface in the darkroom, with the slides pulled out far enough to clear the entire front opening (but don't remove them entirely).

It is conventional to insert the slides into the holder before loading the film, in such a way that the silver-colored, or shiny, top margin of the slide faces out. The other side of the holder clip is painted black. The shiny side is also identified by a deep notch or a row of embossed dots or lumps, a feature that makes it possible to tell which side is which in the dark. As a general rule, a closed holder with the shiny side of its slide showing should contain fresh, unexposed film. If the dull or black side of the slide shows, the holder may contain exposed film or it may be empty.

Film holders are equipped with simple latches which can be swung over the closed slides to keep them in place. Some photographers consider a holder empty if its latches are open, regardless of the color of its slide clips. This is a more elegant code, and entirely feasible if you pay attention to detail. If there is any doubt in your mind, it is prudent to check the contents of a holder in the darkroom.

Holders are designed to contain two sheets of film at a time, one on each side, in separate lighttight compartments. The film sheets are inserted from one end so the edges of the sheets slip under narrow metal guides at the sides of the compartment (fig. 8.4b). When the sheet is pushed all the way in, the entering

a

b

c

d

Figure 8.5
a. Holding the films lightly like a hand of cards, count the corners to be sure you have them all and that they are separate.

b. Keep one hand dry. Insert the first film into the developer solution and pat it down to be sure it is completely immersed.

c. Place the other sheets, one at a time, on the surface of the developer and pat each one down to wet it thoroughly before adding the next.

d. Herd the sheets into one corner of the tray, gently, then . . .

Tank processing is best for quantity production

end slips under a similar guide, and the trailing end of the film is held in place by a hinged flap which closes the end of the holder and seals it against light leakage. Then the dark slide, held in slots just above the film surface, is slid closed, and as it interlocks with the end flap, the film chamber is made lighttight. It is good practice to load the film into the holder so the notches on the short edge of the film sheet lie under the holder flap. When this is done, it is easy to check the notches without unloading the film if the emulsion type must be identified.

Processing Sheet Film in a Tray

Tray development of sheet film is convenient and economical for batches of up to about six sheets at a time (although you'd better not try to do more than two or three at a time at first). For larger quantities of film, done day after day, tank processing may be preferable. Tray development aerates the developer so thoroughly that it cannot be reused, but the volume required is relatively small and the cost-per-sheet is fairly low. Tank development requires a much larger volume of solution and one-shot use of the developer would be prohibitively expensive. Tank developers, therefore, are almost always replenished after use and are protected from oxidation during storage by "floating lids" which, literally, float on the surface of the solution.

Tank agitation is intermittent and must be carefully done to avoid problems of streaking and uneven development. Hand agitation is usually accomplished by lifting the film hangers out of solution several times, and tipping them in alternate directions as they drain briefly. This is done for about 5 seconds every minute during the development interval. Some older commercial installations agitate the various solutions by introducing bursts of inert gas, frequently nitrogen, through perforated pipes laid in the bottom of each tank.

e

f

e. . . . commence the agitation by sliding the bottom sheet out from under the slack and laying it, carefully, flat on the surface of the solution.

f. Pat it down and extract the next sheet from the bottom of the stack. Continue this sequence throughout the development time.

Figure 8.6
Tank and hanger

Tray processing requires constant agitation

And must be done in total darkness

Most of these *nitrogen burst* systems have now been replaced by complex automatic processing machines. For amateur work, tank processing is probably more trouble and expense than it's worth. Tray processing is at least as fast and cheaper and will produce negatives of excellent quality when done competently. It will take practice but you can learn to do it.

Tray processing requires constant agitation because the films are stacked up in the tray and the solutions can't work on them until they're separated. Using spoiled film and plain water in the tray, practice the agitation technique in normal room light, then try it in the dark until you feel confident. You'll soon work out ways of handling the sheets so they don't cut each other with their sharp corners and so you don't gash them with your fingernails. When you've reached that point you can work with real pictures.

Since tray processing is done in total darkness, you must set up the three main solutions—developer, short-stop, and hypo—and adjust their temperatures, before you turn out the lights to unload the film. Set the interval timer for the proper developing time, too, so you can start it quickly as soon as the film is in the developer. Arrange the trays from left to right (developer, stop, hypo), and be sure you can locate them accurately when the lights are off. You may find it convenient to turn the stop bath tray at right angles to the others so you can identify it, as the middle tray, by touch. When you're set up and oriented, dry your hands, stack your film holders where you can get at them, and be sure the table surface, where you'll be handling the film, is clean and dry. Turn out the lights.

**Count the films to be sure
you have them all**

Remove the film sheets from the holders, one by one, and carefully stack them emulsion up on the table surface. Don't remove the holder slides completely as you do this; just pull them out about halfway. (Not all slides are interchangeable and they may get mixed up if you remove them from their holders.) Then pick up the stack of films, touching the emulsion sides as lightly and as little as possible, and fan them out in your left hand like a hand of cards. Count the corners to be sure that you have them all and that they are not stuck together. With your right hand, locate the developer tray; then, as quickly as possible, take the films with your right hand, one at a time, and place them flat, emulsion up, on the surface of the developer solution and gently push them under. Your right hand will get wet, of course, but if you work quickly and avoid heavy or prolonged pressure on the emulsion, the films will not be damaged.

Separate the films to prevent sticking

As soon as the last film is in the developer, start the timer with your dry left hand, and immediately put both hands into the developer to begin the agitation. Speed is important here; if the films are allowed to lie in a pile in the developer for more than just a few seconds, they will begin to stick together as the gelatin softens and swells. Using just the balls of your fingertips, herd the films into a loose stack in one corner of the tray, lifting them individually to free them if they seem to be sticking. As soon as this has been accomplished, begin the agitation routine. Lift the edge of the stack off the tray bottom far enough so that you can slip your fingers underneath, and slide the bottom film out from under the stack. Lift it out of solution, drop the stack, and place the film flat on the surface, patting it down lightly. Repeat this operation, gently and deliberately, throughout the developing interval.

Then, agitate gently and deliberately

To avoid uneven development, turn the entire stack around in the tray from time to time and vary your hand positions so the warmth of your fingers will not cause local patterns of overdevelopment. Don't try to slide the films back together if the stack floats apart. Rebuild it, film by film, and don't touch the film surfaces with your fingernails. Support the sheets on your fingers; don't lift them by pinching a corner. The wet gelatin is quite soft and very susceptible to cuts, scratches, and finger pressure.

**Rinse your hands before you turn
on the lights**

Watch the timer (it should have luminous hands and numbers) and prepare to remove the films to the stop bath so as to complete the transfer just as the time is up. In the stop bath continue the agitation procedure through three or four cycles, then transfer the sheets to the hypo bath. Agitate the sheets in the hypo for several cycles, then let them lie quietly while you rinse and dry your hands. Turn on the lights and inspect the films to see if they have cleared. If so, give them another minute or two in the fix, with agitation, before removing them. If they are not clear, time them and leave them in the hypo for twice their clearing time, whatever that is, with periodic agitation.

Fix the films for twice the clearing time

When fully fixed, the films should be rinsed briefly in a tray of gently running water, adjusted to approximately the temperature of the processing chemicals, and then placed in the clearing bath. Agitate constantly for the recommended time, then transfer to a large tray of slowly running water or a tank-type film washer. A tray siphon or print siphon is a handy washing device; it will provide simultaneous fresh water flow and drain while maintaining a constant water level in the tray. Adjust the water flow so the films move slowly, and separate them by hand from time to time to insure good water circulation around them.

Wash and dry them

The washed films should be treated in a wetting solution, using the same precautions that apply to rollfilms. Soak them for about a minute in the solution, then pick them out individually. Attach a film clip to one corner of each and hang them up to dry in a dustfree place. If you have not used a wetting solution, or if your wetting solution was mixed with very hard water, you should wipe the films, especially their backs, with a damp, folded piece of chamois skin. Gently!

Store the dry negatives in individual envelopes or use the punched storage sheets that fit standard notebooks.

Synopsis

Sheet Film Developing Process Steps

Total darkness

1. Developer: Kodak HC-110, dilution *B*, 20°C (68°F). Use no less than 4 ounces of solution for each 4″ × 5″ sheet of film, a minimum of 8 ounces total. Agitate continuously. Discard after use. Developing time is as recommended. Other developers may be used; follow the instructions supplied.
2. Short-stop: 1% acetic acid, as for printing, 20°C (68°F). Agitate continuously for about 30 seconds. Discard after use.
3. Fixing bath: Rapid fix, prepare as recommended for films, or use Kodak F-6 solution at regular strength, 20°C (68°F) for twice the clearing time. Agitate at intervals. Save after use. Discard when clearing time reaches about 5 minutes.
4. Water rinse: 16°C to 24°C (65°F to 75°F) for 30 seconds or more with continuous agitation. Discard.
5. Hypo-clearing bath: About 21°C (70°F), dilution, time, and agitation as recommended. Save if desired. Discard when hypo is discarded (unless the manufacturer gives other instructions).
6. Wash: Running water, with occasional agitation, at about 21°C (70°F), for time as specified on hypo-clearing bath package. If hypo-clearing bath is not used, wash must be for at least 30 minutes.
7. Wetting agent: Photoflo solution at about 21°C (70°F), prepared according to package instructions. Soak for about a minute. Distilled water may be advisable if tap water is "hard."
8. Dry: Suspend each film sheet by one corner using film clips or wooden spring clothespins. Hang in a dustfree place or in a film drying cabinet, if available.
9. Keep the dry negatives in negative envelopes for protection from dust and fingerprints.

Using the View Camera

An ordinary camera sees objects in perspective just as the eye does. It will record the sharp convergence of railroad tracks receding into the distance and will picture tall buildings as tapering into the sky. In pictures of this kind the perspective effect may be distracting or the depth of field of the lens may be inadequate to record the subject area sharply because the subject cuts through it at an angle rather than lying parallel to the plane of focus.

Shifts and Swings

View camera adjustments can alter image perspective and depth of field

A view camera has adjustments designed to help solve these problems. They are called the shifts and swings and refer to movements of the front and rear standards of the camera which make it possible to change the normal alignment of the lens and film. The *shifts* are movements of either standard, either vertical or lateral, which keep the lensboard and film plane parallel to each other but decenter the lens with respect to the film. The vertical shift of the lensboard is referred to specifically as the *rising front*. The *swings* allow the standards to pivot around either a vertical or a horizontal axis. The rotation around the horizontal axis is often referred to as a *tilt*.

The shifts are often used to reduce or eliminate the normal effect of converging lines in perspective and are particularly effective in architectural photography. The shift adjustments are also valuable for making slight changes in composition of the groundglass image, eliminating the need to move the entire camera. Both of these uses are possible because the image formed by the lens at the film plane covers a much larger area than the film itself, and the film can be positioned to record any portion of it.

Adjust the camera back first

In setting up the view camera to deal with problems that are not as obvious in their solution as those illustrated, much fumbling with the controls can be avoided if you will remember to *adjust the camera back first, then adjust the lensboard*. All significant control of perspective is accomplished with the back shifts and swings, as are some gross adjustments of the depth of field coverage. Save the lens shifts and swings for relatively minor refinements of the image.

Figure 8.7
a. The movements of the view camera lens
and back are easy to describe but their
effects on the image are not so simple. In
general, movements of the back affect
perspective primarily, and movements of
the lens affect depth of field by displaying
the plane of focus; but these adjustments
interact to a considerable extent. It is
usually safest to move the back first. Avoid
extreme swings and tilts of the lens, or
image sharpness will suffer. Your best
guide to using the view camera
adjustments is simply to watch the effect
of the movements on the image and don't
use any more drastic adjustment than is
absolutely necessary to accomplish your
desired result. Here is a view camera in its
neutral position.

b. Both standards can be "swung" in
either direction, together or separately.

c. The standards can be also "tilted"
forward or backward. Tilts and swings of
the front standard are risky because they
move the image circle away from the film
plane. Back swings and tilts alone are
much safer.

d. Displacing the standards laterally, while
keeping them parallel, is called shifting.
Here the back is shifted left and the front
is shifted right, effectively displacing the
film off-center in the image circle. You must
have a lens of wide coverage and fine
quality to produce a useful image with a
shift like this.

e. The back and lensboard can be raised
or lowered. These are shift adjustments,
but the vertical movements of the
lensboard are referred to as the rising (or
sometimes falling) front. Again, in using
any of the adjustments, be careful not to
let the film get too far off the lens axis or
you'll be disappointed by the image
quality.

a

b

c

d

e

Figure 8.8

a. A view camera with its adjustments in
neutral; the planes of the film and the
lensboard are parallel and the lens is
centered with respect to the film. In this
position the image of a horizontal subject
cuts diagonally through the film plane and
a very small aperture is required to provide
adequate depth of field for objects at
close range. This is a way the camera was
set to make pictures 8.9a, b, and d.

b. If the camera back is tilted to coincide
with the plane of the image the depth of
field effectively parallels the subject plane
and you'll get adequate depth with only a
moderately small aperture, as in figs. 8.9c
and e.

c. You can make the image plane fall on
the film plane by tipping the lens forward,
too. See fig. 8.9f.

d. Tilting the back alone may over-
emphasize foreshortening; tilting the lens
alone may risk degraded image sharpness.
This compromise setting is usually best.
It's most effective when the extended
planes of the film, the lensboard and the
subject all meet at a point in space. This
is obviously possible with any number of
positions of lens, film and subject, but, in
general it's best never to tilt both the film
plane and the lensboard in the same
direction (unless it's done to eliminate the
effect of perspective convergence by
bringing them into *parallel* with the subject
plane).

e. Tilting both standards of the camera
forward like this is risky and may result in
degraded image quality. See fig. 8.9 g.

f. This opposite extreme is similarly risky;
see fig. 8.9h.

a

b

c

d

e

f

Figure 8.9
a. When photographing small objects at
close range with a view camera, you'll find
the depth of field extremely shallow, as is
illustrated here. The camera was focused
on the model helicopter, about 3½ feet
from the lens. The calculated depth of
field, using 6½-inch lens at its maximum
aperture of f/6.3, is only about 4 inches.

b. Even at its smallest aperture (f/45) the
6½-inch lens provides a depth of field of
only about 1½ feet—not nearly enough to
include the full eight foot-length of this
architectural site model.

c. Using the view camera adjustments
can't actually increase the depth of field
but they can help you make the most
efficient use of the available depth.
Here the camera back has been tilted so
that the film plane coincides with the
principle plane of the image. The model
surface is in focus from front to rear and
an aperture of only f/16, which provides a
calculated depth of field of about 6 inches
is sufficient to render the trees and
buildings acceptably sharp. Only the water
tower in the background is slightly soft; it's
about 8 inches tall and protrudes through
the depth of field about two inches. If you
use short focal-length lens at small
aperture and work with fairly small objects,
you may be able to produce a
satisfactorily sharp image without using
the view camera adjustments.

d. This old type case, about 32 inches long, was photographed with a 135mm lens; at f/45, it's fairly sharp overall, but close examination of the original print shows that diffraction (due to the very small aperture size) has softened the image appreciably. The fairly extreme effect of perspective is normal for this moderately-wide-angle lens at close range.

e. Illustrating the effect of tilting the back of the camera as was done in fig. c. The effective plane of the depth of field now lies parallel to the plane of the subject and an aperture of only f/16 produces a crisply detailed picture of the type case. The emphasized effect of fore-shortening, typical of back-swings alone, was not apparent in fig. c, but shows clearly here because of the obvious geometry of this subject—we know the type case is a rectangular object and not as long as it appears here.

f. Shows the effect of tilting the lens. This adjustment also aligns the depth of field with the subject plane and, in this case, provides a sharp image at f/16. Perspective is normal but the type case image is enlarged noticeably because it is not being formed near the margin of the image circle where magnification is greater than at the center. Definition is degraded, too, but is still acceptable here.

g. Demonstrates the effect of tilting both the lens and film planes forward. Foreshortening is actually reduced (because of the tilt of the film plane) but the edge of the image circle now cuts through the film area (because of the extreme lens tilt) and the far end of the type case is underexposed and unsharp.

h. The opposite effect occurs if both the lens and film planes are tilted backward; foreshortening is drastically increased and, although the foreground is still reasonably sharp in this example, it's beginning to darken.

a

b

Figure 8.10
a. Tilting the camera back to frame the
church makes the verticals converge.

b. You can eliminate the convergence of
the verticals and frame the building
satisfactorily by tilting the camera back
and lensboard forward until they are
parallel to the vertical lines of the church.

c. You can achieve the same effect, even
more easily, by beginning with the camera
level (as in fig. A) and using the *rising front*
movement to raise the lens until the church
is suitably placed in the frame.

c

Figure 8.11
Tessar lens

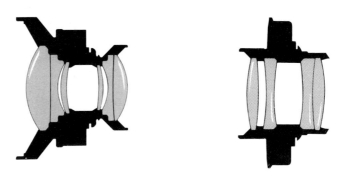

Figure 8.12
Goerz Dagor

**A view camera lens should be
well-corrected and
cover a fairly wide field**

Lens Types

It should be obvious that the lens used for these adjustments should be capable of forming an extensive image area on an essentially flat plane in space, and that the sharpness of the image should be adequate out to its edges. The lens, in short, should be very well corrected for the various aberrations, and should also cover a fairly wide field even at maximum aperture.

Although good lenses of four-element Tessar-type construction (fig. 8.11) are suitable for view camera use in normal focal lengths and at moderate apertures, they do not, as a rule, provide sufficient coverage to permit more than modest adjustments without some loss of image quality. Lenses of more nearly symmetrical construction (fig. 8.12) are probably preferable, since they are likely to provide better coverage and are more likely to maintain their correction at close subject distances.

Some fine lenses, such as the old Protars, the original Schneider Symmars and Goerz Dagors, combine good correction, wide coverage, and moderate speed with the added virtue of being *convertible;* that is, one component can be used alone as a long focal length lens of fairly good quality, which is satisfactory for many purposes when stopped down. This feature has been eliminated from most of the newest designs to permit better correction and enhanced performance for the complete lens.

**Wide-angle and telephoto lenses
may restrict adjustments**

The swings possible with wide-angle lenses will be limited by the inflexibility of the compressed camera bellows as well as the restricted image area available. Some cameras provide recessed lensboards or special bellows units for use with short lenses to allow for some bellows movement, but the swings and shifts should be used with caution with wide-angle lenses. Even in "neutral," the lens field is likely to be only slightly larger than the film area, and deterioration of image quality near the edges of the field will be rapid and extreme. For this same reason long lenses of telephoto construction will permit only moderate swings, since their image circle is deliberately restricted. Long lenses of conventional construction will permit extreme adjustment without much loss of quality.

Figure 8.13
Most lenses for small cameras aren't required to cover an area much larger than the nominal negative size but view camera lenses must cover much more than the film area if the camera's shifts and swings are to be used effectively. In this illustration a 135mm Schneider Symmar lens (moderately wide-angle for a 4 × 5 camera) was used with 8 × 10 film to reveal the limits of the image area. Although this lens illuminates a circle about 8 1/2 inches in diameter (solid outline), it's not all usable; a lighter circle about 7 1/4 inches in diameter (dashed outline) defines the area of acceptable image quality. The vertical and horizontal dashed lines illustrate the tolerable extremes of lateral and vertical shift, and the large dashed rectangle in the center represents the position that the film would occupy if the lens were used on a 4 × 5 camera with all adjustments in neutral. The solid rectangle defines the picture the film would record if the lens were shifted vertically (rising front adjustment) about 1/2 inch and shifted to the left about 3/16 inch. Although you might prefer a bit more sky area in the picture, it's not possible to raise the lens any farther without risking uneven illumination and loss of sharpness.

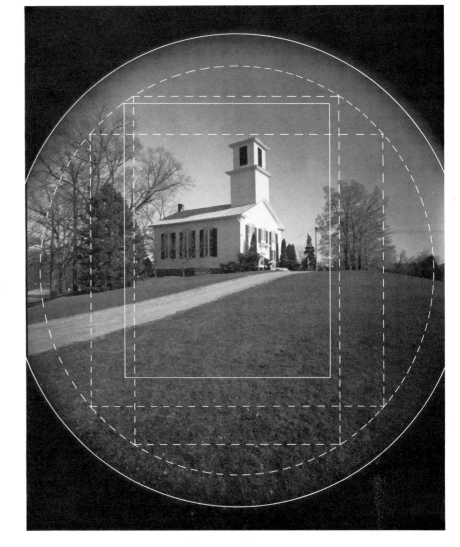

Expose for the shadows; develop for the highlights

The Exposure-Development Relationship

One of the oldest adages in photography is the classic "expose for the shadows and develop for the highlights." This means, of course, that the film must be given sufficient exposure so it can record the darkest portions of the subject; then the development must proceed no further than is required to produce useful negative density corresponding to the brightest areas of the subject. This relationship between exposure and development, and the corresponding relationship between negative density and contrast, is an extremely important one. If you hope to control the medium of photography in any sort of predictable way, you must understand these relationships thoroughly.

Test the effects of exposure and development

An excellent way to investigate the effects of exposure and development is to make a series of negatives to illustrate their possible combinations. Nine negatives will demonstrate the possibilities adequately and the test is easily done. Find a stationary subject of normal contrast in an adequate light condition, and focus and compose it satisfactorily. The camera should be fixed in position so it will not move significantly during the test; nothing should change except the camera exposures. Meter the subject carefully in your usual manner and select a moderately small aperture (for good depth of field) and the appropriate shutter speed.

If you are using sheet film, set the camera controls for normal exposure and expose three films, identically. Then set the camera controls to overexpose the subject by two stops and expose three films. Finally, set the camera to underexpose the subject by two stops and expose three more films. Be sure to mark the holders so you can identify the individual films during processing.

Shoot three sets of three different exposures

If you are using rollfilm, the procedure must be done differently. Either use three separate rolls of film and on each roll expose one-third of the frames normally, overexpose one-third of the frames by two stops, and underexpose one-third of the frames by two stops; or vary the exposures on a single roll in a repetitive sequence (under, normal, over; under, normal, over; under, normal, over; etc.) until the roll has been used up.

In the darkroom, set up a process line of fresh chemicals for film developing and adjust them to the proper temperature. If you are using sheet film, take one normally-exposed sheet, one overexposed sheet, and one underexposed sheet and develop them together for *half* your normal developing time. Similarly, develop the next set of three sheets in fresh or replenished developer for your normal time. Finally develop the remaining set of three in fresh solution for twice your normal developing time. Fix and wash the films as usual and hang them up to dry.

Develop three sets for three different times

If you have used three rolls of film for the test, each roll will contain some underexposures, some normal exposures, and some overexposures. Develop one roll for half normal time, one for normal time, and one for twice normal time, using fresh or replenished volumes of developer for each roll. If you have made all the exposures on a single roll of film, develop it in an open tank in the dark. At half the normal developing time, remove the roll from the developer and snip off about one-third of its length with scissors. Put the cut-off piece of film into the short-stop bath and return the rest of the roll to the developer. At the end of the normal developing time, snip off another third of the roll and put it into the short-stop with the first piece. Continue developing the remaining third of the roll until you have doubled the normal developing time. Add the last film section to the short-stop, then transfer all three pieces to the hypo. Agitate them briefly (wash your hands) and turn on the lights.

You should have nine different combinations

If you have carried out the test properly, you should now have nine different negatives. Arrange them on a light box in a three-by-three array with the normal negative in the center, as shown in figure 8.14. With a little study, you should be able to identify the significant characteristics of each. With more experience you will be able to look at any negative and determine whether it is "normal" and, if not, whether exposure or development was at fault. In general, the negative shadow areas will provide clues to film exposure—thin shadows indicate underexposure; dense shadows indicate overexposure. Contrast is usually a reliable clue to film development—low contrast probably indicates underdevelopment; high contrast probably indicates overdevelopment. Exposure and development interact to some extent and not all films will react in the same way, but these tendencies are usually dependable, at least for preliminary analysis.

Figure 8.14
The nine-negative array. Overexposed negatives in top horizontal row; normal exposures in middle horizontal row. Underdeveloped negatives in left-hand vertical row; normal development in center vertical row; overdevelopment in right-hand vertical row.

If you are unfamiliar with "bad" negatives, try printing this group of nine. In all probability you'll discover that, while most of them are printable, the normal negative will print easily and yield a fine image with the least fuss. You may get good results from some of the others, too, but you'll probably have to change paper grades and work at it a little. It's very likely that the two extreme examples, underexposed/underdeveloped and overexposed/overdeveloped, will be unprintable. Take a good look at them and try not to make any more like them, *ever!*

These exposure-development relationships can be displayed graphically in *characteristic curve* diagrams as illustrated in figure 8.15. Here the horizontal axis of the graph represents values of exposure, such as might be caused by variations in subject illumination or subject value or by changes in either exposure time or aperture setting. On this axis, exposure values increase from left to right. The vertical axis of the graph indicates values of negative density, which result from film exposure and development and increase from bottom to top. Each curve stands for a specific developing time.

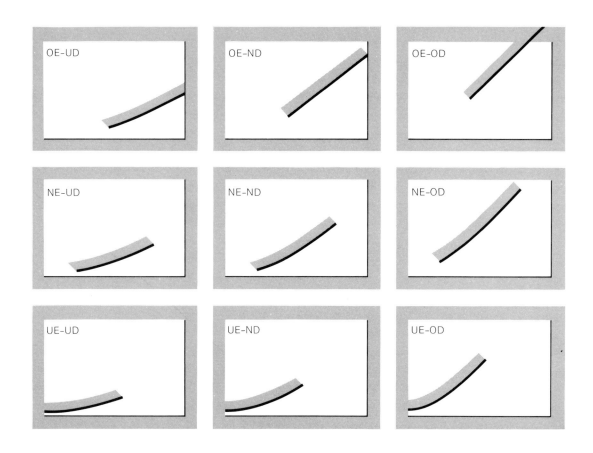

Figure 8.15
Exposure-development diagrams

Curve slope—or gradient—is
an indication of image contrast

Curves for three development conditions are shown. Here curve *A* represents underdevelopment, *B* is normal, and *C* represents overdevelopment. Notice that the slope of the curves changes with development: less-than-normal development produces a gentle slope; overdevelopment results in a steep slope; and normal development produces a moderate slope. (See the curves that correspond to the nine test negatives in fig. 8.14.)

The actual meaning of the curves is easier to explain if they are drawn as straight lines, converting the graphs to simple triangles. In figure 8.17 this has been done, using a base line *B* seven stops long in each case. Seven stops has been chosen as the length of the exposure axes because it represents the range of subject luminance that is considered "normal." In other words, the brightest textured highlight area of a normal subject is seven stops lighter than the darkest useful shadow value of the subject.

Now it is apparent that if *B* is held at constant length and the slope of the curve is changed, the negative contrast, line *A*, must also change. A steep curve slope, corresponding to longer-than-normal development, produces extended negative contrast, while a gently sloping curve results in a negative of short density range. Similarly, if *A* is constant and the curve gradient changes, *B* must vary.

From here it is only a short step to a graphic demonstration of how development can be varied purposely to compensate for abnormal subject contrast. Assuming that a negative range of 3⅓ stops is desirable for printing on normal paper, figure 8.18 illustrates several different subject contrasts, translated into "normal" negatives by different development curve slopes or gradients.

Figure 8.16
Three curve film family

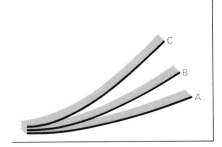

Figure 8.17
a. Normal subject (7 stops), gentle slope (underdevelopment), flat negative (1).

b. Normal subject (7 stops), moderate slope (normal development), normal negative (3½).

c. Normal subject (7 stops), steep slope (overdevelopment), contrasty negative (5).

Figure 8.18
a. Flat subject (4 stops), steep slope (overdevelopment), normal negative (3 1/3).

b. Normal subject (7 stops), moderate slope (normal development), normal negative (3 1/3).

c. Contrasty subject (10 stops), gentle slope (underdevelopment), normal negative (3 1/3).

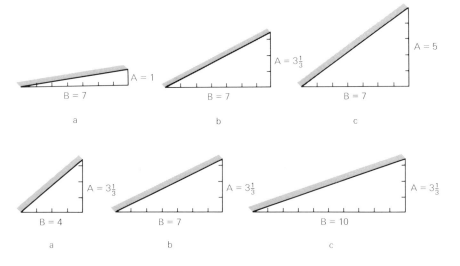

Gamma; average gradient; contrast index

Interpreting the Technical Literature

In technical literature the degree of development, or curve gradient (G), is indicated by the number found by dividing density range (DR) by subject brightness (more correctly, luminance) range (SBR).

When the film curve is actually a straight line, as it has been represented in the demonstration triangles, the number thus found is called the *gamma* number (fig. 8.19). Gamma is not used much anymore, however, because modern films' curves are *really* curves, and a respectable triangle can't be drawn with one curved side. To deal with this problem we sometimes select two points on the film curve that represent useful limits and simply connect them with a straight line to complete the standard triangle (fig. 8.20). The gamma number computed this way is called an *average gradient* number. Most manufacturers publish film developing information based on some form of average gradient measurement. Eastman Kodak calls their method *contrast index;* Ilford, using a more direct approach, describes theirs simply as average gradient and lets it go at that.

Ilford's procedure (fig. 8.21) involves locating a point on the film curve that represents negative density of 0.1 over base-plus-fog or background density; then, using that point as a center, drawing an arc of 1.5 radius to intersect the curve and establish the second point. Connecting the points establishes the average gradient and completes the triangle. Kodak's contrast index procedure is much more complicated than this, but a close approximation can be obtained by following the Ilford method, using a radius of 2.0 rather than 1.5 (fig. 8.22).

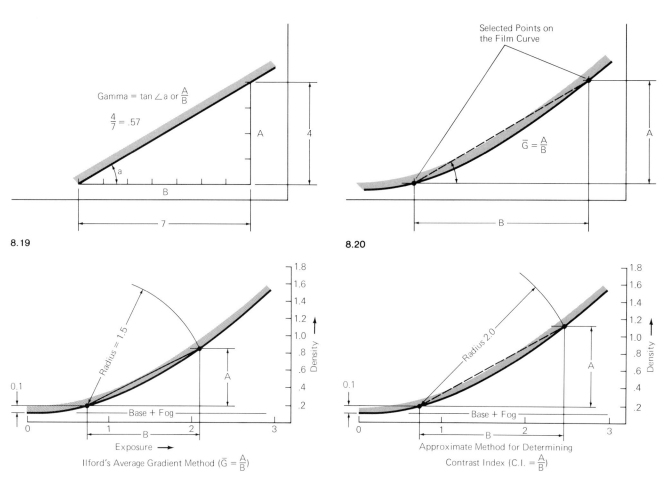

8.19

8.20

8.21

Ilford's Average Gradient Method ($\bar{G} = \frac{A}{B}$)

8.22

Approximate Method for Determining
Contrast Index (C.I. $= \frac{A}{B}$)

Figure 8.19
Gamma

Figure 8.20
Average gradient

Figure 8.21
Ilford method

Figure 8.22
Kodak method, C1

Notice the calibration numbers on these two graphs. They are common logarithms (logs to the base 10) of the actual values of subject luminance and negative opacity. Actually, you don't have to know very much about logarithms to use them effectively in photography. The most important information about them is that the $\log_{10}$ equivalent of the number 2 is 0.3. Therefore, 0.3 is equivalent to 1 stop, and 0.1 equals ⅓ stop. The number of stops equivalent to any range of luminances or densities can be found by dividing the log range by 0.3; thus, Ilford's 0.1 over base-plus-fog represents a negative density ⅓ stop greater than the film background density, and the arc radius of 1.5 is equivalent to 5 stops. Similarly, Kodak's arc radius of 2.0 defines a section of the film curve which is 6⅔ stops long.

Table 8.1 provides a brief list of regular numbers, compared with their $\log_{10}$ equivalents and the intervals in stops between them. Actually, the logs are not exact equivalents of most of the numbers given—for example, the $\log_{10}$ of 8 is closer to .90309 than it is to .9—but these are near enough for our purposes. The log values for 1 and 1000 are correct, and you may be interested to know also that the log of 10 = 1.0, $\log_{10} 100 = 2.0$, and $\log_{10} 1,000,000 = 6.0$ exactly.

Table 8.1	Numbers in geometric sequence	log equivalents	Stops
Comparison of numbers with their log equivalents and intervals in stops	1	0.0	
			1
	2	.3	
			2
	4	.6	
			3
	8	.9	
			4
	16	1.2	
			5
	32	1.5	
			6
	64	1.8	
			7
	125	2.1	
			8
	250	2.4	
			9
	500	2.7	
			10
	1000	3.0	

One final bit of information will help you interpret the published film curves—*positive* logs refer to numbers greater than 1; *negative* logs indicate decimal fractions less than 1. Thus, 2.0 is the log of 100, but minus 2.0 (frequently written as −2.0 or $\bar{2}.0$) is the log of 1/100, or .01. You will frequently see negative log numbers on the exposure axis of film curve graphs because the unit of exposure used in calibration (meter-candle-second) is too large for most film materials and they must be exposed to fractions of the basic unit (fig. 8.23). Most printing papers, on the other hand, are slow enough so the basic exposure unit is not sufficient to affect them at all. Their characteristic curves are calibrated in positive logs indicating multiples of the basic exposure unit (fig. 8.24).

What the curves express: a review

Now let's review briefly. The film characteristic curves display the relationship between values of exposure, film development, and the resulting negative densities. These three variables, graphed simply, form a right triangle (fig. 8.25)—the values of the subject luminance range (from lightest highlight to deepest shadow) fall along the base of the triangle; increments of negative density (from the clearest negative shadow area to the densest highlight) lie along the triangle altitude; and the triangle hypotenuse slope represents the degree of development that the exposed film must receive to produce the desired negative density range or contrast. Development contrast can be identified by a number that compares the negative DR with the subject luminance range, in either stops or $\log_{10}$ numbers. For example, if a negative has only half as much range (contrast) as the subject had, its development contrast number is 0.5 Under some test conditions this number is called gamma, but more usually it will be referred to as contrast index (CI) or, sometimes, average gradient ($\bar{G}$).

Figure 8.23
The sensitometric curves and data in the publication from which these curves were taken (Kodak publication no. F-5) represent current product under normal conditions of exposure and processing. They are averages of a number of production coatings and, therefore, do not apply directly to a particular box or roll of film. They do not represent standards or specifications which must be met by Eastman Kodak Company. Kodak reserves the right to change and improve product characteristics at any time.
Reproduced with permission of the Eastman Kodak Company.

Figure 8.24
Sensitometric curves which represent approximately the characteristics of various grades of Kodak papers with a glossy, ferrotyped surface.
Reproduced with permission of the Eastman Kodak Company.

Figure 8.25
Exposure-development triangle

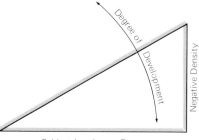

Figure 8.26
CI chart with development time

Using Average Gradient Information

In practice, you know (or can estimate—see appendix 15) the negative density range that prints best for you on normal paper and you can measure the subject range with your meter. Divide the negative DR (it will be given in log numbers) by the subject range (convert stops to log numbers by multiplying stops by 0.3) and you will get the required average gradient number. For this example, you can consider this number to be a contrast index, and by consulting the film manufacturer's published charts, you can find the developing time required to translate the latent film image into a negative of normal contrast. Let's consider a typical situation.

DR/SBR=CI: Consult the chart for developing time

Suppose you discover that your favorite paper and your printing conditions require a negative DR of about 1.1. Suppose also that your measurement of the luminance range (SBR) of your subject turns out to be 8 stops. Convert 8 stops to a log by multiplying by 0.3, which gives you a subject range of 2.4. Divide 1.1 by 2.4 to get .458, call it .46; this is your contrast index. Consult a contrast index/developing time chart (fig. 8.26) to find the appropriate developing time for your subject, in this case 5½ minutes. Be sure to observe the temperature and agitation instructions accompanying the CI chart; proper negative contrast depends upon close control of all development variables.

By definition, CI can only be measured between the points on the film curve defined by its intersections with the 2.0 radius line (fig. 8.22). If your subject tones occupy more or less of the film curve length than this, the average gradient can be determined but it is not contrast index. In spite of this fact, you can use the procedure above in most situations without much danger of error. There will be some discrepancy between your average gradients and published CIs with films that have strongly curved curves (like Tri-X), and there will be greatest chance for error with subjects of extreme contrast, either high or low, but you're not likely to get into serious trouble even in these cases.

Now all you need to know is the SBR

Sheet film is best for this purpose

To make this contrast control system workable, it is only necessary to devise some method of determining subject range with reasonable accuracy. Of course, there must be some provision made for developing the exposed films individually if the subject contrasts are not all the same. This last requirement is no problem with sheet film that can be developed, sheet by sheet, in a tray, but rollfilm exposures are a different matter. The best procedure is to commit a whole roll of film to subjects of similar contrast; this is relatively easy to do if you have several camera bodies or accessory backs for your camera, but is generally impractical for long rolls of 35mm film. If this isn't feasible, be sure that none of the frames on the roll are underexposed and develop either for the average contrast or specifically for the most important pictures on the roll, letting the others do what they will. Probably all, or most, of the negatives will be printable but some of them will probably require paper of other than normal contrast.

Light Meters for View Cameras

For almost all ordinary purposes you'll find the built-in meter in your SLR camera to be highly satisfactory. For view camera use, however, you'll need a separate meter. There are three types to choose from: *wide-field averaging reflectance meters, spotmeters,* and *incident meters.*

Wide-field Averaging Reflectance Meters

Reflectance meters measure luminance

The wide-field averaging reflectance meters are the most common type. They're designed to measure luminance—that is, the light emitted by or reflected from the subject surfaces. They are usually pointed at the subject along the camera line-of-sight so that they measure the same light that the camera sees. A typical reflectance meter has an acceptance angle of about 30°, which means, for example, that from a distance of about 20 feet the meter will read a circular area of the subject about 10 feet in diameter. Furthermore, it will integrate all the variations of light intensity within its field and give you a single *average* reading.

a

b

Figure 8.27
a. Meter in incident mode

b. Meter in reflectance mode

Problem: the meter averages luminance values; the camera doesn't

A spotmeter can help in this case

So can a gray card

Whether this average reading is correct, or even useful, depends not only on the values of luminance represented, but also on their proportionate areas; that is, the meter will be influenced much more strongly by large areas of a given tone than by small areas. If the meter's field includes mostly dark objects with only a few small areas of light tone, it will indicate a low value of average luminance; if the field covers mostly light areas with only a few dark accents, the meter reading will be relatively high. Although this sounds sensible enough, it can create problems for you because that's not the way the camera sees things. The camera doesn't *average* the subject luminances, because it forms a *focused* image, reproducing the individual subject tones on the film.

The film needs enough exposure to record details in the dark shadow areas regardless of their size; that is, the exposure should be the same whether the shadows cover most of the subject area or only a few square inches of it. As far as the camera is concerned only the actual values of luminance are important; neither their relative areas nor the overall average of their luminance values is of any practical importance.

To illustrate the unreliability of average reflectance metering, suppose, for example, that you want to photograph blackbirds feeding in the snow. The film requires an exposure sufficient to render detail and tone in the dark feathers while preserving the subtle texture of the white background. Once you've determined that exposure and set your camera for it, you can photograph one bird or a thousand without changing the camera settings, despite the fact that an overall average reflectance meter reading of a single bird in a field of snow will be considerably higher than a reading of an assembled flock.

Spotmeters

When the extremes of subject tone are represented by very small or inaccessible areas, as in the previous example, you'll find a spotmeter a useful tool. A typical spotmeter can measure a 1° field—equivalent to a circular area about 4 inches in diameter at a distance of twenty feet—and the field is accurately defined in the meter viewfinder. Although they are not suitable for overall average readings, spotmeters make area-by-area analysis of the subject luminances very easy and quite accurate.

Since a reflectance meter is easily deceived by abnormal distribution of tone in the subject, it's often desirable to ignore the subject entirely and take the necessary meter reading from a standard *gray card* placed in the subject space. These cards, available from your camera dealer, are designed to reflect about 18% of the incident light (the light that falls on the subject), and are considered to be representative of an ideal subject. A gray card reading, in other words, will provide correct exposure settings for any normal or near-normal subject, assuming that the card is placed in the same light condition that exists at the subject position, and that the meter is pointed along the camera line-of-sight as the reading of the card is taken.

Figure 8.28
a. Photographer Dave Litschel demonstrates the use of a typical wide-field averaging reflectance meter. Even though Dave is shading the meter cell to protect it from direct sunlight, this is not likely to provide a correct reading; backlighted subjects are difficult to appraise with a wide-field meter.

b. A spotmeter will give more useful information because it allows area-by-area analysis of the subject tones. It will also require thoughtful consideration; Dave will have to decide which subject values are most important, and plan his camera exposure settings to accommodate them.

a

b

Although measuring the incident light with a reflectance meter and gray card is an effective way to determine exposure under ordinary conditions, it isn't foolproof. The card is fairly small, which means that an ordinary meter must be held quite close to it to get an accurate reading, and it's sometimes difficult to avoid casting the shadow of the meter on the card surface. In addition, the card is flat, so it doesn't really substitute for the three-dimensional surface of the average subject and must be positioned with care to avoid highlight or shadow emphasis. Finally, the card is another item that must be carried and handled; if it gets bent or soiled in use, it may not give reliable readings. All these problems were solved when someone invented the incident meter.

Incident Meters

An incident meter is more convenient

An incident meter is really just a reflectance meter with a built-in gray card in the form of a translucent plastic dome covering the meter cell. The plastic dome transmits 18% of the incident light to the cell, and since the dome is hemispherical, it accepts light from the same directions and in the same relative intensities as the subject does. When the meter is held in the subject light condition and pointed at the camera, the reading can be assumed correct for any subject of normal contrast.

Contrary to popular opinion, the incident meter is also suitable for precise metering of abnormal subjects, despite the fact that its readings ignore the subject itself entirely. In fact, when used intelligently, an incident meter allows for a great deal of creative control of image quality. It's also relatively foolproof; incident metering errors usually result in overexposure rather than underexposure, so even fairly inept use of the meter is unlikely to be disastrous.

a

b

Figure 8.29
a. The Incident System requires two meter readings; one in the deepest shadow area where detail must be held and one in the area of brightest illumination. Here Dave Litschel makes the shadow reading. The exposure will be determined from this meter setting.

b. After taking this reading in the brightest illumination Dave can subtract the shadow illuminance value to find the illuminance range in stops; adding 5 to that range will give him the SBR. Once you know the SBR, you can/find both the effective film speed and the appropriate developing time from charts such as those on pages 263 and 268, figs. 8.31 and 8.35.

Measure the illumination contrast; add five stops

An Incident Metering System

This procedure makes two assumptions which sound rather arbitrary but are usually valid: first, that the average subject range is 7 stops; second, that 5 stops of the 7 typically result from local variations of subject color or value and that the other 2 stops are due to local variations in illumination resulting from shade or shadows or from glaring surfaces. Presumably, then, a typical subject in a totally uniform light condition, without either surface glare or shaded areas, will have a maximum range not exceeding 5 stops. If a portion of the subject is shaded and a portion left in full light, the total subject range is the basic 5 stops *plus* the illumination contrast, whatever that is. Since the incident meter is ideally suited to measuring lighting contrast, the rest is easy; simply meter the illumination in the shadows, then measure the brightest illumination level in the subject space and count the stops between these extremes. Add 5 stops and you have an approximation of the subject luminance range.

For example, suppose you measure the subject shadow illumination with your Luna-Pro (in incident mode) and get a reading of 10. Then, measuring the highlight illumination gives you 14. The illumination range is 4 stops; add the basic 5 for the subject values and you get 9, the subject luminance range (SBR).

You'll get reasonably good results most of the time using this method if you base your camera settings on the incident reading of the shadow areas. For greater precision, however, it's necessary to adjust the exposures somewhat for subjects of very long range or very short range because these subjects require abnormal development. Less-than-normal development will effectively reduce the film speed and greater-than-normal development will increase it. The ASA setting of the meter can be changed to compensate for this effect—by using a lower ASA number than normal (to overexpose) when the subject range is long and development is correspondingly reduced, and by using a higher ASA number (to underexpose) when the subject is low in contrast and requires more-than-normal development. Although films and developers are not all alike, the chart shown as figure 8.31 suggests film speed compensation which will be useful with most films under all but the most extreme conditions.

Subject Luminance Range in Stops (12, 11, 10, 9, 8, 7, 6, 5)

ASA Normal

Effective Film Speeds

Figure 8.30
The illumination difference between the sunlit and shaded areas of the table top is 3 stops. The gray scales each represent a 5-stop range. The total range of this subject area is, therefore, at least 8 stops. If holding detail under the table is important, the range must be considered to be even greater.

Figure 8.31
Subjects of abnormal contrast (luminance range) require adjusted development to produce normal contrast negatives. This, in turn, requires exposure compensation if the negatives are to maintain normal density. This chart will provide appropriate film speed settings for subjects of varying contrast and will be effective for all general purpose films developed in the usually available developers. For use, calibrate the chart by labeling the "ASA normal" line with the official film speed of the film you plan to use. Then mark the vertical lines at left with speeds of decreasing value and the lines at right with increasing values. For example, if you are using Plus-X film, mark the "ASA normal" line "125." The left-hand lines would then be labeled "100, 80, 64, 50, 40, and 32"; and the right-hand lines would be labeled "160, 200, and 250."

Using the chart information adds only one short step to the normal metering process. The meter ASA setting is adjusted *after* the subject range readings are made but *before* the camera settings are determined. Here is the procedure:

> With an incident meter read the subject shadow illumination; similarly read the highlight illumination. Subtract the low reading from the high one to get the illumination range in stops. Add this to 5 to find the subject luminance range (SBR). Consult the chart to find the appropriate ASA compensation and adjust the meter ASA setting. Reset the meter dial to the subject shadow reading and consult the meter scales for the camera settings. Take the picture and record the subject range so the film can be developed for the appropriate length of time.

Back in the darkroom, determine your desired negative density range and divide it by the subject range (both ranges must be in the same form, either stops or logs) to find the average gradient desired. Consult an appropriate contrast index/development chart to establish the proper time, and develop the film. With a little practice you'll find that this method gives good results and is more consistent than the usual, uncompensated procedures.

The Zone System

What It Is and What It Can Do

Over the years there have been numerous procedures proposed for the control of image quality by manipulations of film exposure and development. A very comprehensive system, and by far the best-known, is the Zone System, which was originated by Ansel Adams and Fred Archer many years ago. It is a remarkably ingenious approach to image control and one that has been well publicized. Adams himself has explained it thoroughly in his various writings, and numerous other authors have published their own versions. Today the Zone System is taught, more or less authentically, in a large number of schools and colleges and has become a photographic tradition.

The details of the usually recommended empirical testing and calibration procedures required to suit the Zone System principles to individual use are too well known and too extensive to justify further publication. Ansel Adams's book, *The Negative,* and the *New Zone System Manual* by White, Zakia, and Lorenz are the usual recommended references.

The Zone System is based on the principle of *previsualization,* which means that the photographer, before exposing his film, will analyze the subject tonality visually to determine which areas of dark and light he wishes to preserve with adequate detail and what effect of contrast he wants to achieve in the final print. In other words, he attempts to "see" the print in the subject before the negative is made. Then, using a light meter, he measures the tones in the subject that he judges to be significant, and from these meter readings, he determines both the proper exposure for the film and its subsequent development conditions, based on extensive previous testing and experience with these specific materials and processes. If all goes well, he will produce a negative that will print easily to reproduce his previsualized image in tangible form.

The Concept of Zones

The system gets its name from the fact that certain tones of gray in the subject have been labelled as Zones and numbered for easy identification and convenience in calculation. Zone V (Roman numerals are always used for Zone numbers) is identified as middle gray, for example, while a subject value 1 stop brighter than middle gray would be called Zone VI. Zone IV is 1 stop darker than Zone V, and Zone III is 2 stops darker than Zone V.

Minor White's explanation of the Zone System limits the range from Zone I to Zone IX, inclusive, and defines the Zones approximately as follows:

Zone I	Maximum photographic paper black
Zone II	First printable separation of tone
Zone III	Very dark gray
Zone IV	Dark gray
Zone V	Middle gray
Zone VI	Light gray
Zone VII	Very light gray; textured white
Zone VIII	Untextured, but still toned white
Zone IX	Maximum photographic paper white

These definitions are descriptions of print values that will result from proper *translation* of subject Zones into print tones. The actual reflection density difference between these values on the print itself will not be mathematically uniform, nor will the nine zones represent a 9-stop range of print densities (print *reflection* densities can rarely exceed a total range of about 7 stops even under the best conditions). This is a source of some confusion in many descriptions of the Zone System.

How the Zone System Works

Application of the Zone System principles, as they are usually explained, must follow extensive testing to determine the minimum film exposure required to produce the first useful printing density (used to determine the working film speed); the developing time required to produce a printable representation of the nine Zones, as previously described; and variations in development that will effectively *expand* or *contract* the density range of the negative to compensate for unusual subject luminance ranges. Expansion refers to greater-than-normal development; contraction means less-than-normal. A final field test is recommended to verify these experimental conclusions.

Figure 8.32
A homemade Zone Scale applied to a
spotmeter dial.

Careful metering is essential to the success of this system. In essence the exposure meter is used as a reflection densitometer to measure the luminance of subject areas individually. It is almost imperative, therefore, that a spotmeter be employed. No ordinary wide-field averaging meter can supply the accurate small-area readings demanded by the system.

Meters are designed for average readings

Meter scales are designed to deal with average readings. To use them with the Zone System it is convenient to modify them to display the Zones as areas of graded gray. This can be done as indicated in figure 8.32. In this homemade scale, the pointer of the calculating dial, which is usually aligned with the meter light reading, is replaced by the Zone V area, and the other Zones are arranged appropriately on either side of it. The placement of the Zone V gray at the normal pointer position acknowledges the theory that an average gray in the subject, properly exposed and developed, will produce a medium density in the negative, which can then be made to print as a middle gray.

Luminance values are "placed" in selected zones

The other Zones can be used similarly. For example, suppose we place some subject luminance reading opposite the Zone III mark on the meter dial. The resulting exposure recommendations will tend to produce an area of very dark gray (Zone III) in the print. If we place the same subject light value opposite the Zone V mark (Zone System users call this "placing the value *in* Zone V"), we will get a middle gray area in the print. Likewise, placing some subject tone in Zone VIII will tend to reproduce it in the print as an untextured white. Placing a reading in Zone III is the same as underexposing it by 2 stops, and this provides a convenient method of working with meters that are not equipped with Zone scales. Since the normal pointer on the meter scale is equivalent to Zone V, setting the pointer 1 stop higher than any given luminance reading will effectively place that subject value in Zone IV. Setting the meter pointer 3 stops above the reading will place it in Zone II; setting it 2 stops below the reading will place it in Zone VII; and so forth.

If the subject is "normal," development is "N"

If the subject contrast or luminance range is normal (by Zone System definition), placing some subject value in its proper Zone will automatically position all the other subject tones in their proper Zones, too. Under these conditions the recommended development is "normal." For abnormal conditions of subject contrast it is customary to identify the subject value that we want to render as a very dark gray and place it in Zone III on the meter dial. Then we measure the luminance of the area we wish to render as a textured white (Zone VII in the print) and see where that value falls on the meter scale. If the reading falls in Zone VIII it is too high, so the range must be contracted by underdevelopment. In this case, since the error is one Zone, the development recommendation would be "normal, minus one" or "N − 1." If the high value had fallen in Zone VI, it would suggest that the range should be expanded by 1 stop and the proper development would be N + 1. Other high-value reference Zones are sometimes suggested.

Changing development alters effective film speed

One of the shortcomings of the Zone System, as it is usually explained, is its failure to compensate for expansion or contraction (extended or shortened) development by appropriate changes in the effective film speed. This is probably the reason why many Zone System users place their detailed blacks in Zone III or even Zone IV, on occasion. Experience has taught them that if they don't they'll get unprintably thin negatives when dealing with contrasty subject matter. It's a fact of photographic life that reduced development results in loss of effective film speed. Ignoring this loss will lead to underexposure and loss of shadow details (in Zone II at least, and Zone III in extreme cases). But, if the film speed is adjusted to match the development condition, the lower Zones can be adequately and predictably detailed under any subject condition.

Ideally the necessary exposure compensation should be computed for each film-developer combination used. But, since it does not vary greatly from one film type to another and since exact calculation requires the use of a densitometer (which is not available to most students), the charts in figures 8.33 and 8.34 are recommended for use with any film. Although they will not provide exact compensation, their use will improve the quality of negatives made of contrasty subjects and provide a more consistent minimum density than Zone System negatives often exhibit.

Zone System Calibration

Use these charts; calibrate them yourself

To calibrate the effective film speed chart for your own use, label the ASA line with the actual published speed of the film you use. The spaces to the left, then, should be labelled with lower speeds; higher speeds go to the right. Each single space is equivalent to one film speed number in the standard sequence (⅓ stop). Every third line is equivalent to a full stop in the sequence. For example, if you are using Plus-X film, label the ASA point with the number 125. The successive lines to the right will then be labelled 160, 200, 250 and 320. To the left of the ASA point, the numbers should read 100, 80, 64, 50 and 40.

The other chart, figure 8.34, is provided for your own calibration of developing time versus N-numbers. From your personal test results fill in the developing times required for the various expansions and contractions and connect the points with a smooth curve. This will provide an indication of the times required for fractional values of expansion and contraction.

To use these charts, proceed as you normally would to read the subject values with a meter, and place the shadow reading in Zone III. Then read Zone VII tones and see where they fall to determine the expansion or contraction required. When this has been determined consult the effective film speed chart (fig. 8.33) to find the appropriate film speed, set it into the meter (replace the shadow reading in Zone III if necessary), and compute the exposure settings. Make the picture using these settings (modified by such filter, bellows, and reciprocity factors as are appropriate) and mark the holder with the N-number

Figure 8.33
N-numbers vs. effective film speed.

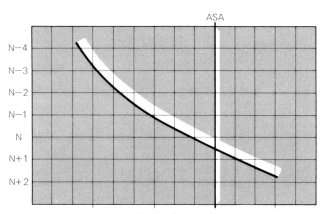

Figure 8.34
N-numbers vs. development time.

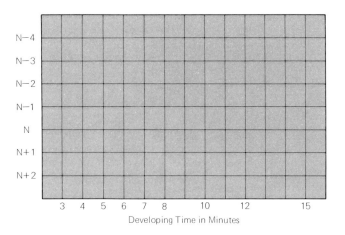

for identification. Back in the darkroom, develop for the time indicated in figure 8.34. Practically speaking, this is not greatly different from normal procedure but it does require the extra step of film speed determination. This compensation will tend to assure adequately detailed shadows and will make Zone II a useful and reliable Zone under all conditions, eliminating any necessity for intuitive "fudging" in the placement of the low values. This procedure is based on Zone III and VII readings only. If you read other Zones for the determination of exposure and development data, you will not get entirely reliable information from the charts as they are given here.

You can also work with manufacturers' data

If you have not completed a personal test of your materials, you will have to rely on the manufacturers' data. The published charts do not include any Zone System information as such, but you can derive developing times for the various subject range conditions from contrast index data. These data are not universal, however; you must use the film and developer specified and follow the chart instructions for temperature and agitation.

CI Charts

First take luminance readings of subject Zones III and VII and count the number of stops between them. If the total is less than the normal 4 stops, subtract it from 4 to get a *plus* N-number. For example, Zone III reads 10 on your Luna-Pro meter and Zone VII reads 13, a difference of 3 stops. Subtract 3 from 4 to get 1. The N-number is N+1.

If the difference between the readings is greater than 4, subtract 4 from the difference and call it a *minus* N-number. For example, Zone III reads 12 and Zone VII reads 18. The difference is 6 (stops). Subtract 4 from 6 to get 2. The N-number is N−2.

Figure 8.35
This chart relates subject contrast (stated either as luminance range in stops or indicated by Zone System "N-number") to contrast index or average gradient. It assumes a desired negative density range (DR) of 1.1—a typical average value. The dotted lines demonstrate that a subject luminance range of eight stops (equivalent to N-½) requires development to a contrast index of about .46 to produce a negative DR of 1.1.

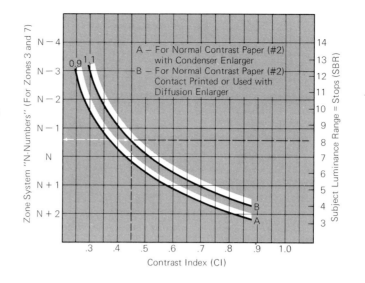

View camera exposures must often be modified

When you have determined the N-number (calculate it to within ⅓ stop if possible), consult the chart (fig. 8.35) to find the appropriate contrast index (development condition) for that subject range. Then, on the manufacturer's contrast index/developing time chart for the film and developer in use, find the correct developing time, temperature, and agitation. Charts for most Kodak films and their recommended developers can be found in the Kodak *Professional Data Book* number F-5, available at most camera shops or directly from the Eastman Kodak Company, Rochester, New York. Other useful CI information can be determined from the charts given in appendix 14.

Much of the work done with a view camera involves filtration, close-up focusing, or very long exposure times, and all of these will necessitate increasing the film exposure beyond the normal calculations. The exposure factors required by filtration and bellows extension are explained on pages 105 and 271. Reciprocity failure due to long exposure times or, more precisely, weak exposing light, varies with the kind of film in use. A very general guide can be given, however, and the chart in appendix 12 will supply information to help you compensate for reciprocity failure by adjustment of both exposure and development. Lacking a more specific guide, this can be used for all normal films with good results.

Apply reciprocity correction last

Notice that the exposure factors are not the same for aperture and shutter speed compensation. This is because opening the diaphragm for compensation brightens the exposing light and tends to nullify the cause of the reciprocity failure. Prolonging exposure *time,* if anything, simply aggravates the problem, although compensation will eventually occur. Reciprocity correction should be the last factor applied to the exposure calculation. Don't forget to apply it if it's needed, however. It affects both negative density and contrast.

Close-up Photography

When it is necessary to produce an image on film, larger than about one-tenth the subject size, special equipment or techniques may be required.

View cameras and SLRs are fine for close-up work

Most small cameras will not focus close enough to allow for greater image size than this without special lenses or accessories, and some are not particularly satisfactory for close-up photography even when modified. Single-lens reflex cameras can usually be adapted rather easily and are generally excellent for the purpose if the relatively small image size is not a drawback. When larger film sizes are desirable, the view camera is the obvious choice.

A great deal of confusion has surrounded the terms that are used to describe photography of objects at close range. It is quite common to hear the terms *photomacrography* and *photomicrography* interchanged with *macrophotography* and *microphotography.* Lenses designed for precision work at close range are often described as *macro-* or *micro-* lenses and are recommended for *close-up* work.

For purposes of standardization we will follow the lead of the Kodak technical writers and define these terms as follows. Close-up photography covers the range from the minimum focusing distance of the basic camera to a distance equivalent to about two focal lengths from the subject, at which range the subject is being recorded at life-size. Accessory lenses, extension tubes, or bellows units may be required.

Photomacrography overlaps this range and more specifically refers to the recording of subjects normally examined visually under magnification, by a reading glass, pocket magnifier, or a low-powered simple microscope. Extra long extension tubes or bellows are required, special lenses are necessary for best results, and magnification may range from $1\times$ to perhaps $50\times$.

Photomacro-, photomicro-, microphoto-, macrophoto-

Photomicrography refers specifically to photography through a compound microscope, a procedure involving highly specialized manipulation and lighting techniques. Magnification may run from as low as about $20\times$ to more than $2000\times$. Electron microscopes overlap this range and extend it to an incredible $200,000\times$ or so.

The term microphotography is used to describe the techniques of producing very small images as, for example, in making patterns for electronic integrated circuitry. This is a highly specialized field in which exotic sensitized materials and meticulous control of processing conditions are required to maintain satisfactory definition in images that are literally invisible to the naked eye. The term macrophotography is assigned to the making of very large images, such as photomurals.

Metering close-up subjects can be difficult

Meter readings of close-up subjects must be taken with extreme care. Incident readings can be difficult to obtain if the camera-to-subject distance is very short or if the subject is likely to be disturbed. Incident readings cannot be relied on if the meter cell is not placed quite precisely in the subject plane and in a typical light condition. Conventional luminance meters are not much better for this purpose. Because of the small subject area and the proximity of the camera, accurate coverage of the subject field is difficult and the meter will probably cast a shadow that will affect the accuracy of the reading. If the camera has a built-in through-the-lens meter, the problem is made much simpler and very accurate readings can usually be obtained.

When a subject is at infinity, the image is formed as close to the lens as it can be under any circumstances, and the approximate distance from lens to focal plane is called the focal length of the lens (fig. 8.36). In ordinary photography, the focal distance is rarely very much greater than the focal length of the lens; in fact, most popular cameras are designed to prevent much focusing adjustment.

At close range the focal distance is greater than the focal length

Although there is some increase in focal distance as the subject approaches the camera from infinity, the percentage of increase, compared to the normal focal length, is insignificant until the subject reaches a point about eight focal lengths in front of the lens (fig. 8.36b).

From this point on, as the subject approaches still closer, the focal distance increases very rapidly until, when the subject has reached a point two focal lengths in front of the lens, the image is formed two focal lengths behind the lens. At this point, the subject and the image are identical in size (fig. 8.36c), and we refer to this as the condition of *unit magnification*.

If the subject is brought still closer to the lens, the image will recede at an accelerating pace (it is now larger than the subject and growing rapidly) until, when the subject reaches a distance equal to one focal length in front of the lens, the image is formed at infinity and is infinitely large (fig. 8.36d).

Focusing is sometimes difficult, too

Focusing a camera is a simple enough procedure when the object is some distance away. At distances approaching unit magnification, however, it is sometimes a very confusing task. At near unit magnification you will probably find that moving the *lens* to focus will become ineffective and it will become necessary to adjust the image sharpness by moving the whole camera or the subject. If you are using a view camera, it may be feasible and effective to use the *back* focusing adjustment. The problem becomes most perplexing when the subject plane and film plane are just a little more or less than four focal lengths

Figure 8.36

(a)

(b)

(c)

(d)

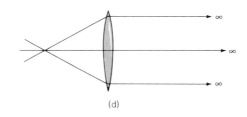

apart. If a little more, some position of the lens will produce a sharp image; but if a little less, no adjustment of the lens will result in good focus. It will be close enough, though, to keep you working at it. The only way out of this dilemma is to increase the subject-to-film distance to four focal lengths or more. A sharp image is impossible at shorter total distances.

As you will recall, the f/numbers marked on the aperture scale of the lens are derived from the relationship between the aperture diameter and the lens focal length.

$$f/ = \frac{\text{focal length}}{\text{diameter}}$$

When focal length is changed, the f-numbers are changed

From this you can see that if the focal length value is changed and the aperture is unchanged, the marked relative apertures are no longer reliable.

This is what occurs in focusing on a very near object. The lens must be racked out to bring the image into sharp focus, and in so doing, the distance from lens to focal plane (focal distance) is increased. This in turn reduces the illumination on the film surface which, unless compensated for, will cause underexposure of the film.

An example should clarify this relationship. Imagine a lens of 6″ focal length with an aperture diameter of ½″. According to the formula above, the lens has a relative aperture of f/12. When this lens is focused on an object close enough so the distance from lens to film measures 10″, the effective relative aperture is f/20, although the aperture pointer on the lens mount will still indicate f/12! If the same lens is focused on an object 12″ away, the image will also be 12″ behind the lens, since this is the condition of unit magnification, and the effective relative aperture will be f/24. Under this condition, if the exposure is based on the marked aperture of f/12, the film will receive only one-fourth the illumination it requires, and the negative will be seriously underexposed. Clearly something must be done to compensate for these errors.

There are several methods of compensating

While there are several methods of computing the required exposure adjustment, perhaps the simplest and most convenient method is the one presented here. (Use of the macro-exposure computer scales, in appendix 6, will save some mental arithmetic.)

1. Focus and compose the image as desired.

2. Stop down for adequate depth of field coverage and note the aperture you have selected.

3. Measure the focal distance (from the approximate plane of the lens diaphragm to the film plane).

4. Divide this measured distance by the lens focal length (printed on the lens mount in inches or millimeters).

5. Square the resulting number. This is the exposure factor.

6. Take an exposure meter reading of the subject and note the shutter speed indicated for use with the aperture you have selected (but don't use this shutter speed).

7. Multiply this shutter speed by the exposure factor from step 5. Use this new shutter speed to make the exposure.

For example, after focusing, composing, and stopping down, you find that you have a bellows extension (total length) of 10″ and the aperture scale reads f/22. The lens focal length is indicated to be 100 mm, about 4″, so:

10 ÷ 4 = 2½, which squared is 6¼.

Increase exposure time by the factor

This is the exposure factor. The meter indicates that an aperture of f/22 will require an exposure time of 1/125 second, but this must be multiplied by the factor just found.

1/125 × 6¼ = 25/500 or 1/20 second

Use the nearest marked speed on your shutter, favoring the longer interval in preference to the shorter one. In this case, if the shutter can be set for 1/15 second, this is the speed that should be used. If the shutter calibrations provide only 1/10 and 1/25 to choose from, the 1/25 speed will probably be adequate, but the 1/10 is a little safer. If you have time and plenty of film, take one shot at each setting since an extra negative is better than none.

Here is another method using simple proportions to achieve the same ultimate result but involves working with the aperture numbers to affect the exposure increase.

Effective aperture: Marked aperture =
Focal distance: Focal length

Using the same values as in the previous example we substitute:

x : f/22 = 10 : 4 then,
4x = 220 and x = 55 or f/55.

Set the camera aperture scale for f/22 but select the shutter speed that the meter indicates for f/55 or the closest marked aperture. An obvious difficulty with this method is the fact that some meter scales do not extend past f/32 or f/45.

Most close-up photographs are of still-life material, and movement is not as much of a problem as is depth of field. Occasionally, though, it is necessary to specify some shutter speed and then determine how to set the lens to provide the proper exposure. Use of the proportion above will also make this possible. If the selected shutter speed requires an effective aperture of f/8, how must the aperture scale be set to achieve this? Using the 4″ lens working at 10″, as above, we substitute.

f/8 : x = 10 : 4 then,
10x = 32 and x (the marked aperture) = 3.2

Or change the lens setting

Use your selected shutter speed, but set the aperture scale at f/3.2. The effective aperture, because of the extended bellows, is f/8.

You can modify these procedures, or perhaps even ignore them, if you are using a single-lens reflex with through-the-lens metering. Most cameras of this type compensate automatically for increases in focal distance because the light intensity is diminished on the meter cells to the same degree that it is on the film surface. In some SLR metering systems the sensitive cell is included in the mirror coating or it may be inserted into the light path at some point ahead of the film. In these meters the light on the meter cell is not diminished quite as much as the actual film image light is and the meter readings may tend to underexpose the film if some compensation is not calculated. Practical experience is the best guide for coping with this condition. Cameras that meter the image light on the groundglass will usually provide almost perfect compensation for any macro-situation.

Because close-up photographs often require long exposure intervals, it is quite likely that the effective sensitivity of the film will be reduced by failure of the reciprocity law (see p. 268). As a rule of thumb, it will be a good idea to double the calculated exposure if it is greater than one second, and double it again if it exceeds about ten seconds. Since films vary in their susceptibility to failure, it will be wise to bracket the exposures or make a preliminary test if the picture is important and cannot be repeated.

Focal length is measured from the rear nodal point

The focal length of a lens can be defined as the distance between the image plane and the rear nodal point of the lens when the lens is focused at infinity. In simple terms this rear nodal point is a hypothetical point in space representing the intersection of light rays as they pass through the lens toward the film plane. It is a point, in other words, around which the lens may be pivoted slightly without displacing the focused image of an object at infinity.

In most lenses of conventional design, the nodal points, front and rear, are actually contained within the lens structure, and the diaphragm is placed between them. The position of the diaphragm, therefore, serves as a convenient and fairly accurate point from which to measure the focal distance in computing close-up exposure compensation.

Retro-focus and telephoto lenses are special cases

Although the focal lengths of telephoto and retrofocus lenses cannot be measured from the diaphragm position, because the nodal points are nowhere near it, the diaphragm position will still indicate the approximate source of light illuminating the film surface and may be used with fairly accurate results as the reference point in computing the bellows extension exposure factor. Simply consider the diaphragm-to-film distance at infinity focus to be the *focal length* of the lens. Measure again after focusing on the object and call it the *focal distance*. Then proceed with the normal calculation. This is admittedly a rather haphazard method because the position of the diaphragm is not easy to establish with any real precision. It will not work, either, with lenses that focus with floating elements. In most cases, though, it is sufficiently accurate to keep you out of trouble. If this, or some similar, compensation is not made, retro-focus lenses will tend to overexpose and telephotos will tend to underexpose when used for close-ups.

Calculate pupillary magnification for accuracy

If the exposure increase is computed from the image magnification ratio, it will also have to be modified for use with these lenses. Exact compensation involves finding the ratio of the diameters of the lens *entrance and exit pupils* and using a formula given in appendix 6. In practice it's unlikely that a very serious error will occur even without this special compensation, because neither lens type is particularly easy to use for extreme close-ups. Many retro-focus lenses, in particular, will actually touch the subject before they will focus a life-size image.

Neither ordinary telephoto nor retro-focus lenses can be expected to produce as good results in close-up work as do normal lenses, and it is unwise to use them in this way if image quality is of critical importance. A number of manufacturers of small cameras produce special lenses for close-up photography which are intended to provide superior correction of the various aberrations in this rather critical range. They are often referred to as macro-lenses, and the prefix sometimes appears in the name of the lens. Such lenses for view cameras are not labelled macro-lenses, as a rule, but are simply called *process* lenses and are also often designated as *apochromats* to indicate that correction of the color aberrations has been carried out to an unusually high degree. There are also some *macro-zoom* lenses featuring ingenious optical or mechanical refinements which permit moderate close-up focusing and provide good macro-correction.

Supplementary lenses are sometimes useful

Cameras that do not focus closer than eight or ten focal lengths can be adapted for close-up work by the use of close-up lens attachments, sometimes inappropriately called portrait attachments. These lenses are generally just simple positive plano-convex lenses of low power designed to slip over the camera lens, and thereby effectively shorten its focal length. The lens then works as if it were a shorter lens *racked out* (working at focal distance greater than its focal length), which is the condition necessary for close-up focusing.

Figure 8.37
Close-up lenses

Since neither the lens-to-film distance nor the actual aperture diameter is changed by the addition of a close-up lens, there is no light loss of any consequence, and no close-up exposure compensation is required. The only real disadvantage of the close-up lens attachment is the generally slight loss of image quality due to the addition of the aberrations of the supplementary lens to those already existing in the normal lens system and the addition of some flare light from the two extra glass surfaces.

Their focal lengths are marked in diopters

Close-up lenses are often sold under the designations plus 1 or plus 2 and so forth. These numbers refer to the lens focal length in *diopters,* a term usually used by optometrists, and not often encountered in photography. A focal length of one diopter is equivalent to one meter or about thirty-nine inches. Two diopters implies a focal length of one-half meter, three diopters means one-third meter, and so forth. If the lens is positive, the description includes the word *plus;* negative lenses are designated *minus.*

Negative supplementary lenses are not as popular as positive lenses, but they are useful as focal length extenders for long lens or telephoto effects if the camera can be physically extended enough to bring the converted image into focus. By lengthening the focal length, minus lenses convert a normal lens into a long lens and reduce its speed, since the aperture is not changed. The effective relative aperture must be computed to avoid underexposure.

Bellows units and extension tubes are available

Some manufacturers provide accessory bellows units for their cameras (see fig. 3.27). These units are fairly common for 35mm cameras, and some are available for rollfilm cameras as well. They can be used only on cameras whose lenses can be removed and are practical for use only on single-lens reflex cameras since focusing and framing of the image are extremely critical at close range.

Bellows units usually replace the normal lens in the camera body, and the lens is attached to the front frame of the unit. The camera can no longer be focused at infinity, using its normal lens, because of the irreducible thickness of the bellows, but extreme close-ups are possible.

Extension tubes provide another means of close focusing. Supplied in sets of three or four rings of different lengths, they can be interposed between camera body and lens, alone or in combination, to provide more or less continuous coverage of the range from infinity to unit magnification.

They are cheaper than the accessory bellows units and allow for moderate close-ups, which the bellows cannot accommodate, but they are awkward in use because of the number of pieces involved and the difficulty of interchanging them. They can, of course, be used in combination with a bellows unit for greater magnification of the image, and if really extreme blowups are desired, supplementary lenses can be added, too. Image quality is likely to suffer considerably, however.

Beware of flare from shiny inside surfaces

A potentially serious problem of flare light can be caused by extension tubes, especially the cheaper varieties, and it is a problem seldom mentioned in discussions of close-up photography. The flare results from light reflecting from the smooth interior surfaces of the tubes. The resulting image degradation can be disastrous (fig. 8.39). If you plan to do much serious close-up work with small cameras (this problem is rare with bellows-type cameras), check the entire camera interior for flare-producing shiny areas by pointing the camera

Figure 8.38
Extension tubes on Pentax

a   b

Figure 8.39
a. A hornet on a windowpane, shot again
the light with well-designed extension
tubes.
b. Same hornet, same windowpane, shot
with "bargain" extension tubes.

Figure 8.40
Although the inside surfaces of these
extension tubes were blackened during
manufacturing, they still reflect enough
light to cause the disastrous flare in figure
8.38b.

Figure 8.41
Reverse adapter

toward a fairly strong light source and inspecting the interior surfaces through the shutter opening (fig. 8.40). A good camera repairman can usually improvise extra baffles to eliminate the reflection or apply matte black lacquer or flocking to reduce it. You may be able to treat the surfaces of extension tubes yourself but it is best to let a professional work on the camera body if it needs extra baffling.

The flare may not be visible in the finder

It's worth mentioning that the flare light from these shiny surfaces is not usually apparent in the viewfinder image, especially when the surfaces causing it are part of the camera body itself. It's quite possible, therefore, to see the subject in the finder quite clearly with excellent visual contrast and still find that the film itself has been badly fogged.

Exposure compensation is necessary with both bellows units and with tubes, since both increase the focal distance of the lens without affecting the aperture. The procedures for computing exposure are identical with those outlined for use with the view camera.

Aberrations are usually worse at close range

It is one of the unpleasant facts of optics that lens aberrations are not uniform in any given lens at various object distances, and the changes become extreme and particularly troublesome in the unit magnification range where the image and object relationships are subject to considerable variation. For this reason, a lens that is superbly corrected for all the aberrations at infinity may be poorly corrected at 1:1 (unit magnification) and vice versa.

Reversing the lens may help

Because the corrections are made for rather specific conditions of image-object relationship, it is sometimes possible to improve the performance of an ordinary lens at close range by reversing it in its mount. If it is designed to work best with a large object distance and a short image distance (infinity condition), it will probably work better at extremely close range when the image is larger than the object, if the front of the lens faces the image. Some manufacturers suggest this practice and supply special adapters to make it possible. Reverse adapters offer no improvement in image quality unless the image is magnified, although they may permit an advantageous increase in the lens-to-subject distance. The lens will probably give better image quality in its normal position until unit magnification is reached.

Figure 8.42
Here is a simple, but effective method for making photocopies from books or magazines. Here the book pages are held flat by a large clip and the book is held open by fastening the vertical half to a brick with a large rubber band. When the camera is positioned so the finder image shows the lens reflection in the center of the mirror and the rangefinder prism circle (in the center of the groundglass) is centered in the lens reflection, the camera is centered over the copy and is facing it squarely. For best accuracy of exposure, replace the mirror with a standard gray card for metering. The single light is sufficient here because the vertical book page acts as an efficient reflector. This is the set-up used to make the copy in figure 1.16.

One of the most troublesome aberrations at close range is field curvature. If the lens provides a flat field for objects at infinity it is quite likely not to at close range. For this reason it is not advisable to use ordinary camera lenses on an enlarger since, of all the possible virtues of a lens, flatness of field in enlarging is most important.

This quality is so necessary in the design of enlarging lenses that premium-quality enlarging lenses are designed for specific magnification ratios. If used for image magnifications outside their intended range, these lenses are still very good but are no longer considered superb. Within their intended magnification range, incidentally, enlarger lenses can be used as camera lenses with excellent results.

Copying Techniques

Copying is easy—if you're careful

Copying material from books or magazines is a typical close-up activity. It's easy to get good results too, if a few precautions are taken. If the page to be copied can be laid out flat and if it is heavy, dull-surface paper, the problems are minimized. Simply position the camera so the lens axis is perpendicular to the page and arrange a pair of lights, one on either side, to shine on the page at an angle of about 45°. This is important because if the camera does not face the page squarely the copy may be distorted and, in extreme cases, a portion of the page may go out of focus. An easy way to get the camera into correct position is to lay a small mirror in the center of the subject space and observe it through the viewfinder. When you can see the reflection of the camera lens centered in the viewfinder image of the mirror, the lens axis is centered and perpendicular to the subject plane. Focus carefully and stop down to a moderately small aperture to insure best definition and adequate depth of field.

Use a moderately small aperture for best sharpness

If you are using an SLR with a built-in metering system, it is best to take the meter reading from a standard gray card, placed temporarily over the page. Be sure that the gray card is large enough to cover the entire field of the meter and that it is evenly illuminated. If a gray card is not available, you can meter

Figure 8.43

a. Flat material must be evenly lighted for best copy results; place a light on each side of the copyboard and position them so there's no apparent surface glare on the copy as seen from the camera position. You can check the relative intensity of the lights by inspecting the shadows of a pencil (or finger) touching the copy board near center. Move one of the lights toward or away from the copy board until the shadows appear to be of equal intensity. In this picture the light at the left is too strong; move it farther away.

b. If you're using a camera without a built-in meter, use a hand-held meter, in its reflectance mode, to read a gray card in the center of the copy area. It's safe to use the reading it gives you without other compensation (except for bellows factor, filter factor or reciprocity compensation if any of them apply.)

c. An incident meter is even more convenient than the gray card. Be sure the meter cell is exposed to the same light intensity that exists on the copy surface, as shown here.

a white card and increase the indicated camera setting by 2½ stops. In any case, it's advisable to bracket your exposures on the first roll to be sure everything is working properly. Lock the mirror up (if you're using an SLR) and use a cable release or the camera's self-timer mechanism to make the exposure. This will reduce vibrations and help to insure sharp images.

Black paper under the copy may eliminate "print-through"

If the book or magazine can't be opened flat without breaking the binding, open it only halfway and support the opened half with stationer's clamps (fig. 8.42). Stretch the page to be copied as flat as possible and clamp it in place, too. If the printing on the other side of the page shows through (with thin papers this is a real problem), insert a sheet of black paper under the page. This will darken the paper very slightly but will practically eliminate any print-through in the photograph.

Use only a single light for this set-up but position it with real care. Again, direct the light at the page at an angle of about 45°, and keep the light far enough away so there is no sign of any hot spot. Angle the light up slightly so some of it strikes the vertical pages of the half-opened book; they will serve as an efficient reflector and take the place of a second light source. With a little adjustment and careful observation, you should be able to provide uniform illumination on the page to be copied.

Don't use glass if you can help it; glare is a problem

If the page cannot be made to lie flat by itself, it may be necessary to hold it down with a sheet of glass. Do this as a last resort because it is awkward to manage and the glass surface is very likely to show bothersome reflections, usually of the camera itself. To eliminate them, keep the camera out of the light and surround it with black paper or cloth.

If the copy page is lustrous or shiny, be sure that the lights are not reflected in its surface. If any sign of glare is apparent, lower the lights until the glare disappears. If the glare can't be controlled this simply, as may be the case if the subject consists partly of acetate overlays, for example, it may be necessary to use a polarizing filter over the camera lens or over the light sources, or (very probably) both.

Reversal processing is fine— when it works

Color slide film is excellent for copy work if the light is suitably balanced by filtration. Even black-and-white originals are reproduced well on Kodachrome or Ektachrome, as a rule, but there is usually a slight color cast and the contrast may be too high for some purposes. Good black-and-white slides can be made by photographing the original on Technical Pan film (for line copy or type) or Panatomic-X (for continuous-tone originals like pencil or wash drawings) and printing the negatives on Fine-Grain Positive film. This process is made simpler if you have a *slide copier* attachment for your SLR or have access to a Repronar or Illumitron copy machine. In either case, the negatives can be fed through the copier and rephotographed on Fine-Grain Release Positive film which is available in 35mm size in 100-foot rolls. This procedure is more complicated than the frequently recommended reversal processing of Panatomic-X film, but the results are excellent. The reversal process itself is not an easy one to control and one of the chemicals (the fogging developer) has been notoriously unstable.

Lighting for Close-ups

Lighting the subject well is not particularly difficult in close-up photography in spite of the limited space available. Bright light, which is usually desirable, both for groundglass focusing and for making the exposure, is relatively easy to provide because the light sources can be placed close to the subject without much danger of unevenness. If the subject is likely to be harmed by high temperature, it may be necessary to focus and arrange the composition by subdued light, turning the bright lights on only for a final focus check and the actual shooting. In extreme cases the subject can be protected by shields of heat-absorbing glass (available from Edmund Scientific Company, Barrington, New Jersey). Electronic flash is also an excellent cool light source, but focusing will have to be done with conventional illumination.

Figure 8.44
Plastic jug tent

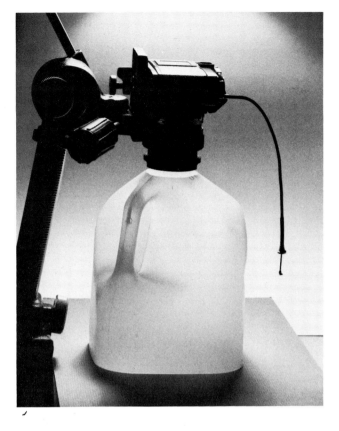

Don't overlook the possibility of tent lighting

There are numerous techniques for lighting close-up subjects. Simply directing a light at the subject from beside the camera will suffice for some purposes but it is frequently necessary to use more than one source or to use reflectors to reduce the contrast and control the surface rendering. Don't overlook the possibility of tent lighting; a paper cone tent will provide excellent light for many sorts of close-up subjects. A semipermanent tent of this sort can be constructed by cutting off the neck and bottom of a large white plastic jug; set it over the subject and poke the camera lens in through the neck hole. Illuminate it from the outside with any sort of light and the subject will glow with a soft brilliance. For more contrasty lighting, cut off a portion of one side to let some direct light in.

Small objects can be separated from their own shadows by placing them on a sheet of glass suspended over some suitable background material. With this arrangement the relative values of subject and ground can be controlled easily and the subject can even be lighted from behind, if desired, to show up some edge details or to dramatize some effect of translucency or transparency. Reflections from the glass surface may cause problems but they can usually be eliminated by surrounding the camera lens with black paper or by tilting the glass slightly to avoid the reflecting light. If necessary, raise the object off the glass surface an inch or more on a little concealed pedestal of wood or wire. This will help throw the glass surface completely out of focus and subdue the reflections.

Axial lighting is frequently appropriate

For some purposes it is desirable to use *axial lighting,* flat frontal lighting that appears to shine onto the subject from the camera lens itself. This is not as difficult to arrange as it might seem. There are *ring light* flash tubes available for several brands of electronic flashguns, and one of these, fitted around the camera lens, will provide shadowless illumination. Their high-speed, high-intensity, negligible heat output and good daylight color balance make ring lights especially suitable for medical and dental work, where the camera must frequently be hand-held and operated quickly and where it is sometimes necessary to photograph hard-to-illuminate spaces such as the interior surfaces of the mouth. For these same reasons, the ring light is an excellent light source for some sorts of nature photography.

Figure 8.45
Ring light strobe

Figure 8.46
a. Axial lighting is convenient and effective for close-ups of small objects, such as this dime. The strong, diffused front light illuminates the subject evenly; the shadows and highlights can be emphasized by careful placement of the light source.

a

b. Here is the setup used to photograph the dime. The bits of black paper and aluminum foil taped to the white board control surface reflections to increase the three-dimensional quality of the subject surfaces.

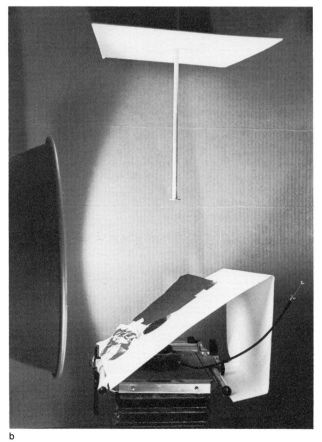

b

Shoot through a hole in a white card

In the studio, still-life objects can be photographed with axial lighting by bouncing light onto the subject from a white card surrounding the camera lens. Be very careful not to shine the light directly into the lens. If this arrangement provides too large a source of light for the subject or if flare light is entering the camera, move the camera behind the card a few inches and shoot through the central hole. This will allow you to concentrate intense light on the card without spilling any into the lens itself.

Or through angled glass

Sometimes these methods are unsatisfactory for use with shiny objects because the image of the lens is reflected as a dark blob in the objects' surfaces. This effect can be reduced, and sometimes eliminated, by shooting through a piece of plate glass angled at about 45° to the lens axis. The subject, in this case, can be illuminated with genuine axial light because the light source is directed at the glass from the side, so its reflection obscures the lens and the light parallels the lens axis. To be effective the glass must be flawless and very clean; any dust or lint spots on its surface will glow strongly in the light and may show up as light blobs or simply cause general flare in the image. It's a good idea to cover the camera with black cloth and keep it out of any direct light to avoid possible reflections, but this is not usually a serious problem. There is a possibility that the angled glass may cause some loss of sharpness in the image but this, too, is usually tolerable.

And so you see close-up photography is not simply a matter of pushing the button. If excellent results are required, the lens must be of fine quality, well corrected for close-up work; focusing must be precise; and depth of field must be accounted for. Both subject and camera movement must be avoided; illumination must be adjusted; light readings must be taken with particular care; and compensation; must be made for the bellows extension if required. Anything less than precision at every stage of the operation will show up in the print as a flaw.

Summary

View and field cameras use sheet film, which must be loaded into holders in total darkness. The film type is identified by notches which appear in the top right-hand corner of the sheet when the film is held vertically and the emulsion faces you. Each holder contains two sheets of film, protected from light by dark slides. Fresh film is indicated when the shiny side of the slide end shows; after exposure the slide is turned over to show the black side.

A view or field camera must be used on a tripod or other firm support, but the operation is straightforward; follow the instructions given.

Processing sheet film can be done in tanks, automatic processors, or by hand in trays. Tray processing is most practical for small batches of film but requires skill and practice for good results. Practice with spoiled film before attempting to work with important pictures. Follow the detailed instructions and be careful to avoid cutting or scratching the delicate film surface.

View cameras have adjustments called shifts and swings which permit some control of image placement on the film, image perspective, and depth of field. All three controls can be exercised by moving the camera back; perspective is not affected by movements of the lens. In general, move the back first, then refine the image with lens movements if necessary.

View camera lenses should be of good quality and should cover a fairly wide field if the shifts and swings are to be used effectively. Camera movements will be restricted if the image circle is small or if the camera bellows is compressed, as is likely if the lens is a very short one.

The exposure-development relationship is a very important one which can be demonstrated by a nine-negative array combining the effects of under-, normal, and over-exposure and development. Follow the instructions carefully. Although there is some interaction, negative density is determined by film exposure, and negative contrast is determined by development. These relationships can be expressed by characteristic curve diagrams which demonstrate that film development can be varied to produce useful negative contrast from any practical subject. *Gamma, average gradient,* and *contrast index* are all terms used to describe negative contrast as it is affected by development.

In these curve diagrams, exposure and negative densities are expressed in $\log_{10}$ values. The log of 2 is .3 and is equivalent to one stop. Other values are given in the chart. You can find the appropriate developing time for film exposed to any subject range by determining the contrast index required and consulting a CI chart for your film and developer. Subject range can be measured fairly accurately with a spotmeter or it can be estimated. One useful method is to take the difference between incident meter readings of the illumination extremes in stops and add five. If the total is other than the normal 7, some exposure adjustment will be required to compensate for the abnormal development required. Consult the charts for recommendations.

The Zone System is a well-known system of exposure and development control incorporating the principle of previsualization. The print density range is divided into seven identifiable tones of gray, plus black and white, each assigned a Zone number. Zone V is considered to represent middle gray; Zone I, maximum black; and Zone IX, maximum paper white. In using the Zone System, the photographer measures the luminance values of significant areas of the subject and tries to visualize how they will appear in the print, comparing them mentally with his concept of the standard Zone values. Scene contrast is usually estimated by measuring the difference between subject areas that are to be rendered in the print as Zones III and VII. If the difference is less than the normal 4 stops, the subject requires N-plus or expansion treatment; if more than 4 stops, development is considered to be N-minus and is contracted from normal. Exposure should be adjusted to compensate for abnormal development; see charts. Zone System information can also be derived from CI charts, as illustrated. Don't forget to apply compensation for reciprocity failure if necessary.

Close-up photography, as distinguished from photomacrography, photomicrography, macrophotography, and microphotography requires some special equipment and techniques. SLR cameras with built-in metering systems are very convenient to use, and most will compensate automatically for the exposure increase required by the lens extension. For other cameras the bellows factor must be calculated. One method is to divide the focal distance by the lens focal length, square it, and increase the exposure time by the factor derived. There are other methods, and a dial calculator pattern is provided in appendix 6. Telephoto and retro-focus lenses are not recommended for close-up work, although some modern zooms offer good correction at close range.

Special macro-lenses are best but ordinary lenses can be used with close-up supplementary lenses, bellows units, or extension tubes. Flare may be a problem with extension tubes. Some lenses perform better at close range if they are mounted in reverse, and special mounting rings are sold for this purpose. Enlarging lenses are excellent for this work if they can be mounted for camera use.

Copying material from books or magazines is not difficult. Hold the page flat with clamps and back it up with black paper if the print shows through. Use the facing pages of the half-opened book as a reflector and meter with a gray card or use an incident reading. Color film can be used for either black-and-white or color originals but black-and-white slides of excellent quality can be made on the Fine-Grain Positive film from good negatives.

Tent lighting is good for small three-dimensional objects. They can be effectively backlighted by supporting them on glass. Axial lighting will provide shadowless illumination and a ring light is often effective for medical, dental, or nature photography. A similar light effect can be achieved by bouncing the light from a white card surrounding the lens or from an angled glass in front of the lens. The reflection of the camera itself can be subdued by draping the camera with black cloth. Careful attention to detail will result in good work.

Special Darkroom Techniques

Outline

Process Manipulations
Dropouts
Posterization
Masking and Tone-Line
Solarization
Screening
Color Manipulations
Introduction to Nonsilver Processes
Making Enlarged Negatives
The Cyanotype Process
The Gum-Bichromate Process

Photographs don't have to be representational

Images can be altered in a number of ways

Untitled, 1979. Michael J. Teres. Teres creates these fantastic images by controlled reticulation and melting of portions of the negative emulsion. The delicate textures of the flowing gelatin, combined with the unmodified fragments of photographic reality, give this mysterious work a weird beauty.
(Courtesy of the photographer.)

Process Manipulations

Most of our photographic efforts are directed toward the production of images that document the subject and represent it more or less accurately. Frequently we will dodge or burn-in some areas of the print to adjust the tonal balance or to influence the mood of the picture, and occasionally we'll use a little Farmer's reducer to accent some highlight area. Finally, many photographers tone their prints, either for visual effect or for greater permanence. All these manipulations can be considered normal if the photographer's intent is to represent the original subject without obvious distortion. Many fine images are made this way, but there are other ways to use photographic techniques— ways that can modify, distort, dramatize, or depart completely from the original subject matter.

Practically speaking, any violation of the normal procedures of negative making or printing will result in an unusual image of some sort, but simply blundering around in the darkroom will not usually produce very interesting pictures. Some knowledge of process is definitely helpful and some sense of craft and control is necessary in even the most destructive distortions of the normal processes if they are to result in images to be taken seriously.

Images can be altered in a number of ways. The images' shapes and outlines can be distorted by optical manipulation in the camera or during the printing process. Tonality can be distorted by increasing the contrast dramatically or by decreasing it until the image is barely discernible. The image can also be distorted by partial or complete reversal, either overall or affecting only a portion of the image area. The sense or identity of the pictured objects can be distorted by juxtaposition or superimposition of other image forms, either photographically or by handwork. Colors or textures can be incorporated into the image and photographs can be printed on a variety of surfaces and materials by several methods. The photographic image can be included as a motif or element in painting, collage, silk screen, etching, weaving, or even three-dimensional arts like sculpture and ceramics. Finally, of course, we are all so familiar with the surreal photographic effects in films and on television that we no longer even think of them as distortions.

Figure 9.1
High-contrast dropout

Dropouts

The easiest and most direct way to depart from photographic reality, which all these processes are intended to do, is to load your camera with a very high-contrast film, such as Contrast Process Pan, or Kodalith, and simply take pictures with it. The film will reduce the subject tonality to black-and-white pattern and the image will resemble a brush drawing in ink, practically devoid of any gray tones (fig. 9.1). Because the grays have been *dropped out* of the photograph, all high-contrast images of this sort are called *dropouts,* no matter how they're done.

High-contrast film will eliminate most gray tones

Kodalith will work well in the camera in bright light but it is a very slow, orthochromatic material (a panchromatic variety is available but not common) which is better suited to printing. It can be handled safely in a light red safelight (series 1A) and is slow enough so that it can be treated like a fast projection paper. It requires its own special developer for highest contrast results but it can be developed in almost any developer if less-than-maximum contrast is desirable. One caution: the film is effectively more sensitive to light when developed in ordinary developers and it may be necessary to reduce the safelight intensity to avoid fog.

Tonal separations can be combined in various ways

Kodalith (or any of the other similar "litho" films on the market) is extremely useful for dissecting images: by printing an ordinary negative onto successive sheets of Kodalith and changing the exposure a little each time, different patterns will be formed, each of which divides the image tones into black-and-white areas of different proportions. These *tonal separations* can be printed individually as simple dropouts or they can be combined in various ways by multiple printing techniques to produce *posterizations,* in either black-and-white or color.

Posterization

To make a simple black-and-white posterization, you should have at least two tonal separations; three would probably be better. Four or more may produce a final image so similar to a regular continuous tone print that the effect will be minimized or lost entirely.

You can work from the original subject, by making the separations in the camera, or you can begin with either a black-and-white positive transparency or a black-and-white negative. You can use color slides, too, but since Kodalith is red-blind it may be difficult to predict the patterns that will be formed. Usually the process begins with a black-and-white negative.

Expose the negative by either contact or projection onto each of two or more sheets of Kodalith, varying the exposures to produce distinctly different patterns. If three separations are to be used, one should be almost entirely black

Prepare a registration guide

Make a test strip

Make the first exposure; identify the top of the image

Register the other images and expose them

Process normally and judge the result

except for a few small accents of clear film; one should be approximately half black and half clear; and the third should be mostly clear with some black accents. These are all positive images. Print these images on Kodalith (by contact, preferably) to produce negatives. These negatives should be small enough to fit into your enlarger negative carrier for projection.

Select the negative that shows the most image detail and put it into your enlarger. Bring the image to the desired size, focus it on a clean sheet of white paper in the easel and move the easel as necessary to compose the image the way you want it. Carefully trace the image outlines on the focus paper with a dark pencil or a felt-tipped pen. This tracing will serve as a registration guide for the projected images. Stop the lens down to its smallest aperture and remove the negative from the carrier. Remove the focus paper but leave the easel in place.

Now make a test strip on the printing paper you intend to use to find out how much exposure is required to produce several shades of gray and a satisfactory black tone. Make the test in your usual manner but remember that because there is no negative in the carrier the light will be quite intense in spite of the small aperture. Suppose, as a result of the test, you discover that it takes 3 seconds to produce a nice light gray, 8 seconds to produce a pleasant dark gray, and 30 seconds to reach a convincing black. Jot these times down.

Replace the focus paper in the enlarging easel and select the clearest negative (the one having the least black image). Put it into the enlarger carrier, check the focus, and be sure that the lens is set at the same aperture used for the test strip. Move the easel, if necessary, to register the projected image with the drawn outlines. Turn off the enlarger light and, being very careful *not* to move the easel (tape it down if necessary), remove the focus paper and lay it aside temporarily.

Put a sheet of printing paper in the easel, positioning it against the edge guides in such a way that it can be removed and replaced exactly. This first negative will provide the light gray tone for the finished image, so it should be given the 3-second exposure. Then (carefully!) remove the printing paper from the easel and immediately turn it over and mark it lightly on the back with a pencil to identify the top of the latent image. Tuck it away out of the light.

Leaving the easel in place, replace the focus paper and project on it the second negative image (half black, half clear). If the images are not in perfect register, move the negative carrier *or* the negative within the carrier until registration is as close as you can get it, then improve it if you can by moving the easel *slightly* (moving it very far may change the image size). Remove the focus paper.

This second negative, which provides the dark gray areas of the print, will require 8 seconds, according to the test; *but* since the paper has already had 3 seconds exposure over the entire area affected by this negative, this exposure should be 5 seconds. Carefully replace the printing paper, being careful to get it oriented correctly, and make the exposure. Remove the paper to a safe place and register the third negative image with the focus paper, as before; then remove the focus paper.

The third negative is mostly black so it will protect most of the previously exposed areas of the print and provide exposure for only the image black tones. They require 30 seconds, but somewhat more won't hurt. The paper has already had a total of 8, so this exposure must be at least 22 seconds. Replace the printing paper and make the exposure. Process the print normally and you should have a posterized image consisting of black, dark gray, light gray, and white.

If the image tones are satisfactory but the picture doesn't look right, it may be because the original Kodalith positives were not exposed correctly to abstract the essential outlines or details of the subject. With a little experience you should be able to select a set of positives that break the image down into a coherent pattern of grays. Don't waste your time trying to correct the Kodalith *negative* exposures, however; the Kodalith positives they are printed from are so contrasty that they won't respond usefully to any printing controls.

Figure 9.2
Black-and-white posterization
a. Posterization negative #1

b. Posterization negative #2

c. Posterization negative #3

d. Posterization positive #1

e. Posterization positive #2

f. Posterization positive #3

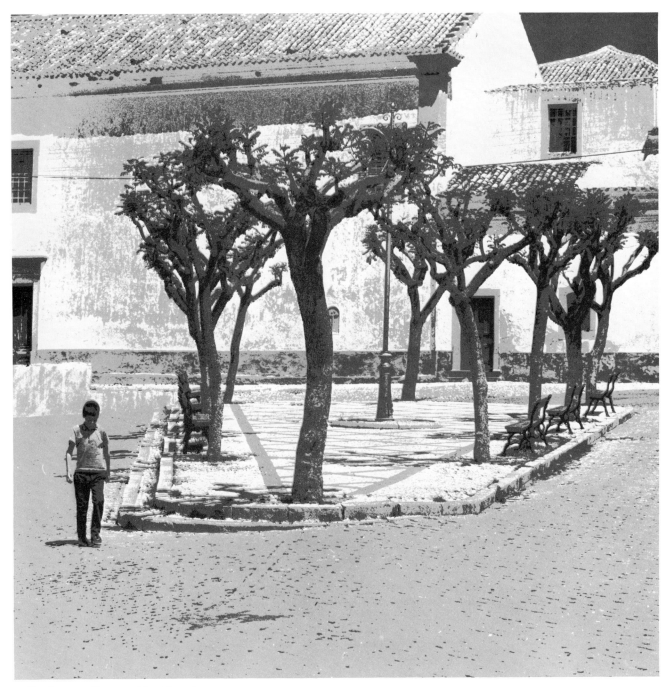

g. The three positives combined to make
the posterized print.

Figure 9.3
Negative and positive mask

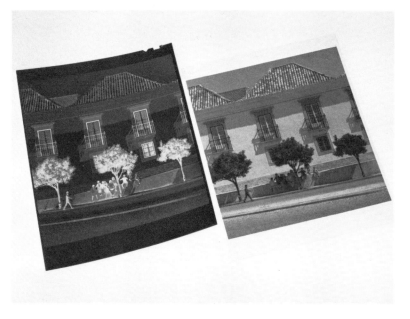

Masking and Tone-Line

Negatives can be masked to alter density or contrast

Negatives can be *masked* to alter their printing characteristics. If a weak positive image is made from a negative by contact printing (so the image sizes are identical) and then registered with the negative, the two can be printed together to form a negative of reduced contrast. If the positive image mask is more contrasty then the negative, the final print may show a partial reversal in the shadows with drastically reduced shadow contrast and density and near-normal highlights. If the mask is much less contrasty than the negative, but still dense enough to function, the effect will be more even throughout the tonal range.

Print the misregistered sandwich for bas-relief effects

If the negative and positive images are similar in density and contrast, their combined density will be high and nearly uniform over the entire picture area; in other words, the contrast will have been cancelled and the image will no longer be printable in the normal way. If the images are slightly misregistered, however, a bright outline will appear around one edge of all the image forms and the opposite edges will be shown as a dark outline. This negative-positive "sandwich," printed heavily, will produce a simulated *bas-relief* image of light and dark outlines on a uniformly gray ground (fig. 9.4).

Spin the registered sandwich for tone-line prints

The outline can be made to resemble a pen drawing if the images are registered exactly, back to back (rather than emulsion to emulsion) so the image layers are separated by the two thicknesses of film base material. Viewed straight on, this sandwich will appear uniformly dark, but seen from an angle of, say, 60° or so, a thin line of light will appear along all the image edges. If this sandwich is printed by contact in a very diffused source of light or, better yet, if a direct light is allowed to strike the printing frame from an angle while the frame is rotated on a turntable of some sort, a complete outline image can be produced on Kodalith film. If this first line image is reprinted, again on Kodalith, the image will be "cleaned up" considerably and a negative image will result. It can then be printed on almost any sort of paper to produce what Kodak refers to as a *tone-line* print. Some photographers call these images *spin dropouts* or *spin-outs*.

Figure 9.4
Bas-relief

Figure 9.5
Tone-line print

Solarization

"Solarization" really isn't solarization

Most films can be made to mask themselves, partially, if they are *flashed* (reexposed briefly to light) about midway through the negative development step, and then allowed to develop further in the dark. This flash exposure must be sufficiently strong to fog the clear areas of the negative image (shadows) but not strong enough to penetrate the relatively dense areas of the negative which correspond to the image highlights. In effect, this procedure prints the partially formed negative image back on its own film emulsion to produce a latent positive image. Further development acts on both images, resulting in a negative that is part positive. While this process is frequently called *solarization* (which it is not), it is correctly known as the *Sabattier effect*.

Mackie lines are an interesting feature

With most films, treated in ordinary developer in the usual way, this partially reversed image simply looks like a badly fogged negative, but under some circumstances the negative and positive areas of the image are separated by distinct light lines which can be quite delicate and precise or broadly smeared, or a combination of both. These are called *Mackie lines* and they result when the immediate border of an actively developing image area is contaminated by the bromide released by the developing action, thereby inhibiting development. The formation of Mackie lines, a highly interesting feature of the Sabattier effect, is encouraged by *still* or *stagnation* development (no agitation) and by the use of a developer type that is both readily oxidized and easily restrained by bromides in solution. Dektol or D-72, diluted 1:2, is usually satisfactory.

Solarization (to use its common name) is not an entirely predictable effect, which, of course, is one of its principal charms. It is most likely to be successful with fairly contrasty films—Professional Copy film, Contrast Process Ortho or Pan films, or even Kodalith. The developer should be partially exhausted, for best results, and should be used without much agitation after the reversal exposure. The timing and extent of the reversal exposure is critically important to the success of the process. If the film is flashed too early in the development, the negative image will not have had time to form sufficiently to serve as a mask and the entire emulsion is likely to be disastrously fogged. If the flashing occurs too late, the positive image will be confined to the shadows of the image only and may not have time enough to develop into a useful density. Too much flash exposure will simply fog the film or produce a very dense positive image; too little will leave it looking like a spoiled negative.

The flashing exposure must be carefully timed

Although it is possible to solarize films that have been exposed in the camera, the relatively unpredictable nature of the process makes this a risky and time-consuming procedure. It's better to make the negative normally, then print it on either film or paper and solarize the print. Any film can be used for the original negative but the print film should be a high-contrast material, as mentioned above. Kodalith and Contrast Process Ortho are preferable to Pan films because they can be developed by inspection in a red (series 1) safelight. Fine-Grain Positive film would be even more convenient to handle but it does not usually solarize well.

Solarization will tend to reduce image contrast

You will have to experiment to find the proper exposure times, but in general, the print film should be slightly underexposed, developed just until the image is clearly visible but not fully formed, then flashed to dim white light for a brief period while still in the developer. Then continue the development until the reversed image nearly matches the original image in density. Typically the reversal exposure can be given at about one-third to one-half the normal developing time, and about a one-second exposure to indirect room light will probably be a reasonable first guess. Don't cut the development short; solarization will reduce the image contrast considerably and (on any film but Kodalith) the images will tend to be too flat.

A paper print from a well-solarized negative will display the best full tonal range and preserve the best highlight whites that are possible, but solarizing the prints themselves is so easy and so fast that it is probably the most satisfactory method of producing these images. The routine is simple: use a very high-contrast paper such as Brovira #5 and print in your usual way,

Figure 9.6
a. Print solarization. First exposure slightly less than normal, flash exposure 1 second to dim room light.

b. First exposure 90% of normal, flash exposure about 2 seconds.

c. First exposure 75% of normal, flash exposure about 5 seconds.

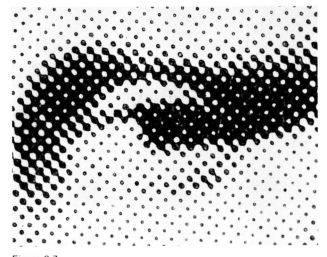

Figure 9.7
Enlarged autoscreen image

Figure 9.8
Detail of nonglare glass screen pattern.

underexposing the print slightly. Negatives of normal or low contrast are usually best, but high-contrast negatives will sometimes produce attractive effects. Develop the print in an ordinary MQ print developer (some other types will also work well), such as Dektol, diluted normally, until the image is visible but not fully formed. Flash the paper to white light (a 15-watt bulb, about 4 feet from the developer tray is probably adequate) for about ½ second and continue the development until the time is up or the image seems to have stabilized.

High-contrast papers solarize best

The quality of the final image is dependent on the amount of original print exposure, the time and extent of development before the flash exposure, the extent of the flash exposure, and, to some degree, the extent of development after the flash exposure. Low-contrast papers do not work well. The formation of the Mackie lines is facilitated if the developer is nearing exhaustion or if a little quantity of potassium bromide is added to the working solution (try about ½ gram per quart at first).

Special developer helps

The process is made even easier and more predictable if the prints are developed in Solarol, a special product (Solarol Co., Box 1048, El Cerrito, Ca.) available in some camera stores. Solarol produces better contrast and allows better control than ordinary developers do. Follow the procedure outlined above, but increase the flash exposure to about 3 or 4 seconds for the first trial. Best results seem to be obtained if the print is developed about 40 seconds before the flash, and about 1 to 1½ minutes after the flash exposure. Agitation can be continuous and the developer should be used at a minimum of 68°F to avoid possible streaking.

Screening

In the normal photographic process the image tones are *continuous* from black to white, through an infinite range of grays. When photographs are printed in magazines or newspapers, or, for that matter, when printmakers employ photographic imagery in their lithographs or etchings, the gray tones are not truly continuous. Instead, they are simulated by patterns of tiny dots of ink, too small for the eye to resolve individually, and the illusion of continuous gray tone occurs. These *halftone* grays are produced in the graphic arts media by *screening* the image. If the screen pattern is fine enough to be invisible, we

Colorplate 11

The simplest way to judge exposure and filtration is to make a test strip, using the manufacturer's recommended filter pack as a starting point. This test, using 30Y + 10C filters and exposures of 3, 6, 12, and 24 seconds, indicated a need for more yellow. Final print was made with 50Y + 10C at 7 seconds.

Colorplate 12

The central image in this array matches the original transparency quite closely and is, therefore, considered "normal." The dark and light prints represent the effect of one-half stop under- and over-exposure. The six color variations represent the effect of 10CC filtration in each of the six CC colors: red, green, blue, magenta, yellow, and cyan. The print material is Cibachrome.

Red

1/2 Stop Over

Magenta

Yellow

Normal

Blue

Green

1/2 Stop Under

Cyan

Colorplate 13

a. During exposure, color negative film separates the subject colors into the three light primaries and forms a latent image of each color on one of its three emulsion layers. Development produces emulsion layers. Development produces both black-and-white and color negative images in each layer. A bleach-fix step removes the silver negative images, allowing the superposed negative dye images to form the final color negative. Controlled amounts of unused couplers are allowed to remain in two of the film layers to form a color-corrected "mask," which gives color negatives their typical yellow-brown appearance.

Red

+

+

Green

+

+

Blue

+

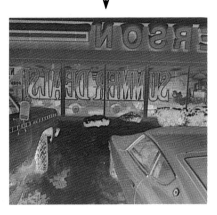

b. During exposure color positive film separates the subject colors into the light primaries and records each of them on one of the three emulsion layers. First development produces black-and-white negative images in each layer. After suitable "fogging" by light or chemical action, the remaining emulsion in each layer is developed by the color developer to form both silver and dye positive images. Bleaching and fixing baths remove the silver, leaving only the positive dye images, superposed, to form the final transparency.

Red

Green

Blue

+

+

+

+

+

+

Colorplate 14

If you live in an area where there are frequent and severe variations in the power line voltage, you should probably get a voltage regulator. Under normal conditions, however, the line voltage rarely varies more than a few volts from the nominal value of 117 vac, and the problem is not usually very serious. This example shows the very slight exposure difference and negligible color shift resulting from 5-volt variations from normal: print (a) was exposed at 112 vac; print (b) at 117 vac; and print (c) at 122 vac. No compensation was made in exposure time, aperture, or filtration. These prints are on Cibachrome, which is relatively tolerant; negative print papers are affected more obviously but, except for critical work, voltage variations of this magnitude are no great cause for alarm.

a   b   c

Colorplate 15

a. "Normal" exposure of 4 seconds @ f/5.6 produced this print.

b. Supposedly equivalent exposure of 32 seconds @ f/16 causes slight under-exposure and very slight shift toward blue.

c. An exposure of 4 minutes and 15 seconds @ f/45 should also be equivalent to "normal" but the reduced illumination causes serious reciprocity failure. Resulting print is distinctly dark (underexposed) and bluish.

a

b

c

Colorplate 16

a. Normal Cibachrome print from contrasty transparency produces harsh effect with serious loss of both highlight and shadow details.

b. Diluting Cibachrome developer 1:1 with water improves detail rendering in excessive.

c. Substituting D-76 for Cibachrome developer causes a green shift and reduces contrast still further. Four-minute development time is barely sufficient to keep whites adequately clean. Yellow tint in bright mirror reflection is due to solarization—reversal due to extreme overexposure. Cibachrome solarizes rather easily and is difficult to use with contrasty transparencies.

d. Reducing D-76 development time to 3 minutes results in low contrast but highlights have not cleared up and whites are putty-colored. No attempt was made to adjust filtration; the greenish shift could be compensated for by red added to, or green subtracted from, the filter pack but the highlight stain would be emphasized. The new Cibachrome papers are somewhat less contrasty than the original product but contrast is still a problem.

a

b

a

b

c

d

Colorplate 17

After your filter pack is approximately adjusted you can proof the slides you
want to print. This will give you a rough idea of both exposure and filtration
requirements as well as providing a convenient record for your files. the step-
tablet image is helpful but not necessary.

Red

1/2 Stop Over

Magenta

Yellow

Normal

Blue

Green

1/2 Stop Under

Cyan

Colorplate 18

"Color-negative" prints seem to be much more affected by exposure and filtration changes than "positive" prints are. These Unicolor prints represent exposure variations of one-half stop from normal, and filtration variations of 10CC in each of the six colors. Notice that filter color is subtracted from these prints and that increased exposure makes the prints darker. Compare this test group with the Cibachrome array in colorplate 12.

Colorplate 19

Colorplate 20

a. Locate the most neutral section of the Duocube image by using the gray comparator card.
b. Count the visible blue-green squares; consider a square "visible" if you can see all four corners.

Colorplate 21

Simple posterizations like these are easy to make on Cibachrome. The colors can be any that you choose and can be made brilliant or muted by controlling exposures.

Colorplate 22

Posterizations made in the camera.

Colorplate 23

Untitled. Bob Routh.
Routh is an acknowledged authority on the subject of manipulation of the
photographic image. In this striking color posterization he demonstrates his
considerable virtuosity by translating a familiar subject into a highly
decorative abstraction that is both complex and subtle.
(Courtesy of the photographer.)

Colorplate 24

a. Cyanatype on cloth.   b. Cyanatype on paper.

Colorplate 25

Three color gum-bichromate print.

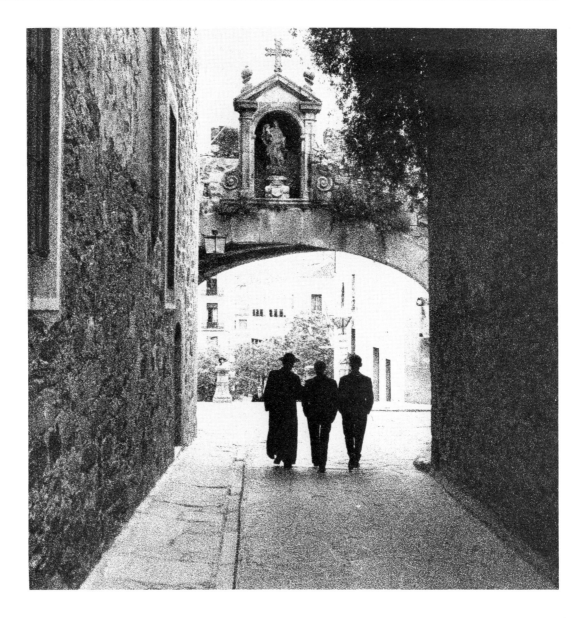

Figure 9.9
Print screened with nonglare glass

Random dot screens are sometimes desirable

perceive the gray tones as smooth and continuous; if the screen is coarse, as it is in newspaper reproduction, we are conscious of the dot texture but are not usually offended by it.

Screened images are occasionally used in photography for graphic or poster effects but they are more frequently employed in silk screen, photolithography, and photoetching. If the images are not screened in these processes, the midtones are automatically dropped out by the process itself and become simple dark and light patterns.

Commercial screens are usually regular patterns of lines or dots, but for some purposes *random dot* screens are preferable because they simulate a natural, rather than a mechanical texture. For ordinary photographic purposes it is not necessary to work with these commercial screens. They are cumbersome and expensive and unnecessarily precise for most simple visual purposes. Relatively inexpensive *replica* screens (printed from the original glass screens on Kodalith) are satisfactory, and an even more convenient technique involves the use of Kodak's Autoscreen film. Photographic images printed on this material are automatically screened in a regular dot pattern, suitable for immediate use.

Nonglare glass serves as an effective
screen

The coarseness of the final image screen pattern is controllable by enlargement; if the screened image is used at same size, the pattern has approximately 125 lines per inch. Enlarging the screened image, obviously, will reduce the number of lines per inch and make the texture more apparent.

Random dot effects, approximating a *mezzotint* screen appearance, can be obtained by printing the photographic image onto Kodalith film through groundglass, matte acetate, or the nonglare glass used for picture-framing. Replace the glass in your printing frame with nonglare glass, then place the negative and a sheet of Kodalith, emulsion to emulsion, in a printing frame and expose through the negative under your enlarger. The best exposure can be determined by trial, and it should produce an image that contains detailed areas of tone in both the near-blacks and near-whites. The contrast of the image can be controlled to some small extent by varying the *area* of the light source: a small lens aperture (on the enlarger) will tend to reduce contrast and emphasize the screen texture; larger apertures tend to *block-up* the light and dark tones, and the image will begin to approach a simple dropout in appearance. The same effects can be achieved by projection. Put the negative in the enlarger and enlarge it to the desired size on a sheet of Kodalith that is held by itself in the printing frame with the emulsion side against the nonglare glass. Be careful to clean the glass. Dirt particles between the glass and the Kodalith will result in unsightly dark blotches in the image.

Color Manipulations

Many of the techniques just described can be worked in either black-and-white or color, but in color they are somewhat complicated. Solarization is a case in point. Just a few years ago when color prints were normally developed in trays, it was fairly easy to flash and partially reverse the color image using either white or colored lights for various effects. Now, with color printing done in drums or in special processors, and with the developing times abbreviated by the high temperatures involved, it is very awkward to get the print out of the processor, flashed, and back into the developer in a reasonable amount of time. Tray processing is still possible, but it is relatively wasteful of chemicals and clumsy because of the necessity of working in the dark (or neardark) wearing rubber gloves.

Color posterization is fairly easy

Color posterization is relatively easy, however, and is done just as it is in black-and-white. It's easiest with Cibachrome. Start with the recommended filter pack for the paper you're using. Set the enlarger at the necessary height and focus it. Stop the lens down to a small enough aperture so an exposure of a second or two will still produce a good black (remember, this is a *positive* process), and with nothing in the enlarger carrier, make test strips on each of the four quarters of the paper using different colors of filtered light—any colors you're interested in. Use the cardboard mask described in chapter 7 to make these four exposures on the same sheet of paper.

Since this is a positive process, use the Kodalith positives, rather than negatives, to produce the posterization. Proceed as in black-and-white (p. 286), using the selected filter colors for each exposure and dividing the exposure times, as indicated by the test strips, so the last (most dense) positive image

Adding light colors together lightens them

supplies enough light to produce a white highlight tone. Develop as usual and you should have a posterized image in brilliant color. Remember, in this process the color is *additive:* red light applied over green light will make yellow; red and blue make magenta; and blue and green make cyan. The accumulated exposures will be lighter in value than the individual colors, too. A little experimentation will lead to some fascinating discoveries about color formation and, no doubt, produce some interesting images. See colorplate 21.

Calculate filter factors and exposures carefully

You may have a little difficulty figuring out the proper times of exposure for the various filters, since the filters will probably not all have the same printing densities (factors) and will produce any given gray tone at different exposure times. To take a simple example, let's suppose your red filter test indicates that 2 seconds is an adequate black exposure and that the times required for dark gray, light gray, and white are 4, 7, and 16 seconds respectively. For a similar range of tones, the green filter requires 3, 6, 11, and 25 seconds. Say the red filter is printed first, for 4 seconds, to form black and dark gray areas. If the next exposure were also made with the red filter, the total required (4 plus 3) would be 7 seconds to make light gray. But, the green filter will require more; if used alone it would require 6 seconds to form dark gray. But dark gray has already been formed, and regardless of *how* it was formed, the green filter would need 5 seconds more (than dark gray) to make light gray. In other words, consult each color test strip to find the appropriate exposure time to move from one selected gray to the next *for that filter,* disregarding the previous exposure times and the accumulated total.

Negative papers reverse the filter colors

Posterization with color negative papers is a little more complicated, mainly because of the heavy original filtration required and the fact that the filter colors will be reversed in the print. Use the Kodalith negatives on this paper and keep in mind that accumulated exposure produces *black.* The filter factors and exposure times can be determined as outlined above. Try to keep some control of the exposures; the temptation is strong to simply experiment wildly. This sometimes works out well, but more often it will simply waste quantities of expensive paper and lots of time.

You can produce experimental posterization effects in great variety if you photograph the Kodalith separations on color film rather than projecting them onto color paper. You will have somewhat less control of the colors and the exposures are a little more difficult to attain, but the process is relatively cheap and fast and is capable of truly bizarre imagery.

Make black-and-white masks and photograph them in color

Begin by making a series of separations from some positive or negative original, using Kodalith for dropout effects and Fine-Grain Positive if you wish to preserve some grays. Positive and negative separations can be combined and printed to produce simulated solarization effects and these, in turn, can be combined and reprinted to abstract the image still further. When you have dissected the image into interesting fractions, select four (at first) and register them on a light box, taping each one to the glass along a different edge so each can be photographed separately or can be folded over each other and photographed in combination. Set up your camera on a tripod and focus carefully on one of the films, using a close-up lens if necessary to fill the image area.

Figure 9.10
Camera set up over masks

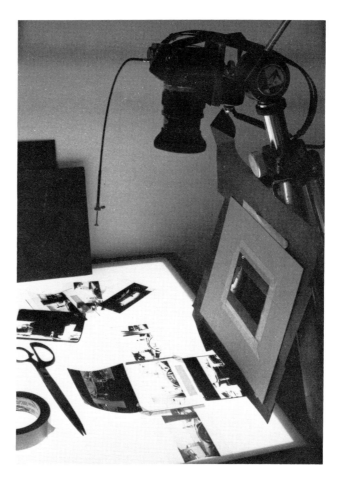

Estimate exposure as well as you can

Reduce the light intensity in the light box by using a low-wattage bulb or by covering the bulb with layers of translucent material until a meter reading of the raw light indicates an exposure of 1/5 second or longer. The basic exposure, then, will be about five or six times longer than this because the meter reading, if followed as given, will render the light as a medium gray. Over-exposure of at least 2½ stops is necessary to record the light as white.

The actual exposures used will have to be estimated and several factors must be taken into account. If there are to be four exposures, and if each of the separations is transparent in a common area, the basic exposure will have to be divided by four so the accumulated total will add up to white. Furthermore, since each of the exposures will be made through a color filter (to add color to the posterization), each exposure will have to be increased by the factor of the filter used.

Use a locking cable release if your camera doesn't have a "T" setting

For example, suppose the corrected meter reading of the light box indicated an exposure of 1 second @ f/16 for the color film in use. Each of the four separations would then require exposures of about ¼ second @ f/16 if no filters were used. But if the four filters had factors of 2x, 3x, 5x, and 10x respectively, the final four exposures would be ½ second, ¾ second, 1¼ seconds, and 2½ seconds respectively.

Sequential exposures on a single frame of 35 mm film are impossible with some cameras, and awkward and unpredictable with others. You'll find it easiest to do the actual photographing in very dim room light, or none at all, controlling the exposure times by turning the light box on and off while the camera shutter stays open on *Time* or *Bulb*. A locking cable release will hold the shutter open on Bulb if the camera is not equipped with a locking release of its own.

The actual procedure is simple enough: flip one of the separations into the camera field of view, dim the room lights, hold the chosen filter over the lens, and open the camera shutter and lock it. Turn the light box light on for the necessary time and then turn it off. Flip another separation into place, use another filter, and repeat the operation, leaving the shutter open. Do the same with the third and fourth, then close the shutter and wind the film.

Experiment, and bracket your exposures

The process can be much more complex than this example. More separations can be used and they can be overlapped in various combinations to isolate or emphasize small areas. The exposure times will become very difficult to calculate under these circumstances but film is relatively cheap (compared to paper) and you can afford to bracket. Remember that the exposures will accumulate if they overlap, but will not accumulate if they don't overlap. One precaution: if direct white light from outside the image area is allowed to strike the lens, it will almost certainly produce a high fog level in the image; it is wise to mask the area around the subject with black paper, especially if more than two or three exposures are used.

Color slide film is recommended for this kind of posterization. When the film is processed you can either project the slides or print them on Cibachrome or one of the reversal papers. See colorplate 22.

Xerox prints offer an appealing alternative

In the last few years, there has been increasing interest in *machine art* of all sorts and quite a number of contemporary photographers have experimented with such things as computer graphics, holograms, and other forms of *generated* images. Although some of these techniques require exotic equipment, one useful machine, the Xerox copier, is generally available. Xerox pictures, especially in color, are interesting transformations of the normal photographic image, ranging from almost representational reproduction to extreme distortion, at the whim of the operator. Although Xerox prints are limited in size and are fairly expensive to produce, they offer an appealing alternative to the usual photographic derivations.

Introduction to Nonsilver Processes

If you like the print as an artifact, try nonsilver

The early photographic processes offer another exciting alternative and are a rich field for exploration. If you are interested in the print as an artifact rather than a mere picture of something or if you are offended by the plastic predictability of the popular RC printing papers, you should investigate the "old processes."

There are, in general, three categories: (1) some salt of silver is used as the sensitive emulsion ingredient and forms the image in metallic silver; (2) a nonsilver light-sensitive compound is used as a sort of catalyst to form a dye image or precipitate some image metal; and (3) some sort of "bichromated colloid" is employed as the sensitive material.

Some of the old silver processes are not unlike our modern ones

The early silver processes include the daguerreotype, the calotype, the ambrotype, and the albumin prints, to name just a few. Some of them are capable of producing images of exquisite quality—a good albumin print is as fine as any contemporary image form—but they are not intrinsically different enough from modern silver print images to be much of more than just technical interest or novelty to most of us. In addition, these processes are not easy to work with and their images are subject to staining and fading to an even greater extent than modern silver prints.

There are a number of interesting and relatively easy processes in the second category. For these processes the most common and useful sensitive material is an iron compound, such as ferric oxalate or ferric ammonium citrate. In most instances the final print image is composed of some metal, usually silver or platinum. But one process, cyanotype or blueprint, forms a dye image. This is one of the easiest of the old processes and is a good one to begin with.

The third category is the largest and most versatile of the group. The bichromated colloids can be used to produce images in a variety of forms, including ink, pigment, dye, or ceramic glazes. The materials are cheap, generally accessible, relatively safe to handle, and very stable; and the images are generally as permanent as the material they're printed on. The colloids generally used are gum arabic, gelatin, casein, and various organic glues; the processes include gum printing, photogravure, photoetching, silk screen, carbon, oil and bromoil, and woodburytype, among others.

The old processes are too slow for projection printing

All the old processes involve materials of very low sensitivity to light and can only be worked by contact-printing methods. It is necessary, therefore, to produce original negatives large enough to print directly or to make enlarged negatives from small original ones. Negative quality is rather critical. Overly dense negatives are unsuitable for all the processes because of the excessively long exposure times required. The contrast of the negatives is also important; some processes, such as multiple gum, work best with negatives of quite low contrast if continuous tone and representational imagery are desired. Others, such as platinotype, work best with negatives of high contrast.

Making Enlarged Negatives

Make enlarged negatives by printing color slides on film

The easiest way to produce enlarged negatives is to project color slides onto sheet film (in total darkness, of course) and develop for the desired degree of contrast. Use panchromatic film if you want to reproduce the colors in normal shades of gray or if you are interested in making color separations for gum or carbon printing. Tri-X film is good because of its extended highlight contrast but you may have to reduce the enlarger light intensity (neutral density filters are useful for this) to avoid exposure times of fractions of a second. These short times may not be a problem if you have an electronic timer for your enlarger or if you can fit a BTL shutter onto the enlarger lens, but the average mechanical timer cannot cope with exposures of less than a second or so.

Make a test strip on the film, just as you would on paper, being sure to include the deepest shadow tones of the image on the test strip. The exposure must be sufficient to produce useful detail in shadow areas; film development will control the highlight density. If you want a soft negative, develop the sheet film in some good film developer, such as D-76, for about two-thirds the recommended "normal" time. Even this may be too much if the transparency is unusually contrasty. For contrasty negatives, suitable for platinum, develop for somewhat more than normal time.

The final negative should show detail in the shadows but not have any unnecessary shadow density. The highlights, for the gum negative, should be thin enough to read through when the negative is placed in contact with a magazine page but should generally appear quite dark. Platinotype negative highlights should obscure the type completely. If you have a densitometer available for measurement, the gum negative should have a shadow density of about .25 and a highlight density of about .9 or 1.0. Platinotype negatives should range from about .25 to about 1.6 minimum.

If you need to make enlarged negatives from existing small ones, you have at least two alternatives. You can project the original negative onto Kodak SO-015 film, or you can make an intermediate positive transparency and print that on film to make the final negative.

Or project black-and-white negatives onto SO-015

Kodak Professional Direct Duplicating film, SO-015, is convenient but expensive and somewhat limited in range. It is also a fairly unstable material that should be used fresh. Because it is a *direct reversal* material, it will produce a *negative* image from the original negative. Keep this firmly in mind. If you've had much experience in photography, it will be difficult to believe that *more* exposure is required to make an image *lighter;* but, with this material, it's true.

Make a test strip (including exposures of up to at least 2 minutes) in the usual manner and develop in Dektol, 1:1, for 2 minutes, using a light red (series 1A) filter in your safelight. Fix the film as usual, and after a brief wash, inspect it carefully in good light to appraise the densities. If the strip is too light, make another and reduce the exposure; if too dark, increase exposure. Contrast is controllable by development: to increase contrast, increase developing time; to lower contrast, reduce developing time or dilute the developer, or both. Under ideal conditions, SO-015 will yield good duplicate negatives, usually with a

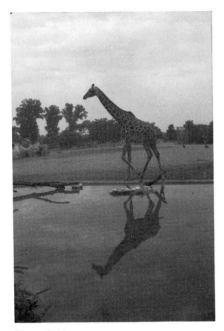

Figure 9.11
Transparency with grayed highlights

**Better yet, make a film positive;
then a negative**

**Adjust negative contrast to match the
process**

**Use litho film, developed to low contrast,
for large negatives**

somewhat greenish image tone, and with a fairly high background density level. Old film is likely to produce foggy, low-contrast images.

Making duplicate negatives from intermediate positive transparencies is less convenient and more time-consuming than using the direct duplicating film, but it permits greater control and usually produces negatives of good quality with minimum fog density. The positive image can be made by either projection or contact, but in the interest of saving material, it need not be as large as the final negative. It's probably best to make it by projection, large enough to handle easily but still small enough to fit into the enlarger carrier for final projection onto the negative film. Fine-Grain Positive film is a reasonable material for this positive image; but, for critical work, something like Gravure Positive film, or Professional Copy film (both of which will enhance the shadow contrast of the positive) may be more suitable.

Fine-Grain Positive film can be handled in the light of an OA or OC filter and has about the same printing speed as Polycontrast paper. The film has no backing dye so it can be exposed from either side, but it is generally preferable to expose the emulsion side. You can identify the emulsion side by the code notch (it appears in the top right-hand corner of the sheet when the emulsion is facing you) or by its very slightly dull appearance when compared to the back. The sheets usually curl toward the emulsion, too, but don't count on it.

Make a normal test strip and develop in Dektol (or other standard print developer), diluted normally, for 2 minutes. Select the time that produces distinctly grayed highlights; this positive is not intended to be an attractive image itself and it must have unusually well-defined highlight details if they are to be retained in the negative. Contrast can be varied to some extent by development but the practical range is not great. Development for less than 45 seconds (with constant agitation) will yield weak shadows and probably result in uneven or mottled tones. Extending development beyond 7 or 8 minutes will not result in a useful increase in contrast.

As a rule of thumb, if the original negative is contrasty (needs a #1 paper to print well), develop the transparency in Dektol, 1:1, for 45 seconds or in D-76 for about 4 minutes. If the negative is normal develop the positive about 2 minutes in Dektol; if the negative is flat (needs a #3 or #4 paper to print well), develop 4 to 8 minutes in Dektol. Development will influence the effective film speed to some extent. Adjust the exposure to obtain the necessary "grimy" highlights if the development is unusually long or short.

Contrast can be modified still further, if need be, in making the negative. Project the positive image onto any standard sheet film or, preferably Kodak Commercial film or Professional Copy film, both of which can be handled in red safelight. If the transparency contrast appears to be about normal (for a print image) when viewed against strong light, develop the negative film to a contrast index of about .4 for low-contrast results and about .7 or more for negatives suitable for platinotype. (See discussion of contrast index, pp. 255–59 and the charts in appendix 14.)

You can use Commercial or Copy film for both the positive transparencies and the final negatives, if you want to, with very fine results. Try developing both negative and positive films in Dektol, 1:1, for about 2 to 4 minutes. If the final negative contrast is too high, reduce development time in either or both steps. If too low, increase it.

When very large negatives are required, it is almost prohibitively expensive to use regular camera film like Tri-X, Plus-X, or Super-XX; in fact, it is now almost impossible to get large sheets of these films even on special order. One alternative which can be quite satisfactory is to use one of the less well-known litho films, which are relatively inexpensive and can often be obtained from graphic arts supply houses. Ordinarily these materials produce extremely high-contrast images, but they can be made to yield negatives of fairly normal characteristics if they are developed in relatively mild film developers. If you try this, be sure to use a safe safelight; ordinary developers enhance the speed of these films and may produce fog if the safelight is too bright. D-76 is a good developer to start with, either straight or diluted, if still lower contrast is desired. For bold, posterish effects, of course, use the film as it is intended to be used and it will give you its natural dropout images.

a

b

c

d

Figure 9.12

a. Cyanotypes are simple and inexpensive to make. Blend the two ingredients in a glass beaker or ceramic cup; don't use a metal container or you may have staining problems.

b. Spread the mixture on the paper rather generously. On some papers two coats may be required to produce a good image. The brush shown is a fan-blender. Its metal ferrule has been lacquered to prevent possible rust stains which would show up as blue streaks. Coating can be done in ordinary room light but avoid direct sunlight or bright fluorescents.

c. Hang the coated paper in a dark place to dry. Quick drying is beneficial and moderate heat can be used. The coating is a light yellowish-green at this point.

d. When the paper is thoroughly dry, put it in a printing frame with your negative, emulsion to emulsion. Contrasty negatives will give the best results.

The Cyanotype Process

The cyanotype process is probably the easiest "old process" there is. It is also versatile, attractive for some purposes, and remarkably stable. Aside from the chemicals involved, there is nothing new to buy; you will need a few trays, a printing frame, a good bright light source—rich in ultraviolet (a sunlamp will work pretty well or you can use sunlight)—some paper or cloth to sensitize, and a flat brush of appropriate size to spread the sensitizer fluid. A natural bristle fan-blender, about #6, is fine for prints of moderate size. Here is the simplest formula I know.

Solution A	
ferric ammonium citrate	25 gms
water	100 mls
Solution B	
potassium ferricyanide	9 gms
water	100 mls

Store the solutions in separate brown "dropper" bottles if you will be making only small prints. If you plan to work on cloth or make very large prints on paper, make larger volumes of both solutions and store them in plain brown bottles.

For use (in dim room light), mix equal parts of the two solutions together in a glass or plastic container and spread the mixture thinly on paper, brushing it back and forth gently until it is even and no longer fluid. Hang the paper in a dark place to dry and hasten the drying, if possible, with gentle heat or air movement, or both. When dry, the paper is ready to print. Place it under a negative and expose to direct sunlight until the coating that is visible around the edges of the negative has changed from its original yellow-green color to a distinct bluish-gray (or some other dark tint).

e   f

e. Expose to a bright light, rich in UV. Daylight is usable but may be variable. This bank of fluorescent tubes is a fine fast source. The exposure will be long—at least several minutes.

f. There will be a strong printed-out image when the exposure has been sufficient, as demonstrated by the undeveloped section of the print in the model's right hand. Development in plain water is almost instantaneous. Acid water gives greenish tones, alkaline water produces purplish tones and will eventually reduce the image density. Strong alkalis will destroy it. No fixing is required. Rinse the paper until no more blue color is discharged, then hang the print up to dry.

There are several ways to intensify cyanotype images

When the paper is removed from the printing frame, a fairly distinct printed-out image should be visible but its intensity is not an absolutely reliable guide to exposure.

Development couldn't be simpler; slip the print into a tray of cool water and agitate it gently. The image will form in a few seconds and progress to a rich blue color. Further washing in several changes of water is all that is really necessary to fix the image but it will be more stable if it is rinsed in a weak solution of hydrochloric acid (commercial Muriatic Acid is all right)—just a few drops in a quart of water will be sufficient. *Caution:* hydrochloric acid is poisonous and corrosive. Read the warning label and handle it with extreme caution.

The color of the image will be altered to greenish-blue by this acid treatment. It can be turned into an intense purplish-blue by immersion in a weak solution of ammonium hydroxide (household ammonia will do as well)—again, just a few drops in a quart of water will do. *Caution:* ammonium hydroxide is a strong base with suffocating vapors. Handle with care in a well-ventilated area. If the ammonia is too strong the image will be lightened and perhaps destroyed, but if the process has not gone too far it can be reversed in the acid bath. The alkaline purple color is elegant, but probably not as stable as the normal blue-green.

There are several ways to improve the richness and contrast of cyanotype images. One direct method simply substitutes a weak dichromate solution for the usual plain water "developer."

| Potassium | (or ammonium or sodium) dichromate | 10 gms |
| Water | | 1 liter |

Immerse the exposed paper in this solution and agitate gently until the image is fully formed—about 1 to 3 minutes, typically. Then wash the print until the yellow dichromate stain is gone and no more blue color is discharged. *Caution:* dichromates are hazardous; wear protective gloves while handling the dry chemical, and while mixing and using its solutions.

If you prefer, you can develop the print normally in plain water, then intensify it to a rich, deep blue in either of the following solutions:

| Hydrogen peroxide, 3% solution | 10 ml |
| Water | 500 ml |

or,

| Household bleach (such as Clorox) | 10 ml |
| Water | 1 liter |

Hydrogen peroxide is a common first aid item, available in the 3% strength at most drugstores. Both intensifiers can be used at somewhat greater strength, but the bleach must not be too strong or it will act as a bleach rather than as an intensifier. It's also possible to skip the preliminary water "developer" and put the exposed paper directly into one of the intensifier baths, but they're a little less effective this way. It's better to use the water bath first, then intensify the image after it is fully formed. Wash the prints thoroughly after intensifying them; then dry them, face up, on blotters or screens, or hang them in a film dryer. See colorplate 24.

Cyanotypes can be made on cloth or paper

Cyanotypes can be made on cloth almost as easily as on paper. Small pieces of cloth can be dipped in the solutions and squeezed dry before hanging them in the dark for final drying. Larger areas can be sensitized with a large sponge well charged with the sensitizer. Spread the cloth out on papers to protect the table or floor, and wet it as uniformly as possible with the sponge. Too much sensitizer is better than too little. The image will use what it needs and the rest will simply wash away.

Some papers are better than others

The cyanotype process is usually quite trouble-free but a few difficulties may arise. Like most of these old processes, the paper used is an important factor determining the quality of the image. Problems of weak or mottled tones, local variations in color, grayed or glazed-over dark tones, and obvious coating streaks in the image may all be due, at least in part, to the paper itself. The best papers are firm, smooth long-fiber papers with good wet-strength. Rag stationery is usually good and so are many good-quality drawing papers, watercolor papers, and some art papers. The real test of paper, however, is in actual use. Try a sample and see what happens. If the image is satisfactory, the paper is good. Cyanotypes are quite permanent in normal handling but launder cyanotype-printed cloth as infrequently as possible and avoid strong soaps or strong bleaches. Alkaline solutions will destroy the dye image.

Contamination is an occasional problem

Chemical contamination is an occasional problem. Blue streaks may form in the coating before development if particles of rust should happen to fall into the sensitizer or if the coating brush has a rusty metal ferrule. It's better to avoid metal ferrules, if you can, or at least to seal them from the sensitizer with lacquer or clear nail polish. For the same reason, don't mix or store the sensitizer solution in any sort of metal container; use plastic or glass.

The Gum-Bichromate Process

The gum-bichromate process, and the similar *casein* and *glue processes,* all produce pigment images. Any color pigment can be used, and the images can be monochromatic or multicolored. The processes are capable of reasonably good photographic representation as well as broad, flat-tone effects and there is plenty of opportunity for hand-modification of the image if that is desired.

Gum prints can be made in monochrome or full color

The equipment required is minimal. You'll need a coating brush, such as the fan-blender previously mentioned, a printing frame, two or three trays a little larger than your print size, and some exposing light—a sunlamp or the sun itself will do. The chemicals needed are gum arabic (sometimes called gum acacia) and one of the following: sodium dichromate, potassium dichromate, or ammonium dichromate (the same chemical used to be called *bi*chromate). Of these, potassium dichromate is the least satisfactory but it will work if that's all you can find. Ammonium dichromate is usually recommended and is available from graphic arts suppliers and, especially, silk-screen supply houses. Sodium dichromate is as good as ammonium dichromate for these processes but is slightly more expensive to use and a little less common. All three are inexpensive chemicals and the quantities used are so small that the cost is almost negligible.

The materials are readily available and not expensive

You'll need some pigment colors and some paper. Watercolor pigments (not casein or acrylic colors), either in tubes or in dry form, are generally good; get tube colors at first to simplify mixing and measuring. The earth colors, such as umbers, siennas, and ochers, are generally good. Ivory black usually works well and some people like lamp black. The modern synthetic colors are generally good, too. Don't get the cheapest "student" grade colors; some of them contain dye rather than pigment and dyes don't work well, as a rule. Start out with ivory black, burnt umber, or burnt sienna.

The paper is very important; some work, some don't

The paper must have good wet-strength so it should be at least part rag and quite well-sized. Watercolor papers are generally usable as are some drawing papers. Avoid soft papers at first; they have a tendency to stain. Very hard or glazed papers have the opposite effect; they tend to give you high-contrast dropout-type images, and the image may flake off in unsightly patches. Try several types of paper to see which works best for you.

Begin by preparing these two solutions:

Solution A

first dissolve	mercuric chloride	3 gms
in	hot water (125°F)	300 mls
then add	cold water	300 mls
and stir in	gum arabic (powder)	250 gms

The gum solution must be preserved— poison!

Caution: Mercuric chloride, used here as a preservative for the gum solution, is a dangerous poison and must be handled with extreme care. Avoid contact with the powder; don't breathe the dust; and wash your hands and utensils thoroughly after handling this material. It dissolves with difficulty even in hot water. Be sure it is completely in solution before adding the cold water and the gum. The gum will not dissolve immediately. Stir it until it becomes thoroughly wet, then let it stand in a covered wide-mouth bottle for a day or two. It will gradually go into solution and turn into a tan-colored, syrupy liquid. Keep it covered to prevent evaporation and it will keep indefinitely. (If mixed without the mercuric chloride, or some other preservative, the gum solution will sour within just a few days.) Be careful to clean off the top of the bottle before screwing the cover on; the gum mixture is an excellent adhesive and is capable of gluing the bottle cap on firmly. If this happens, run hot water over the bottle cap until the dried gum is softened, then remove the cap and clean it thoroughly.

If you prefer, you can substitute some other preservative. Prepare the basic gum solution as described above, but without the mercuric chloride; then stir in about 10 to 15 drops of formalin or about 1 ml of a saturated solution of thymol dissolved in alcohol. If the gum solution is not preserved in some way, it will sour within a few days or weeks. Although soured gum is said to be workable, you wouldn't want to use it; the stench is terrible.

Solution B

ammonium dichromate	150 gms
water	600 mls

or, alternatively (and my personal preference),

sodium dichromate	300 gms
water	600 mls

The dichromates are poisonous, too; protect your skin

If only potassium dichromate is available to you, prepare a saturated solution and use it in place of these as solution *B*. Store the dichromate solution in a brown bottle to protect it from strong light. It will keep indefinitely. *Caution:* dichromates are poisonous and can be absorbed through the skin to cause painful and dangerous dermatitis. They can be handled safely with reasonable precautions, but be careful not to inhale the dry chemical dust or allow the crystals or their solutions to remain on the skin. Rubber gloves will offer complete protection.

a

b

c

d

Figure 9.13

a. To make the pigment test, as described in the text, measure the pigment "worm" to determine quantity. This much is plenty for the entire test.

b. Whip the pigment into the gum solution alone, then when it is thoroughly blended, add the dichromate solution and blend again. Be sure there are no particles of raw pigment clinging to the brush hairs; they'll leave streaks in the image.

c. Press the brush almost dry against the side of the mixing container, then paint a small patch on the paper. Brush it out until it shows no tendency to run, then add a measured quantity of gum and dichromate to the mixture and paint another patch. Repeat, diluting the mixture each time by some known amount, until you have produced a series of patches, ranging from dark to very light tone. Judge the tone by pigment content only, if you can; they'll all be strongly stained with dichromate yellow.

d. Hang the test strip up to dry in a dark place. Strong light will invalidate the test.

e. Don't expose the test strip. Simply take it out of the drying cabinet when it is completely dry and immerse it in cool water. After a few moments the pigment will begin to loosen. Float the paper facedown on the surface of the water and let it stand quietly for a half hour or so. Be sure there are no air bubbles trapped under it while it's developing.

f. When the paper no longer drains any appreciable amount of pigment, consider it fully developed and hang it up to dry. When it is completely dry, pick out the patch that shows just the faintest trace of pigment stain. That mixture is the maximum strength that you can use for printing without risking stained highlights.

e

f

g

h

i

j

g. Mix a batch of the selected emulsion and spread it rather briskly, brushing it out until the brush marks stop blending readily and begin to show. Then, with much lighter strokes, whip the surface gently with just the bristle tips to blend the marks away. The emulsion will begin to feel a little tacky—a sign that it's ready to hang up to dry.

h. Dry the coated paper in the dark.

i. Put it into the printing frame.

j. Expose it. You'll have to determine the exposure time by trial. Gum is faster than cyanotype but the exposure will still be timed in minutes. Tungsten lamps are a poor source of light for these processes; they produce too much heat and not enough UV. Fluorescents are good if you can get enough of them together. Sunlamps are usable.

k. Develop. Don't handle the print after it begins to drip pigment, unless you want granular tones and unsubtle gradation. For best tonality float it until all soluble pigment has been discharged.

l. Multiple-gum is capable of full tonal range and good gradation. Here is a three-layer print in a black and burnt umber mixture.

k

l

For use, pour small quantities of solutions *A* and *B* into separate dropper bottles and measure the working quantities by "droppersfull" or "squirts." Fasten a piece of your selected paper down on a clean washable (or disposable) surface using small bits of tape at the corners of the sheet. Using an old ceramic coffee cup, or other similar container, measure out 2 "squirts" of the gum solution and add to it a 1-inch long section of the pigment "worm" squeezed from your tube of, say, burnt umber. Dampen the fan-blender brush with plain water and slap it as dry as possible against your hand or a towel; then stir the pigment and gum with the brush until the pigment lump is apparently dispersed. Finally, holding the brush vertically in the pigment mixture, twirl the handle rapidly between your palms until the gum mixture is whipped into a fine froth and check to be sure none of the pigment is clinging to the brush hairs.

Test the gum mixture for pigment strength

In moderately dim room light, add 2 squirts of the dichromate solution and stir briskly until blended. Then, after pressing most of the gum mixture out of the brush against the side of the container, paint a small patch on one corner or edge of the paper, spread it out, and brush it back and forth lightly until the brush begins to drag a little. The area should be thoroughly covered but not obviously wet with the liquid. Label this patch "4 squirts." Now add 2 more squirts of gum and 2 more of dichromate, blend thoroughly and paint another patch, labelling it "8 squirts." Continue this process—adding measured amounts of gum and sensitizer, blending, coating, and labelling—until you have a total of, perhaps, 20 squirts of solution, and six or eight patches on the paper. Hang the paper in a dark place to dry. Use warm moving air to hasten drying if possible.

When the paper has dried thoroughly (*don't* expose it to bright light), slip it into a tray of cool tap water, faceup, and immediately pick it out by one corner to let it drain. The dichromate will dissolve almost instantly and drain off in a yellow stream. Reimmerse the paper and drain again. Repeat this procedure until you see some indication that the pigment is beginning to loosen. As soon as this occurs, gently place the paper, facedown this time, on the surface of the water, being careful not to trap a bubble of air under it, and let it float quietly for a half hour. Then rinse it *very* gently in a tray of clean water and let it drain dry, hanging from one corner in a film dryer or on an open line.

The "whites" should remain clean

When the paper is completely dry, the pigment patches (if there are any left) will be durable and you can handle the paper freely. Inspect it in good light. If the test has been successful, one or more of the pigment patches will have disappeared but some will probably still be visible and perhaps even be quite dark. This procedure is designed to test the maximum amount of pigment that you can use and still retain reasonably "white" highlights in the image.

Let's suppose the 16-squirt patch is almost colorless but the 12-squirt patch shows a distinct tone; this indicates that less than 16 squirts risks stained highlights and that the 16-squirt mixture, spread on *this* paper, is an optimum mixture. Other pigments may permit greater concentration or may require less; other papers may stain at lower concentrations or wash clean at much higher ones. If you're interested in predictable control of the medium, you should probably run this sort of test with each pigment and each paper you plan to use.

Some pigments stain more seriously than others

When you have arrived at a paper and pigment combination that pleases you, coat a whole sheet with the optimum mixture and dry it thoroughly. Then expose it, under your (fairly low-contrast) negative, to the printing light and make a conventional test strip exposure series with times running from about 1 minute to about 10 or 15 minutes. You should be able to see a faint image resulting from the exposure but it is not a reliable guide.

Wet and drain the print until the color starts to loosen, then float it, image down, in clean water for half an hour, changing the water once or twice if it becomes badly discolored. Handle the wet print *very* gently; the gum image is extremely delicate and fragile at this stage.

Multiple-gum for normal photographic contrast

Select the best test section and make another print using the indicated time. If all goes well, it should be acceptable. If not, make another, and another, and another. . . .

If you are after normal photographic tonality in your gum prints, you will probably be unhappy with most of them because of their very low contrast. This is an inherent characteristic of the medium and can't be cured by any such apparently logical moves as using more contrasty negatives or adding more pigment to the mixture. If you want better contrast and richer dark tones than a single layer of pigment can provide, you'll have to resort to *multiple-gum printing.* As the name implies, this involves coating the dry print with another layer of pigmented gum, registering the negative over the existing image, developing it, and drying it. If the contrast is still not good enough, do it all again. Some of the old Pictorialists have been reported to have gone through as many as seventeen printings to get a single image, but that seems rather extreme.

For satisfactory contrast in a monochromatic image, using good paper and a good pigment (avoid gouaches or "designers colors" for multiple-gum printing), three printings is usually sufficient.

This process will test your skill as a craftsman

Although this sounds tiresome, consider what you may have when you finish. If all goes well, the print will have a long scale of tones from near-white to a rich velvety dark; it will have a pleasantly soft definition emphasizing tonal masses rather than edges and textures; it will preserve much of the intrinsic surface quality of the paper it's printed on; it will be one of the most permanent of photographic images; it will testify to your skill as a craftsman; and it will be unique, because no two multiple-gum prints can possibly be identical in every detail. Although this medium is certainly not appropriate for every type of photographic image, it is very suitable for some and will certainly attract attention.

Multiple-gum prints can also be made in either natural or arbitrary color. Full-scale prints in natural color will, typically, require six or seven printings, two for each pigment primary color and a final one of a dark neutral shade to accent the blacks. The negatives can be made conveniently from any color slide by direct projection on panchromatic film, using the usual color separation filters (Wratten #s 29, 61, 47B). No color correction masks are necessary. The only requirements are that the negatives be of suitably low density and contrast and that they be approximately matched. As in dye-transfer printing, the red-filter negative (#29) prints cyan (thalo blue) pigment; the green filter negative (#61) prints magenta (alizarin crimson); and the blue filter negative (#47B) prints yellow (azo or hansa yellow medium). They are usually printed in sequence (yellow, magenta, cyan; yellow, magenta, cyan), with a final coating of Payne's gray or ivory black. See colorplate 25.

The images must be registered

Registering the images for multiple-gum printing is one of its most difficult aspects. Because the existing image is practically obscured by each fresh coating of sensitizer, it's almost impossible to register the negative visually. In my opinion, the best (nonmechanical) method of registration is the one outlined by Paul Anderson in the old Henney and Dudley *Handbook of Photography,* published by Whittlesey House about 1939. He suggests scribing register lines on the negative margins and using paper sheets *smaller* than the negative so the register lines can be transferred to the *back* of the print when it is first printed. For subsequent printings it is only necessary to place the coated paper on the negative, facedown, and match the register lines, a relatively simple and foolproof procedure (fig. 9.14).

Unless you want to work with montage or decorative effects

Of course, it isn't necessary to register the images at all if you don't want to, and most contemporary gum-printers don't. Gum is an excellent technique for doing color montages or for incorporating a photographic image into a drawing or watercolor painting. The images can also be produced on some other materials, too, including cloth. It is, in fact, a very versatile and interesting technique but one that will never be widely practiced (except in its crudest forms) because of its difficulty.

Figure 9.14
Seen on a light box, this gum print appears dark gray as it lies facedown on its negative. The registration marks on the negative and the print permit accurate repositioning of the print for each new exposure.

Gum prints can be spotted with watercolors

Gum prints and cyanotypes, and, for that matter, almost all of the old process prints, can be mounted and matted in the same way conventional silver prints are handled. Either high- or low-temperature mounting tissues may be used but you should be especially careful to dry out the mounting press. Gum prints can be spotted with regular watercolor pigments of the appropriate color.

This relatively brief description of two old processes should give you enough information to get started; but it has only scratched the surface. There are many other ways to produce photographic images using these basic materials and each method has certain unique characteristics. There is, fortunately, a great deal of published information available, and if these image forms interest you, you should have no trouble finding formulas and instructions for the technique of your choice. You will find a few readily available reference books listed in the bibliography.

Summary

The normal photographic process represents the subject without obvious distortion, but there are many ways to manipulate the process for dramatic effect. One way is to drop out the image gray tones by using a very high-contrast film material, such as Kodalith—a slow, ortho material requiring a special developer for greatest contrast. By using Kodalith as a print material and varying the print exposures, an image can be separated into several different areas of flat tone and recombined to form a posterization.

Negatives can be masked by printing them on film, then registering the positive with the original negative. Masking reduces image contrast and may alter it selectively. Misregistering the images allows the formation of a thin outline which can be printed as a bas-relief. By slightly separating the registered images, a similar outline can be produced, which resembles an ink line drawing, and is called a tone-line image.

A somewhat similar effect can be obtained by exposing a partly developed film or paper image to dim white light, briefly, then continuing the development. When properly executed, this flash exposure partially reverses the image, causing it to mask itself, and forms white Mackie lines around contrasting forms. This Sabattier effect is commonly called solarization (which is something else entirely) and is frequently interesting.

Screening the image allows it to be printed in silk screen, etching, or lithographic techniques by breaking the tones into tiny dots of pure black and white. The visual illusion of gradation still exists if the dots are small enough. If the image is enlarged, the screen pattern becomes visible as a texture or pattern which may be decorative. Random dot patterns can be produced by printing an ordinary negative or film positive on Kodalith through nonglare glass or some similar material.

Color solarization is possible but rather unpredictable. Color posterization is fairly easy on Cibachrome. Proceed as in black-and-white, but use positive masks, and test for color and exposure. Remember, colors will be additive and filter factors must be applied to the exposures.

Posterization is awkward with negative papers but it can be done on color film by successively photographing different image separations on a light table, through various filters. The separations can be either high-contrast or continuous-tone, positive or negative, or combinations, and may be registered or not. The process is fast and easy once set up, and bizarre effects can be produced. The finished transparencies can be printed, if desired, on Cibachrome.

Machine art and generated images are currently popular. Xerox black-and-white copiers are widely available and widely used. Color Xerox copiers offer an appealing alternative to the usual color processes.

The old processes are becoming increasingly popular. There are three general categories—silver-sensitive systems, iron-sensitive systems, and bichromated colloid systems. All of the old processes are slow and will usually require brilliant printing light and contact-printing procedures.

You can make the necessary large negatives for these processes by projecting color slide images onto regular sheet film and developing to the appropriate degree of contrast. Cyanotype negatives should be quite contrasty; gum negatives (for continuous tone results) should be quite low in contrast. To duplicate existing negatives, you can use Kodak SO-015 but you'll get better results by making an intermediate positive on film and printing it to final size, again on film. Very large negatives can be made on litho film, developed in mild developer for normal contrast results.

The cyanotype process produces deep blue images on almost any material including paper and cloth. The entire process can be carried out in dim room light and the materials are relatively cheap and available.

Gum-bichromate prints are pigment images. They can be made in any color or combination of colors and can be manipulated very easily. Equipment and material needs are minimal. You will have to experiment to find a paper and a procedure that works for you. Use good quality watercolor pigments at first and follow the chemical preparation and testing instructions carefully.

Full-color photographic quality gum prints are the most difficult to make. Work from low-contrast color-separation negatives and use the recommended pigment colors. Registration is difficult; nonrealistic, nonregistered color is much easier. Gum prints are easy to combine with painting or drawing techniques and every print is unique.

What Is a Good Photograph?

Outline

Subjectivity of Definition
    Consumer vs. Producer
    Using Criticism Constructively
Photographic Principles/Personal Expression
    Human Vision vs. Camera Vision
    Composition
    Visual Symbolism
Revival of Early Techniques
Directing Your Image-Making Skills

Subjectivity of Definition

A good photograph—for you—is one you like

What is a good photograph? That depends upon whom you ask and what criteria are being used to make the judgment. In the opinion of the gallery owner, a good photograph is one he can sell easily and at a good price. The scientist considers a good photograph to be one that displays the visual information he wants, clearly and succinctly. The advertising art director and his client call a photograph good if it will glamorize the product and make it appealing to the purchaser. Your photography teacher may call your photographs good if he sees in them some sign of visual awareness, technical ingenuity, or personal expression. To your mother, any photograph of you is good, especially if it shows you smiling. A good photograph, for you, is any photograph you like, whether anyone else likes it or not.

Consumer vs. Producer

"Making" and "consuming" have different criteria

The definitions above relate to the judgment of the consumer of photographs; as a producer of photographs, your criteria of what is "good" should be quite different. Logically, an artist can consider his work good if producing it is an engrossing and gratifying experience and if the finished work measures up to or exceeds his expectations. The process of *making* and his satisfaction with the result reflect the artist's taste. The success or failure of the work in the marketplace reflects the taste of the consuming public.

You should consider carefully the difference between these two criteria. Although a great deal of "fine art" of the past was commissioned by wealthy patrons, much of the work that we consider to be significant or seminal in the history of art reflects the desire of the artist for *self*-expression. It seems unlikely that Picasso's *Guernica,* for example, could have resulted from a commercial assignment. Julia Margaret Cameron's magnificent portraits of the great men of her time resulted from her feeling that photographing them was "the embodiment of a prayer." By comparison, her contrived allegorical illustrations of literary and biblical themes are unremarkable and, in some cases, insipid and silly. More recently, the commercial work of Avedon, Arbus, Davidson, and Michals, although skillful and ingeniously effective for its purpose, is much less interesting and inspiring than their personal work. It seems clear that the "best" work done by any artist is the work he does to please himself solely, unmindful of the opinions or criticisms of others.

Julie and the Judge, from the Seagram Bicentennial Courthouse Project, 1976. Ellen Land-Weber.
One of several photographers chosen to document American courthouses, Land-Weber has transformed what could have been a very plain and ordinary "design" photograph into a whimsical and charming double portrait.
(Courtesy of the photographer.)

We can't operate in total isolation

You shouldn't, however, consider this as license to "do your own thing," regardless of consequences. Only relatively mature and sophisticated individuals who have mastered their craft are equipped to produce work of much lasting significance. Furthermore, as human beings we can't operate in total isolation; communication, sharing of ideas, and approval are all important to us. The work of an inexperienced, unskilled artist, however gratifying it may be for him, will probably seem naive and crude to a sophisticated public, and this rejection can be a painful experience. Far too many young artists react to this rejection by subduing their own instincts and trying to cater to what they perceive to be "public taste." This can only lead to mediocrity. Without the intuitive guidance of personal taste, their work must necessarily mimic that of others and become derivative and "trendy." The better course, by far, is to work harder to develop your own taste and improve your skills until your work merits attention. Then you'll get the approval you deserve.

Using Criticism Constructively

By showing your work, you risk criticism

Although you shouldn't accept other people's pronouncements of what is "good" and "bad" without question, you should consider their reactions to your work carefully and as objectively as you can. By showing your work, you are asking for approval and yet risking criticism. If you get criticism rather than approval, it is obvious that your critic's taste differs from yours or that the fine qualities you see in the photograph are not apparent to him. If approval is important to you (and if you're human, it certainly is), you must find out what the problem is and try to correct it.

Simple differences in taste are not particularly serious. Your critic can express lack of interest in your work but concede that it is well conceived and well executed for what it is. The more serious problem is a difference in perception of the work and this is something that you should consider very carefully. If you are a beginner in photography, you may still be so charmed by the mere mechanics of image formation that *any* picture is a triumph. On an intermediate level you may feel that you have entered the ranks of the Friedlanders and Winogrands with a series of "street photographs" that your critics see as rather pointless snapshots. Even mature photographers can fall into the trap of "wishful seeing" and fail to recognize in their pictures flaws that are distractingly evident to another person. Like a person singing in the shower, exulting in the beauty and resonance of his melodious tones, we all tend to see in our own photographs just those qualities we *want* to see; and just as the singer's efforts may sound, to a person outside, like the bellowing of a wounded moose, so may the inadvertent flaws in our work be distressingly obvious to viewers.

Take criticism seriously, but not personally

Take criticism seriously, then, but not personally. Good criticism can indicate to you the success or failure of your efforts to share your ideas and emotions. It should not be interpreted as an attack on you as an individual. Criticism can help you grow; learn to deal with it objectively.

Photographic Principles/Personal Expression

It's easy to become technically competent

Photography is a complex mechanical medium governed to a very large extent by physical and chemical principles which are reliable, predictable, and inflexible. Because of this, it is fairly easy to become technically competent; all that is required is comprehension of the principles, respect for the materials, and careful workmanship. But this same technical rigidity makes photography a difficult medium of personal expression. Unlike the other visual arts, which permit the gradual building up of a work, constantly subject to review and modification at the artist's whim, photography allows almost no opportunity for review or change during the actual process of image formation. The image can be modified, to be sure, by subsequent manipulation, but it is initially a record of what the lens "saw" at the instant of film exposure.

Most photographic accidents are more disastrous than decorative

In this sort of medium the hand of the artist is well concealed. There are no telltale brushstrokes, no personal idiosyncracies of line, perspective, or color, and very few possibilities for useful "accidents," such as the natural blending of fluid color in a wash drawing or the spontaneous crazing of a ceramic glaze. Accidents, in most photographic processes, are disastrous rather than decorative. "Creativity" in photography is, therefore, limited to the organization or selection of subject matter and manipulation of the image after it is formed.

Photography is a formidable challenge, artistically

Selection and organization of subject matter is the essence of "straight" photography. The choice of camera position, lens focal length, depth of field, exposure interval, film type, filters or other lens attachments, light condition, and development contribute to a certain quality of image which will reflect, to some degree, the taste and sensitivity of the photographer. The work will be still further personalized by the choice of print materials and the presentation style of the finished image. The degree to which a photographer's style is recognizable will depend partly upon the degree to which his personal taste and judgment are involved in making these various selections and decisions. It will also depend upon the extent of his commitment and the lengths to which he'll go to achieve "perfection." Don't be fooled by the apparent simplicity of this medium; technically, it's easy to master; artistically, you'll find it a formidable challenge.

Human Vision vs. Camera Vision

You must learn to see as the camera sees

One of your first problems, as a beginning photographer, will be learning to see things as the camera will record them, and there are a few fundamental differences between human vision and camera vision that you will have to become accustomed to. In the first place, your eyes really see sharply only very small areas of any subject at any given moment. Your visual impression of things you look at is assembled mentally from a series of fragments that you perceive in very brief, scanning glances. Added to this is a general visual orientation of the entire area of the subject obtained by your very wide-angle but unfocused peripheral vision. You use the peripheral vision to establish the relative position of objects in space, then glance at the areas that seem to need more complete analysis with your precise central vision.

This is generally a very brief, totally unconscious act. Your eyes leap from point to point without being willed to do so, and your brain pieces the visual bits together. At the same time, your brain computer is operating to make the impression intelligible. It automatically emphasizes things that it knows will interest you and suppresses things that you have programmed it, by experience, to classify as insignificant.

In addition to the purely visual impressions that you receive, your computer circuits may supply you with some information from your other senses. All of these bits add up to a general impression of the total experience. If you are paying attention, you will experience some sort of reaction, usually a mild one, of interest or boredom, pleasure or displeasure. If you experience pleasure while you are looking for photographic subject matter, you will probably take a picture of the object or scene that prompted it; and if it is done casually for so trivial a reason, it will probably be a rather trivial picture.

The camera can't know what you intend to express

The reason is not complicated. The camera simply does not record what your brain recorded. Your snapshot photograph really does little more than confirm the fact that you were present at the subject area when the picture was taken. It will emphasize none of the points that interested you, suppress none of the areas that bored you, illustrate a very small area of the total subject space that your peripheral vision described to you, and will display the whole distorted mess in smaller-than-life scale, confined within artificially described boundaries, in two dimensions and, perhaps, in black and white. Obviously, there can be no hint of any of the extravisual perceptions that you experienced and that contributed to your total impression.

No wonder your friends fall asleep
when you show slides

If you present confusion, you won't
communicate

Composition—"the strongest way of
seeing"

Fortunately, there are no rigid standards
of good and bad

Sensationalism is unproductive;
so is mindless conformity

Is it any wonder that your friends fall asleep when you show your vacation slides? *You* can enjoy them because they help you relive your trip. They serve for your memory the same function that a prompter serves for an actor who has forgotten his lines. But no amount of prompting can help an actor who has not learned his part, and no amount of simple visual reminding can be of much use or much pleasure to a person who has not had the experience to remember.

If you want to communicate your own impressions to others (and what photographer doesn't), you must supply them with complete, coherent pictures. In very simple terms of straight photography, this means that your print must display clearly, sharply, and without confusion of background details all those areas of the subject that your eye examined with pertinent interest. By the same token, your print must eliminate or subdue those areas of the subject detail that your brain classified as irrelevant or uninteresting. Every visible feature of the print will affect the viewer in some way, and if you supply him with the wrong elements or present them to him in confusion, he will not get your message.

Composition

Another very important factor is the composition or visual arrangement of the image forms for the sake of the design itself. Consider it this way. The photographic print is a picture of something that conveys real information about the subject, and that, with luck and skill on your part, may suggest something of the way you related to the subject while making the picture. In addition to this symbolic aspect, the print is physically a piece of paper coated with gelatin, containing irregular areas of black, white, and gray. Even if they represented nothing at all, these areas of tone create a pattern that nearly everyone can appreciate, to some small degree at least, for its own sake. In fact, whether he is consciously aware of it or not, virtually every viewer will be at least subtly influenced by the abstract design of the image tones and textures.

Edward Weston once described composition as "the strongest way of seeing," and that's not a bad definition. Certainly a well-composed picture is more attractive and more effective for its purpose than one that appears unorganized and chaotic. But how do you distinguish between "good" and "bad" composition; how can you organize the elements of a picture for best effect; and how can you avoid pictorial chaos? These are good questions—obvious questions—but, unfortunately, they don't have good, obvious answers. Furthermore, if you give it some thought for a moment, I think you'll agree they *shouldn't* have answers.

If there were firm and inviolable rules for composition, there would be very little chance for personal expression, and picture-making would become a simple matter of following instructions. Anyone could produce good pictures, one after another, and those closest to the defined "ideal" would be "best." This would also mean, of course, that pictures not adhering to the rules would be automatically branded as "bad," even though they might be powerful images, dramatically presented. Anything new or different would be disqualified, and art museums would soon become dismal wastelands, full of endlessly repetitive, thoroughly tiresome pictures.

That's one hypothetical extreme; now let's consider the other one. If no inviolable rules exist and if a formula approach to picture-making leads to tiresome imagery, does this mean that the traditional rules and conventions should be deliberately flouted, and that anything new and different must necessarily be better than something that's been seen or done before? Of course not! Either extreme is silly. Sensationalism for its own sake is just as unproductive as mindless obedience to the rules. The compulsion to be different is just as hampering to creativity as is the compulsion to conform.

Henry Peach Robinson, in his famous book, "Pictorial Effect in Photography," published in 1869, insisted over and over again on the importance of abiding by the "recognized and certain laws" of composition—but without ever stating unequivocally just what those laws are. He advocated the triangle, the diagonal line, and the circle as guides to be followed in constructing the "most pleasing and agreeable" compositions. "A square," he said, "is much less picturesque than a pyramidal form," and warned that "an important object . . . will never be found exactly in the centre (of a composition)." But Robinson was wise enough to realize that an art governed entirely by rules is no art at all. "Laws become hurtful when carried to excess," he declared; "rules are not intended as a set of fetters to cripple those who use them, and it is not intended that the student should absolutely abide by them."

Robinson was fairly cautious; Hammond was less so

Later authors were less cautious and occasionally inclined to justify their statements with pseudoscientific explanations: Arthur Hammond, an influential magazine editor and author of "Pictorial Composition in Photography," published in 1932, counselled his readers that right angles in a composition are "not good" because they "tax the eye muscles." He advocated scribing the camera groundglass into three equal vertical and horizontal areas so that "the principal object of interest" could be placed at one of the four "strong positions" formed by the intersections of the dividing lines—a principle still sometimes invoked as the "rule of thirds." Finally, Hammond stated flatly, "the laws of principality and unity, harmony and balance, must always be observed."

Things have changed since then

Things have changed considerably since Hammond's time (and certainly since Robinson's). We no longer believe that a triangular relationship of lines or points in a picture necessarily signifies compositional excellence (nothing is simpler than locating triangles or squares or circles or mythological beasts in a picture—or in the stars—if you're inclined to find them there). We're now aware that the eye can't be depended on to "enter" a composition at a designated spot, travel a prescribed route through the picture, and leave (presumably satisfied) at a selected exit point. We now feel much less sure that including an S curve, or observing the rule of thirds, will guarantee a great picture. But, most importantly, we don't think of photography as being restricted to expressing "the sublime, the beautiful and the picturesque" any more. We realize that "good" composition is a matter of taste and we're aware that taste is not a universal verity. Different cultures see things differently; so do different age groups; and so do different individuals. There *are* no rules of taste that we can agree on universally, or depend on to remain unchanged.

There are no rules of taste that we can agree on

If the rules of composition have acquired a bad name over the years (and they have), it may be because they've been interpreted, all too often, by extremists. Furthermore, there's faulty logic at work; while it's absolutely true that a picture we admire *may* contain an S curve, an obvious balance of opposing diagonals, a pyramidal form of some sort, and while it may obey the rule of thirds, it's equally possible that a picture may contain all these "desirable" features and be obviously and offensively dull. The thesis that, "since all good pictures contain S curves (for example), all pictures that contain S curves must be good," is just as ridiculous as concluding that because all dogs have four legs, all four-legged things are dogs.

We should probably divide the rules into two categories

The traditional rules should probably be divided into two categories: (1) rules that define desirable compositional effect—such as unity, variety, harmony, balance, etc.; and (2) rules that specify methods for *achieving* compositional effects—such as preferred shapes, ideal proportions, permissible placement, and so forth. There's not much reason to quarrel with the first category; we can generally agree that it should be obvious what a picture is about (unity, clarity, harmony); that there should be more than just the bare bones of the idea present (variety); and that the picture should appear more or less comfortable in its format boundaries or frame (balance). These generalities are by no means binding but they often apply and can serve as useful guides in studying a composition to see "if it works"; and if not, why not.

The rules for achieving these effects, on the other hand, are at least controversial and perhaps even dangerous. The idea that one physical arrangement of lines or forms or tones is "better" than some other one is unprovable, misleading, and restrictive. If the terms "creativity" and "personal expression" have any significance at all, there is no place in art for regulations of this sort.

You'll learn to compose intuitively if you work at it

You should, of course, be aware of the various visual elements—line, form, tone, texture, color, etc.—and the way in which they can relate to each other—size, direction, juxtaposition, perspective, etc.—because they'll be represented in your pictures whether you like it or not. These relationships will become very important to you if you pursue photography seriously, but merely recognizing their existence is a good beginning. You'll learn to compose intuitively and effectively, sooner or later, if you make a practice of studying your pictures (and other people's), objectively and at length, to see what they *really* look like. Then, if you can decide what you like when you see it, you'll be off to a good start.

Visual Symbolism

You may want to experiment with visual symbolism

As your skill and vision improve, you will probably begin to appreciate the less obvious, more subtle uses of photography. You may want to experiment with visual symbolism to convey part of your message. This may be as direct as presenting the image of a loaf of bread in such a way that it stands for "food," or it may be so personal and complex a symbol that only you will know that it exists in the picture.

Whether you plan them that way or not, people may occasionally claim to recognize symbols in your pictures. This is probably good. It at least indicates that you have managed to avoid being too specific with your imagery. Symbolism is a difficult problem to deal with photographically because of the inherent realism of the photograph. It is very easy to take a picture that means "this is what Billy looked like on his tenth birthday." It's much more difficult to make Billy an anonymous symbol for "boyhood" without getting obvious or corny.

Or manipulated image forms

In the last few years, there has been a renewed interest in the manipulated image. These pictures take many forms, their common characteristic being that they all depart from naturalism. The most common manipulated images are the simple dropouts, solarized images, and screened images of various sorts. Some workers retain the photographic gray scale but distort the imagery in some way. "Weegee" (Arthur Fellig) did it by printing through warped plastic sheets. Uelsmann cunningly combines parts of two or more photographs in one print by multiple printing techniques. Some photographers use simple cut-and-paste techniques to produce photocollages, then work on the prints with dyes, and pencil to enhance the effects. Others work with the Xerox process or other "generative" systems and some are investigating electronic imaging systems and holography.

Revival of Early Techniques

There has been a revival of early techniques

At the same time, there has been a revival of some of the very early techniques. George Tice and others are exhibiting platinum prints, an exquisite method of printing which was popular around 1900. A few photographers have experimented with daguerreotypes and calotypes. Scott Hyde is known for his composite images done in a modern version of the old gum-bichromate process, and Betty Hahn and others combine the older, more traditional methods with handwork to produce very unusual and exciting contemporary images. Todd Walker has experimented with many of the old processes and has produced some elegant solarized nudes in gum-bichromate and in the more modern offset lithographic techniques. He and a few others have also worked in collotype, the beautiful but difficult gelatin equivalent of stone lithography.

The purpose of all these procedures seems to be to free the photographer from the mechanical naturalism of the straight photographic image and the cold, machine-perfect surfaces of the commercial papers. These departures from

Mixed-media expressions can be fresh and exciting

straight tradition should not be thought of as dishonest or bad or nonphotographic even though, at first appearance, many of them are startling and even ugly if judged by conventional camera club standards. Consider them as paintings or prints if that will help you appreciate them. In many cases, it is really difficult to classify them; they are truly mixed-media expressions that can be both fresh and exciting.

Directing Your Image-Making Skills

It's hard to explain the fascination of image-making

It's hard to explain the fascination of image-making to a nonartist. The physical act of photography is a relatively simple procedure which anyone can learn to do passably well if he puts his mind to it. It only becomes really difficult, and engrossing, when the image itself begins to capture your imagination. Then the differences between "good" and "bad" pictures become so important to you that it's hard to think of much else. Where you go from there is up to you.

Your own interest may stop at the snapshot. That's not a bad place to be if you do it well (look up the photographs of Jacques Henry Lartigue to see how intimately delightful a family album can be). Or you may find that the straightforward documentation of your own environment is worth your attention. Look at the straight, beautifully detailed interiors of Walker Evans and the views of Paris that Atget did so naively and with such obvious affection.

Perhaps you will be attracted to social commentary. There is a great deal of material to draw on here—from John Thomson, Jacob Riis, and Lewis Hine, through the incredible FSA record of the depression to the present and people like Gordon Parks, David Douglas Duncan, Bruce Davidson, and Diane Arbus. A more subdued approach to photojournalism, combined with strong visual design, is exemplified by Kertész and, later, by Henri Cartier-Bresson.

Look at the work of others

Look at Weston and Adams for their reverence for form and light. Look at the powerful, brooding photo-essays of Eugene Smith; the cool professional elegance of the work of Irving Penn; and the subtle romantic Polacolor studies of Marie Cosindas. Inspect the composite images that Rejlander and Robinson produced in the 1850s and 1860s and the more recent surrealistic compositions of Uelsmann. Look at the cameraless images of Man Ray, Schad, and Moholy-Nagy, and the bitterly satirical montages of Heartfield.

Investigate the work of the Photo-Secession group, a marvelously varied and skillful group of photographers. Follow the birth and growth of photojournalism from Salomon to the present day. Look at the industrial photographs of Weston, Bourke-White, and d'Arazien, and study the portrait styles of Newman, Halsman, and Karsh.

We inevitably influence each other

As photographers, we inevitably influence each other and this is a healthy thing. Make the most of this interchange of ideas and inspiration and use it as a springboard for your personal expression. It is far more constructive to plagiarize, to deliberately imitate someone whose work you admire, than to wait, without *doing* anything, for the spontaneous arrival of an idea that no other photographer has ever had, or a subject that no one else has ever dealt with. These things simply will not happen.

You'll find your own expressive form

I believe sincerely that it is impossible to copy anyone else's style for very long even if you try to do it seriously. Your own personal vision will certainly intervene and you will gradually find your own expressive form in spite of yourself if you work at it. You can't become a great photographer, or even a good one, by simply thinking about pictures. It's also true, though, that you'll have to involve your mind and your emotions as well as your trigger finger if you want to amount to very much.

Photography will give you more than your money's worth

You'll find, in fact, if you take it seriously, that working at photography will demand as much from you and involve you as totally as anything you have ever done. In return, it will give you more than your money's worth in profound, personal gratification.

Portfolio

Joanne Leonard photographs things that are personally meaningful—her home environment, her friends, and especially her daughter Julia, the subject of this informal portrait. Superficially this is a simple image, but a perceptive viewer will see in it much more than a mere record of a sleeping child. The camera has captured the atmosphere of nap time; it is cool and quiet and the room is dimly illuminated. The viewpoint emphasizes the limp grace of the child's position, the smoothness of her skin and the soft roundness of her young body. The quality of light is dramatically effective and the image is carefully and effectively composed. We can sense in this picture the photographer's love for her daughter and share her obvious admiration for the physical perfection and beauty of this miniature human being.

Although the content of this photograph is clear and uncomplicated, it can have different significance for different viewers. For some it may function as an "equivalent", evoking in some mysterious way an emotional response quite unrelated to the pictured reality. For others it may simply trigger recollections of childhood, or reminiscences of their personal experiences as parents.

Not all photographs are as immediately appealing as this one is but any photograph can function on at least two or three levels: graphic (its two-dimensional design), representational (what it depicts, real or surreal), and evocative (what response it arouses in you); but before it can function at all, you must give it a chance by really looking at it—not casually or out of simple curiosity, but with genuine intent to perceive. The burden of communication is borne equally by the image-maker and the image-viewer!

On the following pages—and worthy of your careful attention— are examples of the work of a number of serious and dedicated photographers. Most of these men and women are well known and in many cases, the choice of images was theirs. This portfolio has no theme. It is intended to suggest some of the vast variety of work that has been done and, although it is by no means a complete summary, I hope you will find it instructive, enjoyable, and inspiring.

Julia Sleeping. Joanne Leonard.
Although Leonard has worked in a wide variety of styles, she is best known, perhaps, for
her sensitive treatment of her home and neighborhood environment. This beautiful
photograph is of her daughter—a favorite subject.
(Courtesy of the photographer.)

Sardinia, 1980. Ralph Gibson.
Gibson's concern with the formal aspects of light, pattern, and space are evidenced here.
In this unusual and dramatic abstraction, light itself is the subject; the human form—
although identifiable—is of secondary importance.
(Courtesy of Castelli Photographs.)

Francis Bacon, artist, April 11, 1979, Paris, France. Photograph by Richard Avedon. Avedon is an acknowledged leader in the field of fashion photography, and has been for years. More recently he has become equally respected for penetrating portraits, such as this one, that combine technical mastery of the medium with interpretive ingenuity and dramatic economy of means.

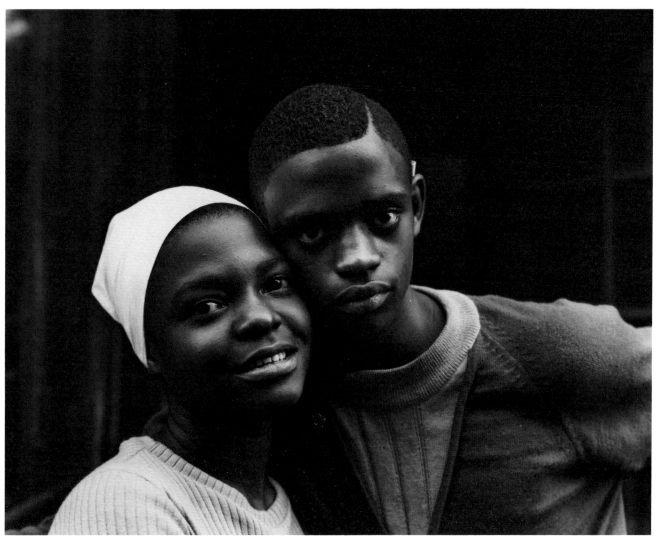

Portrait, from *East 100th Street*. Bruce Davidson.
Of the two years he spent photographing East Harlem, Davidson said, "I entered a
lifestyle, and, like the people who live on the block, I love and hate it and I keep going
back."
(Courtesy of the photographer.)

Marat/Sade. Max Waldman.
(Courtesy of the photographer.)

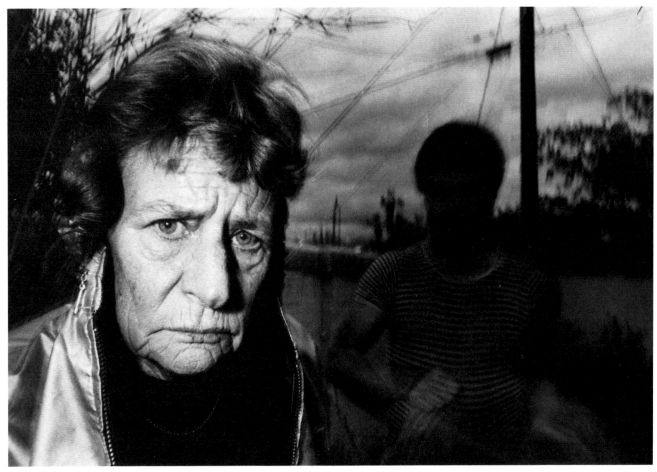

Shelley; from the series: Hot Flash, 1978. Anne Noggle.
This is representative of Noggle's recent work, in which she expresses her emotional
response to the physical process of aging. Her work is typically personal, direct, evocative
and frequently disquietingly surreal.
(Courtesy of the photographer.)

Circumnavigation of the Blood, 1950. Frederick Sommer.
Sommer has been quietly exploring the limits of photographic expression—perhaps more
thoroughly than any other American photographer—for many years. Although his work is
considered seminal, and is highly respected by serious photographers and other artists, he
has never been well-known outside the field. This early avant-garde work is still
mysteriously evocative.
(© Frederick Sommer, Courtesy of LIGHT gallery, NYC.)

Untitled, 1977 / 1980. Ralph Steiner.
Mr. Steiner says of this photograph, "The snow picture is one of my favorites. I call it my
"Mozart" because if Wolfgang Amadeus were a photographer and alive these days and
saw this snow scene, he'd have photographed it. Alas, he is dead (no one knows where he
is buried), so I took the picture for him."
(Courtesy of the photographer.)

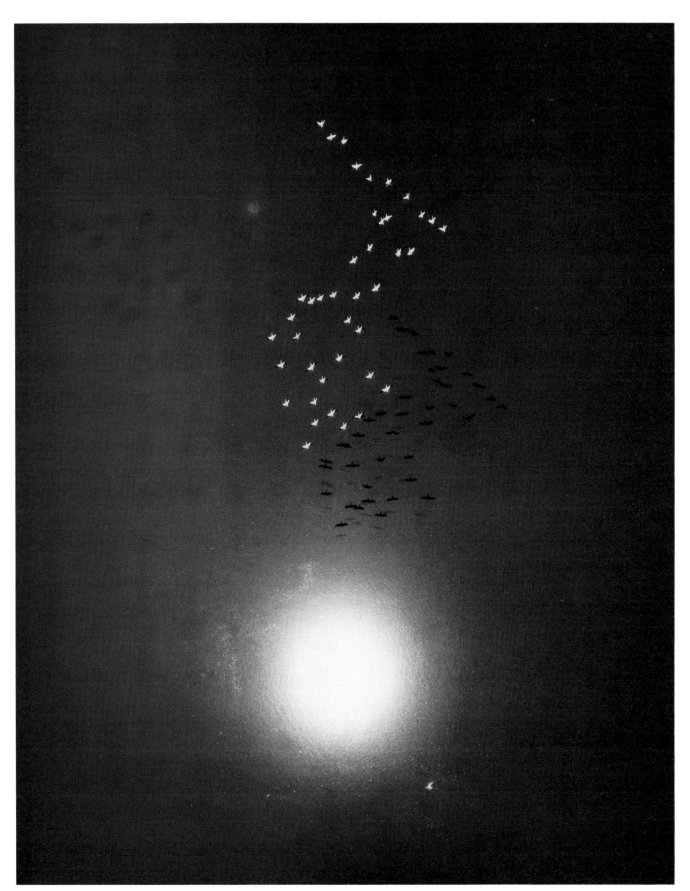

Snow Geese with Reflection of the Sun over Buena Vista Lake, California, 1953.
William Garnett.
Garnett's exquisite aerial abstractions of earth and water patterns have been widely
published for more than thirty years. This relatively early work has an almost oriental
elegance and simplicity.
(Courtesy of the photographer.)

Jerry Uelsmann.
Uelsmann is the acknowledged contemporary master of combination printing. This floating
form in the sky is a recurring theme that has much in common with the work of the
Surrealist painter Magritte.
(Courtesy of the photographer.)

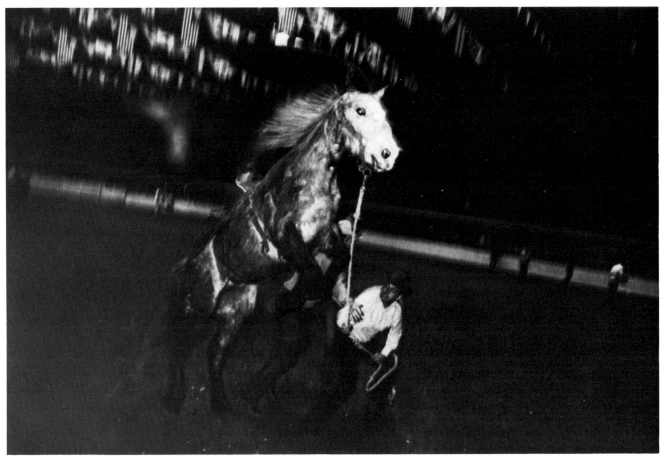

Untitled, from the series, Stock Photographs. Garry Winogrand.
Although he blandly ignores the conventional standards of "good" composition and
lighting, Winogrand—like Cartier-Bresson—photographs "decisive moments." Unlike most
photographers, who use the camera to record what they see, Winogrand uses the camera
for its *own* vision, thereby capturing and dramatizing the unseeable. In this typical
photograph he combines on-camera flash with ambient light to partially arrest the violent
motion of the rearing horse. The horse's glittering eye and flaring nostril, the cringing
figures, blurred flags and tilted horizon convert an invisible split second into a bizarre and
portentous *tableau vivant.*
(© Garry Winogrand, Courtesy of LIGHT gallery, NYC.)

Rose Hill Cemetery, Macon, Georgia, 1977. Lorran Meares.
By working at night and selectively illuminating portions of his subject area with a portable
spotlight, Meares produces these mysterious multiple exposures with a stereo camera.
Even in 2-dimensional reproduction they glow with an unearthly light and are strangely
portentous.

Self-portrait from the Self-portrait series. Vernon Cheek.
(Courtesy of the photography.)

Striped Song, 1981. 22 × 30 silkscreen print by J. Seeley.
Seeley is an acknowledged master of the high-contrast image form. Combining the
undeniable visual appeal of "op art" with the implicit realism of the photographic image,
his black-and-white linear abstractions are boldly decorative, highly complex and a
delightful treat for the eye.
(Courtesy of the photographer.)

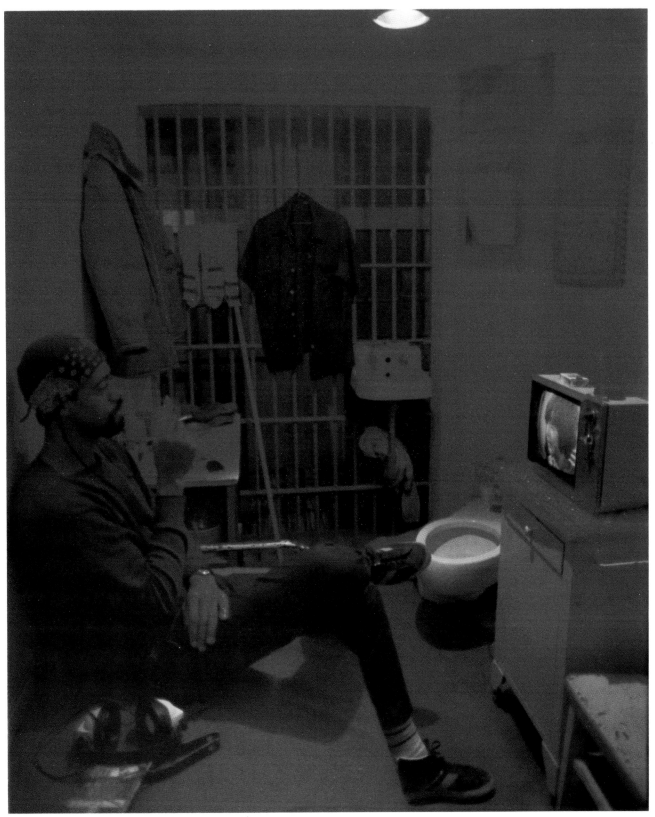

Prisoner, Southern Michigan State Prison, Jackson, Michigan, 1980. Taro Yamasaki.
In the glare of a single red light bulb—the cell's only "decoration"—an inmate passes the
time by watching television. This photograph is one of a series for which Yamasaki—a
staff photographer for the Detroit *Free Press*—was awarded a Pulitzer Prize in 1981.
(Courtesy of the photographer and the Detroit *Free Press.*)

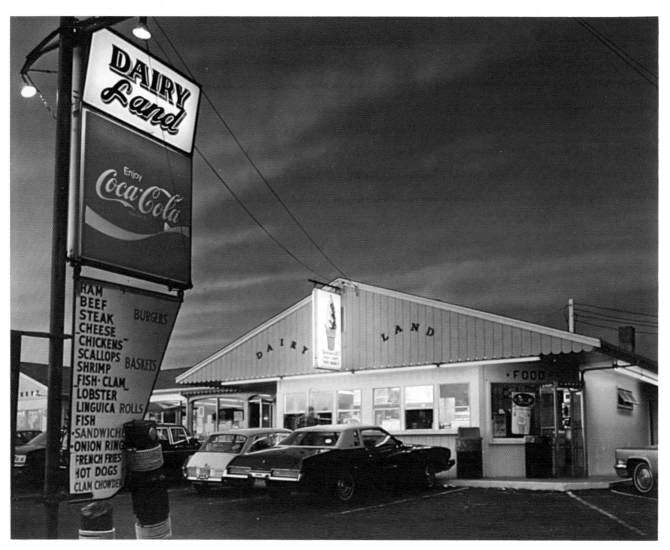

Provincetown, 1976, from the series, *Cape Light.* Joel Meyerowitz.
Meyerowitz is one of several photographers currently working in large-format color, but his
work is notable for the sensuous and dramatic chromatic blends he achieves by working at
dawn and dusk and mixing natural and artificial light sources. In this typical photograph he
captures the gorgeous hues that exist—but are rarely perceived or appreciated visually—
in a familiar and mundane subject.
(Courtesy of the photographer.)

Tarn, Iceland, 1972. Eliot Porter.
Porter is well-known for his beautiful dye-transfer prints that have been featured in Sierra
Club books and widely reproduced. This subtle and delicate image combines the visual
sensitivity and technical mastery for which he is justly famous.
(Courtesy of the photographer.)

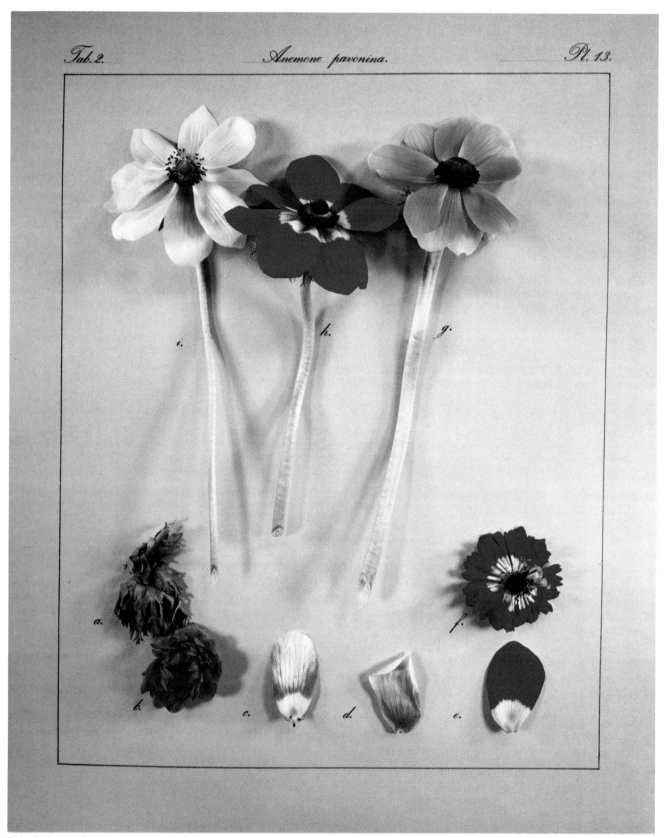

Botanical Layout: Anemone Pavonina, 1980, 20″ × 24″ Polaroid. Betty Hahn.
Hahn is well-known for her experimental works in various nonsilver processes, many of
which she embellishes with stitchery or hand-applied color. In this relatively ''straight''
print she photographs real fresh flowers to create a whimsical parody of a page from a
botanical specimen book.
(Courtesy of the photographer.)

Untitled, 1980. 18″ × 22½″, 3M color-in-color process, transferred to Arches Rag paper.
Ellen Land-Weber.
Land Weber was one of the first to explore the potential of the color-copier as a creative
tool and has become well-known for her fanciful and intriguing arrangements of natural
materials as they are interpreted by the machine. This composition is reminiscent of the
work of the Surrealist painter, Max Ernst.
(Courtesy of the photographer.)

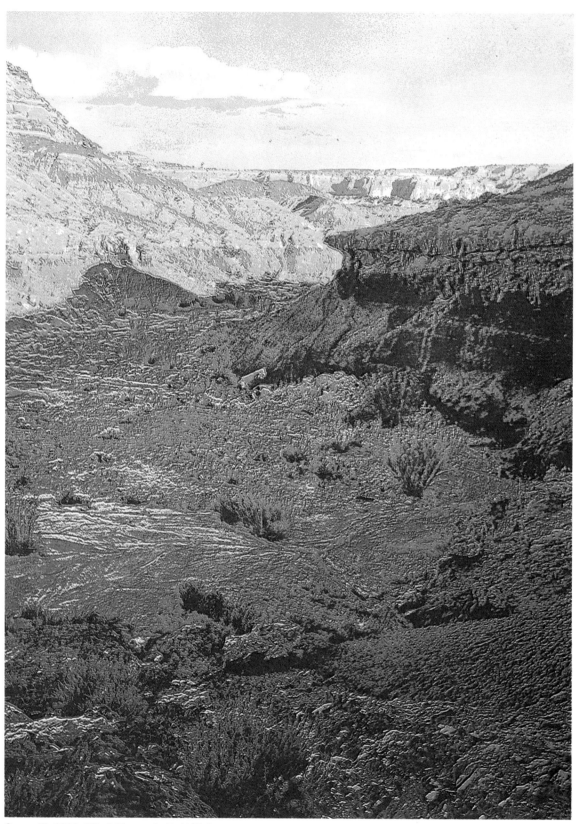

Canon III, 1981. Offset lithograph. Todd Walker.
Walker has worked for many years with various non-silver processes and has become well-
known and highly respected for his skillful and delicate compositions in gum, silkscreen
and—more recently—offset lithography. This recent work demonstrates his sensitivity as a
colorist as well as his mastery of the medium.
(Courtesy of the photographer.)

Appendixes

The reference material and
formulas contained in this
section have been compiled
from a number of sources and
are believed to be accurate at
the time of publication. Specific
product information will change
as the products themselves are
modified or replaced on the
market. It is wise, therefore, to
consult the product manufacturer's latest technical data
sheets for the most reliable
information. Lacking these, the
information given here will be
useful and will keep you out of
serious trouble.

1. Some Currently Available Films and Their Characteristics
2. Currently Available Photographic Papers and Their Characteristics
3. List of Metol-Free Developers
4. Formulas
5. Metric Conversions and Equivalents
6. Close-up Exposure Correction
7. Flashbulb and Electronic Flash Guide Numbers
8. Color Temperature
9. Kelvin Temperature and Filtration Calculator
10. Filter Factors for Black-and-White Photography
11. Development vs Temperature Chart
12. Suggested Reciprocity Failure Compensation
13. Equivalent Lens Focal Lengths and Lens Angular Coverage Chart
14. Contrast Index Developing Charts
15. Matching Negative Density Range to Paper Contrast Grade

1

Table A.1

Some Currently Available Films and Their Characteristics

Film Manufacturer and Name	Sizes Available: Sheets	Rolls	35mm Cart	35mm Bulk	Speed	Contrast	Sharpness	Color Sensitivity	Grain	Recommended Uses
Kodak										
Technical Pan 2415	x		x	x	*100–25	High	Very High	Pan	V.F.	Line and halftone copies
Panatomic-X and Panatomic-X Prof.		x	x	x	32	Medium	Very High	Pan	V.F.	General purpose use in good light, where maximum sharpness is desired
Plus-X Pan Plus-X Pan Prof. Plus-X Pan Prof. 4147	x	x	x	x	125	Medium	High	Pan	V.F. V.F. Fine	General purpose, especially in daylight. Especially studio.
Tri-X Pan Tri-X Pan Prof. Tri-X Pan Prof. 4164	x	x	x	x	400 320 320	Medium	High	Pan	Med. Find	General purpose daylight or studio; available light
Recording Film 2475			x	x	1000	Medium	Low	Pan C	Coarse	Available light; science
Verichrome Pan		x†			125	Medium	High	Pan	Fine	General purpose
Ektapan Film 4162	x				100	Medium	Medium	Pan	Med.	Studio flash; portraiture
Royal Pan 4141	x				400	Medium	Medium	Pan	Med.	General; studio flash
Kodalith Ortho Film	x			x	8‡	Ex. High	Ex. High	Ortho	V.F.	Line copy, dropouts
Fine Grain Positive	x				Low	Med. High	Very High	Blue	V.F.	Transparencies
High Speed Infra-red	x		x	x	Varies	Medium	Low	UV & IR	Coarse	Medical, scientific, unusual visual effects

Film Manufacturer and Name	Sizes Available				Speed	Contrast	Sharpness	Color Sensitivity	Grain	Recommended Uses
	Sheets	Rolls	35mm Cart	35mm Bulk						
Ilford										
Pan F		x	x	x	50	Medium	Very High	Pan	V.F.	General purpose, for maximum sharpness
FP-4	x	x	x	x	125	Medium	High	Pan	V.F.	General purpose
HP-4	x	x	x	x	400	Medium	High	Pan	Med. F	General purpose, for available light (to be discontinued)
HP-5			x		400	Medium	High	Pan	Med. F	Available light
*Ilford XPI-400			x		200–1600	Med.	High	Pan	Fine to Med.	Black and white chromogenic; variable speed, general purpose
AGFA										
*Agfapan Vario-XL			x		200–1600	Med.	High	Pan	Fine to Med.	Black and white chromogenic; variable speed, general purpose

†Includes some obsolete sizes as well as 110 and 126 cartridges.
‡In Kodalith developer; 25 in D-19.
*Chromogenic films: Require C-41 or equivalent color chemistry for development.
*Speed depends on use and developer: see manufacturer's recommendations.

2

Currently Available Photographic Papers and Their Characteristics

Photographic papers come in a wide variety of brands, surfaces, weights, contrast grades, image tones, base materials, and speeds. RC (resin-coated), RD (rapid dry), and similar plastic-laminated papers permit very short processing times, dry quickly in room air, and require low-temperature mounting tissues for dry-mounting. Glossy plastic-laminated papers dry to a mirror-smooth finish without special treatment and should not be ferrotyped. Plastic-laminated papers of all varieties are convenient to use but are not yet considered suitable for archival storage.

Fiber-based or baryta-coated papers require much more thorough washing than plastic-laminated papers, but when suitably treated are considered safe for archival storage. These papers are supplied in greater variety than the plastic laminates and are generally easier to tone and spot. Glossy baryta-coated papers must be ferrotyped to achieve a mirror finish; if dried in air they produce a slightly textured, highly lustrous surface. All fiber-based papers show a pronounced tendency to curl while drying and in response to humidity changes. They can be dry-mounted using either high- or low-temperature tissues.

Table A.2 lists some of the printing papers on the market; papers with similar specifications are roughly comparable in appearance and performance, but there are individual differences that will be apparent to the careful printer. For a more comprehensive listing consult the various manufacturers' literature.

Key to Kodak Surfaces

F   White, smooth, glossy. Single and double weight.

N   White, smooth, lustre. Single and double weight.

A   White, smooth, lustre. Lightweight.

J   White, smooth, high lustre. Single and double weight.

M   Warm white, smooth, matte. Double weight.

E   White or warm white, fine-grained lustre. Single and double weight.

G   Cream, fine-grained lustre. Double weight.

K   Warm white, fine-grained high lustre. Double weight.

R   Cream, tweed lustre. Single and double weight.

Y   Warm white or cream, silk, high lustre. Double weight.

X   Cream, tapestry lustre. Double weight.

Table A.2
Some Currently Available Photographic Papers and Their Characteristics

Brand Name	Image Tone	Surface Texture	Weight	Contrast Grades
Plastic-Laminated Papers (RC, RD, etc.)				
Kodak, Kodabrome RC	Neutral black	F, N	Medium	Soft to ultra-hard
Kodak, Polycontrast Rapid-II SC RC	Neutral black	F, N	Medium	Variable; 1–4 filters
Ilford Ilfospeed	Neutral black	Glossy, semi-matte, silk and pearl	Medium	0, 1, 2, 3, 4, 5
Ilford Ilfospeed Multigrade	Neutral black	Glossy and pearl	Medium	Variable; 1–7 filters (Equivalent to grades 0–4)
Unicolor B&W Resin-coated	Neutral black	Glossy (F)	Medium	1, 2, 3, 6
		Pearl (P)		1, 2, 3, 6
		Fine Grain (J)		2 ,3
		Matte (N)		2, 3
		Silk (Y)		2, 3
Fiber-Based (Baryta-Coated) Papers				
Kodak Medalist	Warm black	F (White)	Single	1, 2, 3, 4
		F, J, E (White)	Double	2, 3
		G, Y (Cream)	Double	G: 2, 3, 4 Y: 2, 3
Kodak Kodabromide	Neutral black	F (White)	Single, Double	1, 2, 3, 4, 5
		N, E (White)	Single, Double	2, 3, 4
		A (White)	Light	2, 3, 4, 5
		G (Cream)	Double	2, 3, 4
Kodak Polycontrast	Warm black	F, N, J (White)	Single, Double	Variable; 1–4 filters
		A (White)	Light	Variable; 1–4 filters
		G (Cream)	Double	Variable; 1–4 filters
Kodak Portralure	Brown black	M, G, Y (Warm White)	Double	Variable; 1–3 filters
		R (Cream)	Double	Variable; 1–3 filters
Agfa-Gevaert Brovira	Neutral black	#1 White Glossy	Single	0, 1, 2, 3, 4, 5
		#111 White Glossy	Double	0, 1, 2, 3, 4, 5
		#119 White Matte	Double	0, 1, 2, 3, 4, 5
Agfa-Gevaert Portriga Rapid	Warm black	#111 White Glossy	Double	1, 2, 3
		#118 White, Fine-Grain Semi-matte	Double	1, 2, 3
Ilford Ilfobrom	Neutral black	Glossy	Single	0, 1, 2, 3, 4, 5
		Semi-matte	Single	1, 2, 3, 4
		Glossy; velvet stipple	Double	0, 1, 2, 3, 4
		Semi-matte, matte	Double	2, 3, 4
		Rayon	Double	1, 2, 3
Kodak Ektamatic SC	Neutral	F (White)	Single	Variable; 1–4 filters
Ilford Galerie	Neutral		Double	1, 2, 3
Unicolor Exhibition	Slightly Warm		Double	2, 3
Oriental (Seagull)	Neutral	Glossy	Single	1, 2, 3, 4
		Glossy	Double	2, 3, 4
		Luster	Double	2, 3, 4
		Semi-matte	Medium	2, 3

3

List of Metol-Free Developers

Although, strictly speaking, all developing agents are capable of causing some sensitizing or toxic effect on susceptible individuals, most can be considered safe to handle in normal use if simple precautions are taken to avoid prolonged or repeated contact with the dry chemical or its concentrated solutions. Silicone protective handcream, applied before contact, will help prevent skin irritation. After contact with any photographic chemical it is advisable to wash your hands, or other affected area, thoroughly.

Whether or not you are troubled by common allergies, you may be affected by some developers, notably those containing the reducing agent p-methylaminophenol sulfate, or Metol—also known as Elon, Pictol, Rhodol, and other common names. This chemical is included in almost all developers manufactured by the Eastman Kodak Company and in many developers formulated by other manufacturers. If you notice any sign of skin irritation, other than simple reddening or drying, after working with standard Metol or MQ (Metol-Hydro-Quinone) developers, you should stop using them immediately or wear rubber gloves while handling them.

The developers listed in table A.3 by their manufacturers contain no Metol. While their use will not guarantee freedom from toxic or allergic reactions, they are presumably less likely to be troublesome than formulas containing Metol.

Table A.3
Film Developers

Edwal Scientific Products Corp.

FG-7	Fine-grain formula for roll and cartridge film.

Acufine, Inc.

Acufine	Fine-grain formula for roll and cartridge films.
Diafine, 2-bath	Compensating formula for roll and cartridge films.
ACU-1, one-shot	Fine-grain formula for roll and cartridge films.

Agfa-Gevaert, Inc.

Rodinal	High acutance formula. Avoid contact with liquid concentrate.

Ilford, Inc.

Microphen	Fine-grain formula for roll and cartridge films.

Eastman Kodak Co.

HC-110	Avoid contact with liquid concentrate. For all films.
D-8	Very high contrast formula, not suitable for general use.
*DK-93	For films or papers.
*D-32	Lantern slide developer.
*D-51,	Containing Amidol, and *SD-1, containing Pyro, are Metol-free, but are at least equally hazardous. Not recommended for users who are sensitive to photochemicals.

*Developer formulas must be mixed from bulk chemicals; not available in prepared form.

4

Formulas

The formulas given here are typical and useful for the purposes indicated. In all cases when mixing chemical formulas from bulk materials, follow the instructions carefully and mix the chemicals in the order given. In general, each chemical should be dissolved before the next one is added. Use clean paper on the scales for each new formula to avoid contamination. Also, avoid skin contact with dry chemicals or their liquid concentrates and don't breathe chemical dust or fumes. Wash your hands and all utensils thoroughly after chemical mixing.

Table A.4
Paper Developers

Acufine, Inc.	
Posifine 16	Neutral tone. For all papers.

Ethol Chemicals, Inc.	
LPD	Neutral tone. For all papers.

Ilford, Inc.	
Bromophen	General purpose paper developer, neutral tone.
Ilfospeed 2	Liquid concentrate for Ilfospeed RC papers, and others.
Multigrade	Liquid concentrate for Multigrade papers, and others.

Eastman Kodak Co.	
Ektaflo, type 2	Liquid concentrate for all papers; warm tone.

Developers

Adapted from Kodak formula D-72, developer printing papers and for vigorous development of sheet films. This is a stock solution.

Water (52°C or 125°F)	500	ml
Elon or Metol	3	gms
Sodium Sulfite (desiccated)	45	gms
Hydroquinone	12	gms
Sodium Carbonate (monohydrated)	80	gms
Potassium Bromide	2	gms
Cold water to make	1	liter

For use with papers, dilute 1:1 or 1:2 and develop 1 to 3 minutes.

Adapted from Kodak formula KD-50, developer for sheet films.

Water (52°C or 125°F)	500	ml
Elon or Metol	2.5	gms
Sodium Sulfite (desiccated)	30	gms
Hydroquinone	2.5	gms
Kodalk (or sodium metaborate)	10	gms
Potassium Bromide	.5	gm
Water to make	1	liter

For conditions of use, see contrast index charts, page 000.

Adapted from Kodak formula D-76 or Ilford formula ID-11

Water (52°C or 125°F)	750	ml
Elon or Metol	2	gms
Sodium Sulfite (desiccated)	100	gms
Hydroquinone	5	gms
Borax (decahydrated)	2	gms
Cold water to make	1	liter

For conditions of use, see contrast index charts, pages 000–000.

Stop Bath

To prepare a standard acetic acid stop bath stock solution (28%) from glacial acetic acid (99.7%), mix 3 parts of glacial acetic acid into 8 parts of water. See page 00 for detailed instructions. *Caution:* glacial acetic acid can cause severe burns and may be fatal if swallowed. Do not get the liquid on the skin or in the eyes; do not breathe the vapor. Keep away from heat or open flame and store at temperatures above 16°C (60°F) to avoid freezing.

To prepare a working solution of stop bath for films, add 30 ml of 28% stock solution to 1 liter of water (1 ounce/quart). For papers, add 45 ml stock solution to 1 liter (1½ ounces/quart).

Fixing Baths

Nonhardening fixing bath for use with papers to be toned in gold or selenium; also recommended for clearing bath, following dichromate, permanganate, or iodine bleach solutions.

Water (52°C or 125°F)	500	ml
Sodium Thiosulfate (Hypo)	250	gms

Stir until hypo is dissolved and solution has cooled to room temperature, then add

Sodium Bisulfite	25	gms
Water to make	1	liter

Stir until dissolved. Potassium metabisulfite may be substituted for the sodium bisulfite in equal amounts.

Kodak formula F-6, acid hardening fixing bath, for general use.

Water (52°C or 125°F)	600	ml
Sodium Thiosulfate (hypo)	240	gms
Sodium Sulfite (desiccated)	15	gms
Acetic Acid (28%)	48	ml
Kodalk Balanced Alkali	15	gms
Potassium Alum	15	gms
Water to make	1	liter

Dissolve hypo completely, then add remaining ingredients one at a time and dissolve each before adding the next.

Hypo Test Solution

Water	100	ml
Potassium Iodide	2	gms

Mix and store in a dropper bottle. Add one drop to the fixing bath; if a yellowish cloud forms in the solution the fixer is nearing exhaustion. For archival purposes discard the fixer if any sign of cloudiness appears in this test.

Hypo Eliminator

Kodak formula HE-1, for prints processed to archival standards.

Water	500	ml
Hydrogen Peroxide, 3% solution	125	ml
Ammonia solution	100	ml
Water to make	1	liter

Ammonia solution is prepared by adding 10 ml of ammonium hydroxide (28%) to 90 ml of water. *Caution:* prepare solution immediately before use and keep in an open container; do not store the mixed solution, evolved gas may break a stoppered bottle.

Treat well-washed prints in HE-1 for about 6 minutes at 20° (68°F). This bath will soften the print emulsion, so be careful not to damage the prints by rough handling. Wash the treated prints for about 10 minutes, and dry carefully. Drying between blotters or facedown on screens may damage the emulsion; use care.

Toners

Gold Toner, for protection of the silver image or for producing bluish-gray tones on most papers.

Solution A

Gold Chloride	1	gm
Water, distilled	100	ml

Solution B

Sodium or Potassium Thiocyanate	10	gms
Water, preferably distilled	1	liter

For archival protective toning, add (with vigorous stirring) 1 ml of solution *A* for each 8″ × 10″ print to be toned, to 500 ml of *B*. Immerse thoroughly washed prints, one at a time, in the toning bath and agitate until a barely perceptible darkening or cooling of the image is apparent. For blue toning, use 2 ml solution *A* for each 8″ × 10″ print and tone until color change is satisfactory. Wash toned prints for at least 10 minutes and dry as usual. Prints must have been thoroughly washed and preferably treated with HE-1 before toning in this solution to avoid possible yellowing of highlights.

Sepia Toner for brown tones on most papers.

Solution A

Water (52°C or 125°F)	700	ml
Potassium Ferricyanide	50	gms
Potassium Bromide	10	gms
Sodium Carbonate, monohydrated	20	gms
Water to make	1	liter

Solution B

Sodium Sulfide, desiccated	5	gms
Water to make	500	ml

Cool solution *A* to room temperature and agitate the well-washed print in it until the image bleaches out to a yellowish-tan color. Rinse the print in running water until the yellow ferricyanide color is gone: then redevelop in solution *B* for a minute or two, until the image is restored. Wash the toned print thoroughly in running water (30 minutes or so), not above 20°C (68°F), and air-dry. This toner softens the print emulsion; it is therefore advisable to harden the toned print before washing it. After removing the toned print from solution *B,* rinse it for several minutes in running water, then immerse it in a hardening bath compounded as follows:

Water (52°C or 125°F)	500	ml
Sodium Sulfite, anhydrous	15	gms
Acetic Acid (28%)	40	ml
Potassium Alum	15	gms
Water to make	1	liter

Dissolve chemicals in the order given and cool to room temperature for use. Harden print for about 5 minutes, then wash in running water for 30 minutes and dry on screens, clean cloth, or blotters.

Selenium Toner, for protection of the silver image or for producing brown or purple-brown tones on most papers. Selenium toner is available as a liquid concentrate from Kodak. To produce brown tones on most papers, treat the prints, after fixing, in hypo clearing bath, wash thoroughly in running water, then immerse them—preferably one at a time—in the toning bath, made by diluting one part of the liquid concentrate with from 9 to about 30 parts of water. Agitate the prints frequently and remove them from the toning bath when the desired color has been attained. The toning action continues for a little while after the prints are removed from the bath, so don't overdo it. Treat the toned prints in fresh hypo clearing bath and wash for at least 20 minutes in running water, or for the time recommended by the manufacturer of the hypo clearing bath. The strength of the toning bath determines the speed of the toning action and, to some extent, the ultimate image color.

Reducer

Farmer's Reducer, for correcting over-exposed negatives; also local reduction of print images.

Solution A (stock solution)

Sodium Thiosulfate (hypo)	12	gms
Water, warm	100	ml

Solution B (stock solution)

Potassium Ferricyanide	4	gms
Water	100	ml

Store solutions in separate bottles. For use add one part *A* and one part *B* to 18 parts water. Use less water for faster action; more water to slow it down. Soak films to be reduced in plain water for several minutes, then immerse in solution and agitate constantly until image appears sufficiently lightened. Rinse films in water to stop reducing action, then treat in hypo-clearing bath and wash as usual. Mixed solution of reducer will not keep; mix it fresh for each use. Stock solutions will keep indefinitely in normal storage conditions.

Bleach Baths

Iodine Bleach for removing dark spots from prints. Use ordinary tincture of iodine, obtainable from any drugstore, or mix the following:

Water	25	ml
Iodine, crystals or scales	.5	gm
Potassium Iodine	2.5	gm

The iodine is virtually insoluble in plain water but will dissolve slowly in the solution of potassium iodide. Store in a small stoppered bottle. It will keep indefinitely.

Permanganate Bleach, for total removal of print image density.

Solution A

Potassium Permanganate	1	gm
Water, warm	200	ml

Solution B

Water, cold	200	ml
Hydrochloric Acid	20	ml

These solutions will keep in separate containers, but working solutions should be mixed fresh for each use. For very rapid action use equal parts of *A* and *B.* For milder action add one part *A* and one part *B* to two parts water. *Caution:* hydrochloric acid is dangerously corrosive and poisonous. Avoid skin contact and don't breathe the fumes. If spilled on the skin, flood with water, then apply baking soda solution, and get medical attention.

5

Metric Conversions and Equivalents

Temperature Conversion Formulas

To convert Fahrenheit to Celsius degrees, subtract 32 and multiply by 5/9. For example,

$$68°F - 32 = 36 \times \frac{5}{9} = 20°C$$

To convert Celsius to Fahrenheit degrees, multiply by 9/5 and add 32. For example,

$$100°C \times \frac{9}{5} = 180 + 32 = 212°F$$

See figure A.1.

Figure A.1
Celsius-Fahrenheit temperature conversion chart. Illustration shows 20°C = 68°F.

Linear Measurements

To convert inches to millimeters, multiply by 25.4. For example,

6″ × 25.4 = 152.4mm

Similarly, divide millimeters by 25.4 to find inches:

127mm ÷ 25.4 = 5 inches

See figure A.2.

Weights

The common Avoirdupois weight units are the pound (lb.), ounce (oz.), and grain (gr.); common metric units are the kilogram (kg) and the gram (g).

1 pound = 16 ounces = 453.6 grams
1 ounce = 437.5 grains = 28.35 grams
1 grain = .0648 grams
1 kilogram = 1000 grams = 2.2 pounds
1 gram = 15.43 grains

Liquid Measure

Our common liquid measurement units are the gallon (gal.), the quart (qt.), the pint (pt.), and the fluid ounce (oz., or fl. oz.); metric units are the liter (l) and the milliliter (ml). The cubic centimeter (cc) is, strictly speaking, a measure of volume, but since it is virtually identical with the milliliter, it is frequently used interchangeably with milliliter in liquid measurements.

1 gallon = 4 quarts = 8 pints = 128 ounces = 3.785 liters
1 quart = 2 pints = 32 ounces = 946.4 milliliters
1 pint = 16 ounces = 473.2 milliliters
1 fluid ounce = 29.575 milliliters
1 liter = 1000 milliliters = 1.057 quarts = 33.82 ounces
1 milliliter = .0034 fluid ounces

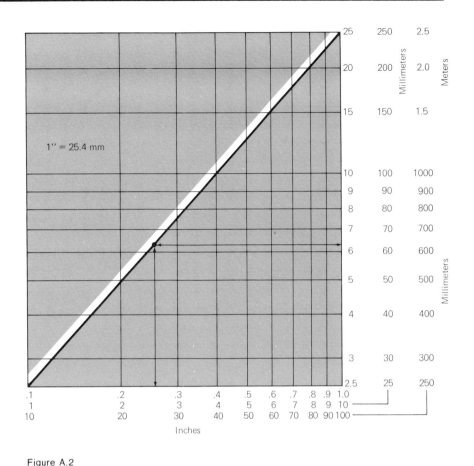

Figure A.2
Inches-millimeters conversion chart. Read matching scales. Illustration shows ¼″ (.25) = 6.35mm or 2.5″ = 63.5mm or 25″ = 635mm.

6

Close-up Exposure Correction

A fairly simple method of exposure compensation, based on the increase in lens focal distance required for close focusing, is explained on pages 270–73. You can also calculate the correction factor by working from image magnification. Find the image magnification by dividing some image dimension by the corresponding subject dimension,

$$M = \frac{\text{Image dimension}}{\text{Subject dimension}}$$

then apply the formula

Exposure Factor = $(M + 1)^2$

For example, some image dimension is found to be .8 inches and the corresponding subject dimension is .5 inches. The magnification (M) is:

$$M = \frac{.8}{.5} = 1.6$$

The exposure factor (EF) is

EF = $(1.6 + 1)^2$ or 2.6^2 or 6.76

The factor found this way is useful for lenses of normal construction but for lenses of telephoto or reversed telephoto (retro-focus) construction, the *pupillary magnification* of the lens must be considered. To find the approximate value of pupillary magnification, divide the apparent aperture diameter, as the lens is held at arm's length and viewed from the rear (the *exit pupil* diameter), by its apparent diameter as seen, similarly, from the front (the *entrance pupil*).

Pupillary Magnification (P) =
$$\frac{\text{Diameter of Exit Pupil}}{\text{Diameter of Entrance Pupil}}$$

then use the formula,

$$EF = \left(\frac{M}{P} + 1\right)^2$$

For example, if the exit pupil measures 12 mm and the entrance pupil measures 18 mm, the pupillary magnification is

$$P = \frac{12}{18} = .67$$

If the image magnification is 1.6 (as in the illustration above), the formula is

$$EF = \left(\frac{1.6}{.67} + 1\right)^2$$

or $(2.39 + 1)^2$ or 3.39^2 or 11.5

Figure A.3
This macro-computer will help you find the amount of exposure increase required for close-up photography if you have trouble with formulas and mathematics. Since it contains both inch and millimeter scales, it can also be used for metric conversions if desired. For example, find the measurement in inches (larger numbers) on either dial and read its equivalent in millimeters (small numbers) on the same dial. Thus, 7″ is seen to approximate 180mm; 4″ is slightly more than 100mm. Reading the other way, 350mm is about 13¾″.

To use the computer for close-up exposure calculations, set up the camera, compose and focus on the subject, then measure the distance from lens-to-film in either inches or millimeters. Find this distance on one of the outer scales. Now move the inner scale until the lens focal length (either inches or millimeters) is aligned with the focal distance just located. Both exposure compensation and image magnification can now be read through the windows. For example, suppose you are using a 100mm lens, extended to a total distance (lens-to-film) of 13″. Set 100mm on the movable scale opposite 13″ on the fixed scale. The image is found to be about 2⅓ times larger than the subject, and the exposure can be compensated by either opening the lens about 3½ stops or by multiplying the shutter speed by 11.

If measuring the focal distance is not convenient, and if the image size can be measured fairly accurately, you can determine the exposure compensation by setting the subject-to-image size ratio in the inner window. For example, if some subject dimension is found to be ½″ and the same dimension of the image measures 2½″, the ratio is 1:5. Set this number (5) in the inner window and read the exposure compensation in one of the other windows. Either open the lens five-and-a-fraction stops or increase the exposure interval by 36 times. This method is convenient if you are using a view camera with inch or millimeter markings on the groundglass.

Copy these scales on Kodalith film and print them to convenient pocket size. Mount them on thin, stiff cardboard, such as Bristol board, and cut them out neatly. You can color the white central area of the larger dial, if you want to, using a light-colored felt-tipped pen or marker; yellow is probably best for visibility. Mount the small disc on the larger one, so it is free to turn, by using a single rivet, grommet, or paper fastener through the center.

7

Flashbulb and Electronic Flash Guide Numbers

A guide number represents the product of a lens f/number multiplied by the subject distance in feet. For example, the guide number "240" indicates that proper exposure will be achieved with the film and flashbulb specified if an aperture of f/8 is used with a subject distance of 30 feet, or f/2 is used at 120 feet, etc. Figure A.4 supplies guide numbers appropriate for the flashbulb types and film speed indicated. This chart applies to single flashbulbs, used at or near the camera position, and pertains to the flashbulb-to-subject distance, not the camera-to-subject distance, if they are not the same. If two similar bulbs are fired together from the same location, multiply the guide number by 1.4. For bounce flash calculation, estimate the total distance the flash light must travel from the bulb to the reflecting surface and then to the subject, calculate the f/number and increase the exposure further by one stop if the reflecting surface is white, two or more if the surface is gray or a dark color. For more specific information consult the information sheet packed with the film in use.

Electronic flash exposure can also be estimated if a regular guide number is known. In some cases electronic flash units are rated in *effective candlepower seconds* (ECPS) or, more usually, in *beam candlepower seconds* (BCPS). Figure A.5 will give you guide number information for various film types if you know the BCPS rating of your flash unit. Since amateur flash units are frequently rated as having a certain guide number "for Kodachrome" or "for Tri-X," you can use this information to determine the BCPS of your unit. For example, if your unit has a guide number of "240 for Tri-X," the chart indicates its BCPS to be 2800, and with this information, it is easy to calculate guide numbers for use with other films.

		Film Speed				
		25	32	64	125	400
Flash Cube	*1/30	48	60	85	120	195
	1/60	32	40	55	80	125
	1/125	27	34	48	68	100
#5B	*1/30	105	135	190	270	400
	1/60	95	120	170	240	380
	1/125	80	100	140	200	320
#22B	*1/30	135	170	240	340	540
	1/60	120	150	210	300	480
	1/125	100	125	180	250	400

Figure A.4
Flash guide numbers for use with "M" synch (or "X" synch at 1/30th or less). This chart is based on the use of efficient reflectors with #5B and #22B bulbs.

Figure A.5
The arrows on the chart show that a guide
number of 240 for Tri-X film (ASA 400) is
appropriate for a flash unit rated at 2800
BCPS.

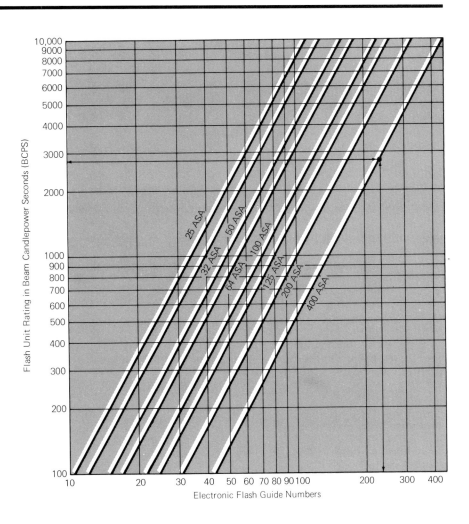

8

Color Temperature

Color temperature is expressed in Kelvin degrees, since it follows the absolute centigrade scale named after the famous British physicist, Lord William Thompson Kelvin. A few common light sources and their approximate Kelvin temperatures are given in table A.5.

Table A.5
Common Light Sources and Their Kelvin Temperatures

Candle flame	1900°K
40-watt bulb	2650
75-watt bulb	2800
100-watt bulb	2900
Professional photographic flood	3200
Amateur "photoflood"	3400
Clear flashbulb	3800
Noon sunlight	5400
Photographic standard daylight (Kodak)	5500
Typical electronic flash (uncompensated)	6100
Light from north sky 15,000 to 20,000 or more	

9

Kelvin Temperature and Filtration Calculator

Figure A.6
The Kelvin Temperature Scale: This scale will help you determine the necessary filter correction whenever the existing light color is not correct for the type of color film you are using. Set the "Film Balance K°" arrow opposite the appropriate film type on the Kelvin scale. The three normal emulsion types are labelled "Day" (5500°K), "A" (3400°K), and "B" (3200°K). Next, on the Kelvin scale, find the color temperature of the existing light. The filter required for proper color rendition will be found opposite this temperature on the mireds scale. For example, suppose you are using clear flashbulbs with Kodachrome II, type "A" film. Set the pointer on "A." Opposite the small "f" (flash) at the 3800°K mark read the required correction: plus 30 mireds. The appropriate filter is the "81B" (plus 27 mireds). Slightly warmer results will be obtained by using the "81C" (about plus 35 mireds). The small letter "s" at 6100°K indicates the approximate color balance of unfiltered electronic flash tubes.

Copy these scales on Kodalith film and print them to convenient pocket size. Mount them on thin, stiff cardboard such as Bristol board and cut them out neatly. Mount the smaller disc on the larger one so that it is free to turn by using a single rivet or grommet or paper fastener through the center.

10

Filter Factors for Black-and-White Photography

Table A.6
Filter Factors for Black-and-White Photography

Wratten Filter Number	Filter Color	Panchromatic Film		Orthochromatic Film	
		Daylight	Tungsten	Daylight	Tungsten
8	Yellow (K2)	2	1.5	2.5	2
11	Yellow-green (X1)	4	3	4	3
15	Deep yellow (G)	3	2	5	3
25	Red (A)	8	6	—	—
58	Green (B)	8	8	8	5
47B	Blue	8	16	6	8
29	Deep red (F)	25	12	—	—
61	Green (N)	12	12	—	—

Development vs. Temperature Chart

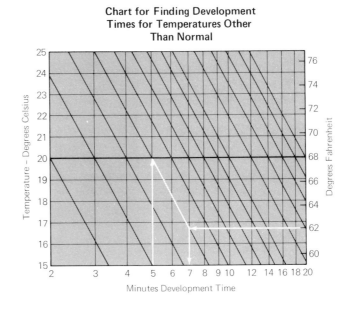

Chart for Finding Development
Times for Temperatures Other
Than Normal

Figure A.7
Development vs. temperature chart for
finding development times for temperatures
other than normal. Example shows that if 5
mins. is correct developing time at 68°F,
then the proper time at 62°F is 7 mins.
Read up from known developing time to
appropriate temperature line (horizontal),
then diagonally up or down to desired
temperature; then straight down to find
new developing time.

12

Suggested Reciprocity Failure Compensation

Figure A.8
Suggested reciprocity failure compensation for all general-purpose black-and-white films.

Compensation for reciprocity failure cannot be determined with real precision. Kodak's published recommendations seem rather extreme in practice and this chart will suggest compensation that differs from the official information. You should use the data that work best for you. To use this chart, lay a straightedge across it so as to connect the reference point *A* with the indicated exposure time in seconds on scale *B*. The straightedge will then indicate the suggested exposure compensation on scales *C* and *D*. If you wish to adjust the aperture to make the compensation, open the lens up by the number of stops indicated on scale *C*. If you wish to compensate by increasing *exposure time*, use the exposure time in seconds indicated on scale *D*. Do *not* make *both* adjustments; use one or the other. The dashed line shows that an indicated exposure time of 8 seconds (scale *B*) will require an exposure increase of one stop (scale *C*) or an exposure time of 19 seconds (scale *D*). With either setting the *normal* developing time for the film should be *reduced* by 7%, as indicated on scale *E*.

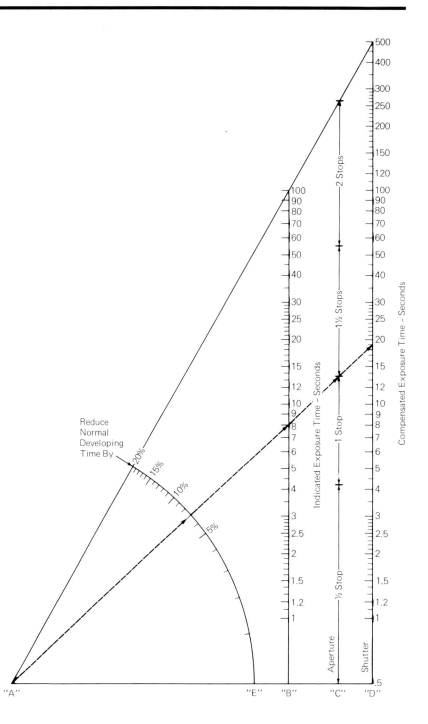

13

Table A.7
Equivalent Lens Focal Lengths for Various Camera Sizes

Image Size	Angular Coverage of Horizontal Field*											
	100° mm.	81°	65°	55°	45°	39°	24°	15°	10°	5°	3.4°	2°
35mm	15	21	28	35	43	50	85	135	200	400	600	1030
1⅝″ × 2¼″ 4.5cm × 6cm ⎫ 2¼″ × 2¼″ 6cm × 6cm ⎬	22	32	42	52	65	76	127	205	308	615	910	1545
2¼″ × 2¾″ 6cm × 7cm	28	39	52	63	80	93	155	250	377	750	1110	1890
2¼″ × 3¼″ 6cm × 9cm	34	48	64	78	100	115	192	311	469	940		
3¼″ × 4¼″ 9cm × 12cm	45	63	85	103	128	150	250	402	605	1210		
4″ × 5″	53	74	100	122	152	180	295	478	720			
5″ × 7″	75	104	140	171	210	251	418	676	1015			
8″ × 10″	107	149	200	244	300	359	597	965	1450			

very ←—wide—→ ← wide ——→ ←—"normal"—→ ← long —→ ← very long ——→

*Lens coverage is usually given for the image diagonal
(corner-to-corner) measurement—an unrealistic statistic.
This table indicates the useful coverage along the *long
dimension* of the image. Focal lengths are given in
millimeters.

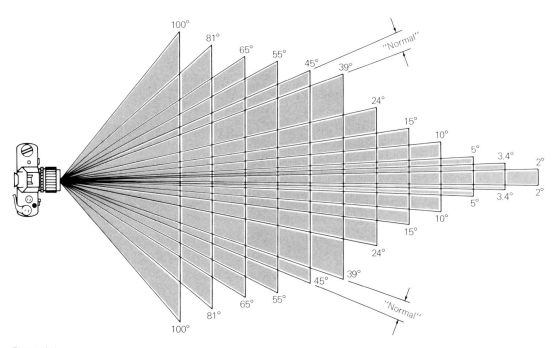

Figure A.9
Lens angular coverage chart

14
Contrast Index Developing Charts

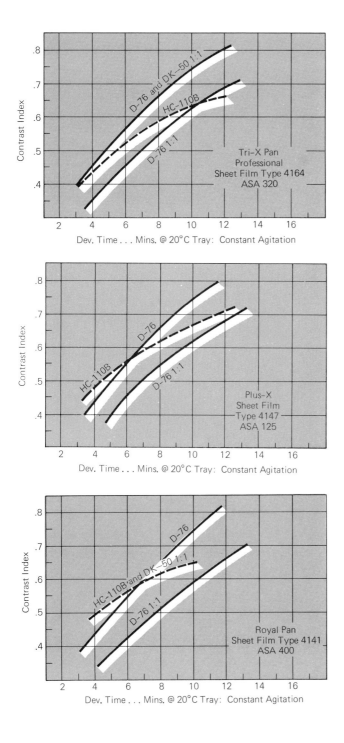

15

**Matching Negative Density
Range to Paper Contrast Grade**

Paper contrast grades are neither as consistent nor as stable as film characteristics. Contrast is apt to vary from emulsion batch to emulsion batch and it generally decreases with age. The contrast grade suitable for any given negative contrast is also dependent upon the type of enlarger used and on such correctable problems as old or exhausted developer, dirty enlarger lens, etc. With these disclaimers in mind, use table A.8 to estimate the negative density range you need to print satisfactorily on your favorite paper type and grade. These data are derived empirically but should serve as a starting point, assuming that your enlarger is average in contrast. Condenser enlargers may require less contrasty negatives than indicated; diffusion enlargers may require negatives of higher contrast for best results with any given paper grade.

Table A.8
Negative Density Range

Paper Types	1.6	1.5	1.4	1.3	1.2	1.1	1.0	.9	.8	.7	.6	.5	.4	.3
						Negative Density Range Suitable for Paper Contrast Grade									
Kodak Graded Papers		0		1	•	2		3		4		5		
Polycontrast Regular and Rapid				1		1½	2 /	2½	3	3½	4			
Kodabrome RC				Soft		Medium			Hard			Extra Hard	Ultra Hard	
Ilfobrom		0			1	2	3			4		5		
Brovira			0		1	2	3			4			5	
Portriga					1		2		3					
Unicolor Resin Coated				1		2	3					6		
Exhibition							2							
Galerie			1				2			3				
Oriental				1			2		3	4				

Glossary

aberrations The several defects of a lens, inherent in its design, material, and construction, which, by deforming the image points in various ways, limit the sharpness of the focused image.

accelerator Same as **activator**, which see.

acetic acid A relatively mild acid used, in highly diluted form, as the rinse bath (stop bath) that follows the developer in the normal film and paper developing processes. The acid in vinegar.

achromat A lens that has been corrected for two colors, thus partially eliminating the effects of chromatic aberration.

acid A hydrogen compound having a pH value less than 7. Most acids will combine readily with certain metals to form salts. Typically, an acid solution feels gritty when rubbed between the fingers and has a sharp sour taste. Acid solutions neutralize alkaline solutions and turn blue litmus paper red. The stronger acids cause severe burns and are dangerous to handle.

activator The chemical ingredient of a developer solution that stimulates the reducing agent to begin its work and accelerates it. The activator in most developers is an alkaline salt, such as sodium carbonate or borax. Also called the **accelerator.**

adapter rings Narrow metal rings, threaded on the outside to fit most popular lenses, and threaded on the inside to accept accessories of other than nominal lens diameter. *Step-up* rings adapt a lens for use with larger-than-normal accessories; *step-down* rings permit the use of slightly smaller accessories than the lens will normally accept.

additive system A name for the principles of color mixing using the light primaries. Mixtures of light colors are brighter and lighter in tone than the individual colors were, and the three light primary colors—red, green, and blue—produce white light when blended.

agitation The process of stirring, swirling, or otherwise causing a liquid to move freely over the surfaces of film or paper during processing.

air-bells Tiny bubbles of air that are apt to cling to a dry surface when immersed gently. In developing films or papers, an initial vigorous agitation is usually recommended to dislodge air-bells so as to avoid pinholes.

air-spaced elements In a compound lens, those elements that are not cemented together.

albumin Commercially, simply dried egg white. Used in the preparation of printing paper emulsions from about 1850, it was replaced by gelatin in the 1880s. The old spelling is albumen.

alkali A compound whose pH value is greater than 7. Alkaline solutions typically feel slippery or soapy when rubbed between the fingers and are difficult to wash off, especially in soft water. They neutralize acids and turn red litmus paper blue. The stronger alkalis can cause severe burns and are dangerous to handle.

ambient illumination The light condition existing at the subject location.

ambrotype A silver image on glass, popular in the 1860s and 1870s, and made by coating a weak collodion negative with black lacquer. Viewed by reflected light, the image appears as a grayish positive. Ambrotypes were usually mounted in plastic or leather cases, like **daguerreotypes,** and were frequently hand-tinted.

anastigmat A lens that has been well corrected for all the aberrations, specifically including astigmatism and curvature of field.

angular coverage The field of view seen or covered by the lens, expressed in degrees.

anhydrous Without water; dry. Used to distinguish the dehydrated form of a compound from its crystalline form which might normally contain a substantial amount of water of crystallization while still appearing to be completely dry. When chemical measurements are made by weight, less of the anhydrous than the crystalline form will be required.

ANSI American National Standards Institute. The present title of the organization that used to be called the American Standards Association (ASA).

aperture An opening, specifically, of the lens and expressed as a fraction of the focal length. The f/ number. See **relative aperture.**

apochromat A lens that has been corrected for three colors, which thus reduces chromatic aberrations to negligible amounts. Apochromatic lenses sometimes include the prefix ''Apo-'' in their names, e.g., Apo-Tessar, Apo-Lanthar, etc.

archival processing Procedures followed during film or print processing to produce a stable image, free from harmful residual chemical compounds and resistant to attack by environmental contaminants.

ASA The American Standards Association, now the American National Standards Institute. A system of film speed rating used in the United States.

astigmatism One of the common aberrations of photographic lenses and the human eye, characterized by the lens's inability to bring into common focus lines that are radial and lines that are tangential to the image circle.

available light The light condition that the photographer finds existing at the subject position. The term usually implies an indoor or nighttime light condition of low intensity, requiring fast film, large lens aperture, and slow shutter speed.

B See **Bulb.**

back That portion of a camera containing the film; specifically, the complete assembly attached to the rear standard of a view camera (usually removable) which includes the focusing screen and accepts the film holders.

back focus The distance from the rear surface of the lens to the focal plane when the lens is focused at infinity.

backlight Illumination from a source beyond the subject, as seen from the camera position, which tends to silhouette the subject. See **rim light.**

barrel distortion One form of the aberration, **distortion,** which is characterized by a bowing-out of lines near the edges of the image. See **pincushion distortion** and **rectilinear.**

baseboard The large, flat board, usually plywood, to which the enlarger column is attached, and on which the enlarging easel is normally placed.

base The transparent sheet material, usually acetate or polyester, upon which film emulsion is coated.

base-plus-fog density The density of an unexposed area of a developed film (negative or positive).

bas-relief A picture printed from the slightly misregistered images of a negative and its positive mask. The print usually resembles the linear shadow pattern of the subject as it would be seen in low relief in strong slanting light.

bellows The center section of a view camera that connects the front and back standards. The bellows is usually made of leather, cloth, or plastic, is accordion-pleated for flexibility, and is, of course, lighttight.

bellows extension A term often used to refer either to the total bellows length or to the additional extension of the bellows (beyond that required for infinity focus) necessary for focusing at close subject distances.

belt The endless canvas strip that carries prints through a motorized or manual drum dryer. Sometimes called an **apron** or **blanket.**

benzotriazole A restrainer, used in conjunction with or in place of potassium bromide in developer solutions, especially those compounded with Phenidone.

between-the-lens shutter A shutter designed to operate in a space between the elements of the lens. See **leaf shutter** and **focal plane shutter.**

bichromate Also, and preferably, **dichromate.** Refers to the chromium salts of sodium, potassium, and ammonium which are used in various bleach baths and in the numerous variations of the **gum** and **pigment printing processes.** They are poisonous and can be absorbed directly through the skin to cause painful dermatitis and ulcers.

black body A hypothetical, unreflecting source of pure radiant energy.

blade arrestor Old term for device similar to **press-focus lever,** which see.

bleach A chemical bath or treatment that either converts the silver image into a less visible form or removes it entirely. See **reducer.**

bleed An image edge trimmed without a border; as, ''the picture bleeds top and bottom.''

blend (1) A composite photographic image whose component parts are so skillfully combined that their boundaries are invisible. (2) The process of producing a blend.

blind An emulsion not sensitive to certain colors; colorblind.

block-up Refers to an area of the negative image so overexposed, and therefore dense, as to obscure textures and details.

blotter book A number of sheets of pure white blotting paper, interleaved with nonabsorbent tissue sheets, and bound at one edge to form a large book. Used for nonglossy drying of relatively small prints.

blue-sensitive The sensitivity of an ordinary silver emulsion; red and green blind.

bounce To reflect light; specifically, light directed away from the subject toward some nearby light-toned surface so as to reach the subject diffused by reflection.

bracket To make a number of exposures (some greater and some less than the one considered to be "normal") in addition to the "normal" one, with the intent of getting one near-perfect exposure.

brightness Our subjective interpretation of luminance or illuminance. Brightness is perceived; luminance and illuminance are objective qualities that can only be measured.

bromide Any salt of hydrobromic acid, but commonly used as a shortened form of potassium bromide. See restrainer.

bromide paper A printing paper sensitized principally with silver bromide.

BSI British Standards Institution. A system of film speed ratings used in Great Britain; essentially, they are similar to the **ASA** and **ISO** speeds.

BTL See **between-the-lens shutter.**

bulb A marked setting *(B)* of most shutters that permits the shutter to be held open for an indefinite period by continued pressure on the shutter release. See **Time.**

burned out Describes an area of the print image in which highlight detail has not been recorded, usually because of severe overexposure of the negative. See **block-up.**

burning-in The process of allowing some relatively small image area to receive more than the normal exposure by shielding most of the printing paper surface from the light. See **dodging** and **flashing.**

cable Abbreviation of **cable release.**

cable release A long flexible cloth or metal braid-covered plunger that screws into a special threaded socket on the shutter or camera body. Compressing the plunger with thumb and finger pressure will release the shutter without much danger of camera movement or vibration.

cadmium sulfide cell A light-sensitive (photoconductive), solid-state device, widely used in exposure meters.

calotype The ancestor of modern photographic processes, invented by William Henry Fox Talbot in about 1840. The camera exposure was made on sensitized paper and developed out. The prints were made by contact on salted paper, printed out, and fixed. The process came to be known as talbotype and was quite popular. It would probably have been much more widely used if Talbot's patents had not been so restrictive.

camera Literally, *room* in Latin. The instrument with which photographs are taken, consisting, at least, of a lighttight box, a lens that admits focused light, and some device or provision for holding the film in position.

camera obscura Latin for *dark room.* Ancestor of the photographic camera; probably originally an actual room in which observers could watch the images of outside subjects formed by light rays entering the room through a small aperture and passing directly to the opposite wall. The camera obscura eventually evolved into a portable box, equipped with a lens and viewing screen, which was used for viewing and sketching, and finally, after the invention of suitable sensitized materials, for actual photography.

carbon process A method of making prints or transparencies using carbon (or some other pigment) suspended in gelatin as the image material. The process is extremely flexible and versatile and is capable of excellent photographic quality. It was popular with the Pictorialists but is rarely practiced now because the materials are no longer widely available commercially and are difficult to manufacture at home.

carrier The negative holder in an enlarger.

carte-de-visite A popular image form of the 1860s and 1870s, they are albumin prints mounted on cards about 2½″ × 4⅛″, usually depicting individuals or small family groups. They were sometimes used as visiting cards but portraits of famous men and women were also collected and exchanged as novelties and keepsakes.

cartridge The disposable metal or plastic container in which lengths of film are sold and used. Sometimes called a **cassette.**

cassette A metal container (usually designed to hold lengths of 35mm film) which can be used repeatedly. Of ingenious design and construction, cassettes are made specifically for a particular camera and will not normally work in any other brand. Sometimes referred to as a **cartridge.**

catadioptric lens A lens system comprised of both reflecting and refracting elements.

cats Slang term for catadioptric lenses.

CC filters Color-compensating filters, intended for use in color photography to modify the overall color balance of the image. They are available in six colors and several degrees of saturation.

CdS Cadmium Sulfide.

CdS meter An exposure meter that employs a cadmium sulfide cell as its light-sensitive element.

cemented lens A lens composed of two or more individual glasses whose adjacent surfaces are ground to fit accurately and are bonded together with some transparent adhesive. Most photographic lenses contain some cemented components as well as some air spaces.

characteristic curve Another name for the **D log E Curve.**

chloride paper Printing paper sensitized principally with silver chloride. A term seldom used any more.

chromatic aberration A general name for the inability of a lens to bring all the light colors of an object point to a common point of focus in the image plane. Chromatic aberration causes simple blurring of the image in black and white, and color fringing of the image in color photography. Two forms are described, lateral and axial, or longitudinal, and the effects are most severe near the edges of the image area.

circle of confusion The tiny, but not necessarily the *most* tiny, blurred circle of light that a lens will form as an image of a point of light at the subject position. It has no significance as a measure of lens accuracy or precision, but is measured and discussed simply as a means of defining tolerable sharpness of the image, and therefore the acceptable limits of depth of field.

clear   The appearance of a negative after the fixing bath has removed all visible traces of undeveloped silver halides.

clearing time   The length of time required to clear a negative. It depends on the strength, temperature, and agitation of the fixing bath and the kind of emulsion being fixed.

click stops   Detents in the diaphragm or shutter scale of a lens that produce a tactile indication and an audible click to mark the significant scale settings.

close-up lens   A positive supplementary lens that, when placed over a camera lens, shortens its focal length and thereby permits closer-than-normal focusing.

close-up photography   The techniques and practice of using supplementary lenses, extension tubes, bellows units, etc., to take pictures at closer ranges than the normal focusing adjustment of an ordinary hand-camera will allow. Refers to image magnification ratios of up to, perhaps, 2×, and therefore overlaps **photomacrography,** which see.

coating   The thin film of magnesium fluoride, or other material, deposited on the surfaces of the lens glasses, which gives photographic lenses their characteristic magenta, amber or greenish color by reflected light. Its purpose is to reduce the intensity of flare light within the lens which in turn increases the brightness and contrast of the image.

cocking the shutter   Winding or tensioning the shutter mainspring prior to making the exposure.

cold tones   Bluish or greenish tinge in the black-and-white image.

collodion   A thin, clear, slightly syrupy solution of pyroxyline in ether and alcohol. It was used in the preparation of wet-plate emulsions, a procedure described by Frederick Scott Archer in 1851.

collotype process   A printing process, similar to lithography, that uses a plate of selectively tanned gelatin, dampened and inked, to produce photographic images in ink on paper. Unlike other ink processes, collotype plates produce halftones without screening. Although capable of exquisite quality, the process has been superseded by faster, cheaper printing methods.

color-compensating filters   A special family of filters—available in calibrated strengths in red, green, blue, magenta, yellow, and cyan—intended for use in color photography. Each is identified by the prefix CC, followed by a number that represents its density (multiplied by 100) for light of its complementary color, and a final letter that identifies the filter color. For example, CC 20Y designates a yellow filter whose density for its complement (blue) is .2.

color fringes   The rainbowlike outlines, caused by lateral chromatic aberration of the lens, that surround dark areas of the image and are particularly apparent in areas of high contrast near the edges of the image.

color head   An enlarger light source containing adjustable dichroic filters which can be set to provide light of any color for color printing.

color temperature   A standard for defining the color of light based upon its similarity to the light color emitted by a black body heated to a known temperature. Color temperature is expressed in degrees Kelvin, or "Kelvins," and is only appropriate for the description of continuous spectrum light such as is emitted by the sun, tungsten filament bulbs, etc.

coma   An aberration of the lens that causes marginal light rays from a subject point off the lens axis to fail to converge at a common image point. The effect is most severe near the edges of the lens field and can usually be eliminated by stopping the lens down. It is a common defect of high-speed lenses.

compaction   Same as **contraction,** which see.

compensating developer   A developer whose activity tends to be inversely proportional to image density. It therefore is self-limiting, working relatively vigorously in areas of underexposure, and slowing down in the overexposed areas as density increases. No practical developer is outstanding in this respect, but those containing the reducing agent Pyrocatechol, or two-solution Metol formulas are sometimes recommended. Almost any developer will tend to be more compensating in action when it is highly diluted and is used with only occasional and gentle agitation.

complementary colors   Any two colors in the subtractive system that produce black or dark neutral gray when mixed in the proper proportion. In the additive system, any two colors whose mixture results in white light.

completion   That state of development when essentially all of the exposed silver halides have been reduced to metallic silver; that is, when further development will produce no more image density.

concave   Hollowed out. The side of a spherical surface seen from the center of the sphere.

condenser enlarger   An enlarger employing condenser lenses to provide uniform illumination of the negative.

condenser lens   A positive lens used to concentrate light rays. Condensers are used in many enlargers to collect the light from the bulb and direct it through the negative into the enlarger lens.

contact paper   A printing paper, usually sensitized with silver chloride, intended for use in contact printing.

contact printing   A method of printing in which the negative is placed in contact with the printing paper, emulsion to emulsion, and held in that position in a **Printing Frame.** The exposure is made by exposing the frame to raw light so that the paper emulsion is exposed by light passing through the negative densities. Contact printers, machines containing a controllable printing light, are also used.

contact screen   Type of engraving screen in which the dots are not sharply defined but, rather, are surrounded by individual haloes of decreasing density. These screens will form excellent halftone negatives by simple contact printing methods. At least two types are used: gray screens for color work, and magenta screens to permit control of image contrast in black-and-white work. Also sometimes called **halo-dot screens.**

continuous spectrum   Light that contains an appreciable amount of all the visible wavelengths or colors. See **discontinuous spectrum.**

continuous tone   Describes an image containing a gradation of grays as well as black-and-white extremes. See **dropout.**

contraction In the Zone System, reduced development that compensates for high subject contrast so as to produce normal contrast in the negative. Some photographers prefer the word **compaction.**

contrast Density difference, usually of adjacent areas of the image.

contrast grade A number or descriptive term assigned to a particular printing emulsion which identifies its contrast characteristic. In the range from 0 through 6, a normal contrast paper is usually considered to be 2, with the lower numbers indicating a tendency toward lower contrast and higher numbers indicating higher contrast. Printing filters for use with variable-contrast papers are numbered similarly. In some cases paper contrast is indicated by such terms as "soft," "medium," and "hard," instead of by numbers.

contrast index The numerical expression of the relationship between the negative density scale and the subject luminance range when, simply, the minimum useful image density is considered to be about .1 above base-plus-fog and the useful curve length is assumed to be 2.0. It might be called the average gamma under the stated conditions.

converter An optical unit that can be interposed between the camera body and lens to effectively double or triple the lens focal length; usually, but not always, with some loss of image quality, and always with a substantial loss of lens speed. Sometimes called an **extender.**

convertible lens A lens whose two major components can be used either together or separately. They were once called "double anastigmats" because each half is separately corrected. When used together the two components yield the "normal" focal length and a relative aperture of about f/5.6 or f/6.3. When used separately the components work as long lenses—about 1.2 to 2.5 times the normal focal length—at reduced aperture. Performance and correction of the complete lens is excellent. The individual components are fair to moderately good.

convex Bulging. The opposite of **concave.** The surface of a sphere seen from outside the sphere.

correction The design and construction refinements of a lens that tend to minimize the aberrations. A practical photographic lens usually consists of several simple lenses (or glasses), since adequate correction normally requires a variety of types of glass and lens shapes, and meticulous spacing of the elements.

coverage The area of the image (formed by a lens) that is of useful quality. Also, the area of the subject that the lens can record as an image of useful quality.

crop To trim, or sometimes to cover, the borders of an image for any reason, but usually to improve the composition.

cross light Light striking the subject from one side.

curtain shutter A shutter variety in which a slit or opening in a strip of metal or cloth is made to travel past the film surface to effect the exposure. See **leaf shutter.**

curvature of field The tendency of a simple lens to form its image on a spherical, rather than a flat, plane.

cut film Another name for **sheet film.**

cyanotype process An iron-sensitive process that produces an image in bright blue dye. The blueprint process.

daguerreotype Generally recognized as the first practical photographic process, it was invented by Louis Jacques Mandé Daguerre and announced publicly in 1839. The image was formed on a polished silver plate, sensitized by fuming with iodine, and developed, after camera exposure, in the vapors of warmed mercury.

dark slide The black plastic or fiber sheet inserted into a film holder through a lighttight slot to seal the film chamber against light.

daylight Sunlight or skylight or any mixture of the two. For the purposes of color photography, daylight is considered to have a color temperature of from about 5500°K to 6000°K; this condition is likely to exist when the sun is high and slightly overcast. Under other conditions the color of daylight is likely to be quite different from the "norm" and must be filtered if "normal" color rendition is desired.

decamired Ten mireds. See **mired.**

dedicated flash An electronic flash unit so designed that it senses and may actually control some camera functions. These units are usually designed for specific camera models and may, among other things, set the camera shutter at the appropriate synchronizing speed and provide "ready" and "proper exposure" lights in the camera viewfinder.

deep tanks Commercial film processing equipment in which large volumes of processing solutions are agitated by nitrogen burst, and controlled replenishment maintains the solutions at optimum strength throughout their life.

delay In synchronized flash photography, the interval between the application of the firing current to the bulb and the opening of the shutter. The delay interval is controlled by the shutter. See **M, F, X.**

dense Descriptive of a negative that is dark overall, or of an area of a negative that has a heavy silver deposit and therefore transmits only a little light.

densitometer An instrument designed to measure the amount of light transmitted by individual small areas of a negative, thus appraising the density of the areas.

density The common logarithm of the reciprocal of transmission. That characteristic of the image silver deposit that absorbs (or prevents it, for any reason, from transmitting) light. Transmission density refers to the absorption of transmitted light, as by areas of a negative. Print tones are described as reflection densities, since they are seen and measured by reflected light.

density range The range of densities represented by a photographic image. It is found by subtracting the lowest density value from the highest and is expressed numerically. Also called **Density Scale.**

density scale Same as **density range.**

depth of field The region of acceptably sharp focus around the subject position, extending toward the camera and away from it, from the plane of sharpest focus. The boundaries of the depth of field are referred to as the near limit and the far limit.

depth of field scale A calibrated scale, ring, or chart—often a part of the camera lens mount—on which the depth of field for any distance and aperture setting is indicated.

depth of focus The little zone including the focal plane of the lens through which the film can be moved, toward and away from the lens, and still record an acceptably sharp image.

desiccated Dried. Describes a substance from which at least some water has been removed. Not necessarily **anhydrous**, which see.

developer The solution that produces the silver image in the normal photographic process. It ordinarily contains a reducing agent, a preservative, an accelerator, and a restrainer in water solution. A practical developer must develop only the exposed silver halide grains in the emulsion, leaving the unexposed grains unaffected. Such a developer is called clean-working. A solution developing an appreciable quantity of unexposed halide is said to produce chemical **fog.**

developing-out The photographic process in which relatively brief exposure produces a latent image which is made visible by subsequent development. See **printing-out.**

diaphragm The assembly of thin metal leaves, usually incorporated into the lens barrel or shutter assembly, that can be adjusted to control the size of the lens aperture. Same as **Iris Diaphragm.**

dichroic filter A filter, usually of glass coated with a thin film of some durable material, having the unique ability to transmit certain colors while reflecting the rest of the spectrum. Because the transmitted and reflected colors are complementary the filter appears to change color in certain lights, hence the name "dichroic." Dichroic filters are highly resistant to heat and fading and are therefore especially suitable for use in color printing applications.

diffraction The tendency of light rays to be bent around the edge of an obstruction.

diffusion Of light, the random scattering of rays as by transmission through a turbid medium or by reflection from a matte surface.

diffusion enlarger An enlarger that employs diffused light to illuminate the negative.

DIN Deutsche Industrie Normen. The German system of film speed determination.

diopter An optician's term that identifies the power of a lens. It expresses the reciprocal of the lens focal length in meters and is usually preceded by a plus or minus sign to indicate whether the lens is positive (converging) or negative (diverging). Thus, a close-up (positive) lens having a focal length of 50 cm (½ meter) would be labelled a +2 lens.

discontinuous spectrum Light radiation from which certain wavelengths (colors) are missing or present in negligible amounts.

dispersion The separation of a light ray into its component colors, as by a prism.

distortion Sometimes referred to as linear distortion or curvilinear distortion, it is an aberration of the lens characterized by variable magnification of the image. The effect increases toward the edges of the image area and will cause straight lines near the edges of the subject field to be formed near the image margins as curved lines. Two forms are identified, **Pincushion** and **Barrel Distortion.**

D log E curve The graphic presentation of the relationship between exposure and density when development is a constant. When several conditions of development are expressed the result is a "family of curves."

Dmax Maximum density.

Dmin Minimum density.

dodging The practice of shading a relatively small area of the image in printing to prevent it from becoming too fully exposed, and thus to render it, in the finished print, as lighter in tone than it would otherwise have been. See **burning-in.**

dodging tool Any device used in dodging. Usually, a thin wire handle on which is mounted a piece of cardboard trimmed to match the shape of the image area to be dodged.

DR Density Range, which see.

dropout A photograph from which certain tones—usually the grays—have been eliminated.

drum dryer A machine (now obsolescent) for drying paper prints. It typically consists of a heated drum or cylinder of metal and an endless canvas belt which holds the prints in contact with the drum surface. The larger models are motorized for continuous operation.

dry-mounting A method of mounting prints on cardboard or similar sheet materials. **dry-mounting tissue** placed between the print and mount board is softened by the heat of a **dry-mounting press** to effect the bond.

dry-mounting press A machine for dry-mounting prints. It has a large flat metal pressure plate that can apply uniform pressure and thermostatically controlled heat on the prints to be mounted.

dry-mounting tissue A thin tissue paper impregnated with shellac or some similar material, which, when heated sufficiently, softens to become an effective adhesive for paper.

dry plate Term used in the 1880s to distinguish gelatin-coated glass plates (dry plates) from the previously very popular collodion-coated plates that had to be sensitized immediately before use and inserted into the camera while still damp.

DS Density Scale. Same as **Density Range**, which see.

dye transfer A method of making very high-quality color prints, in which the final full-color image is produced by separate printings (transfers) of the three primary dye images—cyan, magenta, and yellow—from individual film matrices to a single sheet of prepared paper.

easel The device, usually a frame of metal with adjustable metal masking strips, that holds printing paper flat for exposure under the enlarger, and permits adjustments of the width of the picture borders.

electronic flash   A photographic light source that produces a brilliant flash of light by the discharge of electricity through a gas-filled glass or quartz flash tube. The flash duration is very short, usually less than 1/500 second, and there is no firing delay. Most flash tubes produce a light that approximates daylight in color; therefore, only minor filtration is required for use with daylight color films. Electronic flash is commonly referred to as **Strobe,** an inaccurate nickname derived from stroboscope, a related but different device.

element   Of a lens, one of the unit structures. A term rather loosely used to refer to a single glass unit, a cemented unit of one or more glasses, or even a complete component of several air-spaced and cemented glasses; as, "the front element (component) of a convertible lens."

Elon   Eastman Kodak's brand of p-methylaminophenol sulfate, most familiarly known as "Metol," which is itself a trade name (GAF, Agfa, Hauff, etc.). See **Metol.**

emulsion   The light-sensitive coating on photographic film or printing paper.

enlarger   A printing machine designed to project the image of an illuminated negative onto a sheet of sensitized paper. While all enlargers can be adjusted to make prints larger than the negative image, most can also be adapted to make prints reduced in scale as well, so the name is somewhat misleading.

ES   Exposure Scale, which see.

EVS   A system intended to simplify the determination of exposure. It assigns the EV numbers, 0 through 12, to the shutter speeds, 1 second through 1/1000 second, and the EV numbers, 1 through 12, to the relative apertures, f/1.4 through f/64. Similarly, Additive Speed Values (ASV), 0 through 10, are assigned to ASA Indexes, 3 through 3200, and Light Value Scale (LVS) numbers 0 through 10, are assigned to illumination levels of 6 footcandles through 6400 footcandles. In use, the sum of film speed (ASV) plus light intensity (LVS) yields a number that must be matched by the sum of a shutter speed EV number plus an aperture EV number. The system has not elicited much enthusiasm.

expansion   In the Zone System, extended development that compensates for low subject contrast, so as to produce normal negative contrast.

exposure   (1) The act of subjecting a photosensitive material to the action of light. (2) The accumulated effect of the action of light on a sensitized material.

exposure factor   A number (multiplier) indicating the exposure increase required when, for example, a filter is used. The factor for a condition requiring, for example, four times the normal exposure would be written $4\times$.

exposure index   A number indicating the relative effective light sensitivity of a given film, as determined by any methods other than those proposed by the ANSI or similar organizations.

exposure meter   An instrument used to measure the luminance of the subject or the illumination level at the subject position, and to equate this information with the film speed to indicate appropriate camera aperture and shutter speed settings.

exposure scale   The range of exposures (usually the range of light intensities with exposure time a constant) required to produce, after suitable development, the useful range of densities that a given emulsion can produce. The term is relevant specifically to paper emulsions.

extender   See **converter.**

extension tubes   A set of three or more (usually) rings or tubes of varying lengths, intended to be interposed between the body and lens of a small camera, so as to permit focusing the lens on subjects very close to the camera.

factor   A number by which the duration or effect of some action or process must, for some reason, be multiplied.

failure of the reciprocity law   Refers to the fact that sensitive emulsions, when subjected to extremely intense or extremely dim exposing lights, require more total exposure than would be predicted by the Reciprocity Law. See **reciprocity law.**

Farmer's Reducer   A water solution of potassium ferricyanide and sodium thiosulfate, proposed in 1883 by E. H. Farmer as an effective reducing solution for the silver image. It is still popular.

fast   A term used to describe lenses of large relative aperture or films of high sensitivity. Sometimes also applied to unusually sensitive papers.

feathering a light   The technique of evening the illumination across a set by directing the bright central beam of a light toward the farthest objects, thus allowing the nearest objects to be illuminated by the less intense margins of the beam.

ferrotype   One name for the tintypes. They were also called melainotypes. They were made on small polished and varnished sheets of iron, hence the name *ferro*-type.

ferrotype tins   After gelatin-coated printing papers became popular, prints were sometimes dried by squeegeeing them, emulsion down, on a Japanned (varnished) iron sheet or ferrotype tin. Prints so treated dried with a high gloss and the technique of glossing a print came to be known as ferrotyping. Nowadays glossy fiber-based prints are sometimes dried on chromium-plated brass or plastic sheets or chromium or stainless steel drum dryers, but the term ferrotyping persists.

fiber-based paper   Printing paper whose base material is a high-quality paper, usually coated with a thin layer of barium sulfate (baryta). The term is clumsy but frequently used to distinguish plain paper-based materials from **resin-coated papers,** which see.

field camera   A simple view camera of special light-weight construction, intended for use outside the studio. Field cameras are usually built of wood and are designed to fold up compactly for carrying.

field curvature   See **curvature of field.**

fill light   Light directed into the shadow areas of the subject to reduce the lighting contrast.

film   Generally, the familiar light-sensitive material used in cameras in the practice of photography. It normally consists of a flexible, thin, transparent sheet or strip of acetate or polyester plastic coated on one side with a light-sensitive emulsion, and on the other with a dyed layer of gelatin to reduce curl and halation.

film clip   A spring clip of metal, plastic, or wood designed to hold the film securely as it hangs in the film dryer.

film holder   Thin container of plastic, metal, or wood—usually black—designed to hold two sheets of film in separate compartments, back to back. Film is loaded into the holder in the darkroom and is protected from light by the dark slide. The film is positioned so accurately in the holder that, when it is inserted into the camera and the slide is withdrawn, the previously focused image falls precisely on the film surface, insuring that the photographer will actually get the picture he saw on the groundglass.

film pack   A metal container of several sheets of film, so designed that when the pack is loaded properly into the camera, an exposed sheet can be removed from the focal plane into a lighttight compartment and a fresh sheet can be positioned for the next exposure by simply pulling a paper tab protruding from the end of the pack. After all the films are exposed, the pack can be removed from the camera, but must be unloaded in the darkroom. Film packs are not normally reusable.

film speed   A number indicating the relative light sensitivity of a given film, as determined by some official body such as ANSI or the ISO. The ASA film speed.

filter   (1) To pass light through some material that absorbs selected wavelengths or colors or polarized portions of the light. (2) A sheet or disc of plastic, glass, or other material, usually colored, which can be used to absorb selected components of transmitted light.

fingernail marks   Slang term for little crescent-shaped gray, black, or occasionally translucent marks that appear on negatives, resulting from pressing or crimping the film before development, as, for example, when loading rollfilm (inexpertly) onto a tank reel. The emulsion may be either effectively exposed or desensitized by physical violence of this kind, and the marks are authentic parts of the developed silver image. They will almost always be seen to coincide with a visible crease in the film base. They cannot be removed.

fisheye lens   A type of super wide-angle lens, or lens attachment, capable of covering a field of about 180°. Fisheye images are circular, if the whole image appears on the film, and are notable for their barrel distortion.

fix   To make the film insensitive to further exposure to light, usually by bathing the emulsion with a solution containing hypo or some other effective silver halide solvent. Such a solution is called a fixing bath.

flare   Extraneous light, not part of the controlled image light, that passes through the lens to the film. Flare light resulting from diffusion of the normal image light by dirty lens surfaces, reflections from scratches or chips in the glass, or reflections from bright metal surfaces inside the camera usually causes a more or less general fogging of the film. Actual patterns, usually the out-of-focus images of the lens aperture, are caused by multiple reflections of strong light between the various lens surfaces, and are called ghosts.

flash   General name for any photographic light source that produces a very brilliant, very brief pulse of light.

flashbars   An array of several small flashbulbs, each with its own reflector, mounted side-by-side on a common base, and designed to permit sequential firing. Flipflash is a similar device.

flashbulb   A light source, similar in appearance to an ordinary electric light bulb, but containing a quantity of combustible wire and some priming material in an oxygen atmosphere. When a suitable electrical connection is made to the bulb terminals, the primer fires, igniting the wire which in turn burns very rapidly with a brilliant flash of light. Typically, the flash reaches useful intensity about fifteen milliseconds after the application of the firing current, with the peak intensity occurring at about twenty milliseconds. Total effective duration is in the order of ten to thirty milliseconds. A flashbulb can only be used once, of course.

flashcube   Small, cube-shaped assembly of four tiny flashbulbs, each with its own reflector, in a common housing. A special base design fits the flash socket of certain specialized cameras and permits the flash units to be fired in quick succession. Coupled with motorized film transport, flash-cubes can be used to make four synchronized flash pictures in just a few seconds. Now obsolescent.

flashing   The technique of darkening an area of a print image by exposing the sensitized paper to raw white light. Flashing fogs the image unlike **dodging** and **burning-in,** both of which modify the effect of the image-forming light itself.

flash synchronization   The adjustment of the timing of the application of firing current to a flashbulb and the actuation of the shutter release so that the peak flash intensity occurs while the shutter is open.

flat   (1) A large, free-standing, movable wall or panel, usually painted white, and used as a reflector or background in studio photography. (2) A term used to describe a low-contrast image, usually in reference to a print; it implies that the contrast is *too* low.

floating elements   A glass or group of glasses in a lens, designed to move independently during focusing so the lens spacing is optimized for all subject distances.

flood   A photographic light source designed to illuminate a wide area with light of relatively uniform intensity. Almost without exception, it implies an incandescent or fluorescent source, but flood reflectors are also available for use with flash sources.

f/number   The numerical expression of the aperture diameter of a lens as a fraction of the focal length. See **relative aperture.**

focal distance   The distance from the lens to the plane of the focused image. In practice, it is usually measured from the plane of the lens diaphragm.

focal length   Loosely, the focal distance when the lens is focused on infinity; more accurately, the distance from the rear nodal point of the lens to the image plane when the lens is focused on infinity. See **Nodal Point.**

focal plane shutter   A curtain or blade shutter operating in the camera body just ahead of the film (or focal) plane.

focus   To adjust a camera, for example, so that an image is formed precisely on the film plane. Also a term applied to the adjustment of such instruments as binoculars and microscopes so as to provide a visual impression of sharpness in the image. Generally, the adjustment of any positive lens system so that light rays passing through it converge at a desired point. The convergence of light rays to a point.

focusing cloth   Sometimes also called dark cloth. A large square or rectangular piece of black material, usually cloth, used by photographers as an aid in focusing the image on the groundglass screen of a view camera. It is used to enclose the camera back and the photographer's head, thus excluding outside light to make the image appear bright and clear.

fog   Any tone or density (in the developed emulsion) caused by extraneous light or chemical action not related to the normal formation of image.

forced development   Development deliberately prolonged considerably beyond the normal time. See **Push.**

FP shutter   See **focal plane Shutter.**

Frame   (1) To adjust the position and angle of the camera with respect to the subject for the purpose of containing or composing the image within the boundaries of the viewfinder. (2) The useful area and shape of the film image; the picture.

frame numbers   Numbers printed on the paper backing strip and along the edges of rollfilm, and outside the perforations of 35mm filmstrips, which can be used to identify the individual pictures (or frames).

freckling   Slang term describing a common flaw in ferrotyped prints. Groups or areas of tiny dull spots in an otherwise highly glossy surface.

frilling   The detachment (and wrinkling) of areas of the emulsion layer along the edges of the film or paper base during processing. Likely to occur with, and for the same reasons as, reticulation. See **reticulation.**

GaAsP   Chemical symbol for gallium arsenide phosphide, the compound from which gallium photo-diodes are made. Familiarly known by the initials, GAP.

gallium photo-diode   A solid-state photo-conductor, characterized by fast response time, freedom from memory effects, and relative insensitivity to infrared; used as a light sensor in some camera meters. Also known by the initials GPD.

gamma   A numerical expression of the gradient of the straight-line portion of the film characteristic curve. Loosely, an indication of the contrast of the image as influenced by development. See **contrast index.**

gelatin   A complex protein substance made from animal hides and hooves which is used as a chemical-bearing medium and binder in the manufacture of photographic emulsions. Its many unique properties make it especially suitable for use in silver halide emulsions, but it is also an essential material in some nonsilver techniques such as the collotype and carbon processes.

gelatin filter squares   Thin sheets of dyed gelatin of high optical quality, available in various sizes and colors, and intended for use in the image light path for the selective absorption of color or for the control of light intensity.

glacial acetic acid   The concentrated (99%) form of acetic acid. It is a transparent, colorless, dense liquid with a sharp, powerfully penetrating odor. It freezes at about 16°C (60°F); it is an effective solvent for some plastics; and its vapors are flammable. It burns the skin painfully on brief contact and should be handled with caution. See **acetic acid** and **short-stop.**

glossing solution   A bath in which prints are soaked briefly before being ferrotyped. It is intended to reduce freckling, prevent sticking, and generally improve the luster of the print surface.

glossy   Describes a printing paper with a smooth surface suitable for ferrotyping, or with a mirrorlike luster such as is produced by ferrotyping.

GPD   **Gallium Photo-Diode,** which see.

gradation   Variation in tone. Tonal range or scale.

gradient   Slope, specifically the slope of a film characteristic curve or some section of one.

graduate   A container—usually made of glass, enameled steel, stainless steel, or plastic—that is calibrated in fluid ounces or milliliters, or both, for use in measuring liquid volumes.

grain   The visible granular texture of the silver image, caused by apparent clumping of the individual silver particles, not usually apparent until the image is enlarged or viewed under magnification.

gray   (1) Any of the intermediate tones of a black-and-white image. (2) Describes a print image that is without extremes of tone and is unpleasantly low in contrast. See **flat.**

gray card   A card of known reflectance, usually 18 percent, intended to be placed in the subject area and used as a meter target in the determination of exposure. Also used in color photography to establish a neutral reference for the adjustment of print color.

gray scale   (1) The gradation of an image. (2) A strip of film or paper displaying individually uniform areas of density ranging from light to dark in a series of steps. Also sometimes called step tablets, they are used in testing the sensitivity and contrast characteristics of photographic materials.

gross fog density   Same as **base-plus-fog density,** which see.

groundglass   A general name for the focusing screen in a reflex or view camera.

gum process   Also **gum bichromate process.** A method of printing in which the sensitized surface is a coating of gum arabic, a pigment, and a dichromate. The emulsion is rendered insoluble by exposure to bright light, and the image is ultimately composed of the areas of pigment that are not washed away during development in plain water.

H and D curves   Film characteristic curves, specifically those plotted by F. Hurter and V. Driffield who published their procedure in 1890.

halation   The fringe or halo sometimes occuring around very heavily exposed image points as excess light that penetrates the emulsion layer and is reflected back into the emulsion from the surfaces of the film base. It is reduced in modern films by dyeing the film base material or by applying a dyed gelatin layer, called the antihalation or antihalo backing, to the film back.

halftone Printer's and engraver's term for an image that has been screened so as to produce the effect of continuous tone. This is accomplished by breaking up the image into halftone dots in a regular pattern too fine to be visually resolved under normal conditions. Tones of gray are identified by percentage numbers which indicate the total area of ink in a given area of the image. Thus a 10 percent gray would imply that the dots composing it were 1/10 as large in area as the area of the white paper separating them.

halides Metallic compounds of the halogens, namely the elements fluorine, chlorine, bromine, and iodine. The chloride, bromide, and iodide of silver are the light-sensitive materials upon which most photographic processes are based.

halo-dot screen **contact screen,** which see.

hand camera Little-used term to identify any camera that can be carried and used without a tripod. Also ''hand-held'' camera.

hangers The frames, usually of metal or plastic, in which sheet films are placed for processing in deep tanks.

hard Term occasionally used to describe high contrast in images or lighting arrangements. **Harsh.**

hardener A chemical solution for tanning or toughening the emulsion. Hardeners may be used as separate baths or they may be included in some other solution.

harsh Implies an unpleasant lack of subtlety of gradation or light distribution. Contrasty, glaring.

highlights The brightest light accents in the subject. Also, the areas in the image corresponding to the subject highlights. In the negative, of course, the highlights are the most dense areas.

highlight mask A deliberately underexposed, high-contrast black-and-white negative of a color transparency which records only the highlight areas of the transparency and which is bound in register with the transparency while the principal color correcting masks are being made. Its purpose is to increase the highlight contrast of the final color print image in the dye transfer process. Highlight masks are also useful in black-and-white photography.

holder See **film holder.**

hot-spot An undesirable concentration of light on the subject in studio photography. The brilliant area of illumination produced by the concentrated central beam of a floodlight or spotlight. An area of unusual brightness in the projected light from an enlarger or projector.

hydroquinone Common name for p-dihydroxybenzene, a reducing agent in many popular developers. Its fine, needlelike crystals are white, lustrous, and fairly soluble in plain water and in sulfite solutions. It keeps well in dry form, but only fairly well in solution. It is a high-contrast developer, especially so when accelerated with caustic alkalis, such as sodium hydroxide. It is normally nonstaining but must be heavily restrained to prevent fog. In general use, it is almost invariably teamed with Metol or Phenidone—combinations that not only exhibit the best features of each ingredient, but have some additional desirable characteristics of their own. See **metol** and **penidone.**

hyperfocal distance The distance from the camera to the near plane of the depth of field when the lens is focused on infinity. Also the distance from the camera to the plane of sharpest focus when the far plane of the depth of field is at infinity.

hypo The common nickname for the chemical sodium thiosulfate, which was originally called sodium *hyposulfite* by Sir John Frederick William Herschel who discovered it in 1819 and recommended its use to Talbot in 1839. It is still considered to be one of the best of the few practical solvents for the silver halides and is the major ingredient in almost all of the general-purpose fixing baths. The term *hypo* is commonly used to refer not only to the chemical itself but also to fixing baths compounded with it, and even to those baths made with ammonium thiosulfate—the so-called rapid fixing baths.

hypo eliminator A bath for films and papers, recommended for use following the fixing bath and intended to convert the chemical products of fixation into compounds more readily soluble in water, thus facilitating washing and increasing the stability of the silver image. Most such baths are more properly called hypo-clearing baths since they do not really eliminate hypo but do aid in its removal.

image The photographic representation of the subject photographed. The visible result of exposing and developing a photographic emulsion.

incident light. The light reaching the subject from any and all sources.

incident meter An exposure meter designed, or adapted, for the measurement of incident light intensity, or illuminance.

infinity For photographic purposes, that distance from the camera beyond which no further focusing adjustment is required to maintain a satisfactorily sharp image of a receding object. It varies with the focal length of the lens, the aperture, and the photographer's standard of sharpness, but for most purposes infinity can be considered to be anything beyond a quarter of a mile or so from the camera.

infrared Name assigned to an extensive band of invisible, long wavelength electromagnetic radiations that continue the spectrum beyond visible red light. We can perceive a portion of the infrared spectrum as heat, and some special films are capable of making pictures by infrared.

inspection A method of determining the extent of development by observing the image under dim safelight illumination.

intensifier A solution used to increase the density or contrast of the silver image, usually to improve the printing characteristics of underdeveloped negatives.

interchangeable lens A lens that can be removed from the camera body as a complete unit and replaced by another.

interference The cancellation or reinforcement of light waves, resulting from phase shifts such as may be caused by reflection between surfaces spaced apart by some appreciable fraction of the light wavelength. The effect is frequency-selective and often results in colors or patterns such as those visible in soap bubbles, oil films on water, and lens coatings.

interval timer A device for indicating the end of a selected period of time, usually by ringing a bell or sounding a buzzer. It is used to time development and other procedures that must be carried out in darkness or where a conventional clock cannot be seen.

inverse square law   A statement to the effect that "illumination intensity on a surface will vary inversely with the square of the distance from the light source to the illuminated surface."

iris diaphragm   See **diaphragm.**

ISO   Initials that stand for the International Organization for Standardization (International Standards Organization). In 1974 the ISO adopted a standard for determining film speeds that, in effect, combined our existing ASA (arithmetic) system with the German DIN (logarithmic) system. ISO film speeds, as presently used in this country, include both; so that, for example, Plus-X film is now rated ISO 125/22°—the degree sign indicating the DIN logarithmic value.

Kelvin temperature   Temperature on the absolute Celsius (or Centigrade) scale. In photography, another name for **color temperature.**

lantern slide   A transparency mounted in a cardboard or metal frame or bound between glass plates for projection. Usually implies the 3¼″ × 4″ slide size used in large auditorium projectors. See **slide.**

latent image   The invisible impression on the sensitized emulsion produced by exposure to light in the developing-out processes. Development converts the latent image to a visible one.

LCD   See **liquid crystal display.**

leader   A strip of film or paper, attached to and preceding the useful film area of rollfilm, provided for threading the film into the camera, and in some cases, for protecting the unused film itself from light during storage and handling.

leaf shutter   A type of shutter, usually operating in the space between the major lens components or immediately behind the lens, consisting of a number of thin metal leaves or blades, arranged concentrically around the lens axis, pivoted so they can either form an opening for the passage of light or overlap to block it. An associated mechanism controls the movement of the leaves and the duration of the exposure interval.

LED   See **light-emitting diode.**

lens   A disc of transparent glass, plastic, or other material whose opposite faces are ground into (usually) spherical, nonparallel surfaces (one face, but not both, may be plane) having a common central axis, and capable of forming either a real or a virtual image. If the center of the lens is thicker than its edges, it will form a real image and is called a positive lens. If the center is thinner than the edges, only a virtual image can be formed and the lens is termed negative. A single lens is usually referred to as a simple lens and is used for picture-taking in only the cheapest cameras. In photography, the term "lens" usually refers to the complex composite structures of two or more glasses as used in a camera. See **Correction.**

lens barrel   The metal tube in which a lens is mounted. It usually also contains a diaphragm assembly. A barrel-mounted lens does not have an integral shutter.

lensboard   The wooden or metal panel on which a view camera (or other) lens is mounted.

lens hood   A device for shielding the front element of a lens from direct light from outside the subject area so as to prevent or reduce flare.

lens mount   That portion of the camera body that holds the lens in position.

lens shade   Same as **Lens Hood.**

lens system   A group or series of lenses assembled for the purpose of controlling light.

lens tissue   A special soft, lintless tissue used for cleaning lens surfaces.

light-emitting diode   A solid state device that converts electric current directly into light. LEDs are used commonly as indicator and warning lights in camera viewfinders and electronic flash units.

light meter   A instrument that measures light intensity. If supplied with a suitable computing scale, it becomes an **Exposure Meter.** The term is commonly used interchangeably with *exposure meter.*

light primaries   The three light colors— red, green, and blue—which, when mixed together, produce a color we recognize as white. None of these colors can be produced by mixtures of any other colors, but appropriate mixtures of the primaries can make any color desired.

lighttight   Describes a container, room, or space that light cannot enter or leave, or a door, baffle, or aperture that light cannot penetrate.

light trap   A device (such as, for example, a maze) that will permit the passage of air or water or objects, but will exclude light.

liquid crystal display   A thin-film device whose surface can be selectively polarized by weak electric currents to display patterns such as letters and numerals. Although they are not as brilliant and easy to read as LED display devices, and are susceptible to damage from extreme heat, cold or physical shock, LCDs are becoming increasingly popular as digital readouts in watches, exposure meters, and some cameras, because of their very low power consumption.

long lens   A lens of longer-than-normal focal length. Most accurately applied to lenses of conventional construction, but also commonly used to refer to telephoto lenses as well.

luminance   Light reflected from, or produced by, a surface.

luminance meter   A meter that measures luminance. Also sometimes called reflectance meter or reflected light meter.

LVS   Light value scale. See **EVS.**

mackie lines   The light-toned lines typically formed around areas of heavy image density in the **sabattier effect,** which see.

macro-lens   Also occasionally **Micro-Lens.** A term used to describe lenses especially corrected for use at short subject distances and generally applied only to those supplied for small cameras. The prefixes *Macro* or *Micro* often appear in the lens name.

macrophotography   The process of making very large photographic images; for example, photomurals. See **microphotography.**

main light   The light in a studio setup, usually the brightest one, that establishes the light and shadow pattern on the subject and thus describes the forms. Also sometimes called the modelling light.

masking The process of blocking out portions of the image area or its borders with opaque tape or paint. Also, the technique of modifying image gradation by registering negative and positive versions of the same image and printing them together to produce a new version.

mask A negative or positive transparency made for the purpose of masking the original image.

mat A wide-bordered frame, usually of cardboard, placed over a picture to define the composition, isolate the image area, and improve the appearance for presentation.

mat-knife A short-bladed knife with a large handle and, usually, replaceable blades, intended for cutting cardboard. In use it is generally guided by a straightedge metal ruler.

matrix In dye transfer printing, the final positive film image. The matrix image is in gelatin relief, and it is used to make the actual transfer of dye to the print paper surface. Three matrix images are required, one for each of the pigment primary colors. The plural is matrices, but professional printers call them "mats."

matte Dull, unreflective, nonglossy; referring to surface texture.

maximum aperture The largest useful opening of the lens. Wide open.

meniscus In photography, describes a simple lens, one of whose faces is convex, the other concave.

metol Most common name for the reducing agent p-methylaminophenol sulfate. Also known as Elon, Pictol, Rhodol, Photol, etc. It has low staining tendencies, is easily accelerated by mild alkalis, and produces little fog. It is supplied as a white or slightly grayish powder which turns yellowish or brownish with age and oxidation. It keeps well in powder form, but oxidizes quite rapidly in solution. It works very rapidly, producing an image of neutral tone and very low contrast. It is considered to be a strong sensitizer and will produce an irritating and painful skin rash on those photographers who are unfortunately susceptible. It is generally used in combination with hydroquinone which complements its characteristics very satisfactorily.

M, F, X Markings found on some shutters indicating the flash synchronization settings for use with different flash sources. *M*, medium peak, for use with regular wire-filled bulbs, provides a delay of about twenty milliseconds. *F*, now rarely seen but intended for fast peak bulbs which are obsolete, provides a delay of about five milliseconds. *X*, zero delay, is recommended for use with electronic flash units and makes the flash contact when the shutter blades are fully open.

microphotography The photographic production of extremely small images, as in the preparation of masks for electronic microcircuits.

microprism Descriptive of the structure of a type of focusing aid incorporated into the groundglass viewing screen of some miniature cameras. Consisting of a multitude of minute three- or four-sided transparent refracting pyramids arranged in a regular pattern and placed in the center of the viewing screen, it functions as an area of rather coarse-textured groundglass for viewing, but provides a more sensitive indication of image sharpness than ordinary groundglass does.

millimicron One millionth of a millimeter, one nanometer; formerly, and still occasionally, used to describe wavelengths of light. Equivalent to ten Angstrom Units. See **Wavelength.**

mired Pronounced "my-red," it is a contraction of *micro-re*ciprocal *de*grees. It is a value found by multiplying the reciprocal of a color temperature by 1,000,000. The expression of color temperatures in mireds rather than the usual Kelvin degrees simplifies considerably the problem of filter selection for color photography in unusual conditions of light color.

mirror lens Optical system employing a (usually) spherical mirror surface, rather than a positive glass lens, to form a real image. Most such lenses for photographic use incorporate one or more glass lenses in addition to the main mirror element to improve the system performance. These composite systems are called catadioptric systems.

monobath Processing solution, usually for use with film emulsions, combining the functions of developer and fixing bath.

monohydrate The stable form of sodium carbonate, and the one commonly specified in formulas calling for this chemical. If either the anhydrous or crystalline form is used in place of the monohydrated form, the amount, by weight, must be adjusted. See **Anhydrous.**

motor drive A battery-powered accessory which, when attached to a camera, permits automatic film advance for single-frame exposures as well as continuous, rapid sequence exposures at the rate of several frames per second.

MQ Nickname for developers compounded with the reducing agents *M*etol and (Hydro-) *Q*uinone. Also sometimes called MH, for *M*etol-*H*ydroquinone.

multicoating An improved method of lens coating, employing more than one coating layer on one or more of the lens surfaces.

negative Any photographic image in which the subject tones have been reversed. Specifically, the reversed-tone image resulting from the simple development of the film exposed in the camera in the conventional process of taking a picture.

negative carrier The frame of glass or metal that holds the negative in printing position in the enlarger.

negative lens A diverging lens, thinner at the center than at the edges, which can produce only a virtual image.

neutral density filter A thin sheet or disc of glass, plastic, or gelatin, having plane and parallel faces, toned to some uniform and specific shade of gray, and intended for use over the camera lens during exposure for the purpose of reducing the intensity of the exposing light without changing its color. Sometimes called ND filters, they are available in accurately calibrated densities from 0.1 to 4.0.

nodal point A point on the axis of a lens around which the lens can be rotated slightly without displacing the focused image of an object at infinity. Specifically, the point from which an accurate measurement of the lens focal length can be made.

normal lens Any lens whose focal length is approximately equal to the diagonal measurement of the film frame. See **frame**, 2. The angular coverage of a normal lens is usually about 55° across the film frame diagonal. See **angular coverage.**

notches Specifically, the notches that film manufacturers cut into one of the short edges of a sheet of film which identify the type of film by their number, shape, and position, and which indicate the emulsion side of the film sheet by their placement.

object The thing photographed. Often used interchangeably with subject, but usually applied to inanimate things. See **subject.**

objective In optics generally, the lens or lens assembly that faces the object. The objective normally forms an aerial image which (in a microscope, for example) is then viewed through the eyepiece or ocular lens. In photography, the term objective is sometimes used to refer to a camera lens.

one-shot developer A developing solution, usually compounded and stored in very concentrated form, intended to be highly diluted for one-time use, then discarded.

opal bulb Electric light bulb having an unusually dense, translucent envelope of white opal glass, intended for use where uniform diffusion of light is important, as for example, in an enlarger.

opaque (1) Incapable of transmitting light. (2) A special fine-ground tempera paint, usually brick-red or black, for use in blocking out (opaqueing) unwanted areas of the negative image prior to printing.

open flash Method of taking pictures with flash in which the shutter is opened on *Time* or *Bulb* and the flash is fired manually.

opening Refers to lens opening and is used, loosely, to mean either aperture or relative aperture.

ordinary Refers to emulsions whose color sensitivity has not been extended beyond visible blue light. Ordinary films are not really ordinary any more. The vast majority of available film types are now Panchromatic. See **orthochromatic.**

orthochromatic Type of emulsion that is sensitive to visible blue and green, but not to red. See **Panchromatic.**

overexposed Refers to a photographic image that has received too much light.

oyster shelling A defect in glossy prints dried on flat ferrotype tins, which shows itself as a series of concentric rings or ridges of torn or strained emulsion, caused by uneven drying. Not common in prints dried on glossy drum dryers.

pan (1) Abbreviation of **panchromatic.** (2) To swing a camera during the exposure to follow a moving object, and thus to render the object sharp against a blurred background.

panchromatic Describes an emulsion sensitive to blue and green and some, or all, of the red region of the spectrum. See **Type A**, 2; **Type B**, 2; and **Type C.**

paper The sensitized paper used in making photographic prints.

paper negative A negative image on a paper base, prepared either by exposing the paper directly in a camera or by printing from a positive transparency. The term implies that the image is not in its final form, and that another printing step will follow. If the image is finished for presentation as a negative, it would more likely be referred to as a negative print.

parallax In photography, the differences in both the framing of the subject forms and their spatial relationships between the image seen by the camera viewfinder and that recorded on the film. Sometimes referred to as the parallax error.

PC lens See **perspective control lens**

perspective control lens Typically for SLR cameras, a moderately wide-angle lens in a special mount that allows the lens to be decentered with respect to the film, thus providing image controls similar to those obtainable with the rising front and lateral shifts of the view camera.

phenidone Ilford's trade name for 1-phenyl-3-pyrazolidone, a reducing agent becoming increasingly popular as a substitute for Metol, especially in combination with hydroquinone. PQ developers can be prepared and stored for long periods as highly concentrated liquid stock solutions, and their working solutions are highly active, clean-working, and relatively stable. Phenidone is not significantly affected by bromide and must usually be restrained by benzotriazole. It is not considered to be as strong a sensitizer as Metol and is generally tolerated well by persons who are susceptible to "Metol poisoning."

photoflood A type of incandescent light bulb of high efficiency but limited life, designed to burn at 3400°K. Formerly popular with amateur photographers because of their small size, modest cost, and low current requirements. They are now being superseded by quartz-halogen lights.

photogram A shadow image made by simply placing objects on the sensitized surface of a sheet of photographic paper and exposing it to light. If the light is sufficiently intense and the exposure long enough, the exposed portions of the paper will turn dark, and the image is a light-toned record of the shadow pattern on a dark background. This is called printing-out the image. Relatively brief exposure to light will form a latent image which can be developed-out like a conventional print image. Developed-out images are more neutral in tone and more contrasty. Both types must be fixed to be preserved for any great length of time.

photogravure A process in which the image, etched into the polished surface of a grained copper or zinc plate, is filled with soft ink, scraped or wiped to clean the surface, and printed in a press.

photomacrography The photography of objects under some magnification, usually employing accessory bellows units, extension tubes, supplementary lenses, or simple microscopes. Image magnification may range from about life-size (1:1) to perhaps 50×.

photomicrography Photography through a compound microscope.

pigment primaries The primary colors in the subtractive color system—normally considered to be red, yellow, and blue, but in photography specifically magenta, yellow, and cyan.

pincushion distortion One of the two forms of curvilinear distortion in which image magnification is disproportionately greater near the edges of the field than near the center. Thus, for example, the image of a large square, placed concentric with the image center, would assume the shape of a pincushion. Barrel distortion is the other, and opposite, form.

pinhole (1) A very small aperture in the front panel or lensboard of a modified or contrived camera for the purpose of forming an unfocused but useful image on the film. (2) A small transparent spot, usually circular, in a negative image, marking the position of an air-bell that, by shielding the emulsion from the developer, prevented the formation of silver in that area.

plane of focus The position of the focused image in space; the image plane, as distinguished from the film plane which will usually, but not necessarily always, coincide with it. Actually, the term is misleading, since the image of any three-dimensional subject closer to the camera than infinity is not plane but three-dimensional; even the image of a flat subject is plane only under unusual conditions, usually being warped into one or more spherical curves.

plate A sheet of glass or occasionally metal, coated with light-sensitive emulsion and usually intended for exposure in a camera.

platinotype Another name for *platinum print*. An iron-sensitive process producing an image composed of platinum metal on paper.

polarized light Light waves that have been caused to vibrate uniformly in, or parallel to, a particular plane.

polarizer A transparent material, such as certain natural crystals and some plastics, capable of polarizing transmitted light.

polarizing filter A lens accessory designed to transmit polarized image light.

Pola-Screen Eastman Kodak's trade name for their line of polarizing filters.

portrait attachment An old term (and a rather inappropriate one) for a close-up lens. See **close-up lens.**

portrait lens A lens designed to produce soft-focus images, popular with portrait photographers. See **spherical aberration.**

positive An image in which the tones or colors are similar to those of the subject.

positive lens A converging lens; one having a relatively thick center and thin edges and can focus light to form a real image.

posterization Popular name for a printing process in which the image gradation is arbitrarily limited to two or three tones of unmodulated gray (or color) resulting in a simplified posterlike pattern.

PQ Refers to mixtures of *P*henidone and hydro*q*uinone, as used in developer formulas.

preservative The ingredient in a developing or fixing solution that tends to prevent or retard spoiling, usually sodium sulfite.

press-focus lever A device incorporated in many leaf shutters permitting the shutter blades to be opened, or held open, regardless of the speed setting. On some old shutters this was called a ''blade arrestor.''

primary colors Those fundamental colors, in light or pigment, that cannot be created by mixing any others. See **light primaries** and **pigment primaries.**

print In photography, the term is generally used to identify an image on paper produced by photographic means. It is usually understood to mean a positive image and implies a final image rather than an intermediate one in some longer process.

print finishing The process of producing a permanent, presentable photographic print, sometimes including treatment in the fixing bath and the final wash, but certainly referring to drying, spotting, cropping, mounting, matting, and other related operations.

printing frame A shallow, rectangular frame of wood or metal equipped with a removable front glass and a separate folding back which can be fastened to the frame with leaf springs so as to hold a negative and a sheet of printing paper against the glass smoothly and tightly. In use, light is allowed to shine through the front glass and through the intervening negative to reach the printing emulsion. Also called a contact printing frame. See **contact printing.**

printing-out A method of photographic printing in which a visible image is formed by the action of light directly, and without subsequent development.

printing paper Photographic printing paper. Any paper coated with a light-sensitive substance, for making photographic images, but a term generally used in reference to commercially manufactured papers coated with gelatin emulsion containing silver halides as the sensitive materials.

print quality This term refers to the craftsmanship of the print and whatever evidences there are of the photographer's technical understanding and competence (or lack of them). But there are often intangibles involved which influence the viewer in ways difficult to explain, and these factors, whatever they are, must be included in the term. Print quality is unrelated to pictorial content.

prism-reflex A type of camera, usually small, in which the viewfinder image is focused, right-side-up and correct from left to right, on a groundglass screen and viewed through a magnifying eyepiece. The optical system accomplishing this includes both a mirror and a pentaprism, hence the name.

process (1) To subject photographic films or papers to chemical treatment, such as, for example, development. (2) The sequence of chemical steps required to produce the desired image or result.

process lens A photographic lens especially designed and painstakingly constructed for the purpose of producing images of the highest quality at object distances of only a few focal lengths. Usually nearly symmetrical in construction and corrected apochromatically, these lenses are exceptionally free from distortion, of relatively long focal length, slow, and very expensive. They are used almost exclusively by professionals in industry and the graphic arts. The nearest equivalent for the small-camera user is the *macro*-lens.

projection print Any print made by projection, rather than by contact. Usually interpreted to mean an enlargement.

projector In photography, usually a machine used to project enlarged images onto a viewing screen, such as a slide projector or movie projector.

proofing   The process of making test exposures, frequently of an entire roll of negatives in a printing frame, to obtain a record of the images and aid in their selection.

push   To prolong the time of development of film in an effort to compensate for underexposure. Also, to underexpose a film deliberately with the intention of attempting compensation in development. To force, but only moderately. See **forced development.**

pyro   Common contraction of pyrogallic acid or 1, 2, 3-trihydroxybenzene. One of the first organic reducing agents to be used as a photographic developer, it is usually in the form of white prismatic crystals of irregular size and shape. It is a very active developer. It keeps well in dry form or in suitable stock solution, but oxidizes very rapidly in most working dilutions. It is usual to prepare the stock as three separate highly concentrated solutions: Sol. *A* containing the pyro, the restrainer, and a substantial quantity of an acid sulfite as a special preservative; Sol. *B* containing the normal preservative; and Sol. *C* containing the accelerator. Pyro developers of this kind typically produce a heavy yellowish stain image and also tan or harden the image gelatin as they work so that the final image combines silver, stain, and gelatin relief. Pyro stains the hands and utensils badly and the usual handling cautions should be observed.

quartz light   Also quartz-iodine light or quartz-halogen light. An incandescent electric light of small size and high efficiency employing a tungsten filament burning in an atmosphere of iodine or bromine vapor and enclosed in a quartz envelope. Characterized by long life, exceptional resistance to blackening or dimming with age, and uniform color temperature.

RC papers   Resin-Coated Papers, which see.

racked out   Referring to the bellows of a view camera, the term means extended.

rangefinder   Primarily refers to an optical device consisting of a system of lenses and beam-splitting prisms, which, viewing the subject through two slightly separated objective lenses, presents the images together in the viewfinder. When the two images are made to coincide by turning a dial, the subject distance can be read from a calibrated scale. Now also used to refer to a simple arrangement of two small prisms incorporated into the viewing screen of some single-lens reflex cameras as a focusing aid.

rangefinder camera   A camera featuring a built-in, coupled, optical rangefinder, usually incorporated into the viewfinder and linked mechanically with the focusing mount of the lens so that bringing the rangefinder images into coincidence also focuses the lens.

raw light   Unfocused light.

real image   An image that can be projected on a surface and seen with the unaided eye. See **virtual image.**

reciprocity law   A law stating that exposure varies uniformly with changes in either time or intensity.

rectilinear   Free from linear distortion.

reducer   A solution of chemicals capable of dissolving the developed silver image, thereby reducing its density.

reducing agent   In chemistry, a substance capable of reducing the positive charge of an ion by supplying electrons. Many reducing agents are capable of reducing silver halides to metallic silver, but only a few are appropriate for use as photographic developing agents. See **developer.**

reel   The metal or plastic spool featuring parallel spiral flanges (sometimes adjustable) on which rollfilms are wound for small tank processing.

reflectance   Describes the ability of a surface to reflect light.

reflectance meter   See **luminance meter.**

reflection   The rebounding of light from a surface, especially a plane polished surface. Also the image seen by reflection, such as the image "in" a mirror.

reflector   A surface used to reflect light. Photographic reflectors are usually sheets of cardboard, plywood, masonite, or stretched fabric, painted white or covered with metal foil.

reflex camera   A type of camera in which the viewfinder image is formed by a lens and reflected by an inclined mirror onto a groundglass screen mounted in the top of the camera body. See **single-lens reflex** and **twin-lens reflex.**

refraction   The bending of light rays as they pass obliquely through the interfaces of transparent mediums of varying or different densities.

register   To superimpose one image on another of identical outline so that the forms and edges coincide.

relative aperture   The relationship between the diameter of the lens opening and the focal length of the lens. It is found by dividing the focal length by the diameter and is, strictly speaking, the number so found—as distinguished from the aperture which includes the prefix *f.* This is a niggling distinction— photographers use the terms interchangeably.

replenisher   A solution of chemicals, similar in composition to a developer but usually more concentrated, intended to be added in measured quantities to a developer after each use for the purpose of restoring the strength of the developer and extending its useful life.

resin-coated papers   Printing papers employing a special base material, treated during manufacture with a plastic "Resin Coating" which, by limiting water absorption, allows for very rapid processing and reduces drying time.

restrainer   An ingredient in a developer solution intended to inhibit the development of unexposed halides. In most solutions which contain one, the restrainer is potassium bromide, or benzotriazole.

reticulation   The pattern of tiny wrinkles or tears in the emulsion of a negative which sometimes results when the film is subjected to temperature extremes or harsh chemical treatment during processing. In extreme cases, the emulsion may be detached from the film base in large patches. See **frilling.** Mild cases of reticulation are often overlooked or confused with the image grain. See **grain.**

retro-focus lens   A type of wide-angle lens, supplied for reflex cameras, which has a back focus greater than its focal length. This is made possible by special reversed telephoto design and provides clearance for the reflex mirror.

reversal   (1) The transformation of the original tonal scale from negative to positive or vice versa, which occurs whenever a conventional photographic emulsion is exposed and developed. (2) A special process by which exposed film is made to produce a positive image of the original subject. This is actually a double reversal of the subject tones; the film is first developed to form a conventional negative image which is then bleached out of the emulsion. The remaining unexposed silver halides are then fogged by exposure to raw light or chemical treatment and developed to form the final positive image.

rim light   Backlight that illuminates the edges of the subject, producing a bright outline.

rising front   One of the shifts of a view camera, it refers to that adjustment of the camera lensboard that permits vertical displacement of the lens while allowing the lensboard to remain parallel with the film plane.

rollfilm   Film supplied in rolls rather than sheets, but especially those films protected from light by paper leaders rather than those supplied in protective cartridges of metal or plastic.

sabattier effect   The partial reversal of image tones caused by exposure of the emulsion to light during development, usually after the image has been partially formed. Named after Armand Sabattier who first described the effect in 1862. Commonly referred to as solarization which is a misnomer. See **solarization.**

safelight   Illumination, used in various darkroom processes, having a color and intensity that will not appreciably affect the emulsions being handled. Blue-sensitive emulsions can be handled in a yellow safelight, and orthochromatic emulsions are generally unaffected by orange or red safelight. Image density resulting from excessive exposure to safelight, or to an inappropriate safelight color, is known as safelight fog.

salted paper   Photographic printing paper such as was described and used by Talbot in his calotype process. It can be prepared by soaking a sheet of good-quality paper in a weak solution of salt, then coating it with one or more layers of a silver nitrate solution. The halide formed is silver chloride. The paper is used for printing-out, and the image is an elegant purplish tone which, unfortunately, changes to brown during fixation.

SBC   **silicon blue cell,** which see.

SBR   See **subject brightness range,** for which this is a contraction. "Subject Luminance Range" is preferred.

scale focusing   A method of focusing a camera by measuring or estimating the subject distance and adjusting the focusing controls to align the appropriate mark on the footage scale with the fixed reference mark on the camera or lens body.

scattering   Loss of intensity of light in passing through a turbid medium. The shorter wavelengths are typically absorbed most readily, causing the transmitted light to appear yellowish or reddish. This is the atmospheric effect responsible for the warmth of color in late afternoon sunlight and in sunsets.

screen   (1) The surface upon which images are projected for viewing. Usually made of a special fabric painted white, covered with tiny glass or plastic beads, or metallized for maximum reflectance. (2) The sheet of glass or film containing a fine pattern of lines or dots, through which films are exposed in the production of halftone printing plates. See **halftone** and **screened image.** (3) Occasionally used to refer to the groundglass of a camera, as the viewing or focusing screen.

screened image   A photographic image composed of minute dots which vary individually in size in proportion to the intensity of the light that formed them. Photographs or other continuous-tone images must be screened for reproduction by letter-press or offset techniques in order to preserve the gradation of the original subject. See **halftone.**

secondary colors   Colors resulting when approximately equal parts of any pair of primary colors are mixed together.

sensitivity   In photography, the susceptibility of an emulsion to alteration by light energy.

sensitometry   The science of the measurement of the sensitivity, and related characteristics, of photographic materials.

separation   (1) The characteristics of any image area that make it visible against its background. (2) The process of recording, on individual black-and-white films, the extent and intensity of each of the primary color components of a photographic subject or image. (3) An image resulting from the process of color or tonal separation.

shadow area   Any region of a photographic image that corresponds to an area of shade or shadow in the original subject. Loosely, any dark area of a positive or light area of a negative image.

sharpness   The subjective impression of clarity of definition and crispness of outline in the rendering of detail and texture of the photographic image.

sheet film   Film supplied in individual pieces; also called cut film.

sheet film holder   See **film holder.**

shifts and swings   The various adjustments of the front and rear standards of a view camera, provided for the purpose of facilitating framing, control of perspective, and the efficient use of the available depth of field. See **rising front.**

short lens   A lens of less-than-normal focal length; a wide-angle lens. See **wide-angle lens.**

short-stop   Old term, still occasionally used, to describe an acid stop bath.

shoulder   The upper, diminishing-gradient portion of a film characteristic curve, which represents the region of overexposure.

shutter   The mechanism, sometimes electronically controlled, that opens and closes to admit light to the film chamber of a camera and control the length of the exposure interval. See **leaf shutter, focal plane shutter,** and **between-the-lens shutter.**

shutter release   The lever or plunger that, when pressed, allows the shutter mainspring to operate the shutter mechanism and make the exposure.

shutter speed (1) The duration of the interval of exposure. (2) The marked settings on a shutter dial. The numbers represent the denominators of fractions of which 1 is the numerator.

silicon blue cell A silicon photo-diode (SPD), specially blue-filtered to restrict its infrared sensitivity, and popularly used in exposure meters and camera metering systems.

silicon photo-diode A solid-state photo-conductor device used in many modern cameras and meters as a light sensor. It is characterized by fast response time, freedom from memory effects, and sensitivity extending well into the infrared. Abbreviated as SPD.

single-lens reflex A reflex camera in which the viewfinder image is formed by the camera lens and reflected to a top-mounted viewing screen by a hinged mirror normally inclined behind the camera lens. During exposure of the film, the mirror flips up to seal the groundglass opening, allowing the image light to pass through to the film chamber. In most designs, a focal plane shutter is employed.

slide (1) A transparency mounted in cardboard, metal, plastic, or glass, for projection onto a screen for viewing. (2) A shortened name for the dark slide of a film holder. See **dark slide.**

slow A term used to describe the longer exposure intervals provided by the shutter, as ''one-half second is a slow speed.'' Also applied to relatively insensitive emulsions, as a ''slow film.''

SLR Abbreviation for **single-lens reflex,** which see.

sodium thiosulfate One of the few chemicals that, in solution, can dissolve the silver halides, and one of a still smaller group that is suitable for photographic use. It is the principal ingredient of ordinary fixing baths and is somewhat less active, but is also less prone to attack the developed silver image than is ammonium thiosulfate, which is used in the so-called rapid fixing baths. Available in both anhydrous and crystalline form, the crystals are generally used and are sometimes sold as hypo-rice. See **Hypo.**

soft (1) Describes an image that is not sharp; that is, one that is blurred, diffused, or not accurately focused. (2) Photographic emulsions, specifically printing papers, that tend to produce images of lower-than-normal contrast; for example, the paper grades 0 and 1, and some others of similar characteristics, are called soft papers.

solarization Originally, the reversal of image tones occurring in the early printing-out processes resulting from extreme overexposure; now almost universally used to describe the Sabattier effect. See **sabattier effect.**

spectrum A complete and ordered series of electromagnetic wave-lengths, usually construed to mean the band of visible wavelengths that we perceive as colors. The visible spectrum consists of wavelengths of from about 400 to 700 nanometers, a band representing a gradual color transition from deep violet, through blue, green, yellow, orange, and red. The spectrum colors can be displayed by dispersing white light with a prism. A natural example, resulting from the dispersion of sunlight by raindrops, is the rainbow.

spherical aberration The tendency, inherent in any simple positive lens whose surfaces are spherical, to focus light rays passing through the peripheral areas of the lens at points closer to the lens than the focal point of the central rays. This results in a zone, rather than a plane of focus, and produces a film image that is generally well defined, but overlayed and blended with a kind of ethereal diffusion. It is a common and troublesome defect in fast lenses, but can be greatly reduced by stopping down. It is deliberately left uncorrected in some lenses intended for portraiture so as to produce a pleasing softness of image.

spin dropout Slang term for Kodak's **tone-line process,** which see.

split-image rangefinder A variety of rangefinder in which the opposite halves of the image are displaced along a dividing line when the instrument is not properly focused. Correct distance is indicated when the image halves are adjusted to match. See **Rangefinder** and **Superimposed Rangefinder.**

spotmeter An exposure meter that measures reflected light, or luminance, over a field of only a degree or two. The portion of the subject being read is outlined on a viewing screen to facilitate accurate appraisal of the individual luminances of small areas of the subject.

spotone Trade name of a popular spotting dye available in several shades of warm, neutral, and cool colors to match almost any black-and-white print image tone.

spot reading A measurement of the luminance of a small area of the subject; specifically, a reading made with a spotmeter.

spotting The process of bleaching or painting out blemishes in the print image for the purpose of improving its appearance.

spotting colors The dyes and especially the pigments used in spotting.

spring back The entire assembly attached to and usually removable from the rear standard of a view or press camera, including the groundglass viewing screen and the frame and springs that secure the film-holder in position.

stabilization The process of rendering the unexposed halides in the developed image resistant to further visible change by the action of light. Stabilized prints are not permanent and they are heavily contaminated with chemicals, but the process is a valuable one for many purposes because it is fast and convenient. It does, however, require a special machine called a stabilization processor and uses special papers and chemicals.

stain Colored or toned area, generally of a print, caused by chemical oxidation or contamination and not usually stable, permanent, premeditated, or desirable. The exceptions are the stain images formed by such developing agents as pyrogallic acid, which have certain virtues.

star filter A glass disc etched or scratched in a regular pattern, intended for use over the camera lens for the purpose of producing radiating streaks around the highlights of the image. A square of shiny window-screening or a stretched piece of nylon stocking will produce a similar result.

step tablet A gray scale composed of regular areas of density increasing in incremental progression. Film step tablets are intended for use with transmitted light; paper step tablets are used with reflected light.

stock (1) The base or support material, such as paper, on which sensitized photographic emulsions are coated. (2) The concentrated form of a photographic chemical solution that is commonly diluted into the working solution for use.

stop (1) Originally a metal plate, centrally perforated, and intended for insertion into a slot in the barrel of a lens for the purpose of limiting the amount of light passing through the lens. Sometimes referred to as Waterhouse stops (after James Waterhouse, who devised the system in 1858), these stop plates were supplied in sets with apertures of different sizes. (2) The aperture or f/number of a lens. (3) A change in exposure, from any cause, that doubles or halves the preceding one. For example, changing the shutter speed from 1/25 second to 1/100 second, other things being equal, is said to reduce the exposure by two stops. (4) Contraction of short-stop, the acid rinse bath that commonly follows the developer. (5) To immerse a print or negative in an acid bath to stop development.

stop bath A mildly acid solution (typically about 1% acetic acid) in which films or prints are treated immediately after their removal from the developer. By neutralizing the developer alkali the stop bath halts development and prolongs the life of the fixing bath.

stop down To reduce the size of the aperture of a lens.

straight line portion The central length of the D log E curve, between the toe and the shoulder, representing a progression of image densities that are uniformly proportional to their corresponding increments of exposure. The portion of the curve exhibiting uniform gradient.

strobe Contraction of the word stroboscope. A special form of electronic flash unit capable of firing repeatedly and automatically at rates that can be varied from a few flashes per second to hundreds. This term is applied inaccurately, but almost universally, to ordinary photographic electronic flash units that usually require several seconds to recharge after each flash and do not flash repetitively. See **electronic flash.**

subject The thing or view photographed. There is some implication that the term subject refers to animate things, and that object refers to inanimate things, but the terms are generally used interchangeably.

subject brightness range See **subject luminance range,** a preferable term.

subject luminance range The numerical difference between the light intensities of the shadows and the highlights of a subject as expressed in arithmetic or logarithmic terms, or in terms of the number of stops represented. Sometimes called "Subject Brightness Range."

subtractive system The system of color mixing involving pigments or dyes in which the primaries represent the most intense and brightest colors available and any mixture of them must necessarily be darker and less intense. Pigments and dyes are seen to be colored because they reflect that color of the incident white light, absorbing the remaining wavelengths. The absence of all pigment color is assumed to be white, as represented by the untouched ground or surface that reflects light without selective absorption. Since each of the three pigment primaries absorbs one of the three light primaries, a mixture of the three pigments will absorb virtually all of the incident light, providing, theoretically, the visual effect of black. See **additive system** and **pigment primaries.**

superimposed rangefinder A type of rangefinder in which the two images appear to overlap. One is usually slightly tinted for easy identification, and the instrument will indicate the correct subject distance when the images are adjusted to coincide by superimposition. See **Split-Image Rangefinder.**

supplementary lens A simple lens or lens system to be used over a camera lens for the purpose of altering effective focal length.

surface A term relating to printing paper, referring specifically to the texture of the emulsion coating.

swings and tilts Another name for the adjustments of a view camera. See **shifts and swings.**

synchronizer The device, usually included in the shutter mechanism, that fires a flash unit at the precise moment required to provide peak light intensity during the instant that the shutter is open.

T Time, which see.

tacking iron A small, electrically heated, thermostatically controlled tool used to tack or attach dry-mounting tissue to the back of a print or to the mount board, so as to hold it in place while the print is being trimmed and heated in the dry-mount press.

taking lens The lens that forms the film image in a twin-lens reflex camera, as distinguished from the viewing lens that forms the viewfinder image.

tank A small, lighttight container, usually of plastic or metal, in which film is placed for processing. Also the larger rectangular containers of hard rubber, plastic, or stainless steel used in sheet-film processing, sometimes called deep tanks.

tanning developer A developer solution that hardens the gelatin of the emulsion in the same areas and at the same time that it develops the silver image.

telephoto A type of lens constructed in such a way that its physical length is unusually short in relation to its focal length. Telephoto lenses are usually more compact, and sometimes lighter in weight, than conventional lenses of similar aperture and focal length. They are invariably used as long lenses, since their angular coverage is inherently restricted, and they are more likely to suffer from distortion and chromatic aberrations than are conventional lenses.

tessar A modified and improved version of the Cooke triplet lens, in which the rear element of the triplet was replaced by a cemented pair. Designed by Paul Rudolph for Zeiss in 1902, it was enormously successful and is still considered to be an excellent design for lenses of normal coverage and moderately wide aperture. It has been widely copied, and virtually every lens manufacturer in the world now has a few Tessar-type lenses among his offerings.

test strip A piece of paper or film subjected to a sequence of regular and cumulative exposures and controlled development, so as to sample the estimated range of useful exposures in an effort to determine the optimum one.

thin Describes the appearance of a transparency image (usually the negative) of low overall density.

thin-emulsion film One of a group of modern roll and 35mm films coated with an unusually thin layer of silver-rich emulsion and capable of producing images of high resolution, relatively fine grain, and brilliant gradation. They are typically of medium or low speed and tend to produce high contrast unless specially processed.

time One of the marked speeds on most shutters. A shutter set on *Time* will open when the shutter release is pressed and will remain open until the release is pressed again. It is a convenient setting for exposure intervals of more than a few seconds. See **bulb.**

time-and-temperature The method of controlling film development, when the film is processed in small tanks or in total darkness in large tanks or trays, by maintaining the process solutions at a known temperature and limiting the duration of development to a selected interval. See **Inspection.**

time exposure Specifically, a camera exposure made by setting the shutter dial on *T,* but generally used to refer to any exposure, timed manually, of longer than a second or so.

timer A mechanical or electronic device used to terminate an exposure interval or ring a bell or otherwise indicate the end of some selected interval of time.

tintype Common name for the Ferrotype or Melainotype. Tintypes are collodion images on Japanned (black varnished) iron sheets. Exposed in the camera and treated to appear as positive images, each tintype is unique. They were relatively inexpensive and extremely popular in the 1860s and 1870s.

TLR See **Twin-Lens Reflex.**

toe The lower segment of the D log E curve, characterized by its progressively increasing slope or gradient. Its lowest extreme represents the region of underexposure of the emulsion.

tonal scale The range of grays or densities of a photographic image. Gradation.

tone-line process A method of producing a photographic image that resembles a pen-and-ink drawing. It includes a step in which a high-contrast film material in contact with a fully masked negative is exposed to slanting light while being rotated on a phonograph turntable, and is, therefore, sometimes called the spin dropout process.

toner Any solution of chemicals used to alter the color of the silver image, either during development or, usually, as a postdevelopment treatment.

trailer The length of opaque film or attached paper following the useful image area of the film strip that, when wrapped in several layers around the exposed film roll, serves to protect the image exposures from raw light.

translucent Describes a diffusing material that will transmit light, but not focused light.

transparency An image viewed by transmitted light. Specifically a film image, usually positive, and often in color, intended for projection.

tray The shallow, rectangular, open containers in which prints, and sometimes films, are processed. In England they are called dishes.

triplet A lens of three elements, specifically the three-glass lens designed in 1893 by H. D. Taylor and known as the Cooke Triplet. It was considered a breakthrough in lens design and is the ancestral prototype of a great many modern lenses.

tripod A three-legged stand, usually adjustable in height and provided with a tilting and swivelling head, on which a camera can be fastened for support and stability during use.

TTL Through-the-lens; describes a type of exposure meter, incorporated in the structure of a camera, that reads the intensity of the image light transmitted by a lens.

tungsten light Generally, the light emitted by a heated tungsten filament such as is contained in conventional electric light bulbs. Sometimes used to refer specifically to the light of special photographic tungsten-filament bulbs which are designed to burn at either 3200°K or 3400°K. Also often used loosely to apply to artificial light in general, as distinguished from daylight.

twin-lens reflex A type of reflex camera using separate but similar lenses in separate compartments of the camera body for the individual functions of viewing and recording the image. See **single-lens reflex.**

Type A (1) Refers to those color films that have been balanced or specially sensitized for use in tungsten light of 3400°K. (2) Now rarely used to refer to panchromatic emulsions whose sensitivity to red light is minimal.

Type B (1) The group of color films intended for use in tungsten light of 3200°K. (2) Occasionally, the designation of panchromatic films whose red-sensitivity approximates that of the human eye.

Type C Rarely used designation for panchromatic films whose red-sensitivity exceeds that of the human eye.

ultraviolet The common name for the band of short wavelength, high-frequency electromagnetic radiations bordering the visible spectrum beyond visible violet light.

underexposed Refers to a photographic image that has received too little light.

unit magnification The formation by a lens system of an image identical in size or scale with the subject.

US Uniform system. The name of an obsolete system of lens aperture scale marking that expressed, inversely, the arithmetic relationship of the light transmission of the various apertures. In the system, the number 1 was assigned to the aperture f/4.0, 2 was equivalent to f/5.6, 4 equalled f/8.0, 8 equalled f/11.0, etc.

variable-contrast paper   A type of printing paper coated with a mixture of two emulsions that are separately sensitized to (usually) green and blue light. Since one emulsion has a high-contrast characteristic and the other low, the overall contrast rendition of the paper can be controlled by varying the proportions of green and blue in the exposing light. With most such papers, green light will produce an image of low contrast, while high contrast will result from exposure to blue light. Light color—and therefore image contrast—is controlled by filters, each numbered to indicate the paper grade to which it corresponds.

view camera   A type of camera in which the image is viewed and composed on a groundglass screen placed precisely at the film plane. The viewed image is therefore identical to the one presented to the film during exposure. After the image has been focused and composed, the groundglass is replaced by the film in a suitable holder and the picture is made. Most view cameras provide for considerable adjustment of the relative positions of the lensboard and film plane. They are typically designed to accept sheet film in the larger sizes and must be used on a tripod, or other firm support. **See shifts and swings.**

viewfinder   The aperture or optical device, usually an integral part of the camera, through which or in which the subject can be seen, appraised, and composed.

viewing lens   In a twin-lens reflex camera, the lens forming the viewfinder image. See **taking lens.**

vignetted   Describes an image whose edges or corners have lost density, definition, or contrast. Print images are sometimes vignetted purposely to eliminate or subdue unwanted detail. Vignetting can also occur in the camera if the lens used cannot cover the film area adequately or if lens accessories, such as filters or sunshades, restrict the lens's angular coverage.

virtual image   An image, such as is typically formed by a negative lens, which can be seen in the lens or as an aerial image, but cannot be formed on a screen.

warm tones   In photography, shades of red or orange (browns) in the black-and-white silver image. Generally, similar shades in the color or tone of any material.

washed out   A term to describe a pale, lifeless, gray print image, usually implying loss of highlight detail, such as might typically result from underexposure of the print.

wavelength   The distance from crest to crest, or trough to trough, of adjacent, cyclic waveforms. The completion of a single waveform, including crest and trough, is called a cycle, and the number of cycles completed in a second of time is called the frequency (of vibration) of the waveform. The traditional units of wavelength measurement in light are the Angstrom Unit, abbreviated ''Å'' and equal to 1/10,000,000 of a millimeter, and the millimicron, equivalent to 1/1,000,000 of a millimeter. The preferred unit is now the ''nanometer'' which is equivalent to the millimicron. The unit of frequency is the Hertz, cycles per second.

weak   Describes an image which is not fully formed or which is unpleasantly low in contrast or density. Pale, gray, lifeless.

wedging   The deviation of a light ray in passing, for example, from air through a glass plate with plane, but not parallel, faces. Also sometimes used loosely to describe the lateral displacement of an image being projected through a thick glass or plastic filter that is slightly tilted in the light beam.

weight   The thickness of printing paper stock.

wet-mounting   Methods of attaching prints to their mounts by means of liquid, especially water-based, glues or adhesives.

wet-plate process   Another name for the collodion process, in which glass plates coated with a thin film of salted collodion were sensitized in a solution of silver nitrate and immediately loaded into the camera for exposure while still damp. The process was popular from about 1850 until about 1880 when it was largely superseded by gelatin-coated dry plates.

white light   Generally used (as distinct from safelight) to refer to any light which is capable of exposing an emulsion. Also, in color photography, it describes light of a Kelvin temperature suitable for use with a particular emulsion type. Thus, white light for daylight film is considered to be about 5600°K, while ''Type A'' film white light is 3400°K, etc.

wide-angle lens   Describes a lens whose angular coverage is substantially greater than that of a ''normal'' lens. Also sometimes called ''wide field.''

winder   A battery-powered camera accessory, similar to a motor drive but intended primarily for single-frame operation. Some winders are capable of automatic sequence photography at speeds of up to about two frames per second.

working solution   Any solution used in photographic processing, as distinguished from stock or storage solutions which are usually more concentrated for better keeping qualities. Stock solutions are almost invariably diluted for use, to make the working solution.

zone   In the Zone System, a specific subject tone as it will be rendered in the print. Seven to nine Zones are usually described as covering the useful range of print tones and each is assigned a number; thus, Zone III is considered to represent very dark gray in the print, Zone V is middle gray, Zone IX is maximum paper white, etc. In the subject the Zones are defined as being luminances and the interval between adjacent Zones of a ''normal'' subject is one stop.

zone focusing   Adjustment of the camera controls to achieve depth of field between selected near and far limits in the subject space. Often done in anticipation of the sudden or brief appearance of some subject whose position or movements can be predicted only generally.

zone system   A method of exposure and development determination advanced by Ansel Adams, and later propounded by Minor White, which involves analysis of the luminances of the significant areas and the tonal extremes of the subject and the previsualization of their translation into print densities. It is a logical theory, but one that tends to become pseudo-scientific, if not actually intuitive, in practice.

zoom lens   A type of lens of very complex structure which can be adjusted in use to provide a continuous range of focal lengths within its design limits. They are very popular with cinematographers and are also widely used in still photography with small cameras.

Bibliography

The following bibliography lists only a few of the available books treating the subject of photography in words or pictures. It is not intended to be a definitive list but does represent a selection of titles that would form a fine reference library. I am sure many valuable books have not been included and, no doubt, some of the selections listed could be contested; but within this listing, there should be something of interest for almost any photographer, regardless of his background or specialty. The bibliography emphasizes picture books and books of historical interest because, it seems to me, these are major sources of inspiration for students. The relatively few instructional books listed are basic; extremely technical or specialized scientific works have not been included.

Picture Books

Adams, Ansel. *Ansel Adams: Images 1923-1974.* Boston, New York Graphic Society, 1974.

————. *Yosemite and the Range of Light.* Boston, New York Graphic Society, 1979.

Abbott, Berenice. *Tha World of Atget.* New York: Horizon Press, Inc., 1964.

Abbott, Berenice, and McCausland, Elizabeth. *New York in the Thirties.* Unabridged republication of 1939 edition (formerly titled *Changing New York*). New York: Dover Publications, Inc., 1973.

Aldridge, James. *Living Egypt.* Photographs by Paul Strand. New York: Horizon Press, Inc., 1969.

André Kertesz, Photographer. Intro. by John Szarkowski. New York: The Museum of Modern Art, 1964.

The Appalachian Photographs of Doris Ulmann. Intro. by John Jacob Niles. Pennland, N.C.: The Jargon Society, 1970.

Barbara Morgan Monograph. Foreword by Peter Bunnell. Hastings-on-Hudson, N.Y.: Morgan & Morgan, 1972.

Berenice Abbott, Photographs. Foreword by John Szarkowski. New York: Horizon Press, Inc., 1970.

The Best of LIFE. New York: Time-Life Books, 1973.

Brassai. Intro. by Lawrence Durrell. New York: Museum of Modern Art, 1968.

Brown, Joseph Epes, ed. *Edward Curtis.* Photographs of the American Indian. Millerton, N.Y.: Aperture, 1972.

Bry, Doris. *Alfred Stieglitz: Photographer.* Boston: Museum of Fine Arts, 1965.

Bullock, Barbara. *Wynn Bullock . . . Photographs.* San Francisco: Scrimshaw Press, 1971.

Callahan, Sean, ed. *Photographs of Margaret Bourke-White.* Intro. by Theodore M. Brown, afterword by Carl Mydans. Greenwich, Conn.: New York Graphic Society, 1972.

Capa, Cornell. *The Concerned Photographer.* New York: Grossman Publishers, Inc., 1968.

————. *The Concerned Photographer II.* New York: Grossman Publishers, Inc., 1972.

Capa, Robert. *Images of War.* New York: Grossman Publishers, Inc., 1964.

Carpenter, Edward. *They Became What They Beheld.* Photographs by Ken Heyman. New York: Outerbridge & Dienstfrey, 1970.

Cartier-Bresson, Henri. *The Decisive Moment.* New York: Simon & Schuster, Inc., 1952. (Out of print)

————. *World of Henri Cartier-Bresson.* New York: Viking Press, Inc., 1968.

Clark, Larry. *Tulsa.* New York: Lustrum Press, 1971.

Curtis, Edward S. *Portraits from North American Indian Life.* Intro. by A. D. Coleman and T. C. McLuhan. New York: Outerbridge and Lazard, 1972.

Davidson, Bruce. *East 100th Street.* Cambridge, Mass.: Harvard University Press, 1970.

DeCock, Liliane, ed. *Ansel Adams Monograph.* Foreword by Minor White. Hastings-on-Hudson, N.Y.: Morgan & Morgan, 1972.

DeCock, Liliane, and McGhee, Reginald. *James Van Der Zee.* Intro. by Regina A. Perry. Dobbs Ferry, N.Y.: Morgan & Morgan, 1973.

Diane Arbus. An Aperture Monograph. Millerton, N.Y.: Aperture, 1972.

Dorothea Lange. Intro. by George P. Elliott. New York: The Museum of Modern Art, 1966.

Eisenstaedt, Alfred. *The Eye of Eisenstaedt.* New York: Viking Press, Inc., 1969.

Erwitt, Elliott. *Photographs and Anti-Photographs.* Greenwich, Conn.: New York Graphic Society, 1972.

Evans, Walker. *Message from the Interior.* New York: The Eakins Press, 1966.

The Family of Man. Intro. by Edward Steichen. New York: The Museum of Modern Art, 1955.

Feininger, Andreas. *Forms of Nature and Life.* New York: Viking Press, 1966.

Frank, Robert. *The Americans.* Photographs by Robert Frank, intro. by Jack Kerouac. New York: Grossmann Publishers, Inc., 1969.

Friedlander, Lee. *Self Portrait.* New York: Haywire Press, 1970.

Gernsheim, Helmut, ed. *Alvin Langdon Coburn, Photographer.* New York: Frederick A. Praeger, 1966.

Haas, Ernst. *The Creation.* New York: Viking Press, Inc., 1971.
The Hampton Album. Intro. by Lincoln Kirstein. New York: The Museum of Modern Art, 1966.
Harry Callahan. Intro. by Sherman Paul. New York: The Museum of Modern Art, 1967.
Hendricks, Gordon. *The Photographs of Thomas Eakins.* New York: Grossman Publishers, Inc., 1972.
Hughes, Langston. *The Sweet Flypaper of Life.* Photographs by Roy DeCarava. Philadelphia: Hill and Wang, 1967.
Hurley, F. Jack. *Portrait of a Decade.* Baton Rouge, La.: Louisiana State University Press, 1972.

Imogen Cunningham: Photographs. Intro. by Margery Mann. Seattle, Wash.: University of Washington Press, 1970.

Jerry N. Uelsmann. An Aperture Monograph. Intro. by Peter Bunnell. Millerton, N.Y.: Small, 1971.

Kertesz, André. *Sixty Years of Photography: 1912-1972.* New York: Viking Press, Inc., 1972.
Kirstein, Lincoln. *Eugene Smith, Photographs.* Millerton, N.Y.: Aperture, 1969.

Larry Burrows: Compassionate Photographer. New York: Time-Life Books, 1972.
Lartigue, Jacques Henri. *Boyhood Photos of J. H. Lartigue.* Lausanne, Switz.: Ami Guichard, 1966. (Out of print)
————. *Diary of a Century.* Ed. by Richard Avedon. New York: Viking Press, Inc., 1970.
Levitas, Mitchel. *America in Crisis.* Photographs by Magnum photographers. New York: Holt, Rinehart & Winston, 1969.
Looking at Pictures: One Hundred Photographs from the Collection of the Museum of Modern Art. Notes by John Szarkowski. Greenwich, Conn.: New York Graphic Society, 1972.
Lyon, Danny. *The Bikeriders.* New York: Macmillan Company, 1968.

————. *Conversations With the Dead.* Photographs by Danny Lyon, drawings and writings by Billy McCune. New York: Holt, Rinehart & Winston, 1971.
Lyons, Nathan, ed. *Aaron Siskind, Photographer.* Intro. by Nathan Lyons. Rochester, N.Y.: George Eastman House, 1965.
————. *Photography in the Twentieth Century.* New York: Horizon Press, Inc., 1967.
Lyons, Nathan; Labrot, Syl; and Chappell, Walter. *Under the Sun: The Abstract Art of Camera Vision.* New York: George Braziller, 1960. (Limited edition)

Manos, Constantine. *A Greek Portfolio.* New York: Viking Press, Inc., 1972.
McCarthy, Mary. *Portugal.* Photographs by Neal Slavin. New York: Lustrum Press, 1971.
Michals, Duane. *The Journey of the Spirit After Death.* New York: Winter House, 1971.

Natali, Enrico. *New American People.* Hastings-on-Hudson, N.Y.: Morgan & Morgan, 1972.
Newhall, Beaumont. *Frederick H. Evans.* An Aperture Monograph. Millerton, N.Y.: Aperture, 1973.
Newhall, Nancy. *The Eloquent Light.* A biography of Ansel Adams. San Francisco: Sierra Club, 1963.
————. *Yosemite Valley.* Photographs by Ansel Adams. Redwood City, Calif.: Five Associates, 1959.
Norman, Dorothy. *Alfred Stieglitz: An American Seer.* Millerton, N.Y.: Aperture, 1973.

Parker, Fred. *Manuel Alvarez Bravo.* Pasadena, Calif.: Pasadena Art Museum, 1971.
Paul Caponigro. An Aperture Monograph. New York: Aperture, 1967. Revised and enlarged, 1972.
Paul Strand: Photographs 1915-1968. Text by Alfred Stieglitz, Nancy Newhall, Paul Strand, and others. Millerton, N.Y.: Aperture, 1972.
Porter, Eliot. *In Wildness Is the Preservation of the World.* New York: Sierra Club-Ballantine, 1967.
————. *The Place No One Knew . . . Glen Canyon.* San Francisco: Sierra Club, 1966.

Sander, August. *Menschen Ohne Maske.* Luzern and Frankfurt: C. J. Bucher, 1971.
Steichen, Edward, ed. *The Bitter Years 1935-1941.* New York: The Museum of Modern Art, 1966.
Szarkowski, John. *The Photographer's Eye.* New York: The Museum of Modern Art, 1966.
————, ed. *The Photographer and the American Landscape.* Greenwich, Conn.: New York Graphic Society, 1972.

Tucker, Anne, ed. *The Woman's Eye.* Intro. by Anne Tucker. New York: Alfred A. Knopf, Inc., 1973.

Walker Evans. Intro. by John Szarkowski. New York: The Museum of Modern Art, 1971.
Weiss, Margaret R., ed. *Ben Shahn, Photographer.* Intro. by Margaret R. Weiss. New York: DaCapo Press, 1972.
Weston, Cole. *Edward Weston: Fifty Years.* Millerton, N.Y.: Aperture, 1973.
White, Minor. *Mirrors, Messages, Manifestations.* Millerton, N.Y.: Aperture, 1969.
Winningham, Geoffery. *Friday Night at the Coliseum.* Houston, Texas: Allison Press, 1971.
Winogrand, Garry. *The Animals.* New York: The Museum of Modern Art, 1969.

Instructional and Reference Books

Adams, Ansel. *Camera and Lens*. Hastings-on-Hudson, N.Y.: Morgan & Morgan, 1970.

————. *Natural Light Photography*. Hastings-on-Hudson, N.Y.: Morgan & Morgan, 1965.

————. *The Negative*. Hastings-on-Hudson, N.Y.: Morgan & Morgan, 1968.

————. *The Print*. Hastings-on-Hudson, N.Y.: Morgan & Morgan, 1968.

Crawford, William. *The Keepers of Light: A History and Working Guide to Early Photographic Processes*. Dobbs Ferry, New York: Morgan & Morgan, 1979.

Davis, Phil. *Beyond the Zone System*. Somerville, Mass: Curtin & London Inc., 1981.

Dowdell, John J. III, and Zakia, Richard D. *Zone Systemizer*. Hastings-on-Hudson, N.Y.: Morgan & Morgan, 1972.

Eaton, George T. *Photographic Chemistry*. Hastings-on-Hudson, N.Y.: Morgan & Morgan, 1965.

The Focal Encyclopedia of Photography. New York: McGraw-Hill Book Company, 1969.

Gassan, Arnold. *Handbook for Contemporary Photography*. Athens, Ohio: Handbook Company, 1974.

Life Library of Photography. New York: Time-Life Books, 1970.
The Art of Photography
The Camera
Color
Frontiers of Photography
Great Photographers
Light and Film
Photojournalism
The Print
The Studio

Neblette, C. B. *Fundamentals of Photography*. New York: Van Nostrand Reinhold, 1970.

————. *Photographic Lenses*. Hastings-on-Hudson, N.Y.: Morgan & Morgan, 1972.

————. *Photography: Its Materials and Processes*. New York: Van Nostrand Reinhold, 1972.

Pittaro, Ernest M., ed. *Photo-Lab-Index*. Hastings-on-Hudson, N.Y.: Morgan & Morgan, 1972.

Procedures for Processing and Storing Black and White Photographs for Maximum Possible Permanence. Grinnell, Iowa: East Street Gallery, 1970.

Shipman, Carl. *Understanding Photography*. Tucson, Ariz.: H. P. Books, 1974.

Simon, Michael, and Moore, Dennis. *First Lessons in Black and White Photography*. New York: Holt, Rinehart & Winston, 1978.

Stone, Jim, ed. *Darkroom Dynamics: A Guide to Creative Darkroom Techniques*. Somerville, Mass: Curtin & London Inc., 1979.

Stroebel, Leslie. *View Camera Technique*. New York: Hastings House Publishers, Inc., 1967.

Swedlund, Charles. *Photography: A Handbook of History, Materials and Processes*. 2d ed., New York: Holt, Rinehart & Winston, 1981.

Todd, Hollis N., and Zakia, Richard D. *Photographic Sensitometry*. Hastings-on-Hudson, N.Y.: Morgan & Morgan, 1969.

Upton, Barbara and John. *Photography*. 2d ed., Boston: Little, Brown and Company, 1981.

Vestal, David. *The Craft of Photography*. New York: Harper and Row, 1975.

Wade, Kent E. *Alternative Photographic Processes*. Dobbs Ferry, N.Y.: Morgan & Morgan, 1978.

White, Minor; Zakia, Richard; and Lorenz, Peter. *The New Zone System Manual*. Hastings-on-Hudson, N.Y.: Morgan & Morgan, 1976.

Zakia, Richard D., and Todd, Hollis N. *101 Experiments in Photography*. Hastings-on-Hudson, N.Y.: Morgan & Morgan, 1969.

Aesthetics and Criticism

Brooke, James T. *A Viewer's Guide to Looking at Photographs*. Wilmette, Ill.: The Aurelian Press, 1977.

Coffin, Charles. *Photography as a Fine Art*. Intro. by Thomas Barrow. Hastings-on-Hudson, N.Y.: Morgan & Morgan, 1971.

Coke, Van Deren. *The Painter and the Photograph*. Albuquerque, N.M.: University of New Mexico Press, 1971.

Gernsheim, Helmut. *Creative Photography, Aesthetic Trends 1839–1960*. Boston: Boston Book and Art Shop, 1962.

Hartmann, Sadakichi. Foreward by Thomas F. Barrow. *The Valiant Knights of Daguerre*. Berkeley, CA: The University of California Press, 1978.

Lyons, Nathan, ed. *Photographers on Photography*. Englewood Cliffs, N.J.: Prentice-Hall, Inc., 1966.

Scharf, Aaron. *Art and Photography*. Baltimore, Md.: The Penguin Press, 1969.

————. *Creative Photography*. New York: Van Nostrand Reinhold, 1969.

Sontag, Susan. *On Photography*. New York: Farrar, Straus and Giroux, 1977.

Books of Historical Interest

The following are titles from a recently issued collection of facsimile editions published by the Arno Press, New York, all dated 1973.

Anderson, A. J. *The Artistic Side of Photography.* Philadelphia and London: 1919.
Anderson, Paul L. *The Fine Art of Photography in Theory and Practice.* London: 1910.

Beck, Otto Walter. *Art Principles in Portrait Photography.* New York: 1907.
Bingham, Robert J. *Photogenic Manipulation.* Parts I and II. London: 1852.
Bunnell, Peter C., ed. *Nonsilver Printing Processes: Four Selections, 1886-1927.* New York: 1973.
Burbank, W. H. *Photographic Printing Methods.* 3d ed. New York: 1891.
Burgess, N. G. *The Photograph Manual.* 8th ed. New York: 1863.

Croucher, J. H., and LeGray, Gustave. *Plain Directions for Obtaining Photographic Pictures.* Parts I, II, & III. Philadelphia: 1853.

Draper, John William. *Scientific Memoirs.* London: 1878.

Emerson, Peter Henry. *Naturalistic Photography for Students of the Art,* 3d edition, including *The Death of Naturalistic Photography.* London: 1891; New York: 1899.

Fouque, Victor. *The Truth Concerning the Invention of Photography: Nicephore Niepce—His Life, Letters and Works.* Translated by Edward Epstean from the original French edition. Paris: 1867; New York: 1935.

Gillies, John Wallace. *Principles of Pictorial Photography.* New York: 1923.

Harrison, W. Jerome. *A History of Photography Written as a Practical Guide and an Introduction to Its Latest Developments.* New York: 1887.
Hartmann, Sadakichi (Sidney Allan). *Composition in Portraiture.* New York: 1909.
————. *Landscape and Figure Composition.* New York: 1910.
Hicks, Wilson. *Words and Pictures.* New York: 1952.

Jones, Bernard E., ed. *Cassell's Cyclopaedia of Photography.* London: 1911.

Lerebours, N. P. *A Treatise on Photography.* London: 1843.

Mortensen, William. *Monsters and Madonnas.* San Francisco: 1936.

Pritchard, H. Baden. *About Photography and Photographers.* New York: 1883.

Robinson, H. P. *Picture Making by Photography.* 5th ed. London: 1897.
————, and Abney, Capt. W. deW. *The Art and Practice of Silver Printing,* American Edition. New York: 1881.

Sobieszek, Robert A., ed. *The Collodion Process and the Ferrotype: Three Accounts, 1854-1872.* New York: 1973.
————. *The Daguerreotype Process: Three Treatises, 1840-1849.* New York: 1973.
Sparling, W. *Theory and Practice of the Photographic Art.* London: 1856.

Tissandier, Gaston. *A History and Handbook of Photography.* 2d ed. Ed. by J. Thomson. London: 1878.

Vogel, Hermann. *The Chemistry of Light and Photography.* New York: 1875.

Wilson, Edward L. *The American Carbon Manual.* New York: 1868.
————. *Wilson's Photographics.* New York: 1881.

Other books of historical interest

Andrews, Ralph W. *Picture Gallery Pioneers.* New York: Bonanza Books, 1964.

Braive, Michel. *The Photograph, A Social History.* New York: McGraw-Hill Book Company, 1966.

Camera Work: An Anthology. Millerton, N.Y.: Aperture, 1973.

Daguerre. Intro. by Beaumont Newhall. New York: Winter House, Ltd., 1971.
Doty, Robert. *Photo Secession, Photography as a Fine Art.* Rochester, N.Y.: The George Eastman House, 1960.

French Primitive Photography. Intro. by Minor White. Millerton, N.Y.: Aperture, 1970.

Gardner, Alexander. *Gardner's Photographic Sketchbook of the Civil War.* New York: Dover Publications, Inc., 1959.
Gernsheim, Helmut. *Lewis Carroll, Photographer.* New York: Dover Publications, Inc., 1970.
Gernsheim, Helmut and Alison. *A Concise History of Photography.* New York: Grosset and Dunlap, 1965.
————. *The History of Photography 1685-1914.* New York: McGraw-Hill Book Company, 1969.
Gutman, Judith M. *Lewis W. Hine and The American Social Conscience.* New York: Walker & Co., 1967.

Henney, Keith, and Dudley, Beverly, eds. *Handbook of Photography.* New York: Whittlesey House (McGraw), 1939.
Horan, James D. *Timothy O'Sullivan. America's Forgotten Photographer.* New York: Bonanza, 1966.
Hunt, Robert. *A Popular Treatise on the Art of Photography.* A facsimile edition with intro. and notes by James Yingpeh Tong. Athens, Ohio: Ohio University Press, 1973.

Lothrop, Eaton S., Jr. *A Century of Cameras.* Dobbs Ferry, N.Y.: Morgan & Morgan, 1973.

Mees, C. E. Kenneth. *From Dry Plates to Ektachrome Film,* Ziff-Davis, 1961.
Muybridge, Eadweard. *The Human Figure in Motion.* New York: Dover Publications, Inc., 1955.

Newhall, Beaumont. *The Daguerreotype in America.* Greenwich, Conn.: New York Graphic Society, 1961. Revised in 1968.
————. *The History of Photography.* New York: The Museum of Modern Art, 1964.
————. *The Latent Image.* Garden City, N.Y.: Doubleday & Co., Inc., 1967.
Newhall, Nancy, ed. *The Daybooks of Edward Weston, Vol. I, Mexico.* Millerton, N.Y.: Aperture, 1973.
————. ed. *The Daybooks of Edward Weston, Vol. II, California.* Millerton, N.Y.: Aperture, 1973.

Pollack, Peter. *The Picture History of Photography.* New York: Harry N. Abrams, 1969.

Riis, Jacob A. *How the Other Half Lives.* New York: Dover, 1971.
Rinhart, Floyd and Marion. *American Daguerreian Art.* New York: Clarkson N. Potter, 1967.
Robinson, H. P. *Pictorial Effect in Photography.* Pawlet, N.H.: Helios, 1971. (A facsimile edition first published in 1869.)
Rudisill, Richard. *Mirror Image: The Influence of the Daguerreotype on American Society.* Albuquerque, N.M.: University of New Mexico Press, 1971.

Snelling, Henry H. *Art of Photography.* Hastings-on-Hudson, N.Y.: Morgan & Morgan, 1970. (Facsimile edition)
Steichen, Edward. *A Life in Photography.* New York: Doubleday & Co., Inc., 1963.

Taft, Robert. *Photography and the American Scene.* New York: Dover Publications, Inc., 1964.
Talbot, William Henry Fox. *The Pencil of Nature.* A facsimile of the 1844-46 edition, with intro. by Beaumont Newhall. New York: DaCapo Press, 1969.
Thomson, John, and Smith, Adolphe. *Street Life in London.* New York and London: Benjamin Blom, 1969. (Reissued)
Towler, J. *The Silver Sunbeam.* A facsimile of the 1864 edition, with intro. by Beaumont Newhall. Hastings-on-Hudson, N.Y.: Morgan & Morgan, 1969.

Index

aberrations, 78
Adams, Ansel, 44, 45, 319
adapter rings, 70
additive color
    in posterization process, 297
    primaries, 21, 22, 104, 203
agitation
    effect on negative density and contrast,
        128
    during tank development, 126, 128
    during tray development of film, *241,*
        242
albumin paper, 18, 20
ambrotype, 11
American Place, An, 43, 44
Ansco, 20
aperture
    effect on exposure, 56, 92, 93, 103
    priority, 68, 101
    relative, 92, 93
apochromatic lens, 273
Arago, François, 6, 8
Archer, Frederick Scott, 10
Aristotle, 3
artificial light sources, 181-85
    electronic flash, 183-84
    flash bulbs, 182-83
    fluorescent, 184, 185
    incandescent, 181, 182
ASA film speeds, 95
asphalt, light sensitive, 5
aspheric lenses, 78
Atget, Eugene, 38, 39, *39,* 319
autochrome film, 21, 22, 24
average gradient, 255-57, *256*
    use of, 259

Babbitt, Platt D., 10, *11*
Bacon, Roger, 3
bas-relief, 290, *291*
Bayard, Hippolyte, 8, 9, *9*
"bellows factor"
    in closeup photography, 271, 272, 273
between-the-lens shutter (BTL), 68, *69*
    operation of, *236*
bichromated-colloid processes, 299, 300,
        304-10, *306, 307, 310*
Bisson, Auguste, *14,* 15
bitumen of Judea, 5
Blanquart-Evrard, Louis-Désiré, 10
bleach
    removing spots from prints with, 165
Brady, Mathew, 13, *13,* 15

Brassai (Gyula Halâsz), 29, 30
burning-in
    to adjust print values, *157, 161,* 162
    tools for, *142, 157*
buying equipment, 75, 76

cable release, 72, *73*
cadmium sulfide cell (CdS), 66
Callahan, Harry, 46
calotype, 9, 10, 11
camera obscura, 3, 4, *4, 7*
cameras
    care of, 110
    general characteristics, 61, *62*
    loading, *98-99*
    special purpose, 70
    SX-70, *71*
    types and functions, 61-71
    view and field, 70, *71,* 235-38
camera vision, 315
Camera Work, 37, 42
Cameron, Julia Margaret, 34, *36,* 314
carte-de-visite, 11, *12,* 13, *13*
Cartier-Bresson, Henri, 29, 30, *30,* 31, 319
catadioptric lens, 82
characteristic curves
    average gradient of, 255, 259
        defined, 256, *256,* 257
    calibration of, 257
    contrast Index of, 255
        defined, 256, *256,* 257
    of film, 253, *254-56, 258*
    gamma, 255, *256,* 257
    of paper, *258*
    slope or gradient of (G), 254, 255, *255*
chemical mixing
    for color printing, 216, 223
    general, 121-23
circle of confusion, 56, *81,* 82, 86, 87, *87,*
        88
cleaning negatives in printing, *156,* 157,
        158
cleanup, 131-32
clearing of film in fixer, 129, *130*
closeup photography, 269-82
    axial lighting for, 280, *281*
    calculating exposure factor for, 271-73
    condition of unit magnification in, 269
    focusing difficulties in, 269, 271
    lenses for, 273
    metering difficulties for, 269
    supplementary lenses for, 274, *274*
    tent lighting for, *280*
    terms defined, 268-69

coating, of a lens, 79
Coburn, Alvin Langdon, 37, 40, 41
collodion process, 10, 11, 20
collotype, 19, 21
color
    complements, 29, 203, 309
    early experiments, 21, 22, 23
    filters, 309, colorplate 3
    instant prints, 23, 34
    manipulations, 296-99, *298,* colorplates
        21, 22, 23
    perception of, 205
    primaries, 21, 22, 104, 203, 309,
        colorplates 6, 7
    separation, 204
color compensating (CC) filters, 185
color film
    balance and filtration, 205
    general, 203-5
    processing, 210, 211
color printing, 212-31
    with Cibachrome, 215-22, *218, 219*
    equipment and materials for, 212-15
    filtration for, 216, 220, 221, 228, 229,
        230, 231 colorplates 12, 18
    methods of, 214
    with Unicolor R-2 chemistry, 223-31,
        224-27
color temperature, 181, 205-8
compensating developers, 120
complementary colors, 104, 203, 208, 309
composition, 316, 317, 318
condenser enlargers, characteristics of,
        139, 140
contact printing, papers for, 145
contrast
    appraising negative, 133, 253
    control in printing, 146, *147,* 160, *162,*
        163
    effect of film development on, 252,
        253-54, 258, 259, 301
    of papers, 146, *147*
Contrast Index/development chart, *258,*
        268
copying
    avoiding distortion in, 277
    avoiding glare in, 279
    balancing illumination for, *278,* 279
    film for, 279
    general techniques, 277-82
    gray card metering for, 277, *278*
    incident metering for, *228*
corner mounts for prints, 176, *176*
creativity in photography, 314, 315

criticism, 314
Cutting, J. A., 11
cutting mats, *175*, 176, 177
cyanotype process, 299
    instructions, 302-4, *302, 303*

Dada, 40, 41, 47
Daguerre, Louis Jacques Mandé, 6, 7, 8, 9,
    32
daguerreotype, 6, 9, 10, 11, 22, 32
darkroom cleanliness, 117-18, 131, 132
da Vinci, Leonardo, 3
Davison, George, 35
Davy, Sir Humphry, 5, 7
decamireds, 208
della Porta, Giovanni Battista, 3
density, appraising negative, 133, *253,* 300
depth of field, 57, 61, 88, *88, 89*
    control with view camera swings,
        243-48, *244-48*
    factors affecting, 89, 90, 101
depth of focus, 87, 88
developed-out image, 53
developer
    function of, 118
    ingredients, 118
    skin irritation from, 121
    types, 120
developers
    for printing, 148
    storage of, 116, 120, 122
development
    calculating time of, 259
    charts, *258*
        blank 267, *267,* 268, *268*
    effect on contrast, 252, *253-54,* 301
    effect on film speed, 262, 263, 266,
        267, *267,* 268, *268*
    effect on negative quality, 133, *253*
    equipment for, 115-18
    of rollfilm, 123-32, *124-27*
    process summary, 118-19, *126, 127,*
        128-32, 134
    stagnation or still, 290
    synopsis of process steps, 132
    tanks for, 115
    time for printing, 148
    time of, 128
dichroic filter, 78
    use in enlarger, 140, 213
diffraction, 55, 77
diffusion enlargers, characteristics of, 139,
    140

diorama, 6, 10
direct-positive, 53
Disdéri, Andre Adolphe-Eugéne, 11, *12*
distortion
    avoiding in copying, 277
    wide angle and telephoto, 86
dodging
    to adjust print values, *157, 161,* 162
    tools for, 142, *142, 157*
Draper, John W., 10
Driffield, Vero C., 21
dropouts, 286
drying, film, 127, 131
dry mounting
    with "cold mount" tissue, 172
    with thermoplastic tissue, 168, 169,
        170, 173, 174
du Hauron, Louis Ducos, 22, 40

Eastman Kodak Co., 20
Emerson, Dr. Peter Henry, 34, 35, *35,* 36
emulsion, photographic, 53
enlarger
    color head for, 140
    lenses for, 141
    preparation for printing, 156, 157
    types of, *139, 140*
enlarging
    dodging tools for, *142, 143, 157*
    easel, *141*
    grain focuser for, *141,* 156
equivalents, 43, 46
Evans, Frederick, 35
exposure
    determining film, 98, 259-63, 265-67,
        277-79, *278*
    determining flash, 184
    determining print, 150, 158-62, *159*
    effect of aperture on, 56, 92, 93, 103
    effect on negative density, 252, *253-54*
    effect on negative quality, 133, *253*
    effect on print density, 160
    effect of shutter speeds on, 94, 103
    how controlled, 94
exposure determination
    in closeup photography, 271-73
    in color posterization, 298, 299
exposure-development relationship,
    251-58, 262-68
    displayed, *253-56,* 257, *258*
    testing, 252-54, *253, 254*

exposure meters
    built-in, 66, 98
    functions and use, 259-63, 265-67
    interpreting reading of, 98
    substitute readings with, 100
    types of, 259
    weighted field of, 100
exposure systems
    incident, 262, 263
    Zone, 263-68
exposure values (EV), 103, 104
extension tubes, 81, 274
eye relief, 66

f-numbers
    how determined, 92, 93, 271
f-64, Group, 44
Family of Man, The, 45
Fenton, Roger, 11, *12*
fiber-base papers
    drying, 144, 154, 155
    ferrotyping, *154,* 155
    processing, 151-54
film
    characteristic curves, 253, *254-56,*
        257, *258*
    characteristics of, 95-98
    color balance of, 205, 206
    color negative, 203, 205
    color reversal, 204, 205
    color sensitivity of black-and-white, 96,
        96, colorplate 2
    filtration for color, 206-9
    fixing time of, 129, *130,* 242
    instant-print, 204
    latitude, 204, 205
    orthochromatic, 96
    panchromatic, 96
    processing color, 210, 211
    reciprocity failure of black-and-white,
        268
    reciprocity failure of color, 209
    selecting and using black-and-white,
        95-98
    sheet, 238
        loading, 239-40, *239*
        processing, 240-42, *240*
    speed of, 95
    tank development of, 123-32
    types of color, 206

filters
    color compensating (CC), 185, 208,
        209, 213
    color printing (CP), 208, 213
    conversion and light balancing, 206-8
    effect with black-and-white film, 104-9,
        colorplate 3, *105, 108, 109*
    factors, 105, 106, 107, 109
    neutral density, 107, 300
    Polaroid, 107-9 *108, 109*
    selective absorption by, 104
fisheye lens, 82
fixing bath, 54
    film time in, 129, *130*
    function of, 119
    ingredients, 119
    for prints, 149, 162
    rapid, 119, 123, 162
    testing of, 123
    use in film processing, 129
flare, 49
flare light
    extension tubes as cause of, 274, *275,*
        276
    reduced by lens coating, 79
flash
    bulbs, 182
    determining exposure with, 184
    synchronizing, 182, 183
flash units, general, 74
floating elements, 79
focal distance, 269, 271-73
focal length
    defined, 80, 82, 269, 273
    effect on Image Scale and Perspective,
        82, *83, 84, 85,* 86
    effect on lens speed, 92, 93
    normal, 80, 83
focal plane shutter (FP), 68-70, *69*
focusing
    for IR, 91
    rangefinder, 62, *64*
    reflex, 64
    scale, 62, *63*
Frank, Robert, 45, 46, *46,* 47
Fraprie, Frank, 36, 38
fresnel lens, 65, *67*
Frith, Francis, *14,* 15
FSA, 29

gallium photo diode (GPD), 68
gelatin
    early uses of, 18, 19, 20
    unique properties of, 53
Genthe, Arnold, 26
glare
    control with filter, 107-9, *108-9*
gold toning, 163
Goodwin, Rev. Hannibal, 20
grain
    effect of developer on, 120
    effect of film speed on, 95, 205
grain focuser for enlarging, 141, *141, 156*
gray card reading, 260
groundglass focusing screen, *67*
Group f-64, 44
guide numbers, 184
gum-bichromate process, 304-10, *306,*
        307, 310, 318

Hahn, Betty, 49, 318
halftone, 294
halides of silver, 53
halogen cycle lamps, 181, 182
Hammond, Arthur, 317
Heartfield, John, *40,* 41
Herschel, Sir John Frederick William, 7, 8,
        9, 20
Hill, Rev. Levi, 22
Hine, Lewis, 25, 26, *27,* 29, 42
Hunt, Robert, 21
Hurter, Dr. Ferdinand, 21
Hurter and Driffield, 21
hyperfocal distance, 90, *90*
hyperfocal focussing, 90
hypo, 7, 8, 9, 54
    cleaning up, 118
    mixing, 119
hypo clearing bath
    function of, 119
    preparation of, 123
    use for film, 130
    use for prints, 149, 162, 163
hypo eliminator, 163

image
    first camera, 5
    latent camera, 53
image formation
    focusing effect on, 56, 87, *87*
    general, 54, 55
image sharpness, factors affecting, 100,
        101, 102
image types, defined, 53
incident meter, *260,* 261
    in use, *261-62*
Incident System, 262-63
infrared, 76, 185-86
    focusing for, 91
    image quality, 97, *97*
instantaneous photographs, early attempts,
        17
inverse square law, 192
iodine, used as bleach, 165
iron-sensitive processes, 299, 302-4,
        302-3
ISO film speeds, 95

Jackson, William H., 11, 16, *16,* 17

Käsebier, Gertrude, 37, *38*
Kelvin temperature, 181, 205-8
Kertész, André, 29
Kodak, 20, 21
Kodalith film, 286
    safelight for, 286

Land-Weber, Ellen, 49
Lartigue, Jacques Henri, 39, 319
latent image, 53
LeGray, Gustave, 10
lens, image formation by, 56
lens aberrations, 78, *79*
    correction of for closeup work, 276,
        277

lens accessories, 72
lenses
    angular coverage of, 80, 82, *83-85,* 86,
        250, 251
    aspheric, 78
    care of, 110
    cleaning, *110-11*
    for closeup, 273
    for enlarging, 141, 156, 212, 277
    features and functions, 78
    first application to camera, 4
    floating elements of, 79
    reverse adapters for, 276, *276*
    supplementary, 274, *274*
    types of, 80-83, *83-85*
    for view camera use, 250
lens speed, 92, 93
Lerebours, Noël, 10
Life magazine, 28, 31
light
    analysis and control of, 189-99
    artificial sources of, 181-85
    available, 190, *190,* 191, *191*
    characteristics of, 76, 187, 188
    color primaries, 21, 22, 104, 203, 208
    color temperature of, 181, 182
    as energy, 53, 76
    rays
        how affected, 77
    sensitive materials, 53
    spectral characteristics of, 181, 182,
        184
    visible spectrum of, 76, *77,* 104
Light-Emitting Diodes (LED), 68, 74
lighting
    beginners mistakes in, 192, 193
    general, 186-200
    Inverse Square Law of, 192
    tent, 194, 195, *196, 197,* 198, *198,*
        199, *199*
light meters
    incident, *260,* 261, *261, 262*
    interpreting readings of, 98, 100,
        259-62
    reflectance, 259, *260*
    spot, 260
    types, 66, 98, 259
    using handheld, 259-62, *261, 262, 278*
limbo background, 195, 198, *198*
Linked Ring, 35, 37, 40
Lumiere brothers, 21

Mackie lines, 292, *293,* 294
macro lens, 81
masks, 290, *290*
mat cutting, *175,* 176, 177
matting prints, materials for, 144, *173,*
        174, 175, 176, *176,* 177
Maxwell and Sutton, 22
Metol "poisoning," 121
Meyerowitz, Joel, 48
microprism grid, 65, 66, *67*
mireds, 207, 208
mirror lens, 82
misregistration for bas-relief effects, 290,
        291
Moholy-Nagy, László, 41, *41,* 319
Morse, Samuel F. B., 10
motor drives, 75
mounting press, 168, 169
mounting prints, materials for, 144, 168,
        170, 172, 176, *176*

movements, of view camera lensboard and back, 243-49, *244-49*
multicoating lenses, 79
multiple gum printing, 309, colorplate, 25
Muybridge, Eadweard, 17, *18*

Naturalists, 20, 34, 35
negative image, *58*
  defined, 53
negatives
  appraising quality of, 133, 155
  making enlarged, 300, 301
  storage of, 132-33
Niépce-de-St. Victor, Claude, 10
Niépce, Isidore, 5, 6
Niépce, Joseph Nicephore, 5, 6, 7, 8
Nixon, Nick, 48, *48, 234*
nonsilver processes, 18, 19
  introduction to, 299-310
  three categories of, 299
normal lens, 80, 83, 86

one-shot developer, 120
O'Sullivan, Timothy, 11, *15, 16*
override dial, on meter, 100, *100*

panchromatic sensitivity, 22
papers
  characteristic curve family of, *258*
  processing, 151, 154
  stabilization, 146
  types and characteristics of, 144, 145, 146, 148
  variable contrast, 146, *162, 163*
parallax, 61, 62, 63
Pencil of Nature, 10
personal expression, 314, 315, 316, 317
Perspective Control (PC) lens, 81
  using view camera adjustments, 253-45, *247-49*
Photo-Secession, 36, 37, 38, 40, 42
photogram, 41, *41,* 53, 54
photogravure, 20, 35
Porter, Eliot, 48
positive transparency, *58*
posterization
  black-and-white, 286, 287, *288, 289*
  color, 296
primary colors
  light, 21, 22, 104, 203, 208, colorplate 6
  pigment, 22, 104, 203, 208, 309, colorplate 7
printed-out image, 53
printing
  chemicals for, 148
  in color, 212-31
  by contact, 150, *152*
  enlarger types for, 138-40, *139, 140*
  facilities and equipment for, 137-44
  filters for contrast control in, 146, *162-63*
  by projection, 156-62
  safelights for, 138, 150, 158
prints
  archival processing of, 162, 163
  cold mounting of, 172
  corner mounting of, 176, *176*

determining exposure for, 150, 158-62, *159*
  developer for, 148
  development of, 151
  drying, 144, 151, *153,* 154, *154,* 155, 163
  mounting and matting, 168-77
  post-development control, 164-67
  spotting, 165-67, *166*
  stop bath for, 148, 149
  thermoplastic dry mounting of, 168, 169, *170, 173, 174*
  toning, 162, 163
  use of reducers and bleaches on, 164, 165
  washing, 151
prism-reflex camera, 65, *65,* 66
process manipulations, 285-99
processing
  black-and-white rollfilm, 123-32
  black-and-white sheet film, 240-42, *240*
  color film, 210, 211
programmed shutter operation, 68, 100, 101
proofing negatives, 150, 151, *152, 153*
"pushing" film, 190

rangefinder prism, 65, 66, *67*
rapid fix
  danger of bleaching prints in, 149
  use in archival printing, 162
RC papers
  drying, 144, 151, *153,* 154
  spotting, 167
Reciprocity Law, 94
  failure of, 209, 268, 273, colorplate 15
reducer, Farmer's, 164
  use on prints, 164
reflectance meters, 259, 260, *260*
reflex cameras, 64, 65, *65*
registration
  in gum printing, 309, *310*
  in posterization, 287
Rejlander, Oscar, 33, *33,* 34
relative aperture, 92, 93
replenishment of developer, 120
reticulation, 128
retro-focus lens, 80
Rexroth, Nancy, 48, *49*
Riis, Jacob, 25, *25,* 26, *26,* 29
ring light, 280, *281*
Robinson, Henry Peach, 21, 33, 34, *34,* 35, 316, 317
Root, Marcus Aurelius, 22

Sabattier effect, 292, *293, 294*
safelight
  for fine-grain positive, 301
  for kodalith, 286, 292
  for paper, 138, 150, 158
  not recommended for film, 115, 132, 138
Sala, Angelo, 4
Salomon, Dr. Erich, 27, 28, *28*
Scheele, Carl Wilhelm, 4, 5
Schulze, Johann Heinrich, 4
screen, random dot, 295, *295,* 296
screening, 294, *294, 295,* 296
screen processes, color, 22
selenium toning, 162, 163
shifts, view camera, 243, *244-45,* 249

shutter
  blade, 68, *69*
  BTL, 68, *69*
    characteristics of, 70
    operation of, *236*
  curtain, 68, *69*
  FP, 68
    characteristics of, 70
  setting, effect on exposure, 94, 103
  settings for flash synchronization, 182, 183
  standard speeds of, 94, 96
shutter priority, 68, 101
silicon blue cell (SBC), 68
silicon photo diode (SPD), 68
silver compounds, early experiments with, 4, 5, 6, 7, 8
silver halides, 53
single-lens reflex (SLR), 64, 65, *66*
Smith, Hamilton, 11
Social Landscape, 46
Society for Photographic Education (SPE), 47
solarization, 292, *293, 294*
spin dropout, 290, *291*
spotmeters, 260
  used in Zone System, 265, *265*
spotting prints, 165-67, *166*
stagnation development, 292
Steichen, Edward, 37, 38, *44,* 45
stereoscope, 13
stereoscopic views, 13, *14*
Stieglitz, Alfred, 36, 37, *37,* 38, 42, 43, 46
stop bath
  function of, 118, 119
  indicator, 122
  preparing, 122
  for prints, 148, 149
  use in film processing, 128
stops, defined, 93
Strand, Paul, 38, 42, *42,* 43, 44
subtractive color primaries, 22, 104, 203
supplementary lenses, 274
swings, view camera, 243, *244-45, 246-49*
symbolism, 318
synchronizing flash, 182, 183

Talbot, Wm. Henry Fox, 6, 7, 8, *8,* 9, 10, 17, 18, 20
tank development of rollfilm, 123-32, *124-27*
tank
  effect of improper loading, *129*
  loading rollfilm into, *124, 125*
taste differences, 314, 317
telephoto lens, 63, 80
temperature of processing solutions
  for film, 128
  for papers, 150
tent lighting, 194, 195, *196, 197,* 198, *198,* 199, *199*
Teres, Michael, 48, *284*
test strip
  fixed increment, 158, *159*
  geometric, 159, *159*
  methods for making, 158-60, *159*
Thomson, John, *24,* 25, 29
tilt adjustment of view camera, 243-49, *244-49*

timing
   development, 128
   film in fixing bath, 129, *130*
tintype, 11
tone-line print, 290, *291*
tripod, 72, *73*
   uses of, *102*
twin-lens reflex (TLR), 64, *65*
291 gallery, 42

Uelsmann, Jerry, 48, 319
ultraviolet, 76, 185, 186

view camera, 70, *71,* 235
   basic operation, 235–38, *236, 237*
   lenses for, 250
   shifts and swings, 243–49
vignetted image corners, 72, *74*

Walker, Todd, 49, 318
washing film, *127,* 130
water for chemical mixing, 121
waxed paper process, 10, 11
Wedgwood, Thomas, 5, 7
Weston, Edward, 43, *43,* 44, 316, 319
wet-plate process, 11, 15
   difficulties with, 17
wetting bath for film
   function of, 119
   preparation of, 123
   use of, 130
White, Minor, 46, 47
wide-angle lens, 63, 80
winders, 75
woodburytype, 19, *19,* 20, *24,* 25, 300

xerox, use of in posterization, 299

zone focusing, 90, *90,* 91
Zone System, 45
zoom lens, 81
zoopraxiscope, 17